THE HISTORY OF THE ISLANDS OF THE LERINS

The Monastery and Château Fort.

Reproduced by kind permission of the Most Reverend Father Abbot Dom Patrice.

THE HISTORY OF THE ISLANDS OF THE LERINS

THE MONASTERY, SAINTS AND THEOLOGIANS OF S. HONORAT

by

A. C. COOPER-MARSDIN, D.D.

Honorary Canon of Rochester

Cambridge :
at the University Press
1913

CAMBRIDGE UNIVERSITY PRESS
Cambridge, New York, Melbourne, Madrid, Cape Town,
Singapore, São Paulo, Delhi, Mexico City

Cambridge University Press
The Edinburgh Building, Cambridge CB2 8RU, UK

Published in the United States of America by Cambridge University Press, New York

www.cambridge.org
Information on this title: www.cambridge.org/9781107615465

First published 1913
First paperback edition 2013

A catalogue record for this publication is available from the British Library

ISBN 978-1-107-61546-5 Paperback

PREFACE

THIS *History of the Lerins* has followed upon my earlier work on the life of Caesarius, an eminent son of Lerins. Some account, however imperfect, of the leaders of Christian thought in the fifth and sixth centuries, who owed their training to the monastery of S. Honorat, seemed to fill a gap in English theological literature. Nor can it be devoid of interest to place this study in its historical setting, and trace out the early and later history of the island where these great men of the past lived and moved. French historical and theological literature does not fail in the possession of numerous monographs on this attractive subject, and among those which I have consulted and used, I am specially indebted to the works of M. Henri Moris, and of M. l'Abbé Alliez. On a defect in his work, I have later expressed my opinion. I desire to record my most grateful thanks to my friend the Rev. James S. Hill, B.D., Rector of Stowey, who has afforded me most valuable help, and taken unstinted pains. I am indebted to him for many useful suggestions, and he also undertook to see the volume through the press during my serious illness, correct the proofs and compile the index. Nor can I forget to mention the kindness of my Cambridge Tutor, Canon Foakes-Jackson, D.D., Fellow and Dean of Jesus College, who most kindly read the manuscript, and gave me valuable criticism thereon. The dedication of this book is a sincere, if imperfect, expression of my affection and respect for my Bishop.

A. C. COOPER-MARSDIN

BORSTALDENE
BICKLEY
June 1913

TO

THE RIGHT REVEREND

JOHN REGINALD HARMER, D.D.
BISHOP OF ROCHESTER

THIS TREATISE IS DEDICATED

WITH

AFFECTION AND RESPECT

CONTENTS

ILLUSTRATIONS

CHAPTER I

INTRODUCTION

It is perhaps surprising that a historical account of the home of Vincent of Lerins has never, so far as we are aware, been presented in a monograph to English readers. It is of course a part of the history of monasticism, as the rise of monasticism is a part of the history of religious development. But Lerins has its own special interest. The theme that we have in hand does not require more than some brief remarks by way of introduction. The reader will however be helped towards its more perfect understanding if we commence by giving a short review of the outward history in which the establishment of the monastic institution at Lerins finds its setting. The student of early and mediaeval history will scarcely require even this, but there will we hope be readers of this book who will at least be glad to be reminded of the main parts of that history, treated at length in the graphic and eloquent pages of Gibbon[1], and in the vivid narrative of Professor Dill[2]. And though the history of monasticism has elsewhere been ably treated, a short essay or résumé may likewise prove acceptable, while those who desire more than can be said in these pages may be referred to works where an attractive theme is treated with a power to which we make no pretensions[3].

The foundation of the monastery of Lerins probably dates from A.D. 410 at the commencement of a period of special historical interest. In the opening years of the 5th century barbarian hordes began to pour over the province of Gaul in a

---

[1] *Decline and fall of the Roman Empire.*
[2] *Roman Society in the last century of the Western Empire.*
[3] See Bibliography.

great desolating stream. The remarkable series of alien im- migrations which has been called the " Völkerwanderung," was altering the face of the Roman Empire; startling social movements characterised this period; immense changes were working themselves out through the whole of the 5th and 6th centuries, during which the monastery was at the height of its fame, and again in the 7th and 8th, when its brilliant prosperity showed signs of decline.

This history, however briefly put, of the external and internal condition of the world at least serves to explain the motives which impelled men to withdraw to quiet houses of religious life, and enables us to understand why an Empire seemingly so strong and so advanced in civilisation as that of Rome, could be overcome by barbarous invaders, and fall before their assaults, making social life hard and all but intolerable to the "quiet in the land." It was like a huge and splendid oak tree, immense in girth and grand to look upon, but in reality rotten to the core. Economical abuses were enormous; fraud and greed were everywhere triumphant; firm administration was almost un- known. The old heathen systems of religion were falling into decay and even much of the current Christianity was enervated and corrupt. This partly answers the question which men were then asking, why is the Empire, now that it is Christian, going to pieces? There was indeed a belief widely current among the pagans of this disastrous period that all the heaped up calamities of the time were a consequence of, and a punishment for, the rejection of the gods of their forefathers.

The great S. Augustine sought to refute this delusion when he wrote of another city "not made with hands," the spiritual city of the Church of Christ[1], and this famous work was "a theology of history, a comprehensive attempt to justify the ways of God to man," and as the writer reviews the old world of Graeco-Roman paganism, he exposes its weakness and denies that the decay of the Empire was due to the progress of Christianity. He called his treatise "the city of God." At such a crisis, "civitas" meant more than a city. In his great conception, S. Augustine portrayed an Empire of God, that

[1] *De Civitate Dei.*

had no distinctions of race and religion, of civilisation or barbarism, but which shared the inspiration of faith and law and life that was common to all alike.

Orosius also, a presbyter of Tarragona wrote his seven books of history[1], in which he showed that there is a Providence in human affairs, but he seems to infer that the state of the world was not unsatisfactory and therefore in his optimistic view there was no enigma to be solved. This attitude of his was probably due to the slight but transitory improvement under Honorius in 417 A.D. It was Salvian who with a truer perception faced and solved the enigma. His book made a profound impression, and to this day it is a valuable source of information as to the inner life of the dying Empire. We shall refer to this work in a subsequent chapter.

Alaric.

We do not purpose attempting to trace, in any detail, the successive incursions of Teutons and Slavs, of Goths and Huns, of Vandals, Lombards and Franks[2]. The interest of all this history gathers round certain great names; as of Alaric and Stilicho, Genseric, Attila and Theodoric. Alaric was the first barbarian to win a kingdom. The Visigoths and Ostrogoths, who were merged in one Gothic Empire in the 4th century under Ermaneric, were pressed by the Huns and checked by Theodosius. The Goths, who might have proved a valuable assistance to the Empire, if the sons of Theodosius had been firm and energetic, raised their independent standard, boldly avowed their hostile intentions and spread their hordes from the shores of Dalmatia to the walls of Constantinople. They made Alaric their leader, and his first blows were struck at the Eastern Empire. He made a secret treaty with the ministers of Constantinople, and gained the control of arsenal and taxes, as well as a strong strategic position. He next turned his thoughts westward, for the fame and wealth of Italy tempted him. He thought he heard a voice calling, " Alaric, brook no

---

[1] *Historiarum Libri VII*, " de Cladibus et Miseriis Mundi."

[2] *Italy and her invaders*, 8 vols. Thomas Hodgkin, D.C.L., Clarendon Press. *The Dynasty of Theodosius*, by the same author, and *The beginning of the Middle Ages*, by Dean Church.

delay, thou shalt penetrate to the city[1]." He entered Italy in
A.D. 400, and ten years later Rome was captured and sacked.
The City of the Seven Hills had never in 800 years been entered
by a foreign foe. It was called the "Eternal City" and was
thought inviolable.

Stilicho.

The name of Stilicho stands out prominently among the
defenders of the decaying Empire. To his care Theodosius
had intrusted his son Honorius who ruled the Western Empire.
Stilicho, loyal to his trust, would have gone to the assistance
of Constantinople at the time of Alaric's invasion, but received
a mysterious message, "Let Stilicho withdraw the legions of
Honorius within the limits of his master's Empire." In the
advance on Italy, Stilicho was once more at hand to guard
his trust, and at the battle of Pollentia compelled the invader
to retire for a time; but the loyal soldier's influence began to
wane. He lost the confidence of his troops and forfeited the
trust reposed in him by his king. His friends would have
made him their king, but he hesitated, and his hesitation cost
him his life. While he sat pensive and sleepless, a Gothic
warrior entered his camp at midnight to assassinate him.
Stilicho managed to escape, but a warrant for his execution
was obtained, and he was called in his last moments a traitor
and a parricide, and was put to death in A.D. 408.

Attila.

The conclusion of the first half of the 5th century witnessed
the warlike prowess of Attila, king of the Huns, whose life was
crowded with curious and romantic incidents. He entered Gaul
in A.D. 451. Half a million men, "obedient to his nod," moved
westward carrying devastation and destruction everywhere.
The allied forces of the Empire and the Goths met this enemy
of European civilisation and of Christianity at Chalons in
A.D. 451. In a conflict fierce and obstinate, in which the number
of slain was enormous, Attila could boast no victory, for it was

[1] Rumpe omnes Alarice, moras. Hoc impiger anno
Alpibus Italiae ruptis, penetrabis ad Urbem.
Claudian, *de bello Getico*, 545-6.

a drawn battle. This and the death of Attila freed Western Europe from the barbarism of the Huns. The power of his kingdom was broken up, for only a man of genius in war and skilful in administration could sustain it.

The Vandals under Genseric.

The blow that might have fallen through Attila was only temporarily delayed; it fell four years later in A.D. 455. The Vandals, who were the most savage of the Teutonic invaders, had been allies of the Empire for more than 200 years. They ravaged Spain and Northern Africa under "the terrible Genseric" whose name ranks with those of Alaric and Attila as agents in the destruction of the Empire. He was a man of inordinate ambition, and, as is commonly the case with those of this character, was troubled by no scruples in seeking to justify this passion. In A.D. 455 he arrived at the city gate, where he was met by Leo and his clergy. To them he promised protection, but the promise was not kept. The city was pillaged, and the sceptre of the great world conquering power was broken, and the spell of Empire departed.

Theodoric.

The Ostrogoths were vassals of the Huns and had fought on the side of Attila at Chalons. After his death they recovered their independence under the leadership of Theodoric who was destined to make a name in history and romance, and is, more by way of distinction than from his possession of supreme genius, called "the Great." In A.D. 488 he led his people forth, and fought his way to the confines of Italy. He consolidated his conquests and devoted a reign of 33 years to the duties of civil government. While he adhered to his Arian creed, he strove to show equal justice to all, and never attempted to enforce his own religious views upon his subjects, for as he wisely said, "We cannot impose religion by command, since no one can be made to believe against his will[1]." He was king of the Goths and of the West, and was the first to establish a

[1] Religionem imperare non possumus, quia nemo cogitur ut credat invitus Cassiodorus, *Variae*, 2, 27 (*Patrol.* 69).

state in which Goths and Italians were united in amity, though unlike in manners and customs, in religion and language, and his successful administration is sufficient testimony to his vigour and wisdom.

The Wars of Justinian.

Within ten years all Italy was regained for the Roman Empire by Justinian ruling from the East, the events of whose life were various and important, though it is as a legislator and codifier of the law that his name is best known to-day. He was unweariedly active and inordinately vain; his costly extravagance made an enormous demand upon the people, who groaned beneath the heavy burden of taxation, and his wars weakened rather than strengthened the Empire. Though Italy was regained, it was an impoverished and depopulated country which brought but a small addition of power to the Empire. His reign was also disturbed by a constant succession of border inroads, and the fair prospect was overcast with clouds which presaged the gathering storm that burst upon Italy in the days that followed his death in A.D. 565. Her sufferings, in the midst of turmoil, and revolution, her crimes and factions were at this time greater than those she endured at any other period of her history.

The Lombard Invasion.

During the reign of his successor, Justin II, Italy was invaded by the Lombards, the Italianised name of a Teutonic tribe, called by Roman writers the Langobardi, and described by Tacitus as a race "few in number who held their own against numerous and powerful neighbours by their bravery and love of war." With Alboin their king to lead them, and accompanied by a mixed multitude of barbarians, they descended in A.D. 568 upon this unhappy country, now exhausted by the efforts to conquer the Goths, and meeting with little opposition, they established a kingdom at Pavia which lasted for more than 200 years.

The Throne of S. Peter.

This outline picture of unrest and disquiet is not without its brighter side, for these eventful centuries of change and decay cover a period of the rise of one throne which showed no sign of decadence, but increased in power and brilliance as others tottered to their fall; it was the throne of S. Peter. S. Augustine's Empire of God was no visionary's dream, but an accomplished triumph, for in all the wanderings of the nations, in the rise and fall of tyrant kingdoms, in dissensions and disorganisation, in the overthrow of civilised institutions and in the spread of heresies, there remains " at every step in the tangled history of these times the wonderful life which the Roman name and the Roman power still kept when it was attacked on every side from without and torn in pieces in every quarter from within[1]," and the unity of the Empire was supported by the unity of the Church. " One Church stood beside one Empire," says Archdeacon Hutton, " and became year by year even more certain, more perfect, as well as more strong. In the West the papal power rose as the imperial decayed, and before long came near to replacing it[2]." The growth of this influence marks the earlier half of the 5th century. The bishops of Rome were consulted and courted by the various parties engaged in the factions and disputes of the East, while the bishops of Eastern sees, the prey of mutual jealousies and rivalries, looked to Rome the representative of the Western Churches with its seat in the most ancient and impressive city of the world. The dignity of the Roman see was greatly enhanced and increased by other circumstances, among which the confusion of the civil power was not the least potent. As the wealth of the see increased, the natural influence of riches was felt, and the bishops were able to keep in touch with the ecclesiastical affairs of distant provinces.

The noble character and remarkable genius of the men who filled the papal chair would suffice to make the era memorable. "Upon the mind of Innocent I," says Milman, "seems first distinctly to have dawned the vast conception of Rome's

[1] See Freeman, *Western Europe in the fifth century.*
[2] W. H. Hutton, *The Church and the barbarians*, p. 4, Rivington, 1906.

universal ecclesiastical supremacy." He lost none of the many opportunities of maintaining and extending the authority of the Roman see in all disputes, and of repudiating any conception which narrowed the influence of his office. His successor Zosimus was called upon to intervene in the dispute as to the relative jurisdiction of the sees of Arles and Vienne, and he decided in favour of Arles as it had been founded by Trophimus "sent into Gaul by S. Peter[1]." Zosimus is further remembered in connection with the Pelagian controversy, in which he made an important step towards increasing the authority of his see. His circular letter is the earliest instance of a document from Rome being proposed for general adoption as a standard of orthodoxy. Celestine went beyond all precedents in the extension of the power of his see, when he assumed the right to depose Nestorius, Bishop of Constantinople. His pretensions were not in this case allowed, for the bishop was deposed not by the mandate from Rome, but by bishops in council. Celestine advanced his claims in another direction at Ephesus where his representatives asserted that Rome's supreme judicature rested upon a prerogative exercised by S. Peter through his successors[2], and it must in scrupulous fairness be allowed that though the great Churches of the East as patriarchal sees cannot be said to have accepted the decisions of the Roman see as final, it is still a fact that "the impartial Apostolic See of Rome" generally discovered the true solutions to the questions raised in the Eastern Churches, and which divided them. Hence the power grew.

In Leo I Rome had a bishop of transcendent genius who made claims far in excess of his predecessors in the see. He was an astute politician as well as a learned theologian. He based his pretensions on unbroken apostolic tradition, and in urging that Alexandria should follow the Roman model he alleged that it would be impious to suppose that S. Mark the disciple would have varied the rules laid down by S. Peter the master[3]. Leo exercised sway also over Spain and Sicily, and when Hilary, Archbishop of Arles, at a synod held in A.D. 444 deposed Celidonius, and the latter appealed to Rome, Leo welcomed the

---

[1] Zosimus, *Epp.* 3–5, *Patrol.* 20.
[2] Labbé, III, 625. [3] *Ep.* 9.

opportunity of extending his powers in Gaul. He restored
Celidonius, deprived Hilary of the power to hold synods, and
influenced the Emperor Valentinian to promulgate a law in
which he declared that the Bishop of Rome was the rightful
ruler of the whole Church, and that any bishop who neglected
a citation to appear at the tribunal of the Bishop of Rome would
be compelled to appear by the civil governor of his province.
Further developments of the papal power were made by Felix
towards the close of the 5th century, when he announced the
deposition of Acacius to the clergy and people of Constantinople, and declared that all who sided with the patriarch would
be cut off from the Communion of Rome.

The most eminent representative of the 6th century is the
great Gregory, who was born in Rome A.D. 540. His homilies
describe the depressed state of the Church, which reached its
lowest depths at the end of the 6th century. He compared the
Church to "an old and violently shattered ship, admitting the
waters on all sides, its timbers rotten, shaken by daily storms,
and fast becoming a mere wreck[1]." Once more it is a time of
civil and ecclesiastical decay in which war, disease, and famine
devastated the land. Churches were destroyed; the clergy
deficient in number as in morality; the princes and nobles
sunk in depravity. In these circumstances Gregory showed a
marvellous grasp of affairs, keen insight, business instinct, and
remarkable tenacity of purpose. Nothing was too minute or
unimportant for his close attention. His tolerance was marked
by the protection of the Jews in the exercise of their religion,
and by his disapproval of coercion. His influence and labours
in the conversion of the heathen are too well known to need
more than a passing but none the less grateful reference here.
To our own island home he despatched Augustine, the provost
of his own monastery, with attendant monks, who landed in
the island of Thanet in A.D. 597. The rest of the story is too
familiar to need recapitulation. His strength of character, his
impressive genius, his masterly policy gave him the foremost
place among the bishops of Rome, and his greatness is thrown

[1] *Ep.* 1, 4.

into all the stronger relief by the comparative insignificance of his successors of the next hundred years.

This survey of the secular history of the time and the religious position has not been made without purpose. We are of course not here concerned primarily with the secular life of the centuries during which the monastery of Lerins was a flourishing religious institution, but it is undeniable that the religious life of every age is influenced in its character and form by the secular history of the period, by its prosperity or adversity. It is only by knowledge of the secular history of these centuries that we can form any idea of the world that had to be conquered, and from which many fled. But we must not suppose that monastic institutions, even in their inception, were mere places of refuge, chosen for selfish peace and quiet ; rather were they centres of influence, throwing light upon the surrounding darkness. The light may not have penetrated far ; still it did penetrate. Recluses were not cowards who could not fight against the wickedness of the world. They entered courageously into conflict with it, and were eager to instruct, to purify, and to conquer. In their chosen retirement they sought the strength necessary for this arduous work. With what results, the great names of bishops, scholars and presbyters mentioned in the succeeding pages who obtained their inspiration from Lerins will we trust amply exhibit.

Again and again might the religious recluse exclaim, " The foundations are destroyed, what shall the righteous do?" And so it was to these "isles of the blest" that men turned in their despair, and it is easy to see how these centuries provided devout natures with a powerful incentive to seek escape from the intolerable oppressiveness, and the great uncertainty of social life. The restlessness of the age impelled men of profound devotion and magnetic influence to go forth fortified by their solitude to guide and rule. There were also, of course, other motives at work. When persecution was not so severe as formerly, there were fewer opportunities of displaying the heroism of confession, and the distinction of martyrdom. Others again, overwhelmed by the corruption of Christian society, and despairing of the success of any attempt to hinder it, sought to attain to personal holiness by withdrawing from the world, and by the exercise of austerity to gain a close communion with heaven. There were doubtless other motives which actuated various men; with some it was a personal consciousness of guilt, with others it may have been sloth or even ambition. To the slothful as to the timid the monastery was a refuge from the storms whither they might flee, as to the wilderness, and be at rest. To the ambitious it was a pedestal from which to look down upon their fellow men; for the weak and irresolute it was a defence; to the fanatic it seemed the safest way to heaven.

The history of monasticism, like the history of states and of all human things, exhibits its various stages of growth, honour and decay. From the beginning of the 4th to the close of the 5th century is the age of impulsive enthusiasm; inexperienced and undisciplined "it has all the fervour, and all the extravagance of aims too lofty to be possible, of wild longings, without method, without organisation, of energies which have not yet learned the practical limits of their own power. Everything is on a scale of illogical exaggeration[1]."

The next period is from the commencement of the 6th century to the time of Charlemagne, and in this, monasticism shows a more mature activity. There is now a traditional routine, a division of duties, with stated hours for devotion, for social intercourse, for study and for manual labour. Thus, with the revival of learning, the monks were pioneers of civilisation to barbarian natives. The Lerinensian schools were the forerunners of the Benedictine seminaries in France, and of the professorships in the universities of mediaeval Christendom. After the downfall of Rome it was among the monks that musicians, painters, statesmen were found.

The third stage is that of decay. Its story, as is always the case, makes sad reading. It is now that we begin to see ostentation for simplicity, worldliness for spirituality, rivalry for respect, luxury for poverty. It is the old story; empires and individuals are alike ruined by the material prosperity which

[1] Dr Gregory Smith, *Christian Monasticism*, Introduction, p. 9.

eats into noble ideals like the cankerworm. Pride ever goes
before destruction, and a haughty spirit before a fall. The state
of the world called for an exhibition of stern Christianity, as a
counteractive to the prevalent and growing laxity. It was
needed to act as a check to the undisciplined tendency of the
time. But it could scarcely be hoped that even the old Roman
spirit of austerity could save an empire fast crumbling to pieces.
Numberless families were in distress and misery through the
continuous inroads of barbarian hordes, needing bread for their
bodies and food for their souls. Untamed natures required
discipline and the ignorant needed teaching. The educational
establishments with which Roman munificence had endowed the
principal towns of Gaul had for the most part disappeared in the
3rd and 4th centuries. "Alas for our days, for the study
of letters hath perished from among us[1]." The monastic order
also accepted as its mission the preservation to the world of the
masterpieces of past centuries of culture. All who are not
blinded by strong religious prejudices will ungrudgingly acknowledge the value of the literary services to posterity thus
rendered. It has been well said that "Englishmen remember
monasteries only in their decadence, they have entirely forgotten
that for 1500 years they were the well-springs of living water
from which our faith flowed to fertilise the world. They were
the sacred homes where Christian art, painting, music, architecture and learning were born and nourished. They were the
holy sanctuaries where divine love, that flame from the heart
of God, was cherished and fed by prayer and grace, until it
burst forth in missionary zeal which overturned empires and
claimed the world for God."

Monasticism.

A brief notice here of the rise of the monastic system may
form also a part of our prelude to the main theme. At first,
of course, ascetics or those who regarded life as a severe discipline
did not form a class separated from other Christians; for the
faith was in itself an ascetic practice. Tertullian in his Apology

---

[1] Greg. *Praef.*

expressly says that Christians did not separate themselves from the rest of mankind; nor did distinctive Christian monasticism exist till late in the 3rd century. Asceticism or self-discipline was practised, but then the Christian profession was itself an ἄσκησις as Clement of Alexandria in defence of Christian Gnosticism styles it. The word is used by Cyril of Jerusalem, and the thing was naturally common among the early Christians, but it was not practised in solitude, or in special societies, till a later date. The investigation of its beginnings is not an easy task, for the amount of original information is scanty, and extant documents are few in number. Those best competent to judge declare that the most important of these are the *Vita Antonii*, the *Historia Lausiaca*, the *Historia Monachorum in Aegypto*, and the *Institutes and Conferences* of Cassian. Antony is the prominent type of the monastic ideal and is regarded as the founder of monasticism. The authorship of the *Vita Antonii* was for a time disputed[1], but it is now generally accepted that Athanasius wrote it[2].

The *Lausiac History* written in A.D. 420, and so named from its dedication to Lausus, a chamberlain at the Court of Theodosius II, is a series of short biographies of the ascetics that Palladius had known personally or from hearsay, and is a vivid account of the desert life. Originally written in Greek, it has been translated into Latin, Syriac, Coptic, Ethiopic and other versions. It is generally ascribed to Rufinus, once the friend and later the strenuous adversary of Jerome, and gives an account of a visit to solitaries in the Thebaid during the years A.D. 394–5. We shall have occasion later to describe in some detail the works of Cassian, which give us considerable insight into the thoughts and aspirations of the early exponents of the monastic life, and into the author's own views of its practical value.

[1] For a summary of the controversy, see Bishop Robertson's *Introduction to the Works of Athanasius* in Wace and Schaff's Library of Nicene and Post-Nicene Fathers.

[2] *Ibid.*, Dom Butler comes to the same conclusion. See *Lausiac History of Palladius*, Cambridge Texts and Studies, edited by Dr Armitage Robinson.

The Origin of Monasticism.

Monasticism had its birthplace in Egypt, and three causes chiefly contributed to its origin. They were a general tendency towards a contemplative life, the teaching of the Alexandrian school of Neoplatonism, and the social state of the world external to Christianity, or merely nominally Christian. The crowds of new adherents too often brought with them their vices, delusions, superstitions and worldliness. They thronged the churches on the Christian festivals, and the theatres on the festivals of the pagans[1]. The Cross was not in the hearts of the people and with many the nominal acceptance of Christianity made little difference to their lives. Many relied on the power of the merely outward sign and joined themselves to the new faith with no serious inward call. To some baptism was a refuge in calamity, and was regarded in the light of a magic charm. Communions were carelessly made and often without devout preparation. The merits of outward attendance were magnified; the motives and methods of almsgiving were not considered. It would of course be quite contrary to fact to say that all the converts were worldly, formal, and lax. There were those of whom it might be said, "Ye are the salt of the earth." As in the days when the Christian refused to compromise with the pagan, so now the earnest genuine Christians stood out in relief against the nominal and superficial. Such earnest souls were not satisfied with the cold formality of outward ceremonies, of a parrot creed, and of a nominal orthodoxy. The aims and ideals of the ascetic life with its great renunciations, and its great gain in sincerity attracted and fascinated all who had taken to heart the self-denying precepts of their Lord. Can it be doubted that the life so pictured drew many to it who were dissatisfied with the aimlessness of their own lives, and desired to follow more closely the precepts and footsteps of their Divine Master? Thus was the way prepared for the ascetic life which developed along two lines, the Antonian and Pachomian. If the disturbed state of the world was the

---

[1] Illae turbae implent ecclesias per dies festos Christianorum, quae implent theatra per dies solennes Paganorum. Augustine, *de catechizandis*, p. 48.

outward, this was the inward cause of the trend to monasticism characteristic of the times.

From the life of Antony we note the gradual development of early monasticism. As his fame spread, many came to take up their abode near one whom they wished to imitate. Thus came the institution of the Laura or cluster of cells, in close proximity to each other like wigwams of an Indian encampment. The Antonian system prevailed at the end of the 4th century from Lycopolis to the Mediterranean, and prepared the way for the coenobitic life which was developed south of Lycopolis. Pachomius stands out in history as the founder of the coenobitic life and as the author of the first monastic Rule to be formally promulgated. He established his first monastery in the opening years of the 4th century, and based it upon the military ideal rather than that of family life. He planned a series of different houses, each with about thirty monks who were divided according to trades. His Rule has been handed down to us in two different forms. The first is very brief and is found in the *Lausiac History*. The second and fuller form extends to nearly two hundred chapters or headings, and has been preserved to us in a translation by Jerome. Although there was a minimum obligation, the regulations were far from severe, and much was left to private opinion and choice.

When Pachomius died in A.D. 349[1], his place was taken by Basil, the distinguished theologian, and the eloquent preacher who became Bishop of Caesarea. He was an ardent follower of the monastic ideal, who took a prominent part in the task of the reform of abuses which, parasite like, cling to the system. His Rule absorbed and supplanted all its predecessors. It had no rival and remains to-day the monastic code of the Eastern Church.

Towards the end of the 4th century, the East not merely gave to the West much of her theological speculation, the dominant forms of the creeds, and displayed her overmastering influence in the prevailing philosophy, but also helped greatly to shape Church life. In no respect is this more obvious than in the

---

[1] According to the Bollandists, who say he died about the date that Athanasius returned to his see in the time of Constantius.

spread of the ascetic and monastic ideals of life and piety. Italy was the first European country in which monasticism took permanent root, and it was not until towards the close of the 4th century that it found its way into Northern Gaul, through the instrumentality of Martin of Tours, soldier, hermit, bishop, saint, whose name and reputation excited unequalled admiration in the West. He originated an altogether new and independent system which it is not easy accurately and precisely to describe. He laid down no definite rule and prescribed no special habit of dress. But in his plans there was an effort to combine in reasonable proportions the active and the contemplative life.

We can well understand that when suitable spots in which to live the anchoretic or monastic life were sought, the numerous islands peacefully reposing in the sunshine of the Mediterranean Sea were chosen as sites for settlement and that "the bleak and barren isles from Lerins to Lipari that arise out of the Tuscan Sea" should have provided a refuge for these exiles from social life. Ambrose[1] asks why should he recount the number of the islands which were like "a woven necklace" on the neck of ocean, and where those who had abandoned "the allurements of a dissolute age" had deliberately chosen to forsake the world and escape "the doubtful conflicts of the worldly life." Jerome[2] in his letter on the decease of his friend Fabiola says of him that he visited the lonely corners on the headlands and curving bays of the tossing Tyrolean Sea in which there were *Monachorum Chori*. A heathen poet Rutilius Numatianus in his itinerary from Rome to his native Aquitaine passed their settlements at Gorgona and Capraria (A.D. 417). He notes the islands were full of men "clad in squalid garments," and with a tinge of contempt he says they call themselves by a Greek word (monks)[3]. With greater severity he calls them "shunners of light[3]," as if they were owls or bats. Salvian refers to the jeers which their sombre dress and white faces excited in the streets[4]. There were monastic establishments in

---

[1] *Hexaemeron*, III, 5.   [2] *Ep.* 84, 30.
[3] *De Reditu suo*,
          Squalet lucifugis insula plena viris
          Ipsi se monachos Graio cognomine dicunt.   I, 439–40.
[4] *De Gubern.* VIII, 4.

Sicily, Syracuse, and Sardinia, and there were pious hermits on the island of Ellea still earlier. Orosius had lived on the island of Gorgona, which is some twenty miles south-west of Leghorn, and he mentions it in his history[1]. At Capraria there was an abbot who was a correspondent of S. Augustine.

These monastic societies were formed on the Egyptian pattern. Gallinaria had its S. Martin who lived on herbs and roots. The choice of islands comports with the nature of the monastic life at that time. It was not the coenobitic life nor the eremitical life, but a combination of the two. It was so at Lerins. Cortesius tells us there were two classes of monks as in Egypt. The hermits lived in the grottoes scattered about the island either at Cap Roux or in separate cells, but only embraced the eremitic life after being proved by the exercises of the coenobitic. Free to seclude themselves in the solitudes of the isle, monks were yet circumscribed by the encircling sea; they still remained under the eye of the abbot and his *praepositus*, and they assembled to hear his instructions and to celebrate the Office. Thus, as Butler says, Gallic monasticism was Egyptian both in theory and practice[2]. Bingham[3] mentions that *Insulani* was a designation of monks in Southern France in the 5th century on account of the great reputation of the island monasteries, especially of Lerins. If the enthusiasm of Martin of Tours created the monasticism of Gaul, it was fostered and disciplined at the famous monastery on one of the islands of the Lerins. The far-reaching influence of this "island of the blessed," it will be our purpose and endeavour now to illustrate.

[1] VII, 36.
[2] *Lausiac History of Palladius.*
[3] *Orig. Eccles.* VII, 2, Sec. 14.

CHAPTER II

THE MAINLAND OF THE LERINS

The charms of modern Cannes are known to many who in search of pleasure or of health have basked beneath its sunny skies. Its visitors will descant upon its advantages and sing its praises. Surrounded by hills it is sheltered from the winds. Its winters are mild. There is never any fog. There are no long dreary days of rain. Its amusements are manifold. Its walks are attractive, its views magnificent, its flowers lovely. Do visitors to the Riviera know also that the history of Cannes is full of historic interest dating back through the centuries of the past?

The Department of Provence.

The influence of geographical position is more enduring than the works of man at the highest stage of his civilisation. Physical geography has its unalterable features. Many have feared to visit the Holy Land lest their ideals should be shattered. There is much to disillusionise in the squalid surroundings of human production, but all travellers will agree there is no make-believe or superstition in the hills and in the valleys of Palestine. The spoiling hand of man cannot destroy their charm. The outline of the Holy City and its environs is not changed. The aspect of the Mount of Olives is to-day what it was in olden times. The everlasting hills are there to emphasise the words of the Psalms: "They that put their trust in the Lord shall be even as the Mount Sion which may not be removed, but standeth fast for ever. The hills stand about Jerusalem: even so standeth the Lord round about his people[1]." This is true of all places. Provence was not always as visitors behold it

---

[1] Ps. cxxv, 1, 2.

now, but the mountain crests were always there.   The old order
changeth, but yet there stand the everlasting hills.   The waters
of the sea were ever blue.   The range of the Esterels was always
purple against the sun.

The name of Provence is derived from that of the Roman
province founded in Gaul at the end of the 2nd century
before Christ, and afterwards called the Narbonnaise.   Its limits
varied much during the centuries.   It lies on the high road to
Italy, and has been trodden by the feet of many varying
generations.   In its prehistoric epoch, Iberians, Ligurians,
Phoenicians and Greeks peopled it.   We know little of the first
inhabitants.   The Ligurians made their longest stay in this
region of Gaul, and their memory is still perpetuated in the
walls of large unmortised stones, called by the peasants of to-day
"leis murassos" (the walls), which guard the Celto-Ligurian
camps[1], notably on the plateau of Gourdon surmounting the
valley of the Loup.   The Phoenicians left no durable traces
of their occupation, though they established a new town at
Marseilles about B.C. 600, and later founded Athenopolis,
Antipolis, Nice and other places.   They gave way in their
turn to merchant Greeks.   Then followed the Roman period
when Marseilles, unable to defend Nice and Antibes against the
Oxybians, summoned the aid of its ally, Rome, as is mentioned
later, and the province was founded.   In the next three hundred
years Gallo-Roman civilisation developed almost without interruption.   Then ensued the barbaric period when Celts and
Goths, Burgundians and Franks, Vandals and Huns, invaded it.
To this succeeded the feudal epoch, with the dynasties of the
Bosons (A.D. 934–1113), of the Berengers (1113–1246) and
of D'Anjou (1246–1481).   This was followed by the royal
period.

An Ancient Site.

The modern Cannes in all probability is built on the site
of an ancient Ligurian city.   Before it was Christianised, the
Mediterranean coast was covered with Greek settlements, of
which Nice and Antibes were first in importance.   The Phocean

---

[1] *Maritime Alps*, Vol. I, pp. 52 and 232.

colony extended from Marseilles to Monaco. Its commerce was disturbed, and its existence was threatened more than once by the Ligurians, who were divided into an infinity of small states, each with its own government. Chief among these were the Oxybians in the west and the Deceates in the east.

The Oxybians.

Their territory included the town since called "Forum Julii" (the modern Fréjus) on the banks of the river Argens, so named from the silvery colour of its waters[1]. Their chief port was on the site of the modern Cannes (as we hope presently to show). They lived under a democracy which was a mixture of republican and monarchical government. They had a king who led them to war and distributed the rewards of battle. This was his only prerogative. He was chosen not from the most rich and eloquent but from the bravest and from those who had rendered the greatest services. His authority generally lasted only for a year, but sometimes it was a life appointment. The people made the laws. They did not go to war for mere love of gain, for they sacrificed their prisoners and the riches and booty they had secured. They recognised several gods, and believed in the immortality of the soul. They buried with a man what he loved best, and even the notes of sums that he had lent, that he might exact their payment in the other life. Their occupations were fishing and piracy. They surprised vessels that were tempest bound, and having despoiled them, placed their treasure on the islands of the Lerins. Thus did these islands serve as a pirate's treasure house, a purpose humble enough, long years before they achieved a very different reputation destined to be world-wide. In spite of their savage customs, these Oxybians practised hospitality, and made generous recognition of services rendered to them, or to their cause. To the east of them the Deceates extended from Antipolis (the modern

---

[1] Walckenaer, *Géographie ancienne des Gaules*, Vol. I, p. 182, Paris, 1839. He and most modern geographers believe that the Oxybians' territory ended at the Esterel and extended to the environs of Antibes. Bouche, *Chorographie de Provence*, says, "They should be placed beyond the Deceates, i.e. beyond the Var at the commencement of Italy."

Antibes) to the Var, with a capital between Nicea and Antipolis.

Proofs of this early occupation of Provence are not wanting. Ancient documents show that the portion of the maritime coast between the eastern heights of the Esterel and the river Var was in the possession of the Oxybians. Polybius[1] says the Romans landed "at the town of Aigitna in the territory of the Oxybians." Strabo[2] tells us of the existence of a port between Antibes and the Esterel, but he gave it no name. He calls it simply "the port of the Oxybians." Pomponius Mela[3] refers in his nomenclature of Narbonnesian Gaul to the capital of the Deceates[4]. Pliny[5] is even more precise in his reference to both Oxybians and Deceates[6]. Cluverius[7] in his *Italia Antiqua* says that Egitna is the name of the Oxybian port that Strabo mentions, and he tells us that it is not far from the river Siagne. It is to-day called Cannes[8], and was the ancient Acro of

[1] A Greek historian, born B.C. 200. His great work was a general history in 40 books.

[2] A Greek writer and geographer who was born about the middle of the 1st century B.C. and died about A.D. 20. We know from Plutarch and Strabo himself that he wrote *Historical Memoranda* in 43 books, which commenced at the period where Polybius left off. His great work *Geographica* in 17 books is still extant. The 4th deals with Britain, Gaul, and the north side of the Alps, and the 5th and 6th with Italy and its dependencies.

[3] A Roman writer on geography. It is the only systematic treatise on the subject preserved to us in the Latin language with the exception of the elder Pliny's Encyclopaedia. He lived about the middle of the 1st century A.D.

[4] Nicaea tangit Alpes, tangit oppidum Deceatum, tangit Antipolim deinde Forum Julii.

[5] Caius Plinius Secundus, surnamed the Elder, to distinguish him from his nephew, was born in A.D. 23 and died in A.D. 79. He wrote a *Natural History* which is really an Encyclopaedia of geography, agriculture, commerce, medicine, &c., in 37 books.

[6] In ora autem Athenopolis Massiliensium, Forum Julii Octavanorum Colonia, quae Pacensis appellatur et classica: amnis in ea Argenteus, Regio Oxubiorum Ligaunorumque, super quos Suetri, Quariates, Adunicates. At in ora oppidum latinum Antipolis, Regio Deciatum; amnis Varus ex Alpium monte Cemenus profusus.

[7] An antiquary and geographer born at Danzig in A.D. 1580. He published his *Germania Antiqua* in 1616, *Sardinia et Corsica Antiqua* in 1619, and *Italia Antiqua* in 1624.

[8] The Aigitna of Polybius is in Latin Aegitna, and French Egitna. Pronounced with the *g* hard, it successively becomes Ekitna, Eketna, Ecatna, Catna, Cana, and Cannes. A similar change from the *g* hard to a *c* may be illustrated by Cadiz which was formerly Gades.

Polybius[1]. Papon[2] says the town of Egitna was above the village of Mougins, Latin Mouginum, a name that appears to be derived from Mons Egitna. Barralis calls Mougins "an old town[3]." It is possible that the vanquished inhabitants of Egitna were allowed to settle at a distance, and having chosen some height, it would be natural if they recalled their old home and named it Mons Egitna.

The Oxybians and the Romans.

The two settlements of Nice and Antibes were continually at war with the Oxybians and the Deceates till at length in B.C. 155 they were besieged. Marseilles unable to defend them begged the assistance of its ally Rome. The Roman Senate sent a deputation to negotiate the terms of reparation demanded by them from these Ligurians. According to the narrative of Polybius this deputation consisted of Flaminius, Popilius Lenas, and Lucius Papius. When the Ligurians learnt that these Romans had come to order them to give up the siege, they hastened to prevent them from landing. Flaminius had already landed, but they ordered him to leave at once. On his refusal, they pillaged his property, and maltreated his servants. Flaminius himself was wounded, and two of his slaves were killed. When the Senate was informed of these events they immediately ordered Quintus Opimius, one of the consuls, to set out with an army against the Ligurians. He placed his camp along the river Apron and awaited the enemy. Soon he led his forces against Egitna, took it by assault, and reduced its people to slavery. The Oxybians knew there was no hope of pardon and made a desperate resolve. Without waiting for the arrival of the Deceates they threw themselves upon the Romans. The consul was a man of experience and judgment. He shrewdly concluded

---

[1] Strabo Oxvbium memorat portum, quod oppidum Polybio, proprio nomine dicitur Aegitna ; et juxta hoc flumen Acro. Oppidum id nunc vocatur Canes, inter Forum Julii et Antipolim, ad intimum sinus haud modice recessum positum : juxta quod amnis in sinum effunditur vulgari vocabulo Siagne. Haud dubie antiquus ille Polybii Acro est. *Italia Antiqua*, Vol. I, p. 60, 1624.

[2] *Voyage Littéraire de Provence*, Vol. I, p. 273. He was born near Nice in A.D. 1734 and wrote a history of Provence in four volumes.

[3] Villa Vetus.

that this action was inspired by despair and not by reason. He broke their ranks, slew many of the enemy, and put others to flight. Then the Deceates appeared. They too were conquered. The Oxybians were so powerful and redoubtable that the Romans were not content to destroy their chief town, but they took the most energetic methods to reduce them to impotence. Opimius made good use of his victory. Having become master of their territory he gave part of it to the Massilians, and compelled the enemy to send hostages to Marseilles. He spent the winter of B.C. 154 in the neighbourhood. Three years afterwards the Oxybians asserted their independence again, and a considerable army was necessary to bring them once more to submission. They are quaintly described as "more difficult to find than to conquer." They next allied themselves with a neighbouring tribe of the Salluvians in a war with Marseilles in B.C. 123, but they were again defeated and were forced to the mountains. The proconsul Calvinus, their conqueror on this occasion, ceded to Marseilles all the maritime zone from the Rhone to the Var, in order to ensure communication by land and sea between Italy and Gaul. He forbade the Ligurians to approach within certain defined limits. The Romans extended their conquests and in B.C. 117 founded the colony of Narbonne which later gave the name of Narbonnaise Gaul to the Roman province. After an eight years' war Julius Caesar in B.C. 51 brought the rest of Gaul to submission, besieged and took Marseilles which had espoused the cause of Pompey but as an act of clemency and in recognition of the town's faithful alliance in the past, he left its people free to govern themselves. While the Roman conquest of the country lasted, the Greeks, masters of the shore, and protected elsewhere by the arms of the Republic, raised, on the ruins of Egitna, a settlement which took the name of Castrum Marsellinum.

Greek and Roman Traces.

There are few traces of Greek occupation and civilisation, except in the names of places such as Neapolis (Napoule), Antipolis (Antibes) and Athenopolis (Antea, long since in ruins). At Cogolin has been found an interesting little funeral

monument in white marble with two names in Greek characters[1].
The Greeks established themselves on the spot for the purposes
of commerce, they built settlements but not monuments. The
Greek language and Greek coinage were the great vehicles
of commerce. Coins have been found, and it is interesting to
note that Greek words survive, especially among the fisher-folk.
The relics of Roman occupation are much more numerous.
There are remains of a majestic aqueduct near Grimaud. There
is an interesting inscription now in the Museum at Cannes[2].
It reads, " To Venusia Anthimilla, my dearest daughter, Caius
Venusius Andronicus of the body of the Augustulian men[3]."

The Roman roads everywhere, as in our own island, are
marks of Roman civilisation and attest the early importance
of Provence. The development of Castrum Marsellinum was
stopped by the barbarian invasions and devastated. The
marauding bands of the Saracens sacked and burnt it and
the surrounding neighbourhood. From that time it was without
inhabitants. A crusade was raised against the invaders towards
the end of the 10th century and it came under the suzerainty
of the counts of Antibes.

Castrum Canois.

It was not however until the 11th century that it formally
passed into the possession of Lerins. When William Gruetta,
second son of Rodoard, Count of Provence, exchanged the
soldier's girdle for the garment of a monk, and withdrew to the
monastery of the Lerins, he gave to it all that he possessed at

[1] Ἑρμου Μνεσιλας. See Baron de Boustetten, *Carte archéologique du département du Var.*

[2]
VENVSIAE
ANTHIMIL
LAE
C VENVSIVS
ANDRON SEX
VIRI AVG CORP
FILIAE
DVLCISSIMAE.

[3] In A.D. 746 Augustulus organised the order of the "magistri vicorum" in
connection with the worship of the public Lares. The citizens in municipalities to
whom was confided this duty received the name of "sex viri." They were never
less or more than six.

Mont Chevalier, with its ancient Tower, overlooking
Modern Cannes.

Mougin, Arluc and at Castrum Marsellinum. It is in this donation that the name of Canois figures for the first time. The town was reconstructed, and Genoese families came to repeople it. It is called Castrum Canois. Henceforward it is the camp, castle, hospital, church, or town of Canois.

Castrum Francum.

The name was changed once again in A.D. 1131 to Castrum Francum, and the counts of Provence spoke of it as such in the time of King Edward the Confessor. In Raymond Feraud's *Life of Honoratus*, composed at the end of the 13th century, it is called Vilafranqua, when the wife of Raybaud de Beljuec, in fulfilment of a vow, made a pilgrimage to Lerins and embarked from Vilafranqua[1].

The Lerins and the Fief of Cannes.

Till the close of the Middle Ages the history of Cannes is the history of the Lerins. The abbot of the monastery of S. Honoratus was its feudal lord. In the 11th century Aldebert II was the ruling abbot, and deserves to be called "the Great." It was one of the monastery's periods of prosperity and he used it well. As we shall see later, he laid the foundations of the château fort on one of the islands of the Lerins. He rendered a similar service to the town of Cannes. In A.D. 1070 he began the great square tower which still dominates the town and harbour from the heights of Mont Chevalier, as our illustration shows[2]. It is one of the most beautiful buildings raised in Provence during the Middle Ages. It was not completed till A.D. 1395 by abbot John de Thornafort. There is the same quality and shape of stone as on Lerins. Twice a thunderbolt fell upon it, in 1786 and again in 1796. In 1823 the owner wanted to pull it down in order to sell the materials. The demolition was actually commenced, but was stopped, partly because the materials had lost their value, and partly because the authorities agreed with the complaint of the sailors

[1] A Vilafranque dins el port montan on mar. A MS. of this poem has a marginal note :—Vilafranca tunc temporis castrum de Canois.

[2] Aldebertus...monasterium et ecclesias reparasse arcemque turris Lerinensis monasterii, alteriusque in Castro Canois jecisse fundamenta. *Chron. Ler.* II, p. 157.

that a landmark for ships going towards Cannes ought not to be removed.

In return for the protection afforded by the tower, the monks exacted heavy dues. In recognition also of this service, Raymond Berenger took the monastery of the Lerins under his protection, and ceded all his rights as lord to the abbot and his successors for ever. The abbots claimed a tax whenever a piece of land changed hands; wine, figs, oils and other produce were taxed. The monks of Lerins also built in the middle of the 12th century[1] a hospital, under the name of S. Honoratus.

The greater part of Cannet, an annexe of Cannes, was cultivated by a colony sent by the monastery of the Lerins.

With the commencement of a municipal life and constitution in A.D. 1447, the people of Cannes agreed to take an oath of faith and homage to the abbot on condition that he consented to their statutes. Andrew de Plaisance who was abbot at the time accepted the agreement and received their homage. The heads of families went to the château fort of the island, and in succession took the oath. With heads bare, and with hands upon a missal they promised perpetual obedience and fidelity, and engaged to defend his honour, to take no part in any enterprise against him, and to reveal it to him, if they should know or hear of any such. On his part he promised to maintain the inhabitants of Cannes in all their rights, and to treat them as a true lord should treat his lieges and his subjects. The motive of the abbot in this treaty was to guarantee the privileges of the Lerins against the independence of the new community. The Cannois on their side desired to be rid of a dependence no longer in harmony with the spirit of the times. How great this dependence was may be measured by the letter that had been sent to the abbot, only the year before, to beg for certain concessions. Among them they asked permission to gather acorns for their pigs. This was conceded. They pleaded for half of everything they found on land or sea, and were granted a third part. They desired that every inhabitant might carry "an honest sword" in maritime and suspected places for the purpose of self-defence. This request was allowed. They asked

---

[1] Hospitalis Sancti Honorati. *Cartulaire*, f. 33, 4.

that the abbot would not pursue by his officers men for what they might say at the municipal council. He consented with the proviso that nothing must be said against the abbot or his monks. There were numerous transactions in the 15th and 16th centuries, concerning the feudal rights of the monastery. In A.D. 1449 these were recognised in a public act passed by Andrew in agreement with the consuls of Cannes. Among the provisions are the following :—From Septuagesima Sunday to Easter, every inhabitant of Cannes must buy his wine, in bulk or detail, at the tavern the abbots had held from time immemorial in the town. From the eve of the Ascension to the day after Pentecost, the period of the pilgrimages, every person found on the island must buy wine and eatables only at the abbey shop and market, and it was expressly forbidden to open another shop or market. No one was allowed to take passengers or goods at Cannes to carry them to the island, until the abbot's boat loaded with people and goods had left the port, and even then such an one must pay the abbot a third part of the price of passage, if the proprietor of the boat belonged to Cannes, Fréjus or S. Raphael, and a half, if he belonged to any other place. The abbot had also the right to take from all proprietors a basket of figs during the harvest. They must also give him the eleventh part of the grapes that were gathered, and take them to the island at their own expense. The abbot on his part must give a drink to the bearers ! The tenth part of the wheat and other cereals, and the eleventh part of vegetables, hemp and flax was also to be paid. There were fishing and hunting rights to be paid for in money or in kind[1]. At length in A.D. 1514 the inhabitants no longer humbly asked concessions. They speak of their rights, and in spite of the protestations of Augustine Grimaldi against such attempts at independence, the nomination of arbitrators was necessary to terminate the dispute. In the archives of Lerins there is an arbitration award of A.D. 1519 by virtue of which the inhabitants of Cannes must grind and cook in the abbot's mills and ovens, and then only by his permission, and they are forbidden to build

[1] For further information of this taxation readers are referred to Alliez, *Les Iles de Lerins*, p. 215, and Sardou, *Histoire de Cannes*, p. 67 seq.

such for themselves.   Five centimes of every florin is a due to
the abbot on the sale, alienation or transfer of all landed estate.
On the other hand the abbot and his successors will no longer
have the right of a tavern at Cannes for the sale of wine or
of receiving a basket of figs from each proprietor.   The abbots
were however able to maintain some at least of the feudal
rights for a long time.

In 1579 all the fish of an inhabitant of Cannes was seized
because the percentage of a farthing per florin had not been
paid on all that was bought and taken away from the town.
The people of Cannes did not forget their hopes of independence,
and their relations with the lords of Lerins gradually underwent
a change.   On the one hand the subjects cherished progressive
ideas which gathered force daily ; and on the other the masters,
who were forgetful of their duties, saw the consideration that their
predecessors had received gradually lessened, and as a result
the moral authority of the abbot and monks, formerly exercised
over minds favourably disposed to recognise it, was losing its
hold.   In the closing years of the 16th century, the consuls
of the town claimed the exclusive right of commanding the
garrison which occupied the château on Mont Chevalier.   The
steward of the monastery, acting in the name of the absent
commendatory abbot, opposed this pretension.   The matter
was discussed by the parliament of Aix in 1594, and the request
of the Cannois was upheld.   In 1633 the consuls had obtained
permission to change the coat-of-arms of their town, but a
decision of the parliament of Provence, on the complaint of the
steward representing the Prince of Joinville, another absentee
commendatory, now forbade them to make the change.   The
coat-of-arms which the abbey had given to Cannes was and
still is to-day a silver palm on a blue ground.   Under the
restoration, King Louis XVIII added to it two *fleurs de lis*
of gold.   The palm served as a witness of the benevolence
of the abbey which gave a palm to every person who made
seven pilgrimages to Lerins.   It was also a remembrance of the
refuge which the founder sought when according to legend the
island was freed from serpents by the invading sea.

It was not till the secularisation of the monastery that

Cannes was finally and completely freed from the domination of the monks. To this day the monks of the Lerins pay no municipal dues, and the mayor would be unable to set foot uninvited on the island were it not that the admiralty possess the foreshore rights[1].

Pestilence and Wars.

There was no more fatal year for the town than 1580. A solitary woman was the unconscious cause of it. She had been landed there from a Levantine vessel and was suffering from the plague, from which she died. From her, infection spread all over Provence from town to town. More than 20,000 perished at Marseilles. A poor hermit named Valéry went about tending the sick and was at first venerated as a saint, but afterwards he was accused of spreading the plague and of maliciously prolonging its duration. He was condemned by the parliament of Aix as a sorcerer, and the unhappy man was burnt alive. The burial grounds of the great plague are still spoken of in Cannes and it is said[2] that when the huge boulevards of the Société Foncière were cut, there were old men who shook their heads and hoped that no harm might come of stirring ground which had not been turned since 1580.

Civil war broke out, during the contagion, between the Protestants who favoured the royalist troops, and the Leaguers or Catholic Party, and Cannes was occupied in turn by each, and later by the army of Emmanuel, Duke of Savoy, who was offered the kingdom by the Leaguers on the death of Henry III. The royalists' cause ultimately prevailed, but Cannes suffered severely and was sacked. It recovered from this reverse and its trade revived, but the hoped-for prosperity was not of long duration. At the close of the Thirty Years' War, the Spaniards attacked Cannes, but failed to conquer it. During the War of the Spanish Succession Prince Eugène and the Duke of Savoy crossed the Var with their forces in 1707 in an invasion of Provence. Surrounding villages and towns were pillaged and sacked. Churches were profaned, sacred vessels stolen, images

[1] For some of the rights of the abbey over Cannes, see H. Moris, pp. 81, 122, &c.
[2] *The Maritime Alps and their Seaboard*, Vol. II, p. 186.

broken. Cannet which was in the township of Cannes was entered, and an abbot, who was the curé of the place, was put at the head of some inadequately armed peasants, but was unable to offer effective resistance. The armies marched on Cannes by the road that bordered on the sea. It was then that the cannons of the island of S. Margaret arrested the march, and the invaders were compelled to go by another route.

Forty years afterwards during the War of the Austrian Succession in which France had taken part against the Empress Maria Theresa, the Austrians and Piedmontese assisted by an English fleet entered Provence. Cannes was again occupied and its inhabitants fled to the islands of Lerins but were peremptorily ordered to return. The wars of the empire had ruined the commerce of the town. It had no desire to welcome Napoleon.

Napoleon at Cannes.

An English warship was supposed to be watching between Antibes and Leghorn the movements of the prisoner of Elba. Napoleon had friends who supplied him with money. A brig with a flotilla of three small ships was provided and 400 men of the old guard, together with 200 infantry, 100 Polish lancers and 200 chasseurs and some field guns were at his disposal. The English cruiser was at Leghorn. The moment was opportune. Napoleon set sail and on March 1st, 1815, the ships anchored in the roadstead of Golfe de Juan. Cambronne, one of his generals, with twenty-five of the old guard, landed to go to Cannes. There was in every mouth in Paris a saying that was prophetic, " The violet will return with the spring." It was now fulfilled. We cannot do better than reproduce an extract from an interesting and graphic account of the emperor's visit to Cannes[1]: " In 1815 Cannes consisted of the few dark streets that clustered under Mont Chevalier. The townhall was in the middle of what is now the Rue Centrale, and next door to it was the public or communal school...; on a bench close to the window of that school a boy sat, slate in hand. It was Master

---

[1] *The Maritime Alps*, Vol. II, p. 200 seq.

Sardou....He was supposed to be following the arguments of a teacher who with his back to his scholars was working a sum in simple division on a black-board. The scholar became aware of a strange noise, and then of a stranger sight. Five and twenty grenadiers with queues and tall fur caps were drawn up before the townhall, and an orderly was tying to an elm the horse from which an officer had dismounted. What might this portend? Master Sardou and a companion slipped out of the room to judge for themselves; their example was immediately followed by every boy in the class; and when the pedagogue finished his sum and turned round, he was alone! No doubt he followed his truants, and soon also heard the amazing news— Napoleon was coming, and Cambronne had come and had just asked for the mayor. He was away for the day. He had gone to see his vineyard. As he was returning he met a gendarme with a tricolour cockade. He settled in his own mind that the offender was tipsy. He met another and then another. Cambronne requested him to declare his allegiance to Napoleon. The mayor replied that he could acknowledge but one master, his Majesty Louis XVIII. By this time night had fallen. Napoleon was now ashore....On the military chest to leeward of the camp fire he sat moody, taciturn and preoccupied. The night was nearly a fatal one for him. Under cover of the darkness a butcher stole out of the Grande Rue, carrying an old fowling piece. He detested the smooth faced Corsican, and at midnight went out to have a shot at the man who, having once already turned the world upside down, had now returned from exile to dispute the throne with the Bourbons. The butcher rested his gun on a fence not many yards from the head of which the pale and clear cut features stood out in the light of the blazing bivouac fire. One moment more and the emperor's midnight watch would have been his last; one shot and there might have been no Waterloo and no St Helena. But the butcher was arrested by a neighbour, not out of any sympathy with the Buonapartes, but from an impression that were Napoleon to be murdered at midnight, Cannes would be burnt down before midday." At two o'clock he was in the saddle. At the angle of the road, he met the mayor, asked him the time and the way to Grasse. He reached this place at dawn. We need not follow his journey further.

On March 6th he issued two proclamations, one was addressed to the French people, the other to the army. Both are masterpieces of military eloquence. The same day Louis XVIII signed an ordinance, in the opening words of which " Napoleon Buonaparte is declared a traitor and a rebel....It is enjoined on all governors, commanders of the armed forces, national guards, civil authorities and even simple citizens to attack him, arrest him and to take him before a council of war which after recognition of his identity shall instigate against him the application of the penalties pronounced by the law."

The Tribute of Cannes to a Lord Chancellor of England; and to the King of England.

It was Lord Brougham who revealed to strangers and even to the French the treasures which nature has lavished on this beautiful neighbourhood of the South of France. He went in 1834, was the first to purchase land there and to suggest to the aged and the invalid that their lives might be prolonged on this beautiful shore. In 1838 a pier and harbour were built. It was the commencement of a new prosperity, now at its zenith. It was then an unimportant borough of 4000 inhabitants. To-day the population has quadrupled. In the centre of a palm-planted square facing the quay, stands a marble statue erected by the people to the memory of their benefactor. The eastern face of the pedestal bears a Latin inscription[1]. Translated it reads— " I have found a harbour. Hope and fortune farewell. You have deceived me sufficiently. Deceive others now." They are the words of a philosopher, pronounced on the day when having renounced grandeur he became a simple inhabitant of Cannes.

The Cannois are proud too of a distinguished visitor, his late Majesty King Edward VII. To his honour a stately monument in white marble has been raised in grateful memory of one who appreciated the beauty of the place, and the respite that it gave from the engrossing cares of state.

[1] Inveni portum. Spes et Fortuna valete. Sat me lusistis. Ludite nunc alios.

CHAPTER III

THE ISLANDS OF THE LERINS

Opposite the low peninsula of the Cap de la Croissette, two or three miles south of the mainland of Cannes to which they form a natural breakwater, lie the islands of the Lerins. The two larger, called by the country folk " the green rosettes of the sea " are Sainte Marguerite and Saint Honorat, which float like two rafts of verdure on a lake of blue. The narrow channel of the Frioul divides them. Round them are barren and chalky reefs dignified as islets, for one is named S. Ferreol[1] and lies to the east of the island of Saint Honorat, and the other, the Translero of antiquity, later called Terra de Lhierra, is the Tradeliere of the Cannois boatmen, and is situated to the east of Sainte Marguerite. The two islands have a great renown. Sainte Marguerite is known as the place of confinement of a mysterious and unnamed prisoner; Saint Honorat claims the attention of archaeologists, historians, Christians, in a word of all who desire to preserve the memory of the priceless past. The group is known as the islands of the Lerins. The name is a survival of the Lero and Lerina of antiquity, for they were so called by the Phoenician Greeks who had invaded this part of Gaul in prehistoric ages. This people desired to recall the exploits of a legendary hero. Mythology has left no trace of him. He was probably the personification of the race. Strabo tells us he saw there a temple of this god, at which the pirates offered sacrifice. According to the *Chronologie de Lerins* it was still in existence during the first two or three centuries of the Christian era. The islands are

---

[1] According to the traditions of the Church of Grasse, he was martyred by the Saracens on the islet that bears his name.

mentioned under various names by ancient writers. Strabo calls the larger one Lero and the smaller one Planasia (now Pianosa), perhaps because it is flat, or the word may have signified "trifles," implying bits of land. He says they were well peopled[1].

The Phoenicians founded the naval station of Vergoanum on the island of Sainte Marguerite, but it existed only in name and memory in the time of Pliny[2]. The position is also mentioned in the Maritime Itinerary of Antonine[3]. The Annalist of Lerins states that the Romans built there sumptuous dwellings, fortifications and an arsenal, ruins of which were still to be seen in the 16th century[4]. Sidonius gives the names as Lerinus and Lerus. Ennodius distinguishes Lero from Lerina[5]. Monsieur l'Abbé Goux remarks that the old name of Lerina has been carelessly disfigured by modern orthography[6]. Moroni states that some geographies refer to Lero and Planasia, others to Lero and Lerina, and he adds that Sidonius does not speak in compliment when he uses the word Planasia, for it means a humble island[7]. Ptolemy[8] only mentions one island, of which the name is variously written. The name of Lero or Leros was given to several islands of the Sporades in the Aegean[9] Sea. The troubadour Feraud in his curious poem relates that Honoratus was delivered to the serpents. Two of them were called Rin and Leri respectively. Hence the island was ultimately called Lerins[10].

---

[1] Πλανασία καὶ Λήρων ἔχουσαι κατοικίας.

[2] Lero et Lerina, adversus Antipolim, in qua Vergoani oppidi memoria. Pliny I, 3. c. 11.

[3] Ab Antipoli, Lero et Lerina insulae.

[4] In qua (Lerone)...auleata domicilia, validasque munitiones construxerunt, ut adhuc monstrant antiqua vestigia. Chron. Ler. Descriptio situs.

[5] Vita S. Epiphanii.

[6] Lerins au cinquième siècle.

[7] Dizionario di erudizione. Venezia, 1846.

[8] II, 9. 21. An astronomer whose writings date from A.D. 128. He published a book on geography in 8 vols.

[9] Strabo IV, 10. c. 5, Leros (nunc Lero) prope Patmos. Pliny IV, 25. 5, Leros in Cariae ora.

[10] L'uns serpentz a nom Rin, e l'autre a nom Lery. Per zo fom appellada en l'islla de Lerins, Car laynz si noyrian le lerys e le Rins. XXVIII.

The Cell of "The Man with the Iron Mask."

The Island of Sainte Marguerite.

This, the larger island, is about 2½ miles long, and about half a mile wide. Its reputation is less than that of the sister island of Saint Honorat, and is of a different kind. Its history is not without interest. It is said by some that S. Honoratus broke the statues of Lero[1] and dedicated the purified Temple to the honour of S. Margaret[2], from love to his sister who may have accompanied him to the islands. The tradition rests upon a pretty legend. When they were about to separate, she to form a retreat for nuns, he to found a monastery of worldwide reputation, he promised that though she could not be admitted to his island, he would come and see her once a year. " Let us agree to meet," she said, " when the cherry trees are in bloom." The brother consented. She prayed that if it were the will of Him who created a brother's love, the cherry tree might bloom every month. Later Eucherius, Vincent and other monks of Lerins who desired complete solitude retired to the larger island[3]. It was kept in the possession of the monks until the 17th century, when as we shall record later, it passed into the hands of the Prince de Joinville, who in 1618 ceded it and his rights therein to his brother Charles de Lorraine the king's lieutenant-general in Provence. Charles in his turn sold it with all its rights to John de Bellon for £4500. Its new owner built a dungeon and fortifications.

The islands of the Lerins were next placed under a Court of Government. The staff office consisted of the governor, a lieutenant of the king, a major, a curé, an almoner, a physician and surgeon. De Guitaut was succeeded in 1687 by M. de Saint-Mars.

The Man with the Iron Mask.

The only interest of the island is the cell, of which we give an illustration, where " the man with the iron mask" spent seventeen miserable years of imprisonment. In the spring of

---

[1] Fregit antiquas statuas Leronis. *Chron. Ler.* i, p. 17.

[2] Illa olim vocata Lero nunc dicitur insula sanctae Margaritae, a sacro sacello priscis saeculis inibi in honorem dictae virginis et martyris consecrato. Lecointe, *Annal. Eccles. Francorum*, Vol. i, p. 504.

[3] Lero (nunc insula sanctae Margaritae) erat velut recessus vastae eremi patrum. *Chron. Ler.* Descriptio situs.

1687 the new governor was coming to the island fort, and orders were given for the preparation of a strongly guarded prison house, with a chapel contiguous. Who was the new governor, and who was his prisoner? There was much speculation concerning both; and for two hundred years, gossips have talked, and people have tried to guess the name of the prisoner. That of the new governor was soon known. It was Bénigne of Auvergne, Count of Saint-Mars, a favourite at Court, and tool of the Minister of War. He brought his mysterious prisoner with him. No one saw the face or heard the voice of his charge. To his jailer he was "the prisoner of Provence"; to the world "the man with the iron mask." The mask was really velvet, with a spring of steel. Louvois, the Minister of War, used to write to the governor concerning "the man you know about." His name was never written, but he was "a person of consequence." The orders were that he should be " jealously secluded from all eyes," and should receive "no comforts." The cell is large and lofty and well lighted by a window, to which there were three thick gratings. Two doors heavily barred closed him in. There was no possible way of escape. The governor boasted that the thick walls and the gratings were without comparison in the whole of Europe. There was a narrow corridor for a promenade, walled up at each end, and a little altar, where a priest said Mass. By the side of his cell was another chamber for his servant, who died there. Our imagination pictures the cruelty and weakness of the jailers, or rather of the men who ordered his incarceration. Capable of guarding this unfortunate man for twenty years, why had they not the courage to end his sufferings by one blow of a sword? He was on the island till the governor, promoted to the governorship of the famous Bastille, took him to Paris. Here the unfortunate man was taken ill. Even the physician who felt his pulse and examined his tongue did not see his face. The prisoner did not recover, and died on November 19th, 1703.

It is not of present interest to consider at any length the arguments that have been advanced from time to time in proof of the prisoner's identity. He has been thought to be, alternately, the Count of Vermandois, son of Louis XIV and of Louise de la Vallière, who died of smallpox in 1683; the

Duke of Beaufort who was born in 1616; the Duke of Monmouth, son of Charles II and of Lucy Walters, who died on the scaffold in 1685 ; Avedick, an Armenian Patriarch who was to the mind of the French ambassador to Constantinople "the mufti who governs the empire," and was kidnapped by a French vessel through the machinations of his enemy; Nicholas Fouquet who had endeavoured to bring about a civil war and was arrested at Nantes; an elder brother of Louis XIV, and a bastard prince; a twin brother of Louis XIV; a son of Cromwell; or of the Duke of Buckingham and Anne of Austria. But all these suggestions were set aside in favour of a secretary of the Duke of Mantua, named Mattioli, who sold the secret of a French intrigue and was eventually denounced and arrested.

The writer who claims the credit of thus finally elucidating the mystery[1] has acknowledged that many before him have so identified the prisoner, "while one alone, Alexander Dumas, like M. D'Artagnan, resisted the researches of twenty scholars and rejuvenated the legend of the brother of Louis XIV, originated and favoured by Voltaire." In the course of a clever argument[2], M. Funck-Brentano gives the fac-simile of the burial certificate[3]. Translated into English it reads: "The 19th November (1703), Marchioly, aged 45 years or thereabouts, died in the Bastille, and his body was buried in the cemetery of the parish of S. Paul, on the 20th, in the presence of M. Rosage, Major of the Bastille, and of M. Reglhe, Surgeon-Major of the Bastille, who have appended their signatures." On this similarity of name he bases his contention. "Marchioly is the name of the Duke of Mantua's secretary, and would be pronounced 'Markioly' in Italian. The governor, M. de Saint-Mars, who furnished the information for the certificate always appears to have written the

[1] M. Frantz Funck-Brentano, *Légendes et archives de la Bastille*, Paris, 1898. An excellent English translation has been made by G. Maidment (Downey and Co.), 1899.
[2] The reader will find the whole of the argument expounded in the most lucid and interesting book already referred to.
[3] This fac-simile is reproduced from the 6th edition of *L'homme au masque de fer* by Marius Topin, Paris, 1883. The original, preserved in the city Archives of Paris, was destroyed in the fire of 1871.

name as in the register, and it is not less distorted than Rosage for Rosarges, and Reglhe for Reilhe." M. Funck-Brentano gets out of the difficulty of the age of Mattioli who was 63 when he died by saying "the age is incorrectly given by mistake or carelessness of the officer, or of the parson or beadle." He has every confidence in his decision for he says, " To-day, doubt no longer exists, the problem is solved," and he adds, " Critics with unanimous voice have declared the solution to be correct." In a preface, M. Victorian Sardou says the author " lifts the famous mask and shows us the figure we have waited to see. The demonstration is so convincing that it leaves no opportunity for doubt."

The great Master of Balliol, Jowett, used to say that if a statement is claimed to be indisputable, it is usually one that ought to be disputed. This maxim is certainly true in this case, for "the indisputable conclusion" has been vigorously contradicted by a still later critic, M. Loquin[1], who quotes as the text of his monograph some words of MM. Burgaud and Bazeries[2]: " What use is it to put in evidence the clearest improbabilities, the hypothesis of Mattioli, for example "; and he proceeds to say, " I frankly confess that after the latest discoveries of the modern critics of our country, the last face I expected to find behind the famous mask is most certainly that of Mattioli." With scathing irony he continues : " Mattioli, forsooth, the man imprisoned at Pignerol six years *after* the man in the iron mask, and dead on the island of Sainte Marguerite nine years *before* him! It is the most splendid example of the method of *a priori* that I have ever met in any book! The mask was worn by the prisoner at the Bastille to hide the face of a man who was extremely well-known in Paris ; why should it have been put on an Italian, a stranger, the least known man, assuredly, in the capital of France ?"

It would seem then that time has not yet revealed the identity of the prisoner whose only accepted title still lives as "the Man in the Iron Mask."

[1] *Biographical Tracts*, No. 9, Paris, 1899.
[2] *Le masque de fer*, p. 134.

Ex-Marshal Bazaine.

Another prisoner, in a sense more fortunate, added a further interest to the island fort. It was ex-Marshal Bazaine, who was condemned to death by martial law at Versailles. The capital sentence was commuted to 20 years' detention. In this case, there were reasons that weighed with the authorities. Walls, doors and gratings were as strong as formerly, but a way of flight was made open, and the prisoner after an incarceration that had not lasted a year, made good his escape.

Such interest as the island of Sainte Marguerite enjoys, is due to these two occupants of the prison cell. But they were not its only prisoners. The Protestant clergy, who either had not left France, or who had returned to prevent their co-religionists from embracing Catholicism, were incarcerated there. The correspondence between the king's representative and the governor reveals several of these cases[1]. A letter dated June 29th, 1692, refers to the ministers singing psalms in a loud voice: "You must not allow them to sing psalms loudly. If, after being forbidden, they do so, put them in the most confined places." After the departure of Saint-Mars, there was no resident governor of Sainte Marguerite. The island was under the orders of a king's lieutenant. Insufficiently manned, it capitulated to General Brown in 1746.

After this date, its history is uninteresting. It has been used successively for prisoners of war, and for political offenders in 1841, and as a hospital for wounded soldiers since 1856. The island is covered with a beautiful forest of pines. One of the avenues leads to what is called the great garden, in the middle of which is a curious building, called for no particular reason the Oubliettes or secret dungeon. No tradition attaches to it, and there are no details of its origin or of its use. The thinness of the walls and the number of doors shows it was not built for defensive purposes. It is not in the form of a sacred edifice. It may be of twelfth century date. Its square formation suggests

[1] *Collection of unedited documents on the history of France. Administrative correspondence under the reign of Louis XIV*, Vol. II.

the 16th century. Ornamentation would be the best guide to the date of construction, but this is lacking.

Taking boat, we sail with all the simplicity of ancient seamanship, round the reef of rocks that guards the western point of the island, across the narrow channel that divides the sister isles, and step ashore on the place where Honoratus built cells of another kind, which occupants voluntarily entered for a nobler purpose.

Saint Honorat, " the Isle of the Saints."

The abbey of S. Honoratus has a great renown ; it is among the most illustrious and influential of these island cloisters. Few names in the whole history of the Church in France inspire such interest and admiration as Lerins. For it many shed their blood in martyrdom ; in it many lives of self-sacrifice were spent ; from it came many a brilliant scholar, celebrated bishops and writers, monks of great sanctity, and skilled administrators. The founder Honoratus, who from his childhood loved the poor and deprived himself to minister to their wants, can scarcely have anticipated the fair name and great reputation his monastery was destined to bear through so many centuries. When Leontius offered this island, which was part of his diocese, for this devout purpose, it was overgrown with brushwood and covered with ruins, and was uninhabited on account of its extreme filthiness, and unapproachable from fear of venomous serpents[1]. From the moment of his arrival the days of its solitude were ended and the snakes vanished[2]. According to the legend, S. Honoratus prayed that God would exterminate them. The prayer was answered. They all died, but their putrefying bodies infected the air. He mounted a palm and prayed again. The sea rose up, and the waves inundated the whole island, and in their withdrawal carried away the bodies[3]. On the side of the chest

[1] Vacantem insulam ob nimietatem squaloris et inaccessam ob pavorem veneatorum animalium. S. Hilary, *Life of Honoratus.* Bollandists, January (Vol. ii).

[2] Fugit horror solitudinis, cedit turba serpentium. *Ibid.*

[3] Ingreditur itaque impavidus, et pavorem suorum securitate sua discutit....Inauditum vere illud et plane inter miracula ac merita illius disputandum reor, quod tam frequens, ut vidimus in illis ariditatibus serpentium occursus, marinis praesertim aestibus excitatus, nulli unquam non solum periculo, sed nec pavori fuit. Hilary, *de Vita Honor.* Migne, *Patrol.* Vol. 50, c. 3.

The Well and Palm of S. Honoratus.

Reproduced by kind permission of the Most Reverend Father Abbot Dom Patrice.

given to Lerins by John Andrew de Grämoldi, S. Honoratus is represented on a palm tree, with the snakes and the waves at his feet. By reason of this fact, two palms bound with a serpent became the monastery's coat of arms. On the occasion of the visit of Eugenius (III) in the 12th century to the island, this Pope accorded a plenary indulgence to every pilgrim who after a pilgrimage of seven consecutive years received from the abbot's hands a branch of the venerable tree[1].

The Well of S. Honoratus.

The island was also without water. Honoratus called some of his followers and having selected a place in the middle of the island between two palms he said, " Come, dig here courageously." At first they were unsuccessful. Again they set to work but without result. S. Honoratus descended into the cavity that had been made. Three times he struck the rock, and the waters flowed[2]. Both S. Hilary and S. Eucherius bear testimony to this incident[3]. There is to-day a low round tower which encloses this supposed miraculous well. Over its gate is a marble tablet with an inscription recording the event[4]. Near it is a palm tree several hundred years old. It is called the palm of S. Honoratus. It is supposed to be an offshoot of the one which he had climbed. We give an illustration of the Water Tower and adjacent palm. Soon a temple was raised for Divine worship, and dwellings were erected for the monks.

[1] *Vita S. Honorati*, Book 3, Chap. 31.
[2] Cum e saxo erumperent, in media maris amaritudine dulces profluebant. Bolland. January (Vol. ii).
[3] Hilary, *De Vita Honorati*. Eucher. *De laude eremi*.
[4]
       Isacidum ductor lymphas medicavit amaras
       Et virga fontes extudit et silice.
       Aspice ut hic rigido surgant e marmore rivi
       Et salso dulcis gurgite vena fluat.
       Pulsat Honoratus rupem laticesque redundant
       Et sudas ad virgas Mosis adaequat opus.
               Barralis, *Chron. Ler.* i, p. 36.

CHAPTER IV

THE GOLDEN AGE

The history of the monastery of Lerins may be roughly divided into three periods. The first is from its foundation to the end of the 7th century, which is its golden age. The second is from the abbacy of Porcarius II to the establishment of the abbots-commendatory which covers the Saracen invasion and witnesses the monastery's increase of wealth, its consequent appeals to Rome in cases of aggression, its perpetual disputes under the new régime and its periodical lapses. This is the period of worldly prosperity. The third is from the *Commendam* to the present day, and is the period of its decay and ultimate secularisation in 1788. The first of these periods is by far the most interesting, especially to students of Church History and to theologians. What remains, has nevertheless its own special interest, though of subordinate importance.

The 5th, 6th and 7th centuries, especially the two first, were the golden age of the monastery. It was in this first period of its history that its far-reaching influence was exercised upon religious life and thought. It was during this period that it sent from its cloisters a succession of bishops, a calendar of saints, a stream of ecclesiastical organisers, and theologians of world wide reputation.

Like the celebrated retreats of Mount Athos in the East and of Monte Cassino in Italy, the monastery of S. Honoratus was the inviolable home of faith and hope and the fount of sacred learning. It existed as an independent society, bravely disciplined in an age of laxity; as a depository of intellectual wealth and eternal truth in a world of ignorance and darkness; and as the consolation of all who, baffled by secular storms and troubled seas of strife, sought its hospitable shores. It was the home of peace in which, while the barbarian sword dismembered the Empire, were sheltered, in halcyon calm, knowledge, love, faith, and all that consoles, ennobles and regenerates mankind[1].

Its Service to Literature.

The influence it exerted is best gauged by contrast with the character of the social life and the tendency of the outer world of these early centuries. It has already been indicated that symptoms of decadence and dissolution were everywhere apparent. In the words of Salvian: "The Empire is dead or at least is dying." At such a time there was little or no hope that literature could claim the attention of the people. It was necessary that its study should be entirely transformed, that it might enter into the domain of realities, and be adapted to popular needs. The Christian religion played an invaluable part in this direction, and opened the way for the needful transformation by embracing in its purview the gravest problems and the greatest interests; and by proposing for study nothing less than the whole moral and intellectual life of man. As we pass in review the works of the learned monks which emanated from Lerins during the 5th and 6th centuries, we shall have no difficulty in realising that it was the home of this intellectual development, and one of the early and the most celebrated schools of Christian philosophy. Guizot has said : " When the social state becomes distraught and unhappy, when men suffer much and long, serious studies run great risk of being neglected. The Christian religion furnished the means, and the human mind, fettered and hampered, took refuge in the shelter of the churches and monasteries[2]." As we recall these words, we can have no doubt that Lerins was quickly peopled by those who desired the quiet of solitude with the opportunity it offered for uninterrupted study. Here there was entire security from

---

[1] Lammenais, *Affaires de Rome*, p. 9.
[2] *Histoire de la civilisation en France*, Vol. I, p. 125.

invasion, for the literary treasures, at any rate during the golden age, were not such as to tempt the avarice of invaders athirst for glittering gold and material wealth.

Some distinguished Sons.

The reputation of the monastery at this time was so great that people came from all parts of Gaul to seek their bishops from among its sons. These monk-bishops were of an entirely different type of prelate from the more secular bishops of the later Empire. Those who held such a high office in Roman society were, by reason of their temporal position in the Empire, from the time of Constantine, too easily captivated by the court pomp with which they were surrounded. This inevitably led to an evident diminution of the apostolic spirit. On the other hand those who left a monastery for a bishopric usually maintained even after their elevation the habits of austerity, poverty and self-denial which they had formed in solitude. We are told that when Martin, who had been proposed for the see of Tours, presented himself before an assembly of Gallo-Roman prelates some protests were raised against his election. "We were not accustomed in the West to see a coarse robe spread over the velvet of a prelate's throne. This was soon to come, for the holy Bishop of Tours was to show the world the virtue of such a contrast[1]." The worldly-wise would have said that the pomp of the Gallo-Roman would best serve the interest and advancement of the Church in its dealings both with representatives of the proud Empire of Rome, and with the rudeness of the victorious barbarian. This monastic type of bishop was capable of gaining and did gain the respect of the fiercest barbarian, and exercised over him an ascendancy that at least suspended his fury and sometimes even entirely conquered it. In the words of Littré, "the Church exercised a mysterious influence that completed her empire. The mysticism of the monk is at once the point of her sanctity and of her sword[2]."

[1] Lecoy de la Marche, *S. Martin*, Chap. 4.
[2] *Études sur les Barbares et le Moyen-âge*, p. 141.

As we must not anticipate the subsequent chapters on the men of great renown, and on "the Nursery of Bishops," we shall scarcely do more now than mention the names of those who in this golden age shed lustre upon the history of the monastery of Lerins as abbots or as monks. Though no writings of his own are extant, the name of Honoratus is reverently preserved to this day as the founder of the monastery after whom the island, on which it stood, had with one brief interval been called for fifteen centuries. Eucherius, of noble family and earthly greatness, became still greater through his virtues and his teaching, as Hilary's words concerning him so eloquently imply[1]. The "great and modest Vincent" who is seldom named to-day except as "Vincent of Lerins," thus preserves the memory of the island that was the cradle of his genius. Not less eminent is Salvian, a man of quite a different turn of mind, gifted with a grave and passionate eloquence, with an ardent soul and a fine imagination. Hilary, nurtured amid the distractions of the world, was second to none of his cloister companions in ascetic zeal. Lupus, master of a considerable fortune, and fitted by talents for the highest honours that earth could offer, became, under the sweet influence of Lerins, an illustrious saint. Faustus who ruled over the monastery for nearly thirty years, achieved a great reputation as a bishop and pastor, as orator, writer and administrator, and stands pre-eminent as a distinguished controversialist. Caesarius was an ascetic who more than any other helped to save Christian civilisation from the ruin that was threatening society. His powers of organisation, the simplicity of his fearless preaching, his glowing zeal, his passionate love for the poor whom he seemed to understand so well, combined with other gifts to make him one of the most influential bishops of his time. Cassian, the sound and sane organiser and systematiser of monasticism, and Patrick the saint, around whose name and life sentiment and legend cling with such affectionate zeal, each adds lustre to the name and fame of Lerins, even though they may not actually have sojourned there as monks. The light of renown that would otherwise shine upon others, who came

[1] Splendidus mundo, splendidior Christo.

from Lerins, is dimmed by the dazzling brilliance of those we have just enumerated. Of Maximus, the immediate successor of the founder in the abbacy of Lerins, no higher praise can be given than to say that he sustained in all its pristine fervour the foundation of Honoratus during the seven years that he presided over it. Stephen, the last abbot of the 6th century, earned the praise of Gregory for his charity to the poor of Italy, and was congratulated by him upon the order and discipline that he maintained in the community. Augustine, the Apostle of England, visited Lerins on his way to Rome and was the bearer of the letter which said: " We congratulate you on the unity and peace which reign among your priests, deacons and whole congregation." Chononus Boufort, who succeeded to the abbacy in the first year of the 7th century, continued to merit a similar commendation, for Gregory wrote: " We have heard how wise you are in the direction of your brethren." We learn too from this letter that Stephen later in his life must have forfeited the confidence that he had formerly enjoyed, for it proceeds: " as the imprudent weakness of your predecessor has afflicted us, so the wisdom of your administration fills us with joy[1]." Chononus found at Luxeuil his inspiration for the reform he undertook. Here the austere Columban had just established a colony of Irish monks who lived under the strictest discipline and asceticism. Chononus reformed the monastery on this model and left such an impression of the sternness of his administration behind him, that he was afterwards known as Chononus the stern. He was succeeded by Nazarus, who maintained his predecessor's strict standard. He also gained distinction by his zeal against idolatry. On the banks of the Siagne, not far from Cannes, there was an ancient sanctuary that probably owed its origin to some Oxybian divinity. When the Roman domination was accepted, a temple was raised there in honour of Venus and the name of the mountain of this " altar of the sacred grove," became by corruption Arluc[2] and was so known afterwards. The first abbots of Lerins had endeavoured to draw away the people from this sanctuary. Honoratus had founded there a monastery for nuns, and it was fulfilling this

---

[1] Alliez, I, p. 334.　　　　　　　[2] *Ara luci.*

purpose in the first year of the 6th century, for Caesarius wrote a letter that is still extant to Oratoria its abbess. Towards the end of the century, the monastery fell under the blows of the Lombards. It was Nazarus who restored and re-established it and dedicated it to S. Stephen[1]. It was in ruins when Aygulphus was at Lerins in A.D. 677 and he built it once again and placed there a colony of nuns. It was pillaged more than once by the Saracens, and we hear nothing more about it after the 10th century. In after years, the hill on which it stood was known as St Cassian, and it is extremely interesting to note that this name is preserved to the present day.

Until A.D. 660 the community of Lerins had lived under the Rule given to it by its founder. What that Rule was we cannot precisely determine. It may never have been committed to writing. If it was, it has not survived. We know there was such a Rule, written or unwritten, for the Third Council of Arles in A.D. 454 refers to it and recommends that it be followed in "every point[2]." We know also that Caesarius a monk of Lerins and afterwards Archbishop of Arles wrote a Monastic Rule in which he settled the ceremonies of the Divine Office "as it was celebrated at Lerins[3]," and it is not unlikely that the other requirements of this Rule were fashioned upon the practice of this monastery.

So far this island home had enjoyed a peaceful existence. Frequent revolutions in southern Gaul had not affected it; successive invasions and conquests of Provence had not unsettled its serenity. Now at length, at the very height of its greatest prosperity, it experienced severe trials. Its discipline was relaxed, but the desire for reform seems to have come from within, for the decision to introduce the Rule of S. Benedict was made in a general Chapter. A deputation of monks from Lerins waited upon Aygulphus, a monk of the monastery

---

[1] Raymond Féraud tells us that "Cloaster a great and rich enchanter had built an altar and practised 'sorceries and many follies' there, and that Nazarus made him pull down the tufted woods. Then the altar was broken in pieces, and the chapel was consecrated to S. Stephen."

[2] Regula quae a fundatore ipsius monasterii dudum constituta est in omnibus custodita. Labbé, *Concil.* IV, p. 2055.

[3] Secundum statuta Lirinensium Fratrum. Bolland. Jan. (Vol. ii), p. 735.

of Fleury-sur-Loire, and begged him to undertake the direction
of their community. After some hesitation he consented to do
so, "with the permission of the king," as the Chronologist
of Lerins remarks[1]. He was received with great enthusiasm,
and soon restored regularity, fervour and discipline. His zeal
aroused the enmity of the disaffected, and he ultimately paid
the penalty of this with his life. There were two chief
conspirators named Columbus and Arcadius. They were not
impelled to oppose the reform from any love or zeal for the
primitive Rule and customs of the monastery, but because they
had led an undisciplined life, without check. With the prospect
of perpetual silence and obedience in the cloister, the yoke that
threatened them was intolerable. They managed to spread
their discontent among others, and having gathered together a
band of mutineers, they invaded the oratory where Aygulphus
was at prayer. He rose to meet them, and impressed them by
the majesty of his manner and of his words. "My dear children,"
he said, "I came to this island in answer to your prayers; if you
believe me to be the author of the discord among you, then
throw me, like a second Jonah, into the sea." The two
ringleaders lowered their heads in confusion, and with all the
appearance of sincere repentance, asked his pardon for what they
had done. Arcadius then bribed Mummulus, Count of Vence,
with hopes of pillage, to come to Lerins under pretence of
examining into the conduct of some bishop. Aygulphus received
him hospitably, and soon Arcadius joined him with a band
of followers, and gave orders that the holy abbot should be
bound, beaten, and imprisoned. Mummulus demanded from
Aygulphus the treasures in his possession. "I will show you
the riches of the monastery," was the reply, and stretching his
hands towards the brethren that were his fellow prisoners, he
said: "These are my treasures." In anger, Mummulus set himself to pillage the monastery and did not spare even the most
sacred places. He then took his departure for a time, and Arcadius
and Columbus, in fear lest the news of their violence should
spread, delivered the abbot and thirty-seven faithful monks into
the hands of bandits, and all but one were massacred. Rigomir

[1] Barralis, *Chron. Ler.*

was elected to succeed the murdered abbot, and after him, the monastery was governed in A.D. 690 by Amandus, in whose abbacy it is said that 3700 monks were obedient to his rule[1], and prosperity once again reigned in the island. During all the years of the golden age bishops had been chosen almost exclusively from Lerins for the vacant sees of Gaul, and all of them sought to reproduce the teaching and training of this monastery in the cities to which they were called to live and teach and rule. To mention but a few of them: Honoratus and Hilary, Caesarius and Virgilius were called to the archbishopric of Arles; Maximus and Faustus were bishops of Riez; Lupus was summoned to the see of Troyes; Eucherius to Lyons; Valerianus to Cimiez; James to Moutiers; Salonius to Geneva; Veranus to Vence; Apollinarius to Valence; Maximus, Magnus and Agricola to Avignon. These and others were selected for high office in the Church and it is no exaggeration to say of the island of Honoratus that it numbered among its sons men of great renown, and was in very truth "a nursery of bishops," as we shall hope in these following pages amply to demonstrate.

[1] Sic florebat monasterium ut Amandus sub se haberet trium millium et septingentorum monachorum numerum. *Chron. Ler.* II, p. 80.

CHAPTER V

THE GREAT THEOLOGIAN, VINCENT

A chapter on the great theologian S. Vincent, who has made the name of Lerins famous and is the best known of all its sons, should embrace within its scope: 1. such fragmentary information of his personal history as is known ; 2. an account of the *Commonitorium* ; its doctrine of tradition ; its theological contents ; and its position in regard to the Pelagian controversy.

1. Little is known of the personal history of S. Vincent. According to Gennadius[1] (A.D. 480–500) he was an eminent and highly esteemed theologian of the Gallican Church in the 5th century. He was by birth a Gaul, and died in or about A.D. 450. It is from his own statement that we learn that the stress and strain of the worldly life, in a period so fraught with disquiet, drove him to seek refuge in the "isle of the saints." The exigency of the times and opportunity afforded by retirement suggested to him, "the least of all God's servants," that it would be a matter of no small profit to himself and to the many distressed by theological conflicts to put in writing what he had learned at the feet of the Fathers. Time, he argued, takes from us all earthly things ; we should in turn take from it something of everlasting value. The place, was, he declared, opportune, for having forsaken the company and troubles of cities, he had chosen for his dwelling-place a remote and solitary abbey where he might follow the Psalmist's injunction "Be still then and know that I am God." He speaks also of the storms of the world, from which he found shelter in the

[1] *De Scriptoribus eccles.* 65.

harbour of the cloistered life. It was in A.D. 434 that he wrote the famous *Commonitorium*. In Chapter XXIX he speaks of the sacred council " held almost three years ago at Ephesus." This is the Ecumenical Council of A.D. 431. Other notes of time afford similar evidence of date. In Chapter XXX he again refers to this council and mentions men whose works were quoted there, and among them "the venerable Cyril who now adorns the Church of Alexandria," and Pope Sixtus "now an ornament of the Church of Rome." The date of Vincent's death is uncertain. Gennadius merely says it happened during the reign of Theodosius and Valentinianus. Of his personality we can learn but little, either from outside sources or from his work. He would seem to have received a good general education and to have acquired a considerable amount of theological knowledge. In his *Commonitorium* he lays no claim to any of the graces of style. He presents his work rather as a faithful reporter than as a pretentious author, and then in language unadorned and in "common and easy speech[1]." Yet many of his phrases are echoes of the classical Latin writers. Nor is there any lack of pith and point in his sentences.

2. The *Commonitorium* has been variously regarded. By most of those competent to form a judgment, it is considered a masterpiece of theological reasoning; by others, misleading and untrustworthy as a theological guide. It has been called a "monument of faith," "the golden book," "a work small in size but great in virtue." Its author is pronounced by some a lucid genius, by others a simple-minded theologian. The numerous translations of the *Commonitorium* are a proof both of its popularity and its usefulness. An Italian version was published in 1665; one in French in 1686; in German in 1795; and a Scottish translation was dedicated to Mary Queen of Scots in 1563 by Knox's opponent, the original title of which is "a richt goldin buke written in Latin, passit and neulie translated in Scottis be Niniane Winsot, a Catholik Preist." The fact that the opponent of John Knox published this translation as an aid to the Roman side of the controversy would point to the inference that Romanist divines at the time of the Reformation accepted its

---

[1] Neque id ornato et exacto, sed facili communique sermone.

principles, but for obvious reasons, Vincent's test of catholicity would not now so universally apply.

It is a polemic and apologetic treatise which was published under the pseudonym of Peregrinus. Gennadius tells us that as sheets of the second volume were by some persons purloined and destroyed, the author briefly recapitulated the heads of the perished portions and compacted the two parts into one volume. The title witnessed to by manuscripts, *Incipit tractatus Peregrini*, is not necessarily that of the author and is far more likely that of a transcriber. This indeed ought to be clear from the text in which Vincent five times calls his book *Commonitorium*, or "the Reminder." The closing subscription, *Explicit tractatus Peregrini contra Hereticos*, is also likely to be the work of a transcriber, as is the note at the close of the twenty-eighth chapter[1] that the second Commonitory has been lost and no more of it preserved than the last section, that is to say the recapitulation alone, which Vincent subjoined.

The author explains his choice of title. He considers it profitable to set down in writing what he has received of the holy Fathers, that by daily reading it he may refresh his weak memory. The title *Commonitorium* is not altogether original, for it is used by other writers, Marius Mercator, for example, an Italian or African merchant of ecclesiastical tastes, who wrote the *Commonitorium ad Theodosium Imp.*, and *Commonitorium adv. haeresem Pelagii*. We have already referred to the note of the loss of the second Commonitory. The only reference to it in the text is in the twenty-eighth and twenty-ninth chapters. Vincent concludes the twenty-eighth chapter by saying, "I will here make an end of this Commonitory, and so take another beginning for those things which do follow." He commences Chapter XXIX by saying, "It is now time in the end of this second book to recapitulate what has been said in these two Commonitory books." No doubt then this work lies before us in the same compass as Gennadius knew it. Vincent did not apparently attempt to replace the lost sheets, as did Carlyle when the manuscript of his *French Revolution* perished through

---

[1] There is an unfortunate double numbering of the chapters. That in capitals is the older, following the edition of Baluze, 1684.

the tragic carelessness of Froude. An examination of the recapitulation reveals that it is merely a summary not of the two books, but, with one exception, of only the second. Does this mean that the author considered the first part was accessible to his readers? or is it possible that Vincent of his own accord withdrew the second book, or abbreviated it?

After the brief introduction, the intention of the author appears to be simply to give a summary of traditional patristic doctrine, and therefore a sort of synopsis of doctrinal teaching. From his recapitulation it is evident that his main design is to set up a standard of doctrine, and give a test for the distinction of catholic and heretical doctrine, in other words to define a formal principle of the catholic Church. According to him the catholic Church possesses a twofold canon, Holy Scripture and tradition. Holy Scripture, absolutely sufficient of itself, still needs completion by the added authority of the catholic Church, on account of the possibility of perverted interpretations. The question to be settled is, what is the authoritative interpretation, the ecclesiastical *sensus* to be gathered from a consensus of the Fathers; and what is the catholic tradition? Hence the canon of orthodoxy is supplied which offers us a threefold test of catholicity in the widely known and oft quoted maxim *quod ubique, quod semper, quod ab omnibus*, i.e. universality, antiquity, and general consent; and the testimony of succeeding centuries has proclaimed its wisdom.

The doctrinal value of the *Commonitorium* has never been seriously disputed. "We love," says Abbé Gouz[1], "the neatness of the plan, the easy chain of ideas, the orderly arrangement of proofs, and the purity of expression." Mgr Gerbet[2] says, "Christian antiquity has produced two fundamental works, the *Prescriptions* and the *Commonitorium*. We call them fundamental because the considerations therein developed touch all sects equally whatever be their particular doctrines." As a guard against the tendency to misleading and false citation of the Holy Scriptures, the order of the three criteria is to be emphasised. It is with manifest intention that they

[1] *Lerins au cinquième siècle*, p. 111.
[2] *Coup d'œil sur la controverse Chrétienne*, p. 39.

stand in this particular order, universality, antiquity and general consent. First of all, in any declension from the faith of the Church, the whole Church must decide what the faith is. If the Church has been contaminated at any time or place, there must be recourse to antiquity, which cannot be affected by later heretical contaminations. If again error is found in any teacher or even in a whole ecclesiastical province, then an appeal is made to general consent within the limits of antiquity. This order shows thoughtful deliberation and clear design, and is plain evidence of the intellectual subtlety of the author. General consent includes, as one of its first and most important elements, the decisions of the great councils of the early centuries. Where decisions on points of doctrine have not been promulgated, then the utterances on those points, of the acknowledged Fathers of the Church, are to be examined and their *consensus* of opinion regarded as authoritative. This method is set forth in the second and third chapters, and the several propositions and principles are, in the chapters which follow, illustrated and justified by appeals to church history and the history of Christian doctrine.

There can scarcely be a doubt that it was the Donatist and Pelagian controversies that aroused Vincent and set him to study this question of ultimate authority, especially in matters of theological controversy, as well as S. Augustine's doctrine of grace and predestination then agitating the Church, and the teaching of Origen and Tertullian. Thus in Chapter IV an example is given from the errors of the Donatists to show how the principle of universality may be applied in answer to schismatic propositions. A great part of Africa fell into the error of Donatus, and "preferred the rashness of one man before the judgment of the whole Church of Christ," with the result that all who hated this schism joined themselves to all the orthodox churches of the world, and so left the example to posterity that the sound doctrines of all men should be preferred to the madness of one or of a few.

In the same chapter he deals with "the poison of the Arians," which had affected almost the whole world. Those who preferred the old faith to new error were untouched, even though the emperor and his palace yielded to the infatuation. This was an illustration of the value of the test of antiquity. Once again, in Chapter v, he refers to the defence made by S. Ambrose and others against novelty, and he says that they did not defend any one part but the whole Church, not one or two men, not a small province, but the canons and decrees of the whole hierarchy, the heirs of apostolic and catholic truth. This illustrates the need of general consent.

Vincent next recalls the controversy on heretical baptism to prove that the innovations of individuals are to be resisted. Agrippinus, bishop of Carthage, of venerable memory, for the first time in the history of the Church considered the re-baptism of heretics needful, but when everywhere all men exclaimed against this novel doctrine and all priests in all places opposed it, Pope Stephanus wrote a letter to Africa to this effect that no innovation must be allowed, but that which was received by tradition should be observed. What was the result? "Antiquity was retained, novelty was denounced. The decree of Africa was abolished, disannulled and abrogated."

In Chapter VIII Vincent expounds the words of S. Paul in Galatians i, 8, "Although we, or an angel from heaven, preach any other gospel than that which we have preached unto you, let him be anathema," to show the ungodliness of all innovation, without exception. This he says was not a command to and for the Galatians only. S. Paul cries out again and again in his epistles, to all men, to all times, to all places. Vincent explains in the following chapter that when certain teachers and rulers of the Church preach certain novel doctrines, it is because God is tempting them. As examples of this, Vincent instances Nestorius, Photinus, and Apollinarius, who might have been chief builders of the Church had they not invented new opinions, which were not for the edification but for a trial of the Church.

In Chapter XVII Vincent handles the interesting questions of the writings of Origen and Tertullian as further illustrations of the severe trials of the Church caused by greatly gifted men who despite their genius had yet widely departed from general consent. He cannot forbear to praise the learning, eloquence, and power of Origen, the reverence and honour he gained, but yet the books circulating under his name are a great temptation, so that even if he himself gave no cause of originating erroneous doctrine, yet his cited authority seems to have been the occasion why an error has been received. The case also of Tertullian is similar. He too was learned, quick of wit, but not holding the universal and ancient faith, was more eloquent than faithful, and discredited with later error what he had previously written. Vincent concludes this subject by stating his conviction that antiquity cannot be overridden or set aside by individual teachers, however weighty their personality may be, but as S. Paul says, " There must be also heresies among you that they which are approved may be made manifest among you[1]." Again Vincent appeals to Scripture. Writing to Timothy, S. Paul warns him to safeguard the *depositum*, the faith entrusted to him. *Nove* not *nova*; the doctrine may be presented anew, *nove*, more suggestively, more clearly, more instructively, but never as novelties, *nova*.

Vincent appeals to tradition because the heretic appeals to the Scriptures. He reminds his readers of the scriptural warning, " Ask thy father and he will shew thee, thy elders and they will tell thee[2]." In giving two ways of defending the faith, by Scripture and tradition, he shows the necessity of tradition even though the Scriptures be perfect and sufficient, because every heretic expounds them after his own interpretation. Thus the work of Vincent marks an epoch in the history of interpretation inasmuch as it is the most elaborate statement of the case for tradition.

The doctrine of tradition. What is meant by παράδοσις? What is the tradition of the elders that the disciples of Christ were accused of transgressing[3]? This "tradition of the elders," of which our Lord spoke, is that which, mainly in the Maccabaean time and later, became fixed and consolidated as a great collection of explanations and expositions of the written law, and in process of time was recognized as of equal authority with the authoritative collection of writings, the Pentateuch. In our Lord's time this tradition had not of course been put in writing,

---

[1] 1 Corinthians xi, 19.   [2] Deuteronomy xxxii, 7 (A.V.).
[3] S. Matt. xv, 2, and cp. Galatians i, 14; Hebrews xi, 2.

but had been handed down orally. The oral transmission existed for centuries before it was committed to writing, and at length the accumulations of generations were collected about A.D. 200 into a code which afterwards took the form of the Massorah[1] and Kabbalah[2]. These were superstitiously traced back to Moses. The Talmud[3] closed the tradition, inasmuch as it contains, in addition to individual decisions, all that is necessary for legal and religious decisions of every kind. It has been for the Jews the strongest bond of union, and has kept alive among them the religious idea.

Catholicism and Protestantism in its extremer forms are sharply divided on the critical question of tradition in the Christian Church. The Christian tradition has relation to the New Testament writings. Is it permissible to appeal to the opinions of the Christian Fathers without incurring the charge of making the teachings of the apostles of none effect? On the principles of Vincent these patristic opinions, published in some cases a century from the time of Christ, are less likely to contaminate the Scriptures than twenty centuries of diverse opinion, and they are more likely to be right. Thus antiquity is appealed to as the decisive criterion of truth. It must not however be supposed that Vincent was the first to appeal to tradition. Athanasius, who is the first to quote the "Fathers" as witnesses to the faith, thus appeals to antiquity. Tertullian and Cyprian were great champions of the principle, and Cyril of Jerusalem says that even the catechumen must go to antiquity to learn what were the books to which appeal is

---

[1] It is a Hebrew word meaning "tradition" and is technically applied to the tradition by which Jewish scholars determined the correct writing and reading of the Old Testament text.

[2] This word means "reception" and is applied to "doctrines received from tradition."

[3] The Mishnah is the collection of legal decisions by ancient rabbis, which forms the text on which the Gemara or Commentary rests, and is therefore the fundamental document of the oral law of the Jews. The Talmud, which commonly signifies the combination of the texts of Mishnah and Gemara, exists in two recensions, the Palestinian, which embodies the discussions on the Mishnah of doctors in Palestine, chiefly in Galilee, from the 2nd to the 5th century, and the Babylonian which contains the discussions on the same Mishnah of doctors in Babylonia from the end of the 2nd century to the end of the 6th.

made. There is also the well known and oft quoted statement of S. Augustine that he could not believe the gospel if it were not for the authority of the catholic Church[1].

The position early taken on the tradition of the elders is well illustrated by a remark of Clement of Alexandria in the beginning of the *Stromata*. Speaking of his work he says[2], "This work of mine is not written for display, but my memoranda are stored up against old age, as a remedy against forgetfulness, truly an image and outline of those clear and living words I have been deemed worthy to hear from blessed men, deserving of honour." These teachers, he says, he met in Greece. Of these, the one, "in Greece, an Ionic," is probably Tatian, the other, "in Magna Graecia," may have been Theodotus. He heard also those "living words" in Egypt and the East, in Assyria and Palestine. "When I met with the last (he was the first in power[3]) I found rest." Of him he says, "He, like a Sicilian bee gathering the flowers of the prophetic and apostolic meadow, engendered a deathless knowledge in the minds of his hearers." These men, he proceeds to say, preserved the tradition of the blessed doctrine derived directly from the holy apostles, Peter, James, John and Paul, "the son receiving it from the father." In the further metaphor that "use keeps steel brighter, but disuse produces rust," he desires to proceed to the renowned and venerable canon of tradition, and he thinks his treatise will be agreeable to a mind that wishes to preserve the truth and escape from error.

Christianity of course existed originally and to commence with in the form of tradition. Our Lord wrote nothing. The gospel of the life, death and resurrection of our Lord was taught by word of mouth. The origin was oral, not written. S. Paul too speaks of that which he had "received[4]" as that which he handed on to others. On the death of the apostles, the appeal was to apostolical authority, and the traditions and writings preserved in the several centres of Christian influence, the local

---

[1] Ego vero evangelio non crederem, nisi me Catholicae Ecclesiae commoveret auctoritas.

[2] Book I, Chapter I.

[3] Probably Pantaenus, his teacher, master of the cathechetical school in Alexandria.

[4] I Corinthians xi, 23 and xv, 3.

churches. Only slowly were the written books, to which on one theory sole appeal is to be made, collected into one. In the complete form in which we now have them they existed in the end of the 3rd century at the earliest. Hence in this tradition the first rank must be assigned, as Vincent astutely recognises, to the apostolical writings and to the gospel writings drawn from written sources and from oral tradition, in a word, to the New Testament. It is clear how the early Fathers like Irenaeus and Tertullian appeal to the local church traditions. When the apostles died, the churches they left preserved their traditions. Thus Irenaeus in his work *Against Heresies*, in which he gives an exposition and defence of the catholic faith, expressly states[1] that the true knowledge " is the teaching of the apostles and the ancient system of the Church in all the world "; and again, " the Church holds the tradition firm from the apostles and enables us to see that the faith of all is one and the same "; and again, " in the succession of bishops tracing their descent from the primitive ages and appointed by the apostles themselves, you have a guarantee for the transmission of the pure faith[2]." Tertullian represents this idea of tradition even more strongly. He says[3], " Our appeal must not be made only to the Scriptures, nor must controversy be admitted under circumstances where victory will be either impossible, or uncertain, or not sufficiently certain. Another question must first be propounded. " From whom and through whom, and where and to whom has been handed down the discipline by which men become Christians ? Wherever the reality of the Christian discipline of faith is to be found, there will be also the reality of the Scriptures, and of the interpretations and of all Christian traditions," and again[4], he maintains with equal emphasis that the tradition of the apostolic churches has been preserved by a succession of bishops.

In the 3rd century, with its altered circumstances, when the speculations of heretics were rife and those in doubt asked for a test of truth, this importance of the historic churches as courts of appeal falls into the background for obvious reasons.

---

[1] IV, 33. 8 ; V, 20. I.
[2] See also III, Chapters II, III, IV, v, etc.
[3] *De Praescriptione adv. haereses*, 19.   [4] *Ibid.* 32.

Traditions handed on for several generations are easily corrupted. Still it is surprising how tenaciously religious usages and ideas are preserved for long periods. In this 3rd century, the idea of the unity of the Church as residing in the collective episcopate takes the place of this simple appeal, and it is their voice in the council, after examination of the tradition or Scripture and the works of the Fathers, that is determinative. The germ of this development is found in the teaching of Ignatius, "the staunchest advocate of episcopacy in the early ages," who held that its chief value consisted in the fact that it provided a visible centre of unity. When personal and local ties were withdrawn, it was the episcopate that would safeguard the Church against schism and disunion. Some of his words are almost extravagant, as e.g. " The bishops established in the farthest parts of the world are in the counsels of Jesus Christ[1]." The decision of the episcopate in synod is at this time the essential organ by which the voice of the Church makes itself known, especially in the later development of the ecumenical council sitting *ad hoc*. Thus was decided what was of apostolical authority and therefore *de fide*, that is, what the tradition really was.

It is at this point that the significance of the work of Vincent appears. In his exposition of the apostles' injunction to keep the *depositum*, Vincent asks, who at this day is Timothy? and his answer is either, generally, the whole Church, or, especially, the whole body of prelates. The decrees of councils were for no other end than to give authentic accounts and unmistakable statements of doctrine. He explains in general terms the usefulness and indispensableness of this rule for the refutation of rising errors[2]. He gives an actual example from the decrees of the Council of Ephesus, to prove that the conclusions arrived at were, without additions, taken precisely from the carefully collected statements of the ancient Fathers. In the actually existent *recapitulatio* or second part of the *Commonitorium* we see that this council closely corresponded to his theory, that also the popes of Rome of his day acknowledged these principles, that consequently the proper way consisted in holding firmly to the holy faith of the Fathers, in life and in death, and

[1] *Ep.* 3.   [2] Chapter XXVIII.

to abhor profane novelties. He further considers that the voice
of the majority as at the Council of Ephesus, where 200 bishops
were assembled, safeguarded the Church against the dangers to
orthodoxy exemplified in the decisions of the Council of
Ariminum. He no more expects unity of sentiment than
absolute unity of feeling. While he speaks respectfully of the
popes, referring to Stephanus "of blessed memory" for example,
he never regards them as the ultimately determining factor, but
always as upholding the essential principles of universality,
antiquity and consent. His final court of appeal is to the
collective episcopate in council assembled.

    Still he emphasises that this is only in regard to the "rule
of faith," and not in all questions that concern the divine law.
He is aware of the special danger attaching to the heretical use
of Holy Scripture, and asserts that in this they do but emulate
the father of lies, who himself quoted Holy Writ in the temptation
of Jesus. It is not therefore sufficient to quote Scripture. The
right and wrong use of it are to be discriminated, and the only
canon of interpretation that can be laid down is that of the
general consent of the Fathers of the Church. Irenaeus presses
the point[1] when he says the Church although scattered throughout
the world yet, as if occupying but one house, carefully preserves
the tradition. Although the languages of the world are dissimilar
yet the tradition is one and the same. The churches which have
been planted in Germany do not believe or hand down anything
different from those in Spain or Gaul. The preaching of the
truth shines everywhere. In like manner the councils "register
the agreement of the churches," and as a further safeguard their
decisions must receive the general acceptance of the Church at
large. It is not a matter of a chance majority after an embittered
controversy. Thus Vincent speaks of the Council of Ephesus.
After quoting the names of those whose writings were cited[2],
Peter, bishop of Alexandria, S. Athanasius, S. Theophilus and
S. Cyril, bishops of the same city, he continues, "lest it should
be thought that this was the doctrine of one city or province,

---

[1] *Adv. haereses*, Book 1, Chapter 10, Section 2, and compare Tertullian
de Praescriptione, 24–36.
[2] Chapter xxx.

the testimony of S. Gregory of Nazianzum and of S. Gregory of
Nyssa is added, and for proof that not only Greece and the East
but also the Western and the Latin world were always of the
same opinion, letters of S. Felix Martyr and S. Julian, bishops
of Rome, were read. And that not only the head of the world,
but also that other parts should testify to this judgment, they had
S. Cyprian from the south and S. Ambrose from the north. All
these were alleged masters, witnesses, judges, whose doctrine the
synod holding gave sentence concerning the rule of faith."

The *Commonitorium* is, in its doctrine of tradition, the ripe
fruit of all that had gone before. It gathers up on this subject
the rays of light scattered through Irenaeus, Tertullian, Cyprian,
and S. Augustine, and focuses their thoughts in the already
mentioned remarkable and historic saying, the apostolic tradition
is *quod semper, quod ubique, quod ab omnibus creditum est*.
Hitherto the validity of a custom or doctrine is tested by an
appeal to the tradition of one of the apostolic churches, of which
Rome from its historic and worldwide fame could not but be the
most considerable, as Irenaeus bears witness[1]. Now the appeal
is to the essentially dogmatic principle that the Holy Ghost speaks
through the collective voice of the Church. The *Commonitorium*

---

[1] *Propter potentiorem principalitatem. Adv. haeres.* III, 3. 1. It will be
remembered that Duchesne translates *principalis ecclesia* as "l'église souveraine"
(*Origines Chrétiennes*, vol. 2, Chapter XXIV, Section 6, pp. 427 and 436), but
it may be questioned whether this is a legitimate rendering, if we enquire what
principalis meant to the Romans. Is it not correct to say that *princeps* was
the usual designation of the emperor? (*Dicty. Greek and Roman Antiq.* vol. II,
p. 483.) As the *princeps civitatis* or first man in the state, he had a title that was
quite familiar in the Republic. He was thereby invested with certain powers which
he held on a life tenure. It was a courtesy title which expressed the pre-eminence of
an individual citizen. It formed no part of his official designation, and conveyed no
special prerogative. The senate and people conferred certain powers upon one who
was accordingly raised above them for the time being. This position dates from
Octavian who though undisputed master of the Roman world handed back his
authority and was invested by the senate and people with a limited command. In
the three succeeding centuries to Diocletian the position was considerably changed;
the area of government was enlarged, more direct control was given and authority
ceased to be co-ordinate and became subordinate. Thus *principalitas* may be said
to have had its origin in the State and not in the Church, and even then, it did not
imply sovereignty. In other words, as Archbishop Benson says (*Cyprian*, p. 537),
"*Principalis ecclesia* would mean to the Romans a constitutional pre-eminence
as opposed to despotic rule, the first and highest in a great Republic of
Churches."

is thus of importance in the development of historic theology as the culmination and shaped expression of this theory.

It is evident that the principle of Vincent, without qualification, amounts to a closure of the canon of tradition somewhat resembling the Talmudic closure of the Jewish tradition, though far from completely resembling it. The Council of Trent practically formulated a principle opposed to this closure, for it decided that the hierarchy is a living authority, and that to the end of time the collective episcopate represents the power and capability of the Church to determine in matters of faith and morals, with infallible authority. An example of this was its determination to give canonical authority to the books of the Apocrypha, which the ancient Council of Laodicea had pronounced uncanonical. Lastly in the Roman Church the idea of tradition has undergone another change, for since the Vatican Council it is no longer the conclusion of an ecumenical council that determines matters of faith and morals, but the infallible pope speaking *ex Cathedra Petri.*

On the question of tradition, Protestantism as a principle looks primarily to the books of the Holy Scripture, but yet embodies a number of traditional rites and beliefs, summed up in the sacraments and the authoritative creeds, and the observance of Sunday and feast days. These latter rest entirely on tradition. It will be seen that Vincent represents a principle which is not that of the modern Roman or Greek Church, and far more nearly represents the attitude of the Anglican Communion. It possibly has the misfortune of representing an appeal to a closed canon of tradition whether of the first three or the first six centuries. But Vincent admits a *progressus fidei.* In what sense does he admit it? The theory of development is an endeavour to show that Christ committed certain seeds of truth to His Church, which should in due course develop into definite doctrines. This theory has fallen into the background latterly, for with the doctrine of infallibility it became unnecessary. S. Vincent declares that whatever has been sown in the Church, which is the field of God's husbandry, shall be cultivated and maintained that it may flourish and come to perfection. It is lawful that the ancient articles of Christian belief should be attuned to the time, but unlawful that they be changed or maimed. The Church of Christ, he maintains, is deeper than the doctrines committed to her, changing nothing, diminishing nothing, adding nothing; "novelty must cease to disturb antiquity." He declared that the catholic faith must not be injured by novelties. This does not mean that there can be no *profectus religionis*, no progress in the Church. He admits such development in the sense of the pregnant phrase *profectus, non permutatio*. Progress there may be, but not change. Identity must be preserved throughout. Progress must, maintain the same teaching, the same sense, the same thought. He says again, "It is a crime to change [these ancient dogmas], to mutilate them. To teach anything to catholic Christians besides[1] what they have received has never been allowed, is nowhere allowed and never will be allowed." Thus the Church is "a living witness to a once-spoken voice[2]," and her authority will be gauged by the consent of independent witnesses. This test is applicable alike to churches and to councils.

Vincent is therefore in favour of development[3], but it is very clearly defined. He allows no new dogma, but only such development of old truths as will give completeness to them ; he was much too clear and sound a thinker and too scholarly to commit himself to the negation that no growth or progress in religion could be made. But the growth is organic, there is no foreign innovation. Yet he partially gives up his case. When there are heresies widely spread and deeply rooted, and the error cannot thus be disposed of by the unanimity of the teachers, then the appeal is to Scripture. Tradition is thus after all somewhat lame, but only partially. Vincent is fair minded and desires to face all the difficulties of his position. The Bible is in his view the oldest tradition, it is to him the standard tradition. This too is the view of the Anglican Communion. Scripture is the final court of appeal in matters of faith, " so that whatsoever is not read therein, nor may be proved thereby is not to be believed as an article of the faith, or be thought requisite or

---

[1] Not only *contra.* but *praeter*, Chapters XX and XXVIII.
[2] Gore, *Authority of the Church*, p. 40.　　　[3] Chapter XXIII.

necessary to salvation." The Council of Trent[1], on the other hand, says the revelation of Christian truth is "contained in the written books *and* in the unwritten tradition," and adds that both are received "with an equal sentiment of piety and reverence."

In all attempts to defend the authoritative promulgation of doctrines like that of the immaculate conception, the infallibility of the Pope and other changes of this sort, the real point of dispute may be summed up in a question based on these words of Vincentius: "Is it *profectus* or is it *permutatio*?" Those who say that such apparently novel dogmas are *profectus* will assert that these doctrines are implicit in Scripture statements or accepted doctrines, and that they are no more *permutatio* than the development of the doctrine of the Incarnation or the Trinity; others will declare that they contain absolutely new ideas not implicit in earlier or Scripture teaching. Vincent deals in Chapter XXIII with progress in religion. "Shall we have no advancement of thought in the Church of Christ? let us have the greatest that may be," but he explains the lines of this advancement :—"that it may be an increase in faith and not a change. It is the nature of an increase that things in and from themselves grow greater, but of a change, that something be turned from what it was to another which it was not." He uses the analogy of a child's growth, and he concludes: "The Church of Christ, the anxious and diligent guardian of doctrines committed to her charge, never changes anything in them, diminishes nothing, adds nothing, does not take away what is necessary, or put on anything superfluous, does not lose what is her own, nor usurp what is not, but with all industry studies this one thing, how, by faithful and wise dealing with what is old, to perfect and polish it; to establish what has been already expressed and declared; to preserve what has been already established and defined. What else has she endeavoured to accomplish by the decrees of councils but that what was before believed, should afterwards be more diligently believed." Some would consider it difficult to defend the doctrine, for instance, of papal infallibility on

[1] Session IV.

Vincent's principles.   It is not however our purpose or business
to enter into this disputed question save so far as the allusion to
it may serve to illustrate the meaning of the principles taught
by the author of the *Commonitorium*.   It may however be
mentioned that at any rate one modern Roman theologian[1]
would seem to find it difficult to prove that certain Roman
dogmas were recognised in substantial reality in the early
Church, and so while accepting the truth of Vincent's rule in its
positive sense, cannot accept it in an exclusive sense.   The
cardinal says, " It is enough to have shown a consent of faith
prevailing in the Church at any time in the apostolic succession,
in order to vindicate the Divine revelation and apostolic tradition
as to any head of doctrine."   But this surely would abrogate
part of the threefold test, antiquity, and would allow *permutatio*,
which Vincent rigorously disallows.   The fundamental principle
of the teaching of Vincent is that the Church once for all
received the whole *depositum* ; that therefore the main thing
was to see that no rent was made in what has been called by
others than Vincent, " the seamless robe " ; and that the whole
truth which has been sufficient from the commencement, whether
in conciliar decrees or in patristic utterances, has been fixed in
writing.   " I cannot sufficiently marvel[2] at the madness of some
men that they be not content with the rule of faith once
delivered us and received from of old, but do every day seek
for one new doctrine after another, ever desirous to add to, to
change, or to take away something from religion."   In dealing
with the words of S. Paul to Timothy, Vincent asks[3], " What
is this *depositum* ? "   He answers his own question thus : " That
which is committed to thee, not that which is invented of thee ;
that which thou hast received, not that which thou hast devised ;
a thing brought to thee, not brought forth of thee ; wherein thou
must not be an author but a keeper, not a founder but an
observer, not a leader but a follower."   It is the boast of the
Anglican that he seeks to preserve what was held and taught
by the ancient Church from the first, and in the spirit of

[1] Cardinal Franzelin, *De Divina traditione et scriptura*, 3rd ed., Rome, 1882.
Theses IX, XII, XXIV.
[2] Chapter XXI.   [3] Chapter XXII.

Vincent, adds nothing, diminishes nothing, changes nothing, but "commends the old faith to every man's conscience, and shows her life by rendering it intelligible in view of new needs to new generations of men[1]."

Its theological contents. Vincent is quite clear and definite in his use of terms applied to the Person of Christ. In describing the error of Apollinarius, he speaks of it as a refusal to recognise in Christ two substances[2], the one divine and the other human, the one of God His Father, the other of the Virgin His Mother. He declares that in the matter of our Lord's incarnation Apollinarius openly and manifestly blasphemes. Whereas the truth says there is one Christ of two "substances," he, contrary to the truth, affirms that of the one Divinity of Christ were made two substances[3]. Referring to the heresy of Photinus, he points out that this heretic affirms that God is one and must be acknowledged as by the Jews, and does not believe there is any "Person" of God the Word, or of the Holy Ghost. He maintained also that Christ was only a mere man who had His beginning of the Virgin Mary. Vincent goes on to explain that God the Logos without any change of his essential nature, uniting Himself to man was made man not by confusion of substance, and not by mutation of His nature. While His own Divine substance remained immutable, He took upon Himself the nature of perfect man, not in imitation or counterfeit, but in substance.

Dealing with the heresy of Nestorius, Vincent shows that he believed in two distinct substances in Christ, and so with "unheard-of wickedness" must needs have two sons of God, two Christs—one God and another man, one begotten of the Father, another born of His Mother. With some subtlety Nestorius declares that Christ was born at first an ordinary man and

---

[1] Bishop Gore.

[2] The word "substantia" for οὐσία was practically introduced by Tertullian. On the terms introduced into the theological terminology of Western theologians, there are instructive and illuminative notes in R. L. Ottley's *Doctrine of the Incarnation* (pp. 573–597). Reference also may be made to the *Early History of Christian Doctrine*, pp. 231–8, by J. F. Bethune-Baker, Methuen, 1903.

[3] A reference, apparently, to the fundamental error of Apollinarius that man's nature pre-existed in God.

nothing more and not, as yet, associated[1] in unity of Person with the Word of God ; and that afterwards the Person of the Word descended upon Him, assuming man to Himself; and although the manhood thus assumed now remains in the glory of God, yet once there would seem to have been no difference between Him and other men. Thus Nestorius in effect said that there were either always, or at some time, two Christs. The Catholic Church, on the other hand, confesses one Christ not two, and the self-same both God and man, one Person yet two substances, two substances yet one Person. In order to declare the faith more clearly, Vincent adds that in God is one "substance," yet three " Persons," in Christ are two "substances," but one " Person "; in the Trinity there is a difference in the " Persons " but not a difference of essence ; in our Saviour there is unity of Person, and a difference of essence or οὐσία. How is there in the Trinity a difference of Persons, but not a difference of essence ? Forsooth, because there is one Person of the Father, another of the Son, and another of the Holy Ghost, but yet not a difference in the " nature " of the Father, of the Son and of the Holy Ghost, but one and the self-same " essentia." To explain the two " substances " and the one " Person " of Christ, Vincent uses the analogy of S. Peter and S. Paul. In them the soul is one thing and the body is another thing, yet the body and the soul are not two Peters, nor the soul one Paul and the body another Paul, but one and the self-same Paul subsisting of a double and diverse nature of body and soul, so in one and the self-same Christ there are two substances, the one divine and the other human, the one consubstantial with His Father, the other consubstantial with His Mother. Not only in this world does every man consist of body and soul, but also in the next and never shall either be changed into the other. So in Christ the distinctness of either substance shall continue for ever, the unity of Person remaining notwithstanding. Thus Vincent uses the word "substance"

---

[1] Nestorius would only allow a "conjunction" (συνάφεια) of two Persons, and denied that the two natures (which Vincentius calls "substances") formed a personal unity, ἕνωσις καθ᾽ ὑπόστασιν. This "conjunction" in which they were brought together was only σχετική, one of relation.

throughout his argument defined either as divine or human, and he speaks with the greatest lucidity of the nature of the "substance." He is equally explicit in his use of the word person. He is careful to show that the frequent use of this word must be clearly understood. When we say that God in His Person was made man we must not seem to say that God the Word took upon Him what is ours in imitation, just as in a theatre a man takes upon him many persons or "characters" of which he himself is none, for when men imitate the actions of others, they perform their office, but are not the men they act. Let this madness be confined to the Manicheans, who say that God the Son was not in "substance" the person of man, but feigned the reality of human personality. The Catholic faith affirms that the Word of God became man in such wise that He took upon Him our nature not in pretence and semblance but really and truly, and performed human actions, not as though He were doing the acts of another, but as performing His own: Peter and John were men not by imitation, but in real essence; Paul did not counterfeit the Apostle, or feign himself Paul, but was an Apostle and Paul in real essence, so God the Word did not feign Himself to be perfect man but showed Himself to be very man in reality and truth and without any conversion of Himself, united Himself to man, and became man, not by confusion nor by imitation, but by subsisting in reality of substance while the Divine "substance" of the Logos remained unchangeable and while He took upon Him the nature of perfect man, He was Himself flesh, was Himself a man, and had the person of a man.

Vincent is equally definite in upholding the unity of Person in Christ. We must insistently believe Christ to be not only one, but always one Person. It is an intolerable blasphemy to concede Him now to be one, and yet to say, one after His baptism, but two at the time of His birth. This sacrilegious assertion can only be avoided by confessing that man was united to God in unity of Person, not from the time of His resurrection, not from the time of His baptism, but already in His Mother's womb, by reason of which unity of Person those things which are proper to God are attributed to man, and those which are proper to flesh are ascribed to God[1]. Thus it is written by inspiration that the Son of Man descended from heaven[2], and the Lord of Glory was crucified upon earth[3].

Vincent also defines the phrase "the Mother of God." Since the flesh of the Word was born of an undefiled Mother, God the Word Himself was born of the Virgin, and most impiously the contrary is maintained. The Holy Virgin must not then be deprived of her prerogative of Divine grace and her especial glory, for she is to be confessed to be the "Mother of God," but not according to a certain impious heresy which affirms that she is the "Mother of God" in name only as bringing forth that man which afterwards was made God, just as we speak of a woman as the mother of a bishop, not because she brought forth one that was already a bishop, but because she gave birth to one who became a bishop. Not in this manner is the Holy Mary to be called "the Mother of God," but rather that in her womb that holy mystery was already wrought whereby on account of the unity of Person, as the Word in flesh is flesh, so man in God is God.

Those who have followed, in the history of Christological doctrine, the various errors and ambiguities which arose and misled the wariest, will here appreciate the accuracy of statement characteristic of this monk of Lerins.

There are also brief references by Vincent to other points of Catholic doctrine. He makes a general statement when he asks, Who ever originated a heresy who did not first separate himself from the consent of the universality and antiquity of the Catholic Church[4]? He gives these examples : Who, before Pelagius, presumed so much on the power of man's free-will as to deny the necessity of the grace of God as an aid to it? Who ever before Celestius denied that all men are involved in the guilt of Adam's transgression? Who before Arius dared to rend asunder the Unity of the Trinity? Who before Sabellius dared to confound the Trinity of the Unity? Who before Novatian represented God as merciless in desiring rather the death of a sinner than that he should return and live? Who before

---

[1] Technically called *communicatio idiomatum*.   [2] John iii. 13.
[3] 1 Corinthians ii. 8.   [4] Chapter XXIV.

Simon Magus dared ever affirm that God is the author of evil? Vincent sums all these up as profane novelties which are against the decrees of the Fathers, and are a shipwreck of the faith.

The Pelagian controversy. The theological history of the monastery will not be complete without a reference to the charge of Semipelagianism which has been laid against some of her sons, and notably against Vincent. At the time the doctrines of Pelagius were being hotly debated, a conciliatory party arose which, while exposing the errors of Pelagius, desired to soften the harshness of Augustine. This party appeared almost simultaneously in Northern Africa and Southern Gaul; its special tenet was the co-operation of the human with the Divine Will, a doctrine that in much later theology become known as Arminianism. John Cassian inaugurated the movement which rapidly spread and found favour in Gaul. In fact after Pelagius had been condemned, the controversy mostly centred in Gaul. This does not however necessarily mean that Pelagianism found very many adherents there. The doctrines of free-will and the necessity of grace were alike held with varied insistence as to the place of each. The controversy really became a subsidiary dispute, on a side issue, as to the relative value and extent of grace and free-will. Augustine in his desire to accentuate the triumphs of grace went too far; the Gallican theologians anxious to preserve the doctrine of free-will seemed to favour some aspects of Pelagianism. Between these came a middle party, fittingly called Semipelagians. We have our first intimation of its progress in a letter which Prosper of Aquitaine addressed in A.D. 429 to S. Augustine, whom he greatly admired, and whose teaching he ardently upheld. He speaks with much charity of this new movement and refers to those who originated it as "servants of God, people distinguished for their exercise of all the virtues, and of whom some are in the front ranks of the episcopate." Augustine[1] conceived it to be the absolute will of God to predestinate some to salvation, and to abandon others to perdition for no other reason than that He wished it so. Grace was regarded as a means by which God pursued the realisation of His decree. The logical result

---

[1] *De correptione et gratia.*

was to attribute the entire efficacy of it to God Himself. He admitted that all had not a share in the power to attain salvation and consequently that Christ did not die for all. Such uncompromising severity offended very many, and the Semipelagians did not perhaps, in the heat of the dispute, weigh his words with sufficient precision or accurately gauge his propositions. This was partly Augustine's own fault, for his words are certainly open to misconstruction. They read as though he argued in favour of what practically amounted to fatalism. Yet his idea of predestination did not exclude God's consideration of human merit or man's freewill, which the Semipelagians allowed was enfeebled though not entirely destroyed by original sin, and which the full-blown Pelagian regarded as intact. They admitted that man without Divine help was not strong enough to work out his own salvation ; still he possessed some power and by its exercise he became deserving of grace to supply the defect. The weakness of this position lies in the idea that the commencement of salvation belonged to free-will and not to Divine grace. Prosper urged S. Augustine to enter upon a defence of his position. The latter therefore wrote his works *De dono perseverantiae* and *De predestinatione sanctorum*, of which Tillemont thought so highly that he declared them to be inspired. Though his doctrine is further explained in these writings, they did not alter the impression already made upon the Semipelagians. Prosper was in consequence inclined to regard them as ungrateful for so great a teacher, and he accordingly wrote his *Carmen de ingratis*, an epigrammatic poem of a thousand lines. After Augustine's death, Prosper with the help of a layman named Hilary was bent on a complete defence of his master's views. With this object they proceeded to Rome in an endeavour to induce Pope Celestine I to condemn the Semipelagians. They were partly successful, for he sent a letter to the Gallican bishops, expressing his respect and admiration for S. Augustine, but it was so vague and indefinite on the point at issue that the supporters of S. Augustine were dissatisfied, and the Semipelagians interpreted it as favouring their views.

It should be noted that the term Semipelagianism is capable

of being misunderstood. This middle party never applied it to themselves. Indeed they did not wish to have any connection whatever with the tenets of Pelagius. Their opponents would not however countenance any "between-party" and so regarded their position as simply an offshoot of the heresy. The Semipelagians, sometimes called Massilians from Cassian's connection with Marseilles, did not really deserve the suspicion which attached to them. They were eminently conciliatory, and their distinguishing doctrines that the human and Divine will are synergistic coefficient factors, can only be condemned in so far as it embodied the root principle of Pelagianism, that with man's will rather than with Divine grace rests the beginning of personal salvation.

As we have said, Lerins through some of her sons has been accused of a strong leaning towards Semipelagianism. Reference to a few opinions will serve to emphasise the truth of the statement. Cardinal Noris[1] expressed the opinion that here it was "openly professed and obstinately defended." The authors of *L'Histoire de la France*[2] hold the same opinion when they declare that "from Marseilles where this error had its birth, it soon spread to Arles and to Lerins. At Lerins especially it was stronger than elsewhere." M. Fauriel[3] says, " It was among the men educated at this celebrated monastic school or at that of S. Victor that the doctrines of S. Augustine found their most distinguished adversaries, who tried to defend the merit of human will, reconciling it with the need of Divine grace." Guizot[4] expresses a similar view in these words: " It was in the abbeys of S. Victor and of Lerins that all the great questions of free-will, predestination, grace, original sin, were most agitated, and where Pelagian opinions found for fifty years most nourishment and support." M. Ampère[5] speaks of "the abbey of Lerins whence went the leading champions of Semipelagianism." Neander[6] describes the island as " one of the most distinguished

[1] Hunc Vincentium, cum Hilario Arelatensi, Fausto Abbate, aliisque syncellitis Lirinensibus, contra sancti Augustini *De predestinatione sanctorum* conspirasse.
[2] Vol. II, p. 10.   [3] *Histoire de la Gaule Méridionale*, Vol. I, p. 404.
[4] *Histoire de la civilisation en France*, Vol. I, p. 121.
[5] *L'Histoire littéraire de la France*, Vol. II, pp. 23–28.
[6] *Church History*, Vol. IV, p. 399, T. and T. Clark, 1849.

seats" of it. Robertson[1] says the abbey ' was a chief strong-hold" of this movement.

But it is our purpose to consider the attitude of Vincent towards Semipelagianism, and sharply divided opinions have been expressed concerning both him and his work. The *Commonitorium* has been described as "a treacherous weapon supplied to the Semipelagians," and it has been said of the author that "after having given some admirable rules for the discovery of truth, Vincent fell into error." Remembering that Vincent's work was published in the heat of the crisis, at a time when the struggle was most keen between Augustine's supporters and the "middle party," it is perhaps natural that Vincent was under these circumstances accused of a covert intention of attacking Augustinianism, but how far this accusation is just will be under consideration in the following pages. Reference may here be made to a most interesting article from the pen of Professor Dr Langen[2] in which he expresses the opinion that the *Commonitorium* has once more come into prominence through the Old Catholic movement. Dealing with the question of Vincent's attitude towards Augustine, the professor calls the latter "a speculative and creative genius, with little historical knowledge, still less knowledge of Eastern theology," and it was not until the dawn of the Pelagian controversies that he manifested any desire to treat of such matters as Divine mercy, predestination, and free-will. In harmony with his whole philosophical opinions[3] he threw himself into the controversy with passionate zeal when Pelagius dared to set at nought all supernatural grace in man's salvation, a position unheard of in the Church. Even in the use of the phrases "Divine mercy," and "predestination," the expressions were by this writer robbed of all definitely Christian connotation. Instead of applying the actual teaching of the Church to the refutation of these novel views, S. Augustine falling back on his own extremely speculative ideas said, "God is all," and almost if not quite maintained the

---

[1] *History of Christian Church*, Vol. II, p. 311.

[2] *Revue internationale de Théologie*, Juillet–Septembre, 1900.

[3] See the whole subject ably set forth in Dorner's work, *Augustinus, Sein Theologisches System und Seine Religionsphilosophische Anschauung dargestellt*, pp. 209–232, Berlin, 1873.

position that, in the Divine dispensation of personal salvation, human co-operation is needless. Those who regarded the views both of Pelagius and Augustine as quite novel and entirely unprecedented in either extreme direction, were anxious to turn to the teaching of antiquity. Vincent was their able spokesman. It must not be considered part of our design to give anything like an ordered and complete account in academic fashion of the Catholic as opposed to the heretical position. Vincent's interest is entirely practical, and his aim was to raise a warning note against the uprising of the extreme Predestinarianism that was agitating the Church. His sufficient justification is found in the fact that even the striking personality and immense authority of S. Augustine could not induce men to accept all the consequences of his theories. In fact they never became catholic, and extreme predestinarian views have come to be regarded as merely opinions of sects and parties.

It cannot be asserted that in any passage Vincent openly betrays his leaning to what has been doctrinally distinguished as Semipelagianism. It is far too much to assert that the fact that he was a monk of Lerins is any evidence of his semipelagian point of view. That he does not even mention S. Augustine is equally little proof. If it be argued that Vincent does not mention S. Augustine among the doctors who at the Council of Ephesus were declared to be the masters and regulators of the faith, this great Father's name does not appear in the Acts of the council.

It will be well to examine a few of the passages which seem to betoken a pronounced hostility to S. Augustine, or which are at least a pronouncement against Augustinianism. It has been said that Vincent dared not sign his name to the *Commonitorium* because of the attack therein made against one of such eminence, but if his own introductory words may be any guide, modesty may have been the reason for the pseudonym, for he calls himself "a stranger to this world and the least of all God's servants," and expresses the hope that others will correct and improve upon what he has written. He has been accused of writing with the specific purpose of refuting S. Augustine, and it has been asserted that the whole drift of the work points to this view, but it is admitted that Vincent did not lack courage, but he probably desired to be as forbearing as possible to one of such distinction. An attack upon S. Augustine is read into the words : " The reason is clearer than day why God in His providence sometimes allows certain teachers and masters of the Church to promulgate novel opinions. It is that God may try you. And it is a great trial when one whom you consider a prophet, a disciple of the prophets, a doctor and upholder of the truth whom you have greatly reverenced and most dearly loved, introduces pernicious errors which you cannot easily detect through prejudice in favour of an old teacher, and cannot well condemn through love of an old master[1]." Similarly in Chapter xx when he says that the good and true Catholic is he that loves the truth of God and the Church which is the Body of Christ, that " prefers nothing before the Catholic faith, not the authority of any man, not love, not genius, not eloquence, not philosophy, but despising all these things, and firm and steadfast in faith, determines to hold only what he knows the Catholic Church in old time to have held universally[2]," Vincent is thought to be covertly attacking S. Augustine, but it is surely illogical to take such words as these to prove that Vincent laid down these principles for this one case and for this one specific purpose, and not as a general formula for futurity. Persons and circumstances cannot alter fundamental principles, and those which treat of dogma are eternal and immutable. This is inherent in his threefold test.

When we turn to such phrases in the *Commonitorium* as " the deceitful dealings of new heretics much need our care and attention," and " the frauds of uprising heretics," " the licence of profane novelty," and the like, they all produce the impression that Vincent had a recent example of heretical teaching in his mind which was greatly to be dreaded. What could this be ? It could not, it is said, be the teachings of Nestorius or the Pelagians, for these heresies had already been condemned and finished with, just as much as the errors of Photinus or Apollinarius or Julian of Eclanum. Of this last, Vincent says, " He that treats with contempt what he knows to be the belief

---

[1] Chapter x.   [2] Chapter xx.

of the whole body shall be deemed unworthy to be ranked
of God among those who are united in faith, than which
I cannot imagine a more terrible evil, and which we see to have
fallen upon Julian the Pelagian[1]." Then there is nothing left
for a theologian writing in A.D. 434 but the errors of extreme
Augustinianism and of Predestinarianism. What is the following
but a clear allusion with a certain semipelagian ring about it?
" For who ever before that profane Pelagius "laid so much stress
on the power of the will " that he thought not the grace of God
necessary to aid it in every particular good act[2]?" The phrase
"laid so much stress on the power of will" is compatible with
a semipelagian interpretation, and would so sound to the
extremists in the theological strife on this subject which then
existed. To whom is the following passage an allusion? " For
they dare promise and teach that in their Church, that is in
the fellowship of their sect, is to be found a great and
special, yea, and a certain personal grace of God, so that
whosoever be of their number, they all straightway without any
work, without any study, without any industry have such
dispensation of God that, preserved by angels, they can never
hurt their foot against a stone, that is to say, may never be
made to offend[3]." Is not this clearly a description of the
extreme Augustinianism of the men who exaggerated the
teaching of their master as in subsequent centuries men out-
calvined Calvin? Are we to take it that Vincent here refers to
some sect[4]? Here, when he adds that this "personal grace "
was such that they were made incapable of offence, "they can
never hurt their foot against a stone, that is never be made to
offend[5]," and so all moral striving rendered needless, is clearly
the extreme predestinarian doctrine of grace. It may without
undue exaggeration be thought that so great a teacher as
S. Augustine himself is referred to in such words as : " If there
shall arise," says Moses, " in the midst of thee a prophet or one
which saith he hath seen a dream, that is some master placed in
the Church whose disciples or followers suppose him to teach by
some revelation from God ; what then ? and shall foretell some

---

[1] Chapter XXVIII.   [2] Chapter XXIV.   [3] Chapter XXVI.
[4] Note the phrase :—In communione suae conventiculae.   [5] Scandalizari.

sign or miracle, and that shall happen which he has said[1]."
Here most naturally we have a veiled reference to some or other
"great master" who was at this time disturbing the Church with
novelties. Then again the passages already mentioned as to
the trial to the Church of the errors of such "trusted teachers"
as Origen and Tertullian, who like the modern innovators bring
forth a multitude of biblical citations in favour of their conten-
tions, become far more intelligible and fuller of significance if the
author was thinking of S. Augustine himself rather than his
later adherents and extreme exponents. Indeed who is it that
he is thinking of and has in his eye but S. Augustine when he
writes[2]: "Whatsoever doctrine any person however holy and
learned, even though he be a bishop, a martyr or confessor,
holds beyond or contrary to that of all men, let it be reckoned
among his own private opinions and be separated from general
consent"? It is surely extreme Predestinarianism that is here
meant, for never previously had this doctrine been taught in
such shape as now by any responsible teacher, though it may
possibly be nothing more than the expression of a general
statement, for it is practically an opinion culled from
Tertullian.

The reason for this indirect and allusive, if not covert, attack
on the predestinarian teaching as a recent instance of the
transgression of the principle of antiquity, used as a preliminary
preparation of his readers' minds for a condemnation of the
errors involved, is said by those who regard it in this light
to be obvious. On the one hand it would have been dangerous,
it is alleged, to make a pointed and direct attack on a theologian
and bishop of such eminence. On the other hand his plan was
thus more skilfully carried out. The minds of his readers were
not offended by direct polemic, yet the sections devoted to the
position of Cyprian already spoken of above; as well as to the
question of the possibility of a subsequent corruption and falsifi-
cation of the writings of Origen, of whose "great gifts time would
fail him to tell"; where Vincent says: "Suppose someone asserts
that the writings of Origen are corrupt, I will not deny it, but
rather prefer that it should be so"; and further the reference to

[1] Chapter x.   [2] Chapter xxviii.

"new and upstart" doctrines "which need to be checked before, the poison spreading further, they attempt to corrupt the writings of the Fathers"—all these references seem undeniably intended to pave the way for a separation of S. Augustine from the followers and scholars who appealed to his authority and sheltered themselves under his name.

There are other passages also in the *Commonitorium* which would seem to indicate the opposite. When Vincent describes doctrinal error as lacking the essential foundation of antiquity, he passes in review several heresies and at the close says, "Whoever before Simon Magus unto this last Priscillian dare ever affirm that God was the author of evil[1]?" Thus according to Vincent, Priscillian is the last to propound this theory of the origin of evil, and he died four years before S. Augustine was baptised. Can it then be supposed that Augustine was attacked when everyone knew that he had often contended against Priscillianism? Again, in Chapter XXVI, when Vincent deals with the quotation of Scripture by heretics who, following the devil's example, "cast the unhappy soul from the tower of the Catholic Church into the gulf of heresy," and deceive simple men by daring to promise "a certain personal grace of God so that they can never hurt their foot against a stone," is it not possible that the Donatists and other heretics are meant, who endeavoured to seduce the simple minded by the most exaggerated promises? In reference to the words already quoted "however holy and learned, though he be a bishop," may not this be only a general statement in which the personal importance of the author of a heresy is emphasised to strengthen the argument?

In a reference to the letter written by Celestine to the priests of Gaul blaming them for leaving the old faith unprotected and for allowing profane novelties to arise, Vincent says in Chapter XXXII, "Some may doubt who they are whom he forbids to preach, whether the preachers of antiquity or the inventors of novelty." Celestine himself shall tell us: "let novelty cease," he says, "to molest antiquity," and Baronius commenting on this quotation by Vincent sees therein a proof

[1] Chapter XXIV.

of the adherence of the author of the *Commonitorium* to the teaching of Augustine[1]. On the whole it is perhaps best to say that the opinions of S. Vincent on S. Augustine are not matured, but that he regards the latest developments of doctrinal partisanship and of extreme Predestinarians as dangerous in the highest degree. To him the novelty of this opinion which in our day we should call " Calvinism " is self-evident, and he considers it the wisest plan to combat the position by attacking novelties in general. His *Commonitorium* is an appeal to the Catholic world not to rest content because Pelagius, Celestius and Nestorius are no longer forces to reckon with, but to take up arms for the faith of the Fathers against all profane novelties. To this end he marshals the Catholic ideas and interests in favour of a practically semipelagian position. There is no writing of antiquity which presents so favourable a field for the survey of this position. It is the more interesting as we are all Semipelagians now.

Gennadius clearly did not know of any other books of Vincent's and it is doubtful whether he wrote any, nor does he himself mention earlier works from his pen. He promises further treatment and explanation of the doctrine of the Person of Christ, when he says, "Hereafter, if it please God, I will treat and declare these points more fully[2]." But this is of course no proof that he ever composed such a treatise. He is supposed to have written a commentary on some of the Psalms. It is doubtful whether S. Vincent was the author of the *Responsiones ad capitula objectionum Vincentiarum*, but it is natural that these objections against S. Augustine should be ascribed to this monk of Lerins. Internal evidence can be produced both for and against such authorship. On the one hand the sentiments are distinctly Pelagian and on the other the comparison of this work and the drift of the seventieth and eighty-sixth sections of the *Commonitorium* would seem to show the two are by the same hand.

It is well known that there are some learned scholars well qualified to discuss the question, who are of opinion that Vincent was the author of the Athanasian Creed. The possible

---

[1] *Annales eccles. ad an.* 431.   [2] Chapter XVI.

authors are of course various, and we must refer our readers to the works of Waterland, Ommanney, Burns, Kattenbusch, and more recently Dom Morin, for a consideration of these various claims. It must here suffice to say briefly that a vast amount of learning has been brought to bear upon this most difficult subject, and a wide divergence of views has been expressed. Vossius was the first to cast a doubt upon the authorship of Athanasius. Ussher agreed with this opinion that Athanasius did not write the creed, but he did not suggest who did. In 1675 Quesnel took the first definite step to determine the author, and suggested Vigilius of Thapsus whose claims have not however been since advanced. Antelmi in 1693 vigorously opposed the theory of Quesnel and suggested Vincent of Lerins. Ommanney in 1896 wrote his treatise in favour of this authorship. In the course of his argument he says, "The enquiry is necessarily hemmed in by certain conditions. The *Quicunque* being of Latin origin, the author must have been a Latin theologian ; as it was composed in the Nestorian epoch and reflects the tone of thought then prevalent among the orthodox, he must have been a person who lived at that epoch and was conversant with its theology[1] ; as it re-echoes in all its parts the teaching of S. Augustine both in substance and language, he must have been familiar with the writings of that great doctor[2]. After comparing the *Commonitorium* with the writings of S. Augustine he adds, "Thus in Vincent the three conditions meet. He lived and flourished at the period of the Nestorian controversy for he died in 450; he was thoroughly conversant with that controversy as plainly appears from his *Commonitorium* ; and he was familiar with the writings of S. Augustine, and a disciple of his School so far as regards the great verities of faith." The claims of this author have also been advanced by Swainson, and his knowledge and ability have been acknowledged by Dr Burn. There are undoubtedly a large number of remarkable

---

[1] Kattenbusch in his work on the creeds affirms that the context of the formulary carries us into the period *before* the Nestorian struggle. There is no turn of expression which must necessarily or even with probability be regarded as pointed against Nestorianism.

[2] The same authority suggests that S. Augustine may be using the language of the *Quicunque* itself.

phrases common to the creed and to the *Commonitorium*, as
Dr Burn shows.   Whoever may have been the author, there is
a strong consensus of opinion as to the place whence the creed
emanated.   With the exception of Vigilius, whose claims, as we
have already said, have not been advanced since 1675, all the
suggested authors are connected with Gaul, and to Gaul the
work is traced for the reasons that may be briefly recalled.
It was first received in the Gallican Church ; Gallican councils
and bishops have always esteemed it highly ; it was admitted
to belong to the Psalter by those Churches that received their
Psalter from Gaul ; the oldest version of which we hear is the
Gallican version of Hinckmar ; the first writers that mention it
are Gallican ; the first to quote its words are Avitus and
Caesarius ; the oldest commentator, Venantius Fortunatus,
570 A.D., was bishop of Poitiers ; manuscript copies were
nowhere so numerous or so old as in Gaul : the use of *substantia*
for the *essentia* of Augustine is not without its bearings on its
Gallican origin.   If Vincent be not the author, yet the
monastery of Lerins still provides him, as students of this
subject are well aware, for Dr Burn " clings with some fondness
to Honoratus " and considers him " worthy to be the author";
the deservedly respected authority of Waterland champions the
claims of Hilary ; Dom Morin has set forward the claims of
Caesarius, which we may consider in greater detail subsequently.
It may here be said that Dr Armitage Robinson[1] commenting
on the view that the latinity of the creed bears a striking
resemblance to the writings of Caesarius, says, " there is much
to be said in favour of this," and Professor Turner is favourably
disposed to this authorship.   Whatever be the several opinions
as to the authorship of this creed, we are, in the words of
Dr Burn, " content to trace it to the island home which sent
forth into the world so noble a band of confessors and martyrs."
In a word, this creed emanated if not from the pen of Vincent,
at any rate from the cloisters of Lerins.

---

[1] *Lectures at Westminster Abbey on the Athanasian Creed.*

CHAPTER VI

THE APOSTLE OF IRELAND

In the general transformation of Europe during the 5th century, Ireland, which was still politically and socially aloof, was drawn into the spiritual federation of the Roman Empire, through Constantine's official recognition of the Christian religion. Even before Christianity was tolerated by the state the way was being prepared for it by intercourse and inter-communication of commerce, and when its recognition was accomplished, the influence of Rome gave it prestige and power. And although we have no records of the relations of Rome with Ireland, we know that the question had been raised whether Ireland should be occupied or not; for Agricola, one of Domitian's generals, desired to attempt its conquest, and was overruled by the government, which apparently saw no political reason for the annexation[1]. We know too that the Roman Empire traded with Ireland[2]. It may then be fairly inferred that "by the end of the 4th century Christians, and some knowledge of the Christian worship, should have found their way to the Irish shores[3]." Obscure may have been the beginnings of the conversion of Ireland, but its organisation and establishment are due in the main to one man—Patrick the son of Calpurnius.

That "a biographer of S. Patrick must ever feel that he is the interpeter of a mysterious master[4]" is a proposition which few who have been attracted by the subject will care to dispute. The life and work of the illustrious patron saint of Ireland is "scorched and hot with the fires of manifold controversies." In

---

[1] Tacitus, *Agricola*, chap. 24.
[2] *Ibid.* Aditus portusque per commercia et negotiores cogniti.
[3] Bury, *Life of S. Patrick*, p. 14.   [4] W. B. Morris, *Life of S. Patrick*.

fact there is little that has not at one time or the other been
called in question.   Disputed are his birthplace, his birth name,
his life from the period of his captivity to his return to Ireland,
his authority for the mission he undertook, and the date of his
death.   His very name has contributed to the general obscurity,
for Patricius, like Augustus, was commonly used down to the
7th century, in the sense of gentleman or noble, as rather a title
of honour than a personal name.   The obscurity is further
complicated by the fact that more than one Patrick was at work
in Ireland about the same time.   One was sent under the name
of Palladius by Pope Celestine as bishop to Ireland in A.D. 431,
just one year before "the patron saint" began his mission.
Another is mentioned by Irish writers as Senn Patraicc, the
head of S. Patrick's community.   In fact so much uncertainty
and obscurity have surrounded both name and memory of the
illustrious saint that some have found the usual refuge of those
who are impatient of all mystery, and doubted whether he
existed at all.   This is childish impatience, to ignore the existing
documents, and to doubt so firmly fixed a national tradition
without better cause.

Where then was S. Patrick born? France, Scotland, Ireland
and England have all made a claim to the honour.   The claim
of Ireland, says Professor Stokes[1], "we may at once dismiss."
It is founded on the words of S. Patrick's letter to Coroticus, the
British prince, in which he laments the contempt felt by Britons
for Irishmen, "with them it is a crime that we have been in
Hibernia."   He was evidently identifying himself with his
converts, for elsewhere he speaks of Britain as his birthplace.
In the interests of France some have proclaimed Boulogne as
his birthplace, but this theory is seldom supported.   It may
however be noted that in the *Annals of the four Masters*, it is
said that after Niall, of the nine hostages, had been twenty-seven
years in the sovereignty of Ireland, he was slain "by the sea of
Wight," at Muir-n-Icht, i.e. "the sea between France and England," a spot that has been identified by some with Boulogne.
S. Patrick's own statement that he was born in "the Britains"
can scarcely include this place.   Those who uphold the claim

<hr />

[1] *Ireland and the Celtic Church*, p. 35.

of Scotland assign the honour to Dumbarton, known in ancient times as Alcluith, forming the western end of the Roman wall which extended from the Forth to the Clyde. In the oldest (11th century) MS. of the Hymn of Fiacc, "Patric was born at Nemthur[1]," and this place is identified by a glossator with Ail Cluade, the Rock of Clyde at Dumbarton. In the letter to Coroticus, who was king of Ail (Cluade) Patrick refers to the king's soldiers as "meis civibus" (my fellow citizens), as though his home was there. This may have suggested the gloss. In the same letter Patrick mentioning his noble birth, says that his father was a decurion or member of the municipal council of a Roman town. As each village or town had a council as soon as there were a few hundred inhabitants, it may be assumed that Dumbarton was in such a position, though there is no evidence of this. To this presumption may be added the fact that, as Patrick says, he was carried away captive with thousands of his countrymen, and we know that Northern Britain was devastated by Picts and Scots during a period contemporary with S. Patrick. On the other hand it is asserted by some that this is the last place where the Roman villa of a decurion would be expected. In his *Confession* S. Patrick speaks of his father (or possibly his grandfather) who was "in the town of Bannauem taberniae, for he had a small country place near[2]." It is again difficult to identify this place. Bannauenta may be the name of a station on Watling Street, three or four miles from Daventry, but it is unlikely though not impossible that the Irish invaders penetrated so far. As Dr Bury points out, "the two elements of the name were probably not uncommon in British geographical nomenclature," and "it is not a rash assumption that there were other small places so called besides the only Bannauenta which happens to appear in Roman geographical sources[3]," but as Muirchu says, it was "not far from our sea[4]," i.e. the Irish Channel, and further seems to consider its identity established[5], it can

---

[1] Probus who wrote a life of S. Patrick quotes an alternative reading, "Nentriae provinciae"; which is probably the same as this Nemthur.
[2] Vico Bannauem taberniae, uillulam enim prope habuit, 357. 5.
[3] *Life of S. Patrick*, p. 17.
[4] Haut procul a mari nostro, 495. 9.
[5] Quem uicum constanter indubitanterque comperimus esse uentre.

scarcely have been near Daventry. Dr Bury is inclined to look for it in south western Britain, "perhaps in the region of the lower Severn[1]." We must be content to leave it in the same kind of obscurity that surrounds the birthplace of Homer and of many others of fame in history.

S. Patrick's original name was Saccath, or it may have been customary to give two names, the one Roman and the other British, just as S. Paul had both a Roman and a Jewish name. Tirechan[2] mentions four names, Patricius, Succetus, Magonus, and Cothraige, but the latter is an Irish equivalent for Patricius with the usual change of *p* to *c*.

For the life of S. Patrick there are certain historical documents from which information can be gained. These have been submitted to a most careful and discriminating study by Dr Bury. There are also extant the *Confession*[3] *of S. Patrick*, and his *Epistle to Coroticus*[4]. There are also the *Annotations* on his life written in the 7th century by Tírechán, a bishop. This memoir provides certain chronological details, and maps out his journeys on some basis of geography. A life of the saint was written by Muirchu Maccumactheni son of Cogitosus in the 7th century. This biography, up to Patrick's arrival in Ireland, is free from myths, but afterwards is full of legends. With the exception of the *Epistle*, all these documents are found in the *Book of Armagh*[5] which was written by Ferdomnach of Armagh in the first half of the 9th century. It also contains a brief section called *Dicta Patricii*, a charter from Brian Boru to the church of Armagh, and the only complete copy of the New Testament transmitted by the Irish Church. The heading of the *Confession*[6] suggests that Ferdomnach intended to include the *Epistle to Coroticus*, but was not able to do so from lack of time.

---

[1] *Life of S. Patrick*, p. 17.

[2] *Analecta Bollandiana*, II, 35.

[3] So called from its concluding words, "Haec est confessio mea antequam moriar."

[4] In *Acta Sanctorum*, March 17, from a St Vaast MS.

[5] The MS. known as the *Liber Armachanus* is in the Library of Trinity College, Dublin. The text has been reproduced by Dr Gwynn, and a critical edition was published by Dr Newport White in the *Proceedings of the Royal Irish Academy*, 1904.

[6] Incipiunt libri sancti Patricii Episcopi.

S. Patrick's capture by Irish freebooters is the first crisis of his life. "I was taken captive," he narrates in his *Confession*, "when I was nearly sixteen years old. I knew not the true God, and I was brought captive to Ireland with many thousands of men as we deserved, for we had forsaken God and had not kept His commandments." For some six years S. Patrick tended the cattle of his lord, a chieftain of Dalaradia, into whose family he was sold as a slave. The days of his slavery were also the days of his conversion. He tells us that "he was every day frequent in prayer." We can well imagine his thoughts were often turned to the freedom of his home and to the memories that surrounded it. He must have longed to see it again. It must have been much in mind by day and night, and then to his highly-strung imagination there was a responsive voice, "Thou shalt soon return to thy native land." The words rang in his ears like the catch of a melody. Again the voice seemed to say, "The ship is ready." So Patrick determined to escape. It was not easy. He reached the port, and applied to the crew of a large ship to be allowed to work his passage out. Patrick incidentally mentions that the cargo partly consisted of dogs. In the employ of the Irish chieftain, he would learn something of the management of wolfhounds. The captain, who at first refused his entreaties, may have been induced to alter his mind if he thought Patrick would be useful with this particular cargo, and so took him on board.

The place whence they sailed and that at which they landed are not accurately known, nor can the nationality of the crew be determined, but from the expression by S. Patrick of a hope that they might come to the faith of Christ, we know they were heathens. We learn from the *Confession* that land was reached three days after leaving the coast of Ireland. This must have been either Gaul or Britain, and no part of Britain would have afforded so long a journey. On landing, S. Patrick and his shipmates spent two months wandering through desert country. This again can scarcely apply to Britain. There is evidence that the ship had reached the coast of Gaul, for S. Patrick tells his followers that he had the fear of God to guide him on his journey through Gaul and Italy. We have already sketched in an earlier chapter the condition of Gaul under the desolating influence of barbarian invasions, and on this account the beaten track may have been prudently avoided. The fear of God which guided him through Gaul and Italy was over him also in "the islands in the Tyrrhenian Sea[1]." After the two months' wandering, S. Patrick separated from his shipmates, but where and when he does not tell us. He appears to have reached the coast of Provence. According to M. l'Abbé Alliez[2] he came into Gaul about the year A.D. 400, entered the monastery of Marmoutier, and received the tonsure there, returning to Britain shortly afterwards, with an ever increasing desire to convert Ireland. S. Patrick himself tells us that his kinsfolk welcomed him on his return "as a son[3]" and urged him not to leave them. Once again his ardent desires were guided by a dream, in which an acquaintance—Victoricus by name—gives him a letter. As he read it, he seemed to hear the people's cry, "Come and walk once more among us as before." He doubted his capacity and fitness to obey this insistent voice, but he could not resist it. He returned to Gaul to be trained for his work and to receive his authoritative mandate. Dr Bury thinks it probable that S. Patrick found shelter at Lerins before returning to Britain, and afterwards chose Auxerre, as there is evidence that this town was a resort of Irish Christians desirous to study, but Alliez makes the visit to Lerins the occasion of his preparation for his mission to Ireland, and considering all the varied circumstances, this is not by any means improbable. It is certainly an attractive supposition. Some maintain he received his commission from Pope Celestine in A.D. 432 ; others say with equal certainty that he received no such authority. Into the controversy on this subject it is not of course our purpose to enter. It will suffice to say that Palladius, a deacon, had been consecrated bishop by Celestine and sent to Ireland, but his sojourn there was not of long duration. He came and went within the year.

---

[1] *Dicta Patricii*, 1. " Mare Tyrrene " is probably a reference to the islands of Lerins. Tírechán says Patrick stayed in the "insula Aralanensis," 302. 24.

[2] *Histoire du monastère de Lerins*, 1, chap. 2, p. 68.

[3] It may therefore be inferred that his own parents were now dead.

About A.D. 432 Patrick sailed for Ireland. His previous sojourn there had taught him much, and as he was no longer a stranger, he was not slow to gain a sympathetic welcome. He landed first at the mouth of the river Vartry, where Wicklow now stands, but his stay here was short. Sailing along the coast, he landed on a small island off Skerries, still called Inis Patrick, in the parish of Holmpatrick. Thence he proceeded northwards, and landed at Strangford Lough. The news soon spread, and he and his companions were thought to be pirates. The chieftain, Dichu, met him sword in hand, but not finding a combatant wielding worldly weapons, he sheathed his sword and received S. Patrick kindly, hospitably entertained him, listened to his teaching, and was baptized. According to tradition he gave to S. Patrick the land on which they met, and here was built a church, since called Sabhall Padhrig, or Patrick's Barn. This barn at Saul was the earliest church founded by him; it was his abiding place in life, and his resting place in death, for in the monastery of Saul he died. It is one of those facts of appealing interest, bringing us into contact with a distant past, that there still exists a church and parish of Saul, in the diocese of Down and Connor. From here S. Patrick went to Dalaradia, where he had spent those early years of his captivity. Legend, ever busy to find instances of "poetic justice," relates that when his former master Milchu heard of the approach of his one-time slave, in fear that he himself now in turn would be enslaved, he set fire to his house, and was burnt to death. S. Patrick returned to Strangford Lough, in readiness for a greater triumph. Like a wise general, he knew the value of a strong strategic position. Tara was the centre towards which five main roads converged, and to this point S. Patrick journeyed. It cannot be said that his mission here was very successful, but from it as a centre he conducted his campaign. Knowing the devotion of the tribes to their chiefs, he prudently determined to deliver his message first to them. If they received it, the conversion of their followers was assured. He began by journeying through Meath. At Telltown, the name of the chief was Carbri or Coirpre, who was a brother of Laoghaire, king of Ireland. This king had desired to kill S. Patrick, but relented, and accepted the faith, though his conversion was merely nominal and he died and was buried a pagan. Carbri would not accept the faith, but another brother, Conall, seems to have been a sincere convert, and after his baptism gave a site for a church near his own house, at Donagh[1]-Patrick on the banks of the Blackwater.

From Meath S. Patrick went into Connaught, where he spent some seven years, and where to this day he has left the marks of his influence in place names and dedications. There is, for example, Tempall Phaidrig, or the Church of S. Patrick on the island of Inisghoill in Lough Corrib[2], where a stone is preserved on which is one of the earliest Christian inscriptions in Ireland. Legend has been unusually busy with S. Patrick. It is a well recognised and widely accepted canon of criticism that the simpler the narrative the earlier is the document, the less miraculous and legendary the more trustworthy the record. This is true alike of the wider sphere of Church History and of the narrower subject of a county, or of an individual. A few examples must suffice by way of illustration. The account of the martyrdom of Polycarp, the *Acts of Perpetua and Felictas* and the history of later martyrdoms of Lyons and Vienne in Eusebius contain no miracles. But in the 5th and following centuries writers give full play to a most vivid imagination, and carried away by admiration for their saint or hero, exaggerate their records by incredible stories. So too, there are no miracles in the writings of S. Patrick, but a comparison of these with the Hymns of S. Fiacc and of S. Secundinus will reveal the growth of miraculous legend. Later biographies, in turn, out-legend legend.

It is not our purpose to reproduce a mass of such material, but one or two legendary incidents may be allowed because they bear unmistakable marks of ancient teaching and rites. At Cruachan, or Crochan, stood the ancient palace of the kings of Connaught. To this day the site possesses memorials of its earliest history. Near a fountain (a well is in existence to-day at the Rath of Crochan), S. Patrick and his companions held a council early one morning. The two daughters of Laoghaire king of Ireland, Feidelen and Ethne, came down for their

---

[1] Donagh is the equivalent of domnach, a church.
[2] See Sir William Wilde, on Lough Corrib and its beauties, p. 146.

morning ablutions. Much astonished they accosted the saint, and questioned him as to his home and whence he had come. In fact they overwhelmed him with their questions[1]. The answer of S. Patrick had contained a reproof, " It were better for you to confess to the true God than to enquire concerning our race." "Who is God?" they asked, "Where is His dwelling place? Has He sons and daughters? Is He beautiful? Is He in heaven or in earth, in the sea, in mountain or in valley? How can He be seen? How is He to be loved? How is He to be found? Is it in youth or in old age that He is to be found?" S. Patrick answered, "Our God is the God of all men; the God of heaven and of earth, of the sea and of the rivers, of sun and moon and stars, of lofty mountains and of lowly valleys; He hath a Son co-equal and co-eternal with Himself, and the Holy Ghost breathes in them. I desire to unite you, the daughters of an earthly king, to the Heavenly King." The maidens then desired that he would teach them how to believe in this Heavenly King, and whatever he would say, they promised they would do. Then follows a series of questions that S. Patrick asked them, and the answers that they gave. "Believe ye that by baptism ye put off the sin of your father and mother? We believe. Believe ye in repentance after sin? We believe. Believe ye in life after death? We believe. Believe ye in the resurrection? We believe. Believe ye in the unity of the Church? We believe." They were then baptized and a white veil was placed upon their heads. They then desired to see the face of Christ, and were told, "Ye cannot see His face except ye receive the sacrifice[2] and except ye taste of death." They then received the sacrifice and fell asleep in death. The story contains much that is artificial, not to say impossible. It pre-supposes a somewhat considerable know-ledge of theology on the part of the maidens, acquired with a miraculous celerity, but it may well be thought to reproduce S. Patrick's method of teaching, even as it describes the ritual of a very early date. Thus the legend bears internal evidence

---

[1] See the *Book of Armagh*.

[2] One of the titles of the Liturgy, and applied both to what was offered to God, and to the communicant.

of its antiquity, and is built on a strong foundation of truth. Similarly, the legend of Croagh-Patrick may be recalled. On the summit of a peak overlooking the bay of Westport, S. Patrick prayed and fasted for forty days and nights. This in itself is not an unreasonable conjecture, for the visit is mentioned in the *Book of Armagh*[1]. Legend describes how he brought together all the venomous serpents and toads of Ireland and drove them into the sea. Perhaps the fact of Ireland's exemption from reptiles[2] provided the basis of the legend.

From Connaught, he went to Ulster and founded the church and monastery of Ardd Mache (Armagh) in the year A.D. 445. The pride of those who think of the great age of the see of Canterbury must give place to those who call to mind this historical event of 150 years earlier. It was made possible by a gift of the land by Daire, king of Oriel. From Ulster S. Patrick went south, and there are ancient records of his visits to Leinster and Munster. He preached at Naas, the palace of the king of Leinster, and is said to have baptized the sons of the kings of both Leinster and Munster.

S. Patrick appears to have spent the last three years of his life in retirement. His death, as his birth, is not left without legend. His wish was to die at Armagh, but death overtook him at Saul. Armagh and Down contended for his burial. To settle the dispute, the monks of Saul placed his body in a cart to which two untamed oxen were yoked. They stopped on the site of the present cathedral of Downpatrick. Thus the people of Saul possessed the body, and the people of Armagh knew he had desired to be buried there.

S. Patrick's Writings.

Two acknowledged works of his, as we have already mentioned, are still extant. The *Confession* was written in his old age and its value and interest lie of course in the number of autobiographical details it gives. It is not a confession of his

---

[1] Tírechán, *Analecta Bollandiana*, II, 58.

[2] See Bede, *Eccles. Hist.* Bk I, chap. I, "No reptiles are found there, and no snake can live there, for though often carried thither out of Britain, as soon as the ship comes near the shores, and the scent of the air reaches them, they die."

sins merely, but also of his faith, and chiefly it is a confession of God's wonderful dealings with him; "I must not hide the gift of God" is his inspiring motive in writing. It gave him also the opportunity of replying to those who criticised his lack of education, and impugned his motives. He fully admits his lack of culture, and in justification of his labour for the conversion of the heathen, he says, "I testify before God and His holy angels that I never had any motive save the Gospel and promises of God to return at any time to the people from whom I escaped."

The *Epistle to Coroticus* is considered from internal evidence to be by the same hand and of the same date. Coroticus was the ruler of Strathclyde. In the course of their depredations his soldiers killed some Christians and carried others captive. S. Patrick promptly sent a messenger to demand the release of these captives. His message was received with scornful mockery. He therefore sent a strongly worded protest, which he addressed to the Christian community, and in which he urged them to have no dealings with the tyrant, or with his soldiers, till they should repent. He asked that this letter should be read in the presence of Coroticus. It contained these plain and fearless words: "It is the custom of Roman Christians in Gaul to send good men to the heathen to redeem captives; you kill or sell Christians to a foreign nation that does not know God."

These words do not of course furnish anything like a complete idea of S. Patrick's character, but they provide some evidence. They give some insight into it, for they reveal the facts that he was sensitive to criticism, and that he was bold to rebuke, while his humility was undoubted. Bitter disappointment at the jealousy and suspicions of others is found in both writings: "I am envied"; "If my own do not know me, well, a prophet hath no honour in his own country"; "Some despise me"; he exclaims bitterly. There are clear indications of a strong personality and of a character of unusual spirituality. He was enthusiastic and practical. If he knew not "letters," he knew his Bible.

An Estimate of his Work.

Opinions are sharply divided concerning the magnitude or otherwise of S. Patrick's mission. We have noted that the authority for it has been both confirmed and denied with equal vigour. The extent of it is similarly debated. We have in this chapter designated him "The Apostle of Ireland," but the sphere of his activity has been narrowed by some to a small district of Leinster[1]. Let it be granted that he did not introduce Christianity into Ireland. At any rate it must be conceded that without him it would have been exterminated by the overwhelming forces of heathenism. Again, even though Christianity did not owe its introduction into Ireland to his mission, yet its organisation was due to him, and through him became a living force. Not less important is the fact that through this organisation, Ireland was brought into much more intimate contact with western Europe.

The Influence of Gaul upon Ireland.

If S. Patrick be thus regarded as one of the sons of the island cloister of Lerins, he adds lustre to that famous monastery. His testimony to the value of its teaching will be found in the influence that it, in turn, exerted over Ireland through his instrumentality. He had come under the spell of the monastic ideal, and he turned it to profit in the outer world in which he lived. In his organisation of the Church and especially in the foundation of monasteries, in matters appertaining to discipline, and in the use of a liturgy, the influence of Gaul may be clearly traced.

The monastic character of the Irish Church in the earliest centuries is acknowledged. As Professor Stokes says[2], "The early Irish Church was thoroughly monastic. Monasticism pervaded every department of the Church and was the secret of its rapid success." Monasticism had its origin—as we have already said—in the East. From Egypt it found its way into Gaul, and

---

[1] Professor Zimmer, *Keltische Kirche* (*Realencyklopädie für protestantische Theologie u. Kirche*, 1901.) Translated by Miss Meyer, *Celtic Church in Britain and Ireland.*

[2] *Ireland and the Celtic Church*, p. 166.

from Gaul it travelled northward. The monastery of Lerins was founded, and regular communication between it and Egypt and Syria was established. When Christianity passed over to Ireland, oriental practices followed, and traces of these in the customs, learning, and architecture of the early Celtic Church have been noted. Monastic foundations were a conspicuous though not an exclusive feature of S. Patrick's organisation, and they served a dual purpose, to extend Christianity and to provide schools of education, as well as to supply the spiritual needs of the immediate neighbourhood. In addition to the clergy, there was an abbot who was often also a bishop. As in Gaul so in Ireland there was a scarcity of cities and therefore of centres for bishoprics. Thus centres for ecclesiastical purposes were often formed on the monastic principle[1]. The inevitable result was a multiplication of bishops due to the growth of monasticism, and as a natural consequence each monastery wanted a bishop independent of the diocesan.

A few instances of this custom in Gaul may here be quoted, for bishops without sees were not confined to Ireland. They were common both in East and West in ancient times, nor were they regarded as irregular. That the abbey of S. Denis near Paris had a bishop of its own from an early period may perhaps be gathered from a charter or letter written in A.D. 786 by Pope Hadrian I, confirming a privilege that had been granted by his predecessor Stephen, in which these words occur: "We enact in the aforesaid venerable monastery that it be altogether lawful to have a bishop there, as from ancient times and up to this present there hath been." The confirmation of a similar privilege enjoyed by the monastery of S. Martin at Tours was obtained from the same pope. Sometimes the bishop was also abbot, as was the case with Wickerbus at S. Martin of Tours in the 8th century. The monastic bishop is most commonly found outside Ireland in Benedictine monasteries[2]. The very fact that the monastic foundations desired to be independent of diocesan bishops is a

---

[1] The word "civitas" means a town within a state and is not only used where there is a corporate existence, but can be applied to a geographical district, e.g. to "loca sacra in civitate."

[2] For fuller information on this subject our readers are referred to Dr Todd's *S. Patrick*, pp. 51 sqq.

proof that S. Patrick also had a system and organisation based upon the see or territory. He knew by experience what the tribal system meant, and conceivably his bishoprics would be coterminous with tribal boundaries. If we are reminded that according to Tírechán the number of bishops under S. Patrick's organisation was four hundred and fifty (although the names of only some forty are given), this is capable of two interpretations. It may have meant that there were many bishops without sees, but with equal truth and probability it can be urged that the territorial areas of the sees were small.

In matters appertaining to discipline, we may here make reference to the *Ecclesiastical Canons* of S. Patrick. Their authenticity has been disputed, but there is much to strengthen the assumption that they are genuine. They are contained in a manuscript (No. 279[1]) in the library of Corpus Christi College, Cambridge. It was written, apparently, on the continent in the 9th or 10th century and was given by Archbishop Parker. There are four principal pieces, all transcribed by a very inaccurate copyist. The Canons have only survived to modern times through the preservation of this volume. It is otherwise known only from the citations from it to be found in the *Hibernensis*. Professor Bradshaw says, in the first of his two unfinished papers (which was written to Dr Wasserschleben in the form of a letter), that he agrees that the *Hibernensis* is not a collection of Pontifical decretals or a book of canons of the ancient Church, but rather a digest of authorities from Scripture, councils and ecclesiastical writers. He differs however in being unable to accept the suggestion that the Canons permit the acceptance of a papal imperium. He further thinks that the work originated probably in Ireland at the close of the 7th or early 8th century, and thence found its way into Brittany, and from there spread to neighbouring districts and elsewhere, reaching the Anglo-Saxon Church towards the end of the 9th century. These words form part of the opening sentences: "To the presbyters and deacons and all the clergy, Patricius, Auxilius, Iserninus, bishops,

For fuller information concerning this MS., see Henry Bradshaw's *The early Collection of Canons known as the Hibernensis*, two unfinished papers, Cambridge University Press, 1893.

(send) greeting." Here follow thirty Canons[1]. It is evidently an episcopal encyclical sent out in the names of the three bishops. Dr Bury wisely remarks that the association of these lesser known bishops with S. Patrick is in itself in favour of the authenticity of the document, for a forger would have given the names of more conspicuous colleagues. S. Patrick had known Auxilius and Iserninus at Auxerre, and they were sent from Gaul to assist him in his work in Leinster. They would naturally add to the influence of Gaul in Ireland. These Canons may not unnaturally bear evidence of similar influence, and not least in following the practice of the Gallic Church in cases of dispute. One of these Canons therefore enacts that "should any questions arise in this island, they shall be referred to the apostolic see." It may be noted further that S. Patrick prescribed the form of tonsure that was followed in western monasteries, though it was given up in favour of the native form after his time[2]. It should also be noticed that S. Patrick introduced the Paschal Table as in use in the West, in place of an older system in use in Ireland before his own arrival there. Once more we may refer to the baptism of the two daughters of Laoghaire, after which S. Patrick placed a white veil or chrisom on their heads[3]. This was a very ancient rite. In the Gallic and Irish Churches in the 5th century only one unction was used.

It remains to consider the liturgy that was introduced by S. Patrick into Ireland. There is no direct evidence, but it is confidently surmised that the Irish and Gallican liturgical uses were identical. The connection of S. Patrick with Lerins would explain certain oriental customs and ideas in the ritual introduced by him. Very little was known until recently of the liturgy used in the Celtic Church both before the Anglo-Saxon conquest and subsequently. The theory of the Eastern origin of the Celtic Church is now generally regarded as untenable, though it will be remembered that Neander states that the British Church

---

[1] See Haddan and Stubbs, *Councils of Great Britain and Ireland*, Vol. II, pp. 328–30.

[2] The Eastern form was entire tonsure, the Roman form allowed a circle of hair to grow round the top of the head, the Celtic form shaved all hair in front of a line across the head from ear to ear.

[3] Crismati neophyti in veste candida, dum fides flagrabat in fronte ipsorum.

C. M. 7

in many ritual matters departed from the usage of the Roman Church and agreed much more nearly with the Church of Asia Minor. It is of course conceded that it is oriental in the sense that its Christianity originated like all Christianity in Asia Minor. It penetrated to Britain probably through Gaul, and any Greek or oriental traces found in the Celtic liturgy may well be due to the Eastern origin of the Gallic Church, which was really a colony from Asia Minor. The churches and books of central England were destroyed by heathen invaders towards the end of the 5th century, but in inaccessible parts of England, as well as in Scotland and Ireland, liturgical independence was retained. An examination of the few extant service books has been made possible by the publication of the books of S. Patrick and other Celtic saints, as well as by the discovery of liturgical remains in the Irish *Book of Dimma* and *Book of Mulling*, the *Stowe Missal*, and in the *Antiphonary of Bangor*[1]. Without going into details at any length[2] it may be stated briefly that the Celtic liturgy owes its origin to the Ephesine group. Ireland possesses a style of architecture peculiarly its own. A study of ancient writings shows a distinctive style of ornamentation that suggests, if it does not necessarily prove, an Eastern origin. It is of some

---

[1] The *Book of Dimma* is a book of the gospels. It is preserved in the Library of Trinity College, Dublin. It also contains a *Missa de Infirmis*.

The *Book of Mulling* is so called because it contains the entry "nomen scriptoris Mulling," and ascribed therefore to Mulling Bishop of Ferns who died A.D. 697. Also in Trinity College Library.

The *Stowe Missal* is the earliest surviving Missal of the Irish Church, and is of a monastic character. It was taken abroad about the 12th century, and was discovered by an officer who left no information concerning his discovery. It came into the possession of the Duke of Buckingham with whom it remained till the sale of the Stowe Library in 1849, when it was bought by the Earl of Ashburnham.

The *Antiphonary of Bangor* is an early liturgical manuscript. Its Irish origin and execution are self-evident. A monastery was founded at Bangor in A.D. 558 by St Comgall, a famous Irish saint. He became its abbot and died there in 602. This Bangor must be carefully distinguished from Bangor Deiniol in Carnarvon and Bangor Iscoed in Flintshire. The *Antiphonary* was probably removed from Bangor to the Irish monastery at Bobbio by one of the refugees at the time of the massacre by the Danes, who for some two hundred years pillaged the greater part o Ireland. The manuscript was transferred to the Ambrosian Library at Milan in 1606.

[2] The whole subject is very fully treated by Rev. F. E. Warren in *The Liturgy and Ritual of the Celtic Church*, Clarendon Press.

interest also to point out that the Celtic bishops wore crowns and not mitres[1].

We cannot better sum up S. Patrick's life and estimate his character than in the words of S. Ervin[2] who describes him as "a just man indeed; with the purity of character of the Patriarchs; the gentleness and forgiveness of Moses; the master of psalmody like David; a seeker after wisdom, as Solomon; the preacher of truth as S. Paul; full of the grace of S. John; a fair flower-garden, a fruitful vine, a glowing fire; a lion in strength and power; a dove in humility and gentleness; a serpent in wisdom, cunning to do good, merciful to the sons of life, and ungentle to the sons of death."

Of all the links that bound Ireland to Gaul, not the least strong, and certainly one of the most interesting, is the "Apostle of Ireland." He owed not a little, we do not doubt, to the inspiring influence of the sheltered cloisters of Lerins, and was only one of many who must have been grateful for the thought that prompted S. Honoratus, himself storm-tossed on the waves of this troublesome world, to seek a haven of shelter for the shipwrecked. S. Vincent had found peace and inspiration within its walls. S. Patrick, from his own confession, was restless and unsatisfied till the great enthusiasm seized and took possession of him: "Woe is me if I preach not the Gospel," and his ambitions here were sanctified, and strengthened, and from its sequestered cells he had gone forth to win a name and fame alike for himself and for this island home.

---

[1] There is a representation of an Irish bishop, so crowned, in a sculptured bas relief of great antiquity in the ruined chapel in the valley of Glendalough.

[2] *Tripartite life*, p. 500.

CHAPTER VII

JOHN CASSIAN, THE GREAT ORGANISER,
SYSTEMATISER AND WRITER

We have indeed no direct evidence that this celebrated monk
was ever at Lerins. But that he must have exercised a powerful
influence over the monastery at its foundation seems almost a
foregone conclusion. There is a blank in the history of Cassian
after his visit to Rome in A.D. 403 until A.D. 415 and it is not
without probability that Lerins was the place of his retreat.
His history in brief is that of a man of more than ordinary force
of character who left his impress on the whole history of
monasticism, and whether he was at Lerins or not, this saint,
monk, and literary genius is so intimately bound up with the
whole period in which monastic establishment began to take
shape, that some notice of him seems almost indispensable to
completeness. How far the predominant influence of Cassian
may have affected the early fathers of Lerins is a question not
easy to answer. It affords some presumption that Vincent was
more or less affected by him, and, in any case, an exposition of
his theological position must help us to see what the teaching
and practice of Lerins was.

He was one of the first founders of monastic fraternities in
Europe, and was the great organiser and systematiser of
monasticism in the 4th and 5th centuries. His writings
are still a fount of inspiration on the subject. No one knows
precisely where he was born, for several places are mentioned.
There is no definite statement in his own writings accurately
to guide us to his birthplace. He only tells us that his
ancestral home "stretched away to the desert, and the woods

delight the heart of a monk and supply him with food in plenty[1]." In another passage Cassian answering a question whether a desire for greater quietness should take him back to his own country, said, "It is impossible; no one, or scarcely any one, adopts this manner of life [i.e. the monastic] there[2]." Again in the preface to the *Institutes*, Cassian who wrote this work at the request of Castor, bishop of Apta in Gallia Narbonensis, says, "Your province is at present without monasteries," and further on he proposes "to exercise a certain discretion in laying down rules in order to make allowance for differences of climate or habit." These passages may point to his Western origin. Gennadius speaks of him as a Scythian[3]. That seems not without probability. He appears to have been born sometime between A.D. 350 and 360. Of his family we know practically nothing except from isolated sentences in his writings. Recalling an old maxim of the Fathers still current in his day, that "a monk should avoid women and bishops, neither of whom will allow him the quiet of his cell," Cassian cannot produce it "without shame, since I could not avoid my own sister[4]." His parents were wealthy, and of their piety he speaks with obvious gratitude and clear remembrance. "We remember that our kinsfolk were endued with piety and goodness[5]." His financial circumstances enabled him to visit the Holy Land when he was quite young. He received his early training at Bethlehem. It was here too he formed his friendship with Germanus, who accompanied him to the East to visit the ascetics in Syria and Egypt. Cassian never paid a second visit to the East.

During the Origenistic controversy in which Chrysostom was involved[6], Cassian and Germanus were chosen as bearers of a letter to Pope Innocent I from the clergy who espoused the cause of Chrysostom[7], but we have no direct evidence of the

---

[1] Cf. *Instit.* XXIV, 1.   [2] *Ibid.* 18.

[3] Natione Scytha (*Catalogus*, c. 62), but this may possibly refer to the desert of Scete, in Egypt.

[4] *Instit.* XI, 18.   [5] Cf. *ibid.* XXIV, 1.

[6] For a full account of the persecution of Chrysostom see Robertson's *History of the Christian Church*, Vol. II, Bk III, chap. 1.

[7] Palladius, *Dial.* 3. Sozomen, *H.E.* 8, 26.

length of Cassian's stay at Rome.   He probably left there about
A.D. 415 and went to Marseilles.   Of Germanus, his friend, we
read nothing more after Cassian had settled down in the West
on the shores of the Mediterranean.   At Marseilles Cassian
made good use of his monastic experience and founded two
monasteries, one for men and the other for women.   The abbey
of S. Victor founded by Cassian was built over the grotto where
the body of a Roman legionary named Victor had been buried.
It is said to have accommodated five thousand monks within its
walls and in the houses beneath its shadow.   It is interesting to
note that though this foundation rivalled Lerins in its importance, yet its work was altogether different.   Cassian was
most anxious to strengthen the barriers between monks and the
secular clergy.   As we recall the number of times that deputa-
tions came to Lerins in search of a bishop, we can understand
Cassian's reason for recommending the monks to avoid bishops,
for they were ever ready to offer ecclesiastical positions.

Cassian wrote the *Institutes*, the first of his three great
works[1], between the years A.D. 419 and A.D. 426, as Castor, to
whom they were dedicated, died in A.D. 426[2].   They are in
twelve books.   The first four deal with the rules of monastic
life, and the remainder treat of the eight deadly sins which
are obstacles to monastic perfection; gluttony, impurity, covetousness, anger, dejection, accidie, vainglory, and pride.   He
prescribes the remedies against these vices, and descants upon
the virtues which are their opposites.   Milman speaks of
Cassian's "severe and inflexible code[3]," but it is perhaps more
correct to say that he compiled materials suggestive of legisla-
tion, than to call him a legislator.   Indeed he complains that
there were as many Rules as there were monasteries, and even
that every cell had its Rule[4].   In his preface he speaks of Castor
"planning a temple not with inanimate stones, but with a
congregation of holy men," and "consecrating precious vessels
not of gold and silver, but saintly souls of innocence and purity,"
and now "desiring the establishment of the institutions of the
East and of Egypt."   He does not desire to weave a story of

[1] Migne, *Pat. Lat.* Vol. 49.   [2] *Acta Sanctorum*, Sept. 6, 249.
[3] *Latin Christianity*, 1, 167.   [4] *Instit.* II, 2.

marvellous signs and wonders, but to avoid all that is in the nature of legend. A study of this work abundantly reveals the practical bent of Cassian's mind.

He had inherited many of his Teacher's thoughts, and dwelt much upon the love of God. With this thought predominant he counselled the monks rather to strive after practical purity of heart than be content with a speculative system. He thus mediates between the excess of the contemplative and that of the active life. If it must be admitted that he had perhaps an exaggerated regard for asceticism, and gives evidences of unreasonable, fanatical, and almost puerile insistence in the way he presses a blind obedience, yet it will also be acknowledged that the life of a monk as portrayed by him is no formal and mechanical routine. This first book is a disquisition on the dress of the monks. They must have a girdle, even as soldiers of Christ prepared for battle, who are exhorted to have their loins girded, and thus resemble Elijah and Elisha who originated this life. By his girdle and uncouth appearance Elijah was recognised[1]. S. John the Baptist also, a link between the Old and New Testament, being in himself both a beginning and an ending, had a leathern girdle about his loins[2]. He instances also S. Peter in prison charged by the angel to gird himself[3], thus showing that his limbs had been freed from the girdle. S. Paul also wore his girdle, for the prophet Agabus, who met him at Caesarea, took it and bound his hands and feet in token of the injuries he was about to suffer at the hands of the Jews in Jerusalem[4]. The habit of monks must be plain, remarkable neither for its colour nor its fashion. They must not by their dress separate themselves from the common life of men. He refers to the very small hoods worn by the Egyptians who desired to preserve the simplicity of little children by imitating their dress, and also to the linen tunics with short sleeves symbolising that they had cut off the deeds and works of this world. They were to cover their necks and shoulders with a cape to avoid the expense of a cloak ; to refuse shoes[5] because the Gospel forbade them, but on account of bodily weakness, the

[1] 2 Kings i.   [2] S. Matt. iii, 4.   [3] Acts xii, 8.
[4] Acts xxi, 11.   [5] S. Luke x, 4.

morning cold, or the mid-day heat, they could wear sandals as
by the Lord's permission. Cassian was very anxious that all
such usages should be modified in accordance with climate or
custom.

The second and third books deal with the canonical system
of prayers and psalms, and the author mentions that throughout
Egypt and the Thebaid the number of psalms was fixed at twelve
for vespers and nocturns. This number was fixed (he states)
from the teaching of an angel. The story runs : The monks had
met together to discuss plans for daily worship so that they might
hand on a legacy of piety and peace. Each man, in proportion
to his own fervour and unmindful of the weakness of others,
desired what he personally considered easy, and when, with
different standards, some strove to fix a large number of psalms,
some fifty, some sixty, and others even more, there arose such
difference of opinion that they had not decided the question by
the time of vespers, and as they were going to celebrate their
daily rites and prayers one rose in the midst to chant the
psalms and when he had sung eleven interspersed with prayers,
he finished the twelfth with a response of Alleluia and suddenly
disappeared[1]. He refers to the conciseness of collects and
prayers offered up by the Egyptians, and to the quietude of
their worship. Though a large number of the brethren might
be assembled, it was only one who stood up and chanted the
psalm in their midst, and when prayer is offered up "there is
no spitting, no clearing of the throat, no yawning, no groans,
or sighs."

The fourth book deals with the *Institutes of the re-
nunciants*[2]. He speaks of the perseverance, humility and
subjection of the Egyptian monks, some of whom remain in
the monastery till extreme old age. He describes the ordeal
by which those to be received are tried ; they must first lie
outside the doors for at least ten days as evidence of perseverance and of a desire to learn humility and obedience. They
are deliberately repelled and scorned by all, but this gives proof

[1] See second Council of Tours, A.D. 567, Canon 18.
[2] In the first chapter, the writer says, "We pass to the training of one who
renounces this world." This title is applied by some to the whole work.

of steadfastness amid insults and affronts. When received into the monastery they lay aside their own clothes and are fresh clothed by the abbot. The discarded clothes are given into the care of the steward; if the renunciant gives proof of his fervour they are given away to the poor, if he is guilty of murmuring or disobedience he is reclothed in his own garments and sent away. There must be eagerness to answer a knock at the door, even if one is practising the writer's art and has just commenced the composition of a letter. He must not wait to finish the letter he has begun. No monk must let fall such an expression as " my coat, my book, my pen." It is considered wrong to say any-thing, however trifling, is one's own property. The accidental breakage of a jar is only expiated by public penance. No food or drink must be taken except at the regular meals of the common table. As an example of the fidelity and care that is required, the instance is quoted of a certain monk who had dropped three beans as he was preparing for cooking. The steward consulted the abbot, who adjudged the monk a pilferer, careless of sacred property. He was suspended from prayer, and made atonement by public penance.

In the final chapter of this fourth book Cassian recapitulates the steps by which a monk can reach perfection. The fear of the Lord brings compunction, from which springs renunciation. This begets humility and the mortification of desires, by which faults decay, and virtues spring up. Thus purity of heart and the perfection of apostolic love are gained.

The other eight books deal, as we have said, with the struggle against the eight chief faults. Gluttony[1] he calls "the pleasure of the palate." The mind choked with the weight of food cannot guide and govern thoughts. Sodom was not overthrown through its drunkenness but because she ate her bread in fulness[2]. The practical mind of Cassian is seen in his insistence that there can be no uniform rule of fasting[3]. "Soaked beans do not agree with everybody." He also emphasises the fact that it is not an external enemy that is to be dreaded but an internal warfare that is to be daily waged and therefore an external fast from

[1] Bk v. [2] Ezek. xvi, 49.
[3] See the later section in this chapter.

visible food cannot suffice for perfection without a fast of the soul, which has its harmful foods. Dealing with the sin of covetousness[1] he says it can easily be avoided, but once a victim the remedy is difficult. It is possible, he says, for one who has no money to be deemed covetous. The opportunity of possession may be wanting, but not the will. Judas could not have been persuaded to sell the Redeemer if he had not been contaminated by covetousness. In another passage Cassian calls covetousness spiritual leprosy. To gain a perfect victory over it no "shred of the very smallest scrap of it" must remain in the heart. Writing, in Book VIII, of the spirit of anger, which some endeavour to extenuate by misinterpretation of Scripture saying that God is said to be angry, Cassian says this and similar things said of God cannot without profanity be understood literally of Him. He points out that not only apostolic precept but the old law guards against it. Again his practical mind is seen when he says, "Sometimes when we want to improve our rough manners we complain we need solitude, as if we could find the virtue of patience when there was no one to provoke us. While we lay the blame on others we shall never reach patience and perfection." Patience therefore does not depend on another's will but on our own control. He gives an apt illustration from the brute creation. "Poisonous serpents and wild beasts while in solitude are not harmless just because they are not actually hurting anybody." Cassian is very practical also when he says that it is not only against human beings that man can show anger. Irritation is manifested against a pen or a knife, and men get rid of their perturbation by swearing at the senseless matter, or at any rate at the devil. His reference to the words "Whosoever is angry with his brother without a cause[2]" is interesting because he says the words "without a cause" are superfluous and were added by those who did not think anger for just causes should be abandoned, and that those who added the words did not understand the intention of Scripture to reserve no opportunity whatever for anger. The remedy for anger, he concludes, is to make up our

---

[1] Bk VII.

[2] S. Matt. v, 22. Western and Syrian texts retain the words, but, as our readers will know, they are omitted in the Vulgate and in the R.V.

minds never to be angry for a good or a bad reason, otherwise we immediately lose the power of discernment. All our renunciation, all our fastings will be unavailing if, on account of anger and hatred, the Judge of the world awards eternal punishment.

His chapters on dejection are few and short. He says the Divine Spirit has expressed the force of this fault, "As the worm injures the wood, so dejection the heart of man[1]." He traces dejection to previous anger or disappointment, but sometimes there is no apparent reason for it except the instigation of the crafty enemy who so depresses us "that we cannot receive with civility the visits of those who are near and dear to us"; we can give them no civil answer, for every corner of the heart is possessed with bitterness. The fault is our own, for no one is provoked by another unless the evil is in his own heart. God therefore does not desire us to give up intercourse with our brethren, for perfection is not secured by separation but by patience. If we correct our manners, we shall be at peace not only with man, but with the brute creation. A worse form of dejection or low spirits is that which despairs of amendment, as did Cain and Judas. This injurious fault will be expelled by occupying the mind with hope of the future.

The tenth chapter deals with accidie[2]. "When a 5th century poet, controversialist and preacher[3] of the Eastern Church under the dominion of the Saracens, or an anchoret of Egypt[4], or an abbot of Gaul, in the 6th century, tells us, in the midst of our letters and railway journeys, and magazines, and movements, exactly what it is that on some days makes us so singularly unpleasant to ourselves and to others—tells us in effect that it is not simply the east wind, or dyspepsia, or overwork, or the contrariness of things in general, but that it is a certain subtle and complex trouble of our own hearts, which we perhaps have never

---

[1] Proverbs xxv, 20. Cassian has quoted from the Septuagint. The A.V. reads, "As vinegar upon nitre, so is he that singeth songs to an heavy heart."

[2] The word sounds strangely unfamiliar to English ears, though it will be found in Murray's *Dictionary*. It is derived from the Greek ἀκηδία and its Latin equivalent is *acedia*.

[3] Cassian.

[4] John Climacus, who was called from his solitude to be abbot of the monastery of Mount Sinai.

had the patience or the frankness to see as it really is; that he knew it quite well, only too well for his own happiness and peace, and that he can put us in a good way of dealing with it— the very strangeness of the intrusion from such a quarter into our most private affairs may secure for him a certain degree of our interest and attention[1]."

This is just what Cassian does secure, when he considers the spirit of acedia[2], and says that it is specially disturbing to a monk about the sixth hour. Some of the elders, he tells us, declare it to be "the midday demon," or as the 91st Psalm has it "the sickness that destroyeth in the noonday[3]." In Cassian's description it takes the form of a dislike of the place, the cell, and the brethren. The victim becomes sluggish and dissatisfied. He imagines he will never be well unless and until he leaves his

---

[1] *The sorrow of the World*, introductory essay on *accidia*, by the late Dr Paget, Bishop of Oxford, Longmans, 1912. The perusal of the whole essay will repay the reader.

[2] Since Cassian wrote of this subtle temptation, others have drawn attention to this "enimie to every estate of man." John Climacus, "the Anchoret of the 6th century" already mentioned, wrote the κλῖμαξ or *Scala Paradisi* (from which his title "Climacus" is taken), while he was abbot of Mount Sinai. It is founded upon his long years of experience of the anchoretic life. In it he deals with accidie. It is equivalent to charging God with being merciless and unloving. He personifies it and makes it declare that "Psalms, work, and the thought of death are my enemies. Prayer kills me outright" (*Scala Paradisi*, 13).

John of Damascus expresses an entirely opposite view, for he defines it as "dumbness" (*de orthod. fide*, 2. 14). In the Middle Ages, S. Thomas Aquinas regards accidie and envy as akin, but distinguishes between the accidie which is deadly and that which is only a venial sin. In Dante's *Purgatorio*, Benvenuto says, "Accidie is a defective love of the highest good, a kind of negligence, a tepid lukewarm condition, and, as it were, a contempt for acquiring the desirable amount of goodness" (Vernon's *Readings in the Purgatorio*, 1, 455). Chaucer describes it in the *Persones Tale*, "Bitterness is the mother of accidie," and again, accidie "maketh a man hevy, thoughtful and wrawe" (angry); "loveth no business at all"; "is like hem that ben in the peine of helle, because of hir slouthe and of hir hevinesse." (Quoted by Dr Paget, *Introductory essay*, p. 16.)

To quote an opinion of modern times, we may conclude with Professor Henry Sidgwick's description: "The state of moral lassitude and collapse, of discontent with self and the world, which is denoted by acedia" (*Outlines of the history of Ethics*, 3, sect. 5). Gloom, sloth, irritation, who has not felt their bitterness? No wonder that, when Cassian speaks to us from across the intervening centuries, he seems very near to us and at once claims and arrests our interest and sympathy, and finds in the hearts of to-day a willing and attentive ear.

[3] The Psalm, in the Vulgate "daemonio meridiano," follows the LXX. δαιμονίου μεσημβρινοῦ.

cell. The devil suggests all manner of duties that he ought to perform to friends and kinsfolk, instead of staying where he is, useless and profitless. Thus he is tempted to forget his profession, and becomes a runaway from Christ's service. Slumber and flight are his special temptations. He becomes either restless or lazy. Cassian points out that S. Paul saw this disease creeping in, or foresaw through the Holy Spirit that it would arise among the monks, and so anticipates it by the healing medicine of this instruction : "We beseech you, brethren, that ye study to be quiet and to do your own business, and to work with your own hands[1]." Cassian interprets this to mean that the monk should stop in his cell, undisturbed by gossip, and doing his own work. Following the apostle's emphasis of the duty and value of work, he counsels work as the cure, even as the Egyptian Fathers did, who never allowed monks to be idle. He recalls a saying of theirs that "a monk who works is attacked by one devil only, but the loafer is tormented by many"; and the case is quoted of a certain abbot who destroyed all the produce of his work every year, lest he should have an excuse to be lazy, and so fall a prey to acedia. Cassian also quotes from the writings of Solomon, "He that tilleth his land shall have plenty of bread, but he that followeth after vain persons shall have poverty enough[2]," and again, "Drowsiness shall clothe a man with rags[3]." Cassian suggests the reason why there were no monasteries in the West is that they are not supported by labour, and that if they were provided through the liberality of others, the love of ease would prevent monks from remaining long in them. He concludes with the advice of abbot Moses. To the excuse "I was terribly troubled yesterday by an attack of acedia and can only be freed by running at once to abbot Paul," the answer is, "A fit of acedia should not be evaded by running away, but overcome by resistance."

Vainglory, Cassian says, attacks a monk both carnally and spiritually. This temptation is subtle, and changes its character, appearing sometimes as though it were a virtue. It endeavours to ensnare the soldier of Christ through dress, gesture, voice, work, fastings, and prayer. It pursues him even in his solitude, in his

[1] 1 Thess. iv, 10.   [2] Proverbs xxviii, 19.   [3] *Ibid.* xxxiii, 21.

readiness to obey, his industry, his humility, his knowledge. It is encouraged, not discouraged, by the virtues of the man it assails. The example of Hezekiah whose heart was lifted up is given as an illustration[1]. This fault seeks to ensnare a monk by puffing up his mind because he sings well, or is of a good figure, or of rich and noble descent, or it suggests to him that he should seek a priesthood or diaconate. The remedy suggested is the avoidance of anything that renders one remarkable among others.

The last fault dealt with is pride, which, like a disease, attacks the whole man and injures the entire body by its evil influence, not sparing even those who have reached perfection of the virtues. By reason of it Lucifer was cast out of heaven. It is the cause of the first fall, it is the beginning of all faults, and destructive of all virtues. It assails the great and the small alike; and "God resisteth the proud." Cassian quaintly says it has no angel opposed to it, for God himself is its adversary. Pride says, "I will be like the Most High[2]." Humility says, "He emptied Himself and took the form of a servant." It is only by the grace of God that this snare can be avoided. Cassian in conclusion gives certain signs by which this evil can be discerned. The voice is loud in conversation, there is bitterness in his answer, his laughter is excessive, his words are not weighed. He ever seeks to gain his own ends, and though incapable of giving good advice, he will emphasise his own opinion. He is eager to build a monastery where he may teach and instruct others, and become instead of a bad disciple, a worse master.

The " Conferences[3]."

In the book of which we have just given some details, there is more than one reference to a forthcoming work, notably when Cassian says of the character of the Eastern Fathers, "we shall deal with it when we relate the conferences of the elders[4]."

[1] 2 Chron. xxxii, 25.   [2] Isaiah xiv, 14.
[3] *Collationes Patrum.*
[4] Bk II, I. See also V, 4 and other places.

The *Conferences* were undertaken at Castor's suggestion, but he died, as we have seen, in A.D. 426. The first part of this work was probably finished shortly after this date. The second part must have followed quickly, for it is dedicated to Honoratus and Eucherius, who are called *Fratres* and not *Episcopi.* Honoratus was bishop of Arles in 426, and Eucherius was Bishop of Lyons in A.D. 434. The third part cannot have been written later than A.D. 429, the year in which Honoratus died, for he is spoken of in its preface as still alive. These *Conferences* are the substance of Cassian's conversations with the more experienced of the monks in the East, and are of deep interest. Even Protestants may well learn much that is edifying and instructive in the ways of piety, and work them up into profitable books of devotion. This is little wonder when we note that it is Cassian who makes prominent the original view, as it then was, that the life of the anchorite and ascetic is not in itself holiness, but only the means thereto. Man may give up gold and silver and estates and yet fail to subjugate the soul. Cassian points to the supreme aim and end of all renunciation; it is that singleness and purity of heart may be attained, without which no man may see God Whose mysteries will remain obscure and unintelligible to those that have fleshly eyes. He emphasises the same truth in the preceding work of which we have just treated.

The reader will be interested even from the modern point of view in the characteristic teaching of this great man. The monks of Lerins certainly could not fail to be influenced by it. At the commencement, he paid gracious tribute to the desert of Scete "where all perfection flourishes," and to Germanus "my closest companion," in token of whose friendship everyone would say "one heart and soul existed in our two bodies." When questioned as to the reason why the love of kinsmen and fatherland and the world is given up and all kinds of trial and privation endured, Cassian answered, "For the sake of the Kingdom of Heaven." When asked what should be the aim and aspiration of a monk here and now, the questioner himself answered, "Purity of heart." Everything that can disturb purity and peace of mind, even though it may be useful and of value, must

be avoided. As an illustration the example of Martha and
Mary is recalled. Practical work, rich in its fruit, may nevertheless crowd out "that good part" which is found in the devout
contemplation of the Lord[1].

Cassian enumerates three sources from which our thoughts
arise; they are God, the devil, and ourselves, and as illustrations
he quotes, "I will hearken what the Lord God will say," "Why
hath Satan tempted thy heart to lie to the Holy Ghost?" and
"The Lord knoweth the thoughts of man that they are but vain."
The need of discretion is emphasised, and is defined as in some
sense the fountain and root of all virtues, and is only secured by
humility. An illustration of his practical mind is given when
he says, "We ought to take food and sleep at the proper time,
even if we dislike it, for excessive abstinence is more injurious
than careless satiety," and again, " The mind enfeebled by want
of food loses vigour in prayer.

In conversation with the abbot Paphnutius, Cassian learned
that vocation to the monastic life may arise as the direct call of
God; from the inducement of a saintly example; or from such
loss of a worldly sort as may point to this refuge. There are
also three kinds of renunciation; we may count wealth of no
account; we may reject the passions and affections of both mind
and body; and we may separate ourselves from things temporal
and contemplate the eternal. Abraham is given as an illustration of this threefold renunciation: Get thee from thy country,
(this world's goods), kinsfolk (former life and habits) and thy
father's house (all recollection of this world)[2].

An interesting answer is given by abbot Daniel who was
asked to explain why monks full of happiness and contentment
could be suddenly filled with dejection and despair. This is
due either to their own carelessness, or to the devil or to the
permission of God. There are two reasons why God may
permit this; that by momentary desertion weakness may be
felt, or that perseverance may be tested. An instructive explanation of the word "flesh" is also given. It may mean the
whole man, as "the Word was made flesh"; or it may signify

[1] 1, 8. Cassian has a Western reading, "few things are needful, or only one."
[2] Genesis xii, 1 (cf. iii, 6).

"sins" as "flesh and body cannot inherit the Kingdom of God";
or it may stand for human relationship, as "if by any means I
may provoke to emulation them which are my flesh." A
warning is given against the danger that those who have
renounced wealth may transfer their affections to small and
trifling things. The vice of covetousness in unimportant
matters may still be manifested, in which case the old greed
has merely changed its object. Monks can be tempted to
keep as their own what really belongs in common to all the
brethren.

In the fifth *Conference*, with abbot Serapion, the eight chief
faults are enumerated, and their remedies are reviewed. They
are the same as mentioned in the *Institutes*. To emphasise the
hold that gluttony can get and retain, an example is given of
one who reduced the quantity of his food and still failed to
avoid the force of the daily temptation[1]. It is therefore the
duty of monks, who by abstinence have overcome the passion
of gluttony, to fill their minds with virtues, lest concupiscence
and other sins should again find an entrance. In the account
of the conversation with the abbot Serenus, there is a curious
statement that Holy Scripture bears witness that a good and
bad angel hover near to every man[2]. "It is his angel," was
said of S. Peter[3], and of Judas, "Let Satan stand at his right
hand[4]." In the *Conference* with abbot Isaac, the value of
prayer is illustrated by comparing the soul with a feather which,
if not affected by moisture, soars to heaven, but, when weighted
by it, is carried to earth. So in like manner the soul not
weighted with faults and cares rises[5] Godwards.

True to the intention stated in the preface to the *Institutes*,
Cassian, dealing with the miracles of the saints, says the Fathers
who possessed miraculous powers never used them unless
compelled by absolute necessity to do so[6]. Recounting some
of them he adds that these men took no credit to themselves
for them, as they were mindful of the Lord's instruction,
"Rejoice not that the spirits are subject to you but rather
rejoice because your names are written in heaven[7]," and the fact

---

[1] v, 21. [2] VIII, 17. [3] Acts xii, 15. [4] Ps. cix, 6.
[5] IX, 24. [6] XV, 2. [7] S. Luke x, 20.

is emphasised that it is a greater miracle to cast out one's own faults than to cast out unclean spirits from the bodies of others[1], and that upright life is more important than the working of miracles.

Some monks will fast for two days without feeling it, simply because they are angry. These are said to be guilty of sacrilege, because with the devil's rage they endure fasts, which should be offered to God in humility[2]. Akin to this is a spurious patience manifested by some who have incited their brethren to smite them, and then offer " the other cheek," and so ignore the meaning of this command. It was given to mitigate anger, which they sought to incite[3].

There is a series of remarkable chapters on the old ethical discussion of the application of the moral law to individual action. There is so much that is complex in life that it is not easy to define duty in precise terms. The difficulty lies in the manifold variations of the moral situation[4]. Speaking generally, duty is a matter of personal conscience dependent upon circumstances. There are certain master questions, the chief of which centres round the conflict of duty. Take as an illustration the conflict of duty in regard to truth. Is it right to save an innocent person through an untruth? Is a lie sometimes justifiable, and even necessary? Sharply divided opinions have been held by theologians of the highest type in all ages. There have been two schools on this principle from the days of Jerome and Augustine. S. Jerome, S. Chrysostom and Luther held that absolute truth was on some occasions impossible, and that a departure from it is permissible in certain extreme cases. S. Augustine and Calvin on the other hand would not countenance this view. This is the old ethical question, how far and when a departure from strict truth can be excused on the principle of accommodation. Simple illustrations will indicate the point at issue. If I meet a man with murderous intentions, brandishing a knife and in pursuit of another, of whom he has lost sight at a turning in the road, and he asks

[1] xv, 8.   [2] XVI, 19.   [3] *Ibid.* 20.
[4] See Haering's *Ethics of the Christian life*, pp. 214 seq., translation by Rev. J. S. Hill, Williams and Norgate's Theological Translation Library.

THE GREAT ORGANISER, SYSTEMATISER AND WRITER 115

me which way his designed victim has gone, is it a lie if I show
him the wrong road? No! it is the choice of two evils. Or
again, if I am asked a question, the answer to which will betray
another's secret (given for instance in confession), what am I to
do? My first duty is to my friend or my penitent. Am I
to say, "I know nothing"; and if I do, is that a lie? It is a
conflict of duties. Concisely, the question is, "Can conscious
deviation from the truth, in a definite situation, become the
moral duty of an individual?" It is this question that Cassian
discusses and answers. This is the whole of his argument
properly understood, and so far as it is justifiable. There are
many "classic" examples in books of ethics and casuistry.
We shall not be disposed to disagree with Cassian's views. He
says that holy men and those approved of God, Rahab and
David, for example, told lies that were guiltless. In such cases
a lie is like hellebore[1] which "is useful in some deadly disease,
but otherwise may cause immediate death[2]." A lie therefore
must be resolutely avoided unless the necessity be urgent on
the principle of accommodation. God examines the purpose and
aim, and will have regard to the will rather than to the words
actually spoken. It may therefore so happen that one may be
guiltless in telling an untruth, and another may be guilty in
speaking the truth. Cassian gives instances of justification
from the New Testament. He quotes the case of S. Paul who
declared unto James and the elders at Jerusalem what God had
wrought among the Gentiles by his ministry. They reminded
him of many thousands of Jews zealous of the law who were
informed how he, Paul, was teaching the Jews among the
Gentiles to forsake the law of Moses. He was therefore bidden
to take four men who had a vow and to purify himself with
them. This course was recommended so that by so doing his
preaching might not lose its effectiveness. Cassian gives a
somewhat strange interpretation of S. Paul's words, "To the
Jew became I as a Jew[3]." This shows, he says, that S. Paul was
always prepared to relax something of the rigour of perfection
by accommodating his life to less strictness where circumstances

---

[1] A herb once in medical repute in cases of epilepsy, madness and the like.
[2] XVII, 17.   [3] 1 Cor. ix, 20–22.

seemed to call for it. He was "all things to all men," just because he held that there were times when the full truth was not called for, and when reservation was justifiable. If in response to the question whether we have had supper, we conceal that we had of set purpose abstained from it, Cassian justifies this reservation which was made in order to satisfy the Lord's command, "Thou shalt not appear unto men to fast[1]." Is it a lie? That is the whole ethical question involved. A lie is an intention to deceive for one's own advantage, and to the injury of another.

The third part of the *Conferences* opens with a word of warning from the abbot Piamun, "the senior of all the Anchorites," and like "some tall lighthouse." "Whoever desires to attain skill in any art will not reach it by idle wishes for likeness to those whose diligence he will not copy"; and he adds, "Some have come from your country only to go round the monasteries for the sake of getting to know the brothers, without meaning to adopt the rules." He informs us that there are three kinds of monks in Egypt, two of them admirable, and the third "a poor kind of thing." The two first are the coenobites and the anchorites, and the third the order of the sarabaites[2]. The system of the coenobites began with the apostles when "the multitude of believers were of one heart and one soul, and they had all things common[3]." This common life gave its name to those who, when the multitude of believers began to wax cold, cut themselves off from intercourse with their kinsmen. Out of the coenobites were produced the anchorites, the originators of whom were Paul[4] and Antony. But it is when reference is made to the sarabaites that the language is most severe; they are "a plant which first sprang up in the persons of Ananias and Sapphira"; they are anxious to be called by the name of monks without imitating their pursuits, they make their vows of renunciation before men but continue in their own homes, or having built cells, call them monasteries but remain in them their own masters[5]. In reply to the question, what is the aim

---

[1] XVII, 21.
[2] Epistle 22, *ad Eustochium.* Jerome too speaks scornfully of these monks.
[3] Acts iv, 32.   [4] Jerome calls him "Auctor vitae monasticae" (*ibid.*).   [5] XVIII, 7.

of the coenobite and of the anchorite, the distinction is thus drawn :—The coenobite's aim is to crucify all his desires and to "take no thought for to-morrow." The aim of the hermit is to have a mind free from earthly things and to unite it with Christ[1]. We confess that the difference does not seem particularly clear.

The twentieth of the *Conferences* deals with the need and character of penitence. A full and perfect penitence is such as never yields to those sins for which we did penance, and the truest test of penitence is found in the full approval of the personal consciousness.

There is some very practical teaching on fasting, in the twenty-first *Conference*. If it is said that fasting is included in the list of virtues, then the partaking of food will be wrong. Fasting brings justification when observed but does not bring condemnation when it is broken. It must be observed with due regard to reason, place, manner and time. If done incongruously, it becomes foolish and harmful. If when a brother comes and needs a kindly welcome, a man should choose to keep a strict fast, he would be guilty of incivility. If the body requires strength that can be gained by food, and a man will not relax his abstinence, he is a murderer of his own body. If on a festival a man observes a fast, he is unreasonable. So too, men, who desire praise of men for their fasts, and gain credit for sanctity by a sanctimonious show of pallor, have received their reward in this life. Thus fasting is not a " good " in its own nature, for there are times when it should be practised, and times when it should be given up, whereas things that are enjoined as good, or are forbidden as evil, are subject to no exceptions of time or place. There are times when fasting ought not to be observed. The disciples were not to fast while they were companions of the Heavenly Bridegroom, "the days will come when the Bridegroom shall be taken away from them, and then shall they fast."

There is a curious explanation of the fast of Lent as being " in obedience to the law of Moses[2]." We are enjoined to offer tithes of our fruits, but it is still more necessary to offer tithe of

[1] XIX, 8. [2] Exodus xxii, 29.

our life, and both these are clearly arranged for in the calculation of the length of Lent. The exact division of time is still more remarkable. The tithe of the number of the days of the year is thirty-six days and a half. In seven weeks, Sundays and Saturdays excluded, there are thirty-five days for fasting ; by the addition of Easter Eve when the Saturday's fast is prolonged to the dawn of Easter Day, the number of thirty-six days is made up, as well as the tithe of the five days which seem to be over and above that number. The perfect man is not restricted to submitting to that " paltry rule which the habits of the Church have established for those who are throughout the year engaged in pleasure or business." The law is not appointed for the righteous who devote not a tenth, but the whole time of their life, to their spiritual duties. The observance of Lent did not exist while the primitive Church retained its perfection, it was only when apostolic fervour relaxed and believers did not portion out their wealth for the good of the faithful that the fast was enjoined.

Each monk must choose the system he prefers. We cannot say that because the anchoretic life is good, it is therefore suitable to everyone, for to many it is not only useless but even harmful. The strictness practised by the brethren in the *coenobium* is not obligatory upon all. Then too the climate of different countries must be considered. Some nations are subject to extremes of cold or heat, which others could not endure however strong they might be. To show that the proximity of kinsfolk need not interfere with the solitary life, the case of abbot Apollos is quoted. His brother came to him in the middle of the night, and begged him to come out from his monastery, and help him to rescue an ox which had stuck in the mire, as he could not rescue it alone. The abbot replied, " Why do you not ask our younger brother who is nearer to you as you passed by, than I am ? " The brother imagined the monk had forgotten the death of his brother who had been long buried and thought he was weak in mind from excessive abstinence so he said, 'How could I summon him who died fifteen years ago ? " The abbot replied, " I have been dead to this world for twenty years, and I cannot from my tomb in this cell give you any assistance in the affairs of this present life."

A word is also said of the value of relaxation even to the most experienced and perfect. The arrival of brethren demands courtesy even though it may seem tiresome, but if the tension of mind is not lessened by relaxation, coldness of spirit, or bodily ill-health, may be the result. Therefore, even the frequent visits of the brethren must be gratefully welcomed by the wise, for they will stimulate the desire for retirement, and will give the opportunity of refreshing the body and of showing kindness. A pretty story, and not less pointed, of S. John the Evangelist is given to emphasise this moral. He was stroking a partridge and looking up saw a philosopher in the garb of a hunter, who was astonished that he should demean himself by so trivial an amusement. "What is it," said S. John, "that you are carrying in your hand?" "A bow," replied the philosopher. "Why do you not always carry it bent?" "It would not do," was the answer, "for the force of its stiffness would be relaxed by being continually bent and it would be impossible to shoot the stouter arrows." S. John replied, "Do not, my lad, allow this short relaxation of my mind to disturb you. Without relaxation the spirit would lose its strength and would be unable to follow what is right[1]."

Doctrine of the Incarnation.

Cassian was of unimpeachable orthodoxy in the other theological controversy which broke out at this time. Nestorius, shortly after his consecration as bishop of Constantinople in A.D. 428, was associated with Anastasius (whom he brought with him as chaplain) in saying that God could not be born of a woman, and in the development of the heresy connected with his name. No less a person than Leo, then archdeacon of Rome, and afterwards bishop, encouraged Cassian to take up this subject. Accordingly he wrote seven books on the Incarnation of Christ[2] against what he calls in the preface "a fresh heresy, and a new enemy of the faith." It was written about A.D. 430 and is an appeal to the Scriptures in proof of the Incarnation, and in support of the correctness of the Virgin's title of

[1] This story is quoted by S. Francis de Sales, *The Devout Life.*
[2] *Pat. Lat.* Vol. 50, pp. 11 seq., Paris, 1846.

"the Mother of God." He explains the word *symbolum*, when applied to the creed, as an epitome of the teaching of the twelve apostles. "It is a combination (or symposium) because the faith of the whole Catholic law is condensed by the apostles of the Lord into the perfect brevity of the *symbolum*[1]." He also speaks with reverence of Chrysostom his teacher, the great bishop who ordained him deacon, and perhaps priest.

A brief survey of this work will indicate Cassian's doctrinal position. In his opening chapter he compares the Nestorian heresy to the hydra of poetic fiction, the fecundity of which was at last ended by the use of fire. In a similar way the fiery sword of the Holy Spirit may cauterise the fertility of this new heresy. Cassian passes in review various heresies or, as he calls them, "tares of the Church," and he specially mentions Leporius, formerly a monk and now a presbyter, who was among the greatest champions of the error of Pelagius in Gaul. He is praised for acknowledging the perversity of his opinions in a recantation addressed to the Gallican bishops[2]. In this he confesses "that our Lord and God, Jesus Christ, who was made Man, was God at His birth, and he says that from the time when He took flesh upon Him, all that belonged to God was given to Man, even as all that belonged to Man was joined to God"; that is to say, two whole and perfect natures were joined together in one Person, each substance continuing perfect in itself. Further, "the God Man is truly born for us of the Holy Ghost and the ever-virgin Mary."

Cassian proceeds to prove that the Virgin was not only *Christotokos* (i.e. Mother of Christ, not of God) but also *Theotokos* (i.e. Mother of God), because Nestorius was then affirming that the Virgin Mary is only Mother of Christ, not of God[3]. Nestorius in A.D. 428 preached a series of sermons at Constantinople, of which he was bishop, against the use of the term *Theotokos* and the implicate doctrine. The stages of Cassian's proofs against the Nestorian heresy are as follows: Quoting the message of the angel "to you is born this day in

[1] VI, 3.
[2] Accessible in *Biblioth. Maxima Patr.* Vol. VII, p. 14, or *Pat. Lat.* Vol. 31, pp. 12 to 21. [3] II, 2.

the city of David a Saviour who is Christ the Lord," he says the words " Lord " and " Saviour " are added that there may be no doubt that the Saviour is God ; and if you are not convinced because the angel did not term him " God " or the " Son of God," the words of the angel Gabriel are mentioned : " The Holy Ghost shall come upon thee, and the power of the Most High shall overshadow thee, therefore also that Holy Thing which shall be born of thee shall be called the Son of God." Thus the Holy Ghost communicated Himself to human nature, taking it to Himself by His own power and majesty, and the weakness of the Virgin was strengthened by the Divine overshadowing. If a mere man was to be born of a pure virgin, a command alone might have done it. Thus the Word, the Son, descended, the Majesty of the Holy Ghost was present, the power of the Father overshadowed, that in the mystery of the conception the whole Trinity might co-operate. How then can she who brought forth God, fail to be the Mother of God ? The prophet Isaiah[1] is also quoted in proof that the birth of God from a virgin had been foretold. Cassian makes reference to S. Paul, "the firmest and clearest witness who can tell us everything about God in the most trustworthy way." S. Paul writes : " The grace of God that bringeth salvation hath appeared to all men...looking for the glorious appearing of the great God and our Saviour Jesus Christ[2]." To the mind of Cassian, the words " hath appeared " indicated a new grace and birth, in the same way that the star appeared to the wise men in the East. In this passage nothing is wanting, it is pointed out, concerning the titles of our Lord, for here is seen God, and the Saviour, and Jesus, and Christ. The heretic cannot say that Jesus was born of the Virgin and was not God, for an apostle supports the fact that He was God; " there is no way of escape."

Later on in the work, again quoting S. Paul's words, "Of whom as concerning the flesh Christ came, who is over all, God Blessed for ever[3]," Cassian shows that it was not a temporary application of the word of God to man, as when God said to Moses, " I have given thee as a God to Pharaoh," for although this should

---

[1] vii, 14, ix, 6. [2] Titus ii, 11-13.
[3] Romans ix, 3-5.

sufficiently indicate the power of God the Giver, and not the
divine nature of the recipient, yet the addition of the words
" Who is over all, God blessed for ever" denotes the true
and real nature of Christ. Cassian then contends against the
idea that when he says the Divinity was born with Jesus Christ,
and his opponents say the Divinity was afterwards infused into
Him, there is only a difference in time. We, who hold the
catholic faith, says Cassian, " know that He is both Son of Man
because born of a woman, and Son of God because conceived of
Divinity." Nothing that is proper to God was lacking to God.
Everywhere God is present in His perfection. He was the same
Person on earth as in Heaven.

Having established the Godhead of Christ, Cassian proceeds
to prove His true Manhood. Again he refers to S. Paul "that
splendid Teacher" who, knowing that Jesus Christ must be
proclaimed true man as well as true God, always sets forth the
Divine in Him in such manner as not to lose hold of the confession
of the Incarnation, and so excluding Marcion's docetism and
Ebionitic asceticism[1]." Quoting the apostle's words, "Paul an
Apostle, not of men neither by man, but by Jesus Christ and
God the Father Who raised Him from the dead[2]," Cassian
declares that the words " Who raised Him from the dead " are
a confession of the Incarnation, and clearly teach a real body.
He next shows from Christ's appearance to S. Paul the existence
of two natures in Him. In the voice he hears Jesus; in the
majesty he sees God. Once more S. Paul says, " We preach
Christ crucified, Christ the power of God and the wisdom of
God[3]," thus speaking not only of Christ as God, but also of
Christ the crucified. Cassian then explains the reason why this
apostle's preaching was rejected alike by Jew and Gentile. It
is not because he taught that the crucified was merely a Man,
for there is nothing novel or strange in this, but because he
declared that this Christ was also God. If the testimony of
S. Paul, " The teacher of the whole world, who is good enough
for me " is not sufficient, Cassian proceeds to teach us the truth
from the lips of a woman, Martha, who declared, " I believe that
Thou art the Christ, the Son of God, which should come into

[1] III, 5.   [2] Gal. i, 1.   [3] 1 Cor. i, 22–24.

the world[1]," and this testimony God did not refuse to accept. But if a woman's faith may seem to be rudimentary, S. Peter proclaims the same truth. He held "the chief place[2] in the priesthood and in the faith," and he says, "Thou art the Christ, the Son of the Living God[3]." Moreover Christ accepted this confession as the truth, "Flesh and blood hath not revealed it unto thee, but my Father which is in Heaven[4]." S. Thomas also, "countryman and ignorant fellow, holy and straightforward," touched the body of his Lord and declared that He was God, and thus testifies that "Jesus whom I touched is God." All this witness is substantiated by "a sign from heaven," by God the Father Himself, who spake these words at the baptism: "Thou art my Beloved Son." Cassian is still not satisfied, he will heap proof upon proof, and so informs us that Christ before His Incarnation was God from everlasting[5]. Through the mystery of the Word of God joined to man, the Word can be called "Saviour," and the Saviour called "the Son of God," and the interchange of titles (implicating the *communicatio idiomatum*) does not interfere with His Divinity. Speaking of the Virgin Birth, he recalls the words "When the fulness of the time was come God sent forth His Son," and he adds, "The creed declares that He has come." By the word "come," it is shown that He was already in existence. If any one objects that "no one ever gave birth to one who had existed before her," Cassian replies that no one "should bring human impossibilities as an objection against Divine omnipotence."

"Is it to be thought that the Nativity of Almighty God is liable to the considerations that apply to the birth of earthly creatures?", and he adds the testimony that he believes that "all living creatures that bear things younger than themselves, could, if God gave the word, bear things much older than themselves." Nor need the one born be of one substance with the one who bears. It is certainly true to say this of earthly creatures, but in the birth of God precedents from nature are not to be considered. Even if they were, whence originated the quails? It is nowhere said that they were previously born of

---

[1] S. John xi, 27.   [2] principatus.   [3] S. Matt. xvi, 16.
[4] v, 17.   [5] IV, I.

mother birds. So too the few loaves and small fishes that fed a great multitude were multiplied by an extraordinary increase. The wine at Cana was produced from water. How could a nobler substance be produced from what was inferior? The omnipotence of God then was all sufficient to bring about His own Nativity. The devil himself was compelled by many reasons to believe that Christ was God. Had he not heard from the lips of John the Baptist, "Behold the Lamb of God"; and again, "I have need to be baptized of Thee"; and when Satan asked, "If thou be the Son of God," he did not doubt the impossibility, but was anxious to know the truth. Nor did he lay aside his suspicions when the temptations were ended, or when he saw Christ scourged and spat upon, for he saw the day darkened, and knew the veil of the temple was rent in twain, and so he asked in the persons of those who crucified Christ, "If Thou be the Son of God"; and he hoped that Christ might be induced by the reproach of the words to destroy the mystery. Cassian closes with an appeal to the citizens of Constantinople to stand fast in the ancient Catholic faith.

His Relation to the Pelagian Controversy.

Another point in which Cassian is of importance in our subject is his relation to the Pelagian controversy. He was a semipelagian, though his expressions are always characterised by a remarkable clearness. The following extracts from his writings will show his position: The will of no one, however eager to reach the palm of uprightness, is sufficient "unless he is protected by the divine compassion[1]." Cassian quotes David and the penitent thief as illustrations of the grace of God. Of David he writes, "The merits of his works were not sufficient to gain pardon for so great a sin," and of the thief, "He did not gain such happiness by the merits of his life, but through the gifts of a merciful God[2]." The need of man's co-operation is also emphasised. Cassian does not wish to discourage men from doing their best, but he feels it necessary to say that while perfection cannot be attained without man's own endeavour, yet

---

[1] *Instit.* XII, 10.   [2] XII, 11.

by this alone "without the grace of God," no one can attain to
it[1]. If Christ said, " I can of mine own self do nothing[2]," shall
we who are but dust and ashes think that "we have no need of
God's help in what pertains to our salvation[3]?" We have to
thank God for free-will, for the grace of baptism, and for the gift
of His daily Providence, in that He works with us so that we
can overcome the sins of the flesh, and protects us from falling
into sin[4]. Once again this free-will, which is inclined to sin, is
turned to a better purpose by the promptings of God. And
further, we are sometimes drawn to salvation against our will[5].
The position of Cassian is still more clearly demonstrated in his
Conferences. In that with Paphnutius, Germanus asks, " Where
then is there room for freewill if God both begins and ends
everything that concerns our salvation[6]?" The answer is quite
definite. The beginning and the end are not everything. There
is a "middle in between." God creates opportunities ; He commands Abraham, " Get thee out of thy country," and Abraham
has the opportunity of showing obedience. Christ teaches the
feebleness and weakness of human faith without the help of
God : "I have prayed for thee that thy faith fail not." A
possible objection is anticipated from the words, "My people
would not hearken to My voice[7]." Does not our salvation then
depend upon ourselves? It is answered by the argument that
"free-will" is evidenced by the disobedience of the people, and
God's oversight is also manifested, for the words imply that He
had often admonished them, and would have vanquished their
enemies, if they would have hearkened[8]. In the *Conference*
with the abbot Daniel, it is shown that free-will without grace is
insufficient, and that human efforts without grace are unavailing.
Without the grace of God " the efforts of the worker are useless[9]."
Yet this grace is conditional upon the free self-determination of
the human will ; perseverance and steadfastness may be proved
when we seek for the return of the Holy Spirit[10]. In the
Conference with Serapion, it is said there are countless passages
of Scripture in proof that foes cannot be overcome by man's

[1] *Instit.* XII, 14.   [2] S. John v, 30.   [3] *Instit.* XII, 17.   [4] XII, 18.
[5] XII, 19.   [6] *Conf.* III, 11.   [7] Ps. lxxxi, 11.   [8] *Conf.* III, 16.
[9] IV, 5.   [10] IV, 4.

own strength, without the help of God. It is "an impious notion and impertinence" to ascribe everything to man's own exertions. In all struggles victory would be impossible without God's help[1]. To the question asked by Germanus of the abbot Chaeremon, why chastity which is gained by the earnestness of man's will may not be ascribed to his exertions? and why the fruits of a husbandman's efforts in cultivation may not be ascribed to those efforts? the answer is given that efforts are vain without seasonable rains. The toil is in vain because the toilers were not under the guidance of God. A man must weigh the fact that he does not apply his efforts without God's gift of physical strength. No good work of any kind can be done without God's assistance. God initiates good thoughts and works, and supplies us with the opportunity of carrying our desires into effect[2].

Cassian is thus ready to acknowledge the universal corruption of human nature through the fall, but with his paramount idea of the love of God, he extended it to all men and taught that God was willing to save all. He says in effect that a man cannot cure himself, but he can at least desire the doctor. In the *Conferences*, the augustinian denial of free-will is opposed on the one hand, and the pelagian infringement of grace on the other. There is, to his mind, human presumption in both these extremes. He prefers therefore to blend free-will and grace. In his view, grace is not always dependent on man's merit, nor is it always prevenient. "If we say that the initiative of the will is always due to God, what about Zacchaeus? If it is due to man, what of Balaam? The penitent thief anticipated divine grace, but in the case of S. Paul, God was prevenient[3]." Thus he allowed more efficacy to the merits of man himself, and said that his moral amelioration was partly the work of his own will.

We have already noted Cassian's determined opposition to Pelagianism in his book on the Incarnation. He is the first to declare the connection between the teaching of Pelagius and Nestorius[4], though it is acknowledged by later writers. In the fifth book he gives many refutations of Nestorian teaching, drawn from the Scriptures and the testimony of the Council of

---

[1] *Conf.* v, 15.   [2] XIII, 3.   [3] XIII, 11, 12.   [4] *De Incarnatione Christi*, v, 2.

Antioch. He challenges Nestorius to profess the creed of Antioch and accuses him of forsaking the catholic faith. "In one of your pestilent treatises you maintain that since the devil shattered the image of the divine nature, God grieved over the image like an emperor over his statue and formed without generation from the Virgin a nature like that of Adam who was born without generation." With great severity Cassian says, "Some poisoners disguise their poison that the injurious ingredient may be concealed by the sweet," and his argument proceeds: "With all your professions, you deceitful plotter, you have, though naming God in the beginning, degraded Him to the condition of a man[1].' In this book he closes, as we have already said, with an appeal to the citizens of Constantinople to stand fast in the faith. He begs them also to "separate themselves from that ravening wolf who devours the people of God. Touch not, taste not anything of his, for all those things lead to death[2]."

As a writer Cassian is more practical than profound, and his writings, based on a thorough knowledge of the Scriptures, are expressed with much quaintness of language and with not a little originality of thought. His style is forcible and clear, but would not be regarded as either polished or graceful in diction. They were highly esteemed by contemporary and later founders of monasticism. The *Conferences* were called by S. Benedict "a mirror of monasticism[3]." They received the warm commendation of Ignatius Loyola, founder of the Jesuit Order, and Cassiodorus recommended them to his monks.

The year of Cassian's death is uncertain. It took place either in A.D. 435, or between A.D. 440 and 458. Though more than one church honoured him as a saint, he was never formally canonised. Perhaps the highest testimony paid to him is that which refers to him as "the most blessed Cassian who in the monastery of Lerins has, as his compeer, the blessed Honoratus[4]."

[1] *De Incarnatione Christi*, VII, 6. [2] VII, 31. [3] Speculum Monasticum.
[4] Wilkins' *Concilia*, Vol. IV, App. p. 741, London, 1737.

CHAPTER VIII

THE FOUNDER OF LERINS
S. HONORATUS, ARCHBISHOP OF ARLES

A special interest most naturally attaches to the man who gave his name to the smaller but more renowned island of the Lerins, who founded the monastery thereon, and gathering round him a brotherhood of remarkable men made for it a new and glorious history. S. Honoratus was eminently fitted by temperament and disposition for the organisation and the administration of a monastic brotherhood. He learned in his childhood to love the poor, and denied himself to minister to their needs. His biographer recounts a pretty story of his early life which is not without its moral to all who read it. Tired and hungry, S. Honoratus was about to eat, when on a sudden there came to him a leper full of sores; the young Christian ran towards him, tenderly embraced him, took him to his chamber and offered him his food, and as he washed the leper's hands, the face immediately shone bright as the sun and Honoratus recognised in it the face of Jesus[1].

Honoratus belonged to a rich pagan family of distinction. His desire for baptism aroused the bitter hostility of his father who vainly endeavoured to oppose it[2]. The devotion of the brilliant gifts of his son, who gave such promise of added lustre to the family name, would, in the proud father's mind, be wasted and lost in a religious life. But all his efforts to avert this dreaded course were unavailing. The son sold his goods, distributed the proceeds among the poor, and leaving friends, family, and fortune behind him, went with his brother Venantius

---

[1] Ecce facies egroti sicut sol splendida apparuit, agnovit hunc esse Jesum Christum.
[2] Pater a baptismate quantum potuit avertit.

and under the guidance of Caprasius to Marseilles, where his brother died. In grief Honoratus sought for solitude in the mountains of the Esterels, of which the headland of Cap Roux is the most marked feature in colour and outline. It forms the western side of the Curde which includes the Bay of Cannes. It was always very dear to the monks for the grotto or " baumo " of Cap Roux was the first hermitage of their founder. Barralis says that in his time it was known under the name of Sainte Beaume, as it is to-day[1]. Part of the rock seems shaped like the imprint of a human body and is called by the people "the bed of Honoratus[2]." Tradition says that he went to this place to seek consolation from God on the loss of his brother. He found the isolation that Leontius, bishop of Fréjus, had promised him, until visitors found him and came to him in great numbers. It was then that he went to Lerins. Eucherius, who had previously spent some time on the island of Sainte Margaret, had also occupied a grotto at Cap Roux. It was from it that he wrote "in praise of solitude" to Hilary who had just returned from Arles. The inhabitants of Fréjus used to go in procession to Sainte Beaume to pray for the cessation of any scourge or trouble[3].

According to the tradition of Lerins, as Barralis tells us, Honoratus retired to Cap Roux about A.D. 375 and to Lerins in 391. Baronius accepts this date, as does Père Giry who says, " Honoratus governed the abbey of Lerins for 35 years, and he was promoted in 426 to the bishopric of Arles." Tillemont, Mabillon and others give A.D. 400–410 as the date of his establishment at Lerins. Men had sought Honoratus in his grotto-dwelling[4], and when later, at the suggestion of Leontius, bishop of Fréjus, he betook himself to the isle of Lerins, at that time squalid and deserted, inaccessible and uninhabited, disciples came to him from all directions[5]. " He was to Lerins

---

[1] Specu seu antro...qui a nostratibus dicitur la sancta Bauma de Sant Honorat. *Chron. Ler.* I, p. 37.

[2] Quo in loco visitur saxum veluti in forma putei concavum. *Ibid.*

[3] Forojuliensibus qui cum ariditatibus, sterilitate, imbribus aliisque pressuris urgerentur, ad placandam iram altissimi Dei processionali pompâ.

[4] Tanta visitantium fratrum irruens multitudo.

[5] "Quae natio in monasterio illius cives suos non habet?" asks Hilary.

what the sun is to the sky," says S. Salvian.   It was Honoratus
who reclaimed this snake-infested sterile land.   Wells were dug
and water, hitherto withheld, flowed in abundance.   Vineyards
were planted and flowers added their fragrant beauty to the
uninviting and even repulsive place, so that in later years
Barralis could describe it as "our favoured healthy island
covered by shady pinetrees, olives, myrtles, laurels, sweet
smelling furze, and cypress trees, a variety of herbs and flowers
in a thousand colours[1]."   Here, as we have already seen, earlier
cells were built, and formed the beginning of the monastery
destined to fill so honoured a place in the religious history of
the world.

S. Hilary has provided the chief source from which the
historians of S. Honoratus draw, in the panegyric which he
pronounced as a funeral oration[2], and which, in the opinion of
Tillemont, "surpasses in spirit and eloquence every utterance of
a similar kind in ecclesiastical antiquity[3]," and has been
unanimously praised by writers of every age.   From it we see
the attractiveness of the character of Honoratus.   Around him
gathered a body of distinguished men assembled in Lerins.
Indeed from this famous place came, as we shall see, some of
the best known men in the Church of Gaul, literature of world-
wide fame, a possible share in the development of two creeds,
and a liturgy.

Hilary gives a most touching picture of the founder's
influence over his monks.   The griefs of all he regarded as his
own, the progress and labour of all he considered to be his.
Active, diligent, indefatigable, his tender love took account even
of the moments of the sleep of each brother.   It was as by a
divine instinct that he seemed to know the strength and courage
of each and all under his care.   He watched over their health,
nourishment, and work, in order that each might give to God
the best possible service.   He inspired them with a more than
filial affection.   "In him we find," they said, "not only a father,
but a whole family, a whole country, a whole world."   When he
wrote to one or other of those who were absent, they would say

[1] *Chron. Ler.* I.   [2] *Sermo de Vita Honorati.*
           [3] *Mémoires*, Vol. XII, p. 464.

when receiving his letters (written on wax tablets, according to the custom of the times), "It is honey that he has poured into this wax, honey drawn from the inexhaustible sweetness of his heart." It was Eucherius who in a pretty compliment exclaimed as he recognised the writing, "You have restored to the wax its honey." We can only regret that none of his many letters have been preserved, for we know that Hilary spoke of them with high praise. He was guide and helper of many beyond the confines of the monastery. "With arms constantly outstretched to invite all Christians to come and rest in the love of Jesus Christ" is Hilary's tribute. Maximus, afterwards bishop of Riez, was among the first to come under his influence; Eucherius, of illustrious birth and rank, was another disciple; Salvian, the Jeremiah of his age, sought at his side an aid and incentive to greater perfection. Cassian says that his virtues were so perfect that his disciples could with difficulty follow him. Eucherius calls him, "Master of bishops, a doctor of the churches." Faustus describes him as "an angelic man." Hilary remarks that "if charity desired to have her portrait painted, she would borrow the features of Honoratus." A modern writer regards him as "one of those men chosen by Providence to console the sorrows of the people of the West[1]."

The utterances of some of its sons demonstrated the impassioned affection this island home inspired. Caesarius exclaims, "O sweet and happy habitation in which the glory of the Saviour is daily increased by virtues manifold, and whence the wickedness of the devil is menaced by the defeats he receives." In enraptured metaphor the tiny island assumes magnificent proportions, equal in his imagination to the massive mountains which he saw beyond the gulf. "Fortunate Isles of Lerins, thou art small and flat to look upon, and yet thou hast raised to heaven numberless mountains! It is thou that dost nourish perfect monks, that sendest illustrious prelates into all countries, for all those whom thy beneficent shelter receives, thou dost raise upon the wings of love and humility to the highest virtue[2]."

---

[1] M. L'Abbé Alliez.

[2] O felix et beata habitatio insulae hujus, ubi tam sanctis quotidie et tam spiritalibus lucris gloria Domini Salvatoris augetur, et tantis damnis diaboli nequitia

Eucherius, the great layman who became a bishop, whose two sons, trained at Lerins, were subsequently bishops, tenderly loved the place : " I embrace my Lerins with special honour[1]." " How many lofty mountains," says Sidonius Apollinaris, the foremost man of letters in Gaul in the 5th century, "this isle so flat has raised to the heavens[2]." The praise of later centuries is just as great. Isidore, in the 7th, challenges the world : " The whole world offers no more beautiful abode[3]." His contemporary, Gregory Cortesius, can find no words of sufficient eulogy : " Small in extent, illustrious in glory ! what saints of ardent piety, what anchorites of insatiable austerity, it has produced ! Stars in a serene sky shine less numerous. O land that no one can ever praise enough ! Oh dwelling of the saints, placed as a shelter from the tempests of a wicked world[4]." Denys Faucher desires no place in preference to it. Offering his verses to a friend he says, "I was happy to sing in the shade of tufted trees, when Lerins offered me peaceful leisure. The silence of its banks inspired my soul, and the forest seemed to repeat my words as my skilful hand caused the chords of my lyre to vibrate. The laurel was responsive to my accents, the pine and the myrtle caressed by gentle zephyrs joined their sweet murmurs to them. Now amid the willows and the noisy frogs, my lyre is dumb, as once on the banks of the waters of Babylon the joyous songs of Zion were turned to mourning. The songs that once charmed my leisure have given place to sad regrets. The chords of the lyre now are stretched in vain. My thoughts return to Lerins. I cease not to weep over my exile. I love not magnificent palaces inhabited by kings ; this little island suffices for my happiness[5]." The island became a haven of

minoratur. Beata, inquam, et felix insula Lerinensis, quae cum parvula et plana esse videatur, innumerabiles tamen montes ad coelum misisse cognoscitur. Haec est quae eximios nutrit monachos, et praestantissimos per omnes provincias erogat sacerdotes. Ac sic quos accipit filios, reddit patres, et quos nutrit parvulos, reddit magnos, quos velut tyrannos excepit, reges facit. Nam omnes quoscunque felix et beata habitatio ista susceperit, charitatis et humilitatis pennis ad excelsa virtutum culmina Christo sublimare consuevit., *Biblioth. Maxima Patr.* Vol. VIII, *Hom. Caesarii*, 25.

[1] *De laude eremi.*
[2] *Carmen* 16, *ad Faustum*, Quantos insula plana miserit in coelum montes !
[3] Pulchrior in toto non est locus orbe Lerina.   [4] *Chron. Ler.* 1, p. 18.
[5] Nec mihi vestra placent augusta palatia ; deliciis satis est insula parva meis.

peace and faith amid the convulsions of the old world, and we shall note that its influence continued through much of the troublous period of the Middle Ages, and reached even to modern times.

Mamertus, a presbyter in the diocese of Vienne—in his description of the period, during which there was a prevailing neglect and even contempt of the Roman language, an abandonment of grammar, dialectics and rhetoric, a contempt for geometry, arithmetic and even music, and a disdain engendered by philosophy—refers to the fact that Lerins offered a brilliant exception, for some of its sons preserved the best traditions of the purest literature, and in an age of misgovernment and licentiousness, of failing culture and crude theology, kept brightly burning the lamp of learning and enriched the world with literature that occupies to-day no insignificant place in Christendom. The young nobility of Gaul came to this monastery as to "the most renowned emporium of literature and virtue[2]." He says : "In our age it is not capacity but study that is lacking."

Manual labour was a feature of the life at Lerins, and served as a means not only of personal discipline, but also of provision for the sick and poor, and for the requirements of the monastery. Many kept up the habit after they had left the monastery to undertake the direction of the churches. S. Hilary of Arles did not disdain the work of the field, even when it was beyond his strength, for he was thus enabled to succour the hungry[3]. Here too considerable austerity was practised by some who desired to emulate the penances of the Egyptian monks. Sidonius[4] describes the severity to which Faustus, bishop of Riez, subjected his body when in his old age he returned to Lerins; he refers to Antiolus, another bishop, who by his strictly frugal methods of living, tried to follow the Syrian ascetics. Caesarius too practised severe austerities during his sojourn there.

It is not surprising that the reputation of Honoratus was

---

[1] Nostro saeculo non ingenia deesse sed studia.
[2] *Chron. Ler.* II, p. 130.
[3] Gennadius, *De Scriptor. Eccles.* chap. 69.
[4] *Carmen Eucharist.* XVI.

made known far beyond the island boundaries, and, when the clergy and people of Arles lost Patroclus their bishop, it was to Lerins and the founder that they turned for a successor. S. Honoratus was chosen with unanimous enthusiasm, but the burden of so eminent a see overwhelmed him, and the sight of the island where God had wrought so much, and of the disciples that were under his fatherly guidance, filled him with sorrow and anxiety. He told the Arlesians that he was quite unknown to them, but the diocese was insistent. He was reminded of the divisions within it, and of its need of such an one as he for ruler; he was told that the flourishing state of the monastery rendered it a favourable opportunity to leave, and among so many examples of piety and culture a successor would be found without difficulty. S. Honoratus still hesitated to take a step that meant a great sacrifice of his personal desire, for he longed to remain at Lerins. But at last he consented to go, and with him took S. Hilary, whose companionship gave him some solace in the grief that departure from Lerins caused. The love of the founder for Lerins was strongly implanted also in his disciple, who soon returned to the monastery.

In his new position S. Honoratus was not long in impressing his personality upon the diocese. He was to it what he had been to Lerins. He entered sympathetically into the great needs of his Church. There was naturally a close bond of affection between the two places. From time to time he visited the monastery, and the monks sought their old master's help at Arles. As his years drew to their close and he felt his end approaching, he sent for his favourite disciple Hilary, who hastened to his side in the hope that his presence would prolong his master's life. Desiring to implant in those that gathered round his bed a love of things eternal, he said, "You see how fragile is the house that we inhabit. Whatever rank we hold death comes upon us, and neither riches nor honour can escape from this necessity. Live in such wise that you fear not the last hour, and look upon death as a journey. My dearly loved children, follow my advice, it is the heritage that your dying father and bishop leaves with you. Do not allow yourselves to be deceived by love of the world; free yourselves voluntarily of what one day you must of necessity relinquish[1]." Thus did the old man, grown white in devotion and penitence, speak of the vanity of temporal things. When he had finished, his outstretched hand evoked the blessings of heaven upon them. There was ever a strong link between Lerins and its founder and through Hilary he sent his last blessing to its sons whom he had remembered constantly before the throne of God. S. Hilary tells us of the last moments of his master. As I tried in vain to stop my tears and to stifle my sobs, he asked, "Why do you weep over the inevitable destiny of the human race?" I replied that I did not weep for his loss, as his prayers which had never failed us would be more powerful when he had gone from us, but that I grieved to see the anguish of his last moments. "What have I suffered," said he, "compared with what many saints have experienced?" Those present then desired that he would name his successor, and he pointed to S. Hilary. He died in peace in A.D. 430 at the age of 76. His body was carried into the city through the midst of an immense concourse of people who proclaimed his virtues. On the morrow the clergy went forth to bury his remains, and as the coffin was lowered into the grave the vestments were torn in shreds, for each one desired to take away a piece of them as a precious relic. S. Hilary in his funeral oration eloquently declared that "to think of Honoratus is very sweet, but to be separated from him is very cruel."

It has been maintained by Dr Burn[2] that S. Honoratus may have been the author of the Athanasian creed, a theory to which he "still clings with some fondness." All the available evidence, internal and external, points to the south of France as its home, and it is generally acknowledged that the sons of Lerins were men of more than average learning and intelligence. Dr Burn finds support for his contention that "Honoratus was worthy to be the author," from the testimony that such men as Hilary and Faustus bear to the dogmatic teaching of their much revered master[3].

---

[1] S. Hilary, *Sermo de vita.*
[2] *An introduction to the creeds*, p. 148.
[3] S. Hilary, *Vita*, c. 38, Quotidianus siquidem in sincerissimis tractatibus confessionis Patris ac Filii ac Spiritus Sancti testis fuisti : nec facile tam exerte tam

But his authorship of the creed, if it were conclusively proved, would add nothing to the reputation of him whose " beautiful countenance shone with a sweet and attractive majesty[1]," and by the force and affection of whose character, a desert was made a paradise, in which those who had renounced the worldly life sought for happiness, and felt and proclaimed that they had found it there. His name cannot be forgotten, for it is linked with the monastery of Lerins which sent forth its sons, as bishops, theologians and saints, to spread the knowledge of the gospel far beyond the boundaries of Gaul.

lucide quisquam de Divinitatis Trinitate disseruit, cum eam personis distingueres et gloriae aeternitate ac majestate sociares.

Faustus, *In depositione S. Honorati*, Sed et modo minus potest gaudere is...qui fideliter sanctam regulam custodierit ab illo allatam...teneamus in primis fidem rectam, credamus Patrem et Filium et Spiritum Sanctum unum Deum.

[1] Eucherius, *De laude eremi*, p. 342.

CHAPTER IX

A NURSERY OF BISHOPS
CAESARIUS, BISHOP AND SAINT[1]

His Personal Character.

We know but little of his early life and youth. He was born in A.D. 468–470, at Châlon-sur-Saône. His parents were in affluent circumstances. Caesarius, however, did not expend his ample allowances on selfish gratifications but early showed the unselfish aspirations which characterised him throughout his life. At the age of eight he would even give away his clothes to the poor he met, and on returning home found refuge in evasion, even asserting by way of explanation, on one occasion, that he had been robbed ! His account of himself up to the age of eighteen is that he had been " a young man of few hopes, walking the primrose path of dalliance strewn as it was with rocks and precipices, on which he blindly stumbled." His endeavour to find happiness in this world failed.

The crisis of his life came. As the eldest of the family, he felt, as others have before him and since, the conflict of duty to his family and what he felt to be the call of conscience. After a brief delay at most of two years he sought the cloister at Lerins, where he was supremely contented. " Happy island of Lerins," he called it. The memory of the great men who had

---

[1] The sources of information concerning his life are found (*a*) in a Biography in Migne's *Pat. Lat.* Vol. 67, pp. 1000–1042, (*b*) in the deliberations of those councils at which he presided, Agde in A.D. 506, fourth Council of Arles and Carpentras A.D. 527, second Council of Orange and second Council of Vaison A.D. 529, and a synod at Marseilles in A.D. 533, (*c*) in his sermons, of which over 100 are accessible in the *Appendix to S. Augustine's Works*, Migne, *Pat. Lat.* Vol. 39, and M. de la Bigne, *Biblioth. Patrum*, (*d*) in his *Regula ad Monachos* and *Regula ad Virgines*, and (*e*) his will.

lived there became the inspiration of his life, and to read their works his daily delight. The writings of Faustus, and his high ideal of monastic life especially attracted him.

The keynote of his character was his intense reality. This is equally seen in the rigour of his daily self-examination and in the ideal which he kept always before him, of seeking continually to help and edify all with whom he came into contact. It was also continually exhibited in his insistence that the inward thought should, especially in worship, correspond to the outward action and profession; "Let your life," said he, "accord with your language." The sweetness of the chants might rob prayers of all savour. They might sing, "Let pride be confounded," while concealing pride in the depths of their own hearts.

The monastery, at the time he entered it, was under the rule of abbot Porcarius. When the office of steward became vacant, his practical ability was recognised by the abbot, and, with the consent of the seniors, he was appointed to the vacancy. His duty was to attend to the bodily needs of the brethren; to look after the sick; to provide for the traveller. His early training and traditions eminently fitted him for this work, and here his experience trained a nature, generous to a fault, to that wiser charity which knew when to give and when to withhold his hand. He used a gentle and generous constraint with those who were in need and who were too diffident or self-denying to ask, while to those who were in need of nothing he gave nothing. He dealt fairly with all, and while the glove was velvet the hand was iron. It is true that his severity of discipline was at times more than either he himself or others could endure with safety to health, or without murmuring and discontent. Protests were made which were too strong for the abbot to resist, and he learnt to graduate discipline according to the ability of each to bear it. Still he did not relax the discipline he applied to his own life. In the isolation of his own little cell he lived in the strictest simplicity. Herbs were his only nourishment, of which he prepared a week's supply at a time, and he occupied himself entirely with reading, meditation and prayer. His austerity impaired his health, and he broke down under the excessive strain.

He went to Arles and exchanged the severe solitude of a lonely island for the stir and stress of a civil and commercial centre. Here he came under the notice of the bishop, Anonius, who ordained him deacon and priest. Just at this juncture the post of superior in a suburban monastery was vacant. It was one of those early monasteries bound by no definite rules, governed by no effective head, where each man was a law to himself. The bishop recognised the organising and disciplinary powers of the monk of Lerins and appointed him to the vacancy as abbot with plenary powers. By his force of character it was placed on such an excellent footing that it became the model of similar institutions.

On the death of Anonius, Caesarius was appointed to succeed him in A.D. 502, greatly against his own will and taste, but was urged to the acceptance of so onerous and responsible position by clergy and laity alike. The manner of his appointment as bishop is interesting. The aged Anonius, knowing his end was near, summoned his clergy and took counsel with them. With sadness he spoke of his growing weakness, and of his desire to be assured of a worthy successor to take up the work he must reluctantly give up. He spoke to them of the wisdom and energy of that servant of God, Caesarius. If they would see their way to promise their suffrages for him, their old bishop would find consolation for his last days in the knowledge that the work he had so much at heart would be faithfully and thoroughly carried on. They replied that the bishop's nominee was worthy. The shrewd old man sent a deputation to the court of Toulouse to ensure this selection. The chief opposition seems to have come from Caesarius himself. And here again does the intense reality of the man manifest itself, as he realises the great responsibility of the episcopate, and his own unfitness for so difficult a task. It is almost amusing to read that he tried to escape consecration by hiding himself among the funeral monuments of the city. Though he shrank from such high office, he was not slow to rise to its great duties. He did not change his ordinary manner of life to any extent, for he was a monk to the last, and closely followed the rules of monastic life as far as possible, consistently with his new work. Though outwardly he conformed to the bishop's dress and affected no startling singularity, he yet fulfilled his love of simple poverty by innumerable austerities.   There was no silver upon his table ; all that was presented to him was sold, and the proceeds given to his works of charity.   His clothing other than his official vestments was of the plainest and poorest material.   Better than the trappings of state was the reverence accorded to the man, a reverence superstitiously attaching to his very garments when the wearer had departed this life.   It is related that a man came to the deacon Stephen in a high state of fever, and asked for a piece of cloth which had been used for Caesarius : " Give me some of the cloth to cure my shivering."   Stephen having brought him a linen kerchief with which the body had been wiped, the man refused to take it.   " Why do you lie ? " he said, with indignation, " I know well that the saint did not wear linen."

Having himself learnt to obey, Caesarius was well qualified to command, and was very impatient of disobedience, whoever was the author, and whatever the cause.   It is told us by his biographer, how on one occasion he was travelling with another bishop, when they met an old woman with body bent, dragging herself along, rather than walking.   Moved with pity, Caesarius made his companion get out of the carriage, bless her, and take her by the hand and raise her up.   Eucherius—for it was he—sought to excuse himself, and suggested that his brother should carry out his own request.   But Caesarius cut short the dispute ; his impatience would brook no opposition to his wishes : " Come, give your hand to this woman in the name of the Lord and raise her up."   But if the will of our saint would not brook disobedience even when it had the colour of reasonableness, we may imagine that it was imperious in more important matters.   On one occasion, when he found that the rules of abstinence, silence, and prayer were being relaxed, he went in person to the monastery of Lerins and having spoken very severely to the delinquents, he threatened that unless things were altered he would come again ; " not with the simple rod of speech, but with the chastisements he held in reserve for hardened hearts."

That he had a tender heart concealed beneath this severe exterior may be seen by the practical manner in which his pity for the poor and the sick found expression. In these days of hospitals, infirmaries, and provision for coping with all sorts of disease, we look back and find a great forerunner in this 5th century bishop. He had built, close by his episcopal residence in Arles, a spacious hospital where a large number of beds were at the service of the poor and infirm. It has a modern touch about it to find that he had a doctor specially appointed to serve there, to give advice and medicine gratis. The church hard by ministered to the needs of their souls.

The poor were his constant thought. If he had a weakness it was an excess of generosity; the doors of his house were never closed to the needy. Those who had the care of his cellars and treasury found it no easy matter to practise needful economy; through his desire to give to others his companions often endured compulsory fasts. This self-denying bishop, whose theological interest we shall presently consider, presided over his see for forty years, and during this time he did not escape suspicion and misconception. On one occasion indeed he was accused before Alaric, by a notary named Licinus, of a plot to bring the state of Arles under the subjection of the Burgundian rulers. The accusation was for a time believed, and he was exiled to Bordeaux. It was not long, however, before he was able to prove his innocence and gain his recall. It is noteworthy that he bore no malice to his false accuser, and it was characteristic of the reality of his religion that he interceded for the calumniator's life.

Another great trial came upon him as a result of the Burgundian invasion of the Mediterranean provinces which Theodoric was anxious to re-conquer and re-organise. Owing to the vigorous resistance of the defenders of Arles against the combined forces of the Franks and Burgundians, Theodoric arrived in time to relieve the city. This success was of material advantage to him in his endeavour to weld the conflicting interests of Ostrogoths and Visigoths. But just outside the city walls a monastery which was in course of construction by

Caesarius was razed to the ground. A still less endurable trial was the suspicion of treachery that fell upon him. A young relative foreseeing the capture of the garrison, and dreading the consequences, succeeded in entering the besiegers' camp, and, unfortunately, failed to satisfy either them or the besieged. He accused Caesarius of sending him, and of a deliberate attempt to deliver the city into the enemy's hands. The Goths, on the other hand, believed the youth was his emissary, and invading his home, seized the bishop, and were about to send him to a fortress, but being prevented, kept him prisoner in his own house. When events took another turn, and their attention was drawn elsewhere, he was set at liberty.

His freedom, however, was no joy to him when he contemplated the horrors of the war. There were the usual attendant miseries and consequences—devastation, suffering, massacre, pestilence. To alleviate the distress and repair the ravages was the bishop's first thought and chief desire, and he applied all his resources to this work. Even the enemy, who were prisoners, were allowed to share in his solicitous care. His religion, as always, coloured all his actions ; humanity, brotherhood, was its keynote. He even sold the furniture and sacred vessels of the church to provide necessaries, not, of course, without a grave and loud protest against this sacrilege. In defence Caesarius nobly replied, " I should like to know what my critics would have said were they in the place of the captives ? God who gave Himself as the price of man's redemption, will not begrudge my redeeming captives with altar metal." To the objection that there were now no costly vessels for communion, he answered that Christ "did not use silver." He was as generous with his own possessions as he had been with those of the church ; his cellar and his table were at the disposal of the hungry, and on one occasion he had absolutely nothing left. His dependents somewhat anxiously asked how much longer they themselves must go without food, when, almost as if by magic, a royal gift of three shiploads of wheat arrived. Apart from the generosity, it was a significant recognition, by Gondebaud and Sigismund, of the value of the services the bishop had rendered to their subjects.

Theodoric's sovereignty included the country under the metropolitan jurisdiction of Caesarius. He sent messages from Ravenna to Arles: " Let the people consider themselves delivered, not conquered." He only fears one possibility, namely, that the barbarian influence may have left an abiding impression upon them, and he urges them to remember their Roman traditions, and to rid themselves of the manners of strangers. Under his laws and government the province changed for the better, and began to recover from its disasters. Caesarius commenced the rebuilding of his monastery ; it was ready for consecration when he was summoned to Ravenna to see the king, and to answer for the third time an accusation with which the local governor was evidently not competent to deal. It was a strange irony that his wide charity provided the pretext. From the first, however, Theodoric seems to have been convinced of the bishop's innocence, and when he entered the king's presence the latter went to meet him, spoke to him most affably, and was greatly impressed by his attitude and bearing. After the bishop's departure Theodoric expressed his regret and displeasure that so good a man should have been dragged like a prisoner so great a distance. The king further sent Caesarius a valuable present of money and a gold plate, which he promptly sold, and devoted the proceeds to the relief of the poor and the captives.

His reputation soon reached Rome. The pope (Symmachus) wanted greatly to see him, honoured him with the bestowal of the pallium, confirmed him as Metropolitan, and made him " Vicar of the Holy Chair." He returned to Arles, like a conqueror crowned with the glories and honours of victories. At length the possibility of suspicion and mistrust is over ; he had gained the confidence and admiration of the highest, and the popular acclamation of the lowest. We must pass over the details of this journey, which are very fully described by Cyprian, who was responsible for this part of the life-history of Caesarius. It is noticeable how this strong-minded, level-headed bishop recognised authority ; " the holy pope of the city of Rome has ordered " was a favourite formula of his, and he appealed to him in any matter of unusual importance.

His Influence at Councils.

Reckoned among the chief sources of information for an estimate of the character and powers of Caesarius, must be the councils at which he presided, the deliberations of which he guided by his master mind. At each we may trace the influence, and note the ideas, of a great bishop who has helped to make Lerins famous as a school of training.

First in date and ranking in importance with the second of Orange, is the council which met at Agde in A.D. 506, in the 22nd year of Alaric, Arian king of the Goths; in this council the influence of Caesarius is clearly manifest. His name stands first in the list of signatories. Modern collections contain seventy-one canons of this council, but these were not all passed at Agde. The first forty-seven and the last one are doubtless genuine, the remainder being either resumés or extracts from the deliberations of other councils. It has historical, political and ecclesiastical interest; historical because it marks the transition between the Gallo-Roman and Gallo-French Church; political, in that it throws light upon the extent of Alaric's kingdom; and ecclesiastical, in so far as it treats of the institutions of the Gallic Church. The contact with far distant churches reflects the comprehensiveness of Caesarius' catholic mind. The canons are imbued with the disciplinary zeal and methodical precision of its president. The council assembled "by permission of our lord, and king[1]" (i.e. Alaric), without any mention of the pope Symmachus.

The prologue states the objects and aims of those assembled in council: "to discuss matters of clerical discipline and ordination, and of the temporalities of the church." Among the questions debated was the relation of the clergy to their bishop. It appears that the former had complained of episcopal severity, and Caesarius does not, by any means, exonerate his brother bishops of blame, and the council decided that "if a bishop forgot moderation, and excommunicated a cleric without good reason, or for some trivial offence, the neighbouring bishop

---

[1] Ex permissu domini nostri gloriosissimi, magnificentissimique regis.

should interpose and not refuse communion to the victims of severity." The powers of those who were inclined to abuse their authority were thus checked, but it must not be supposed that justice was by any means irregular in administration. Priests were distinctly given to understand that they were under ecclesiastical jurisdiction; those however who appealed from the ecclesiastical to a secular tribunal were threatened with excommunication. The age of ordinands was also fixed; the deacons must be twenty-five and priests or bishops, thirty. This, it was thought, would guarantee reality of vocation. The question of discipline in its moral bearing upon the individual cleric was discussed, and rules of great severity were promulgated. The perusal of the canons, and a knowledge of his requirements from ordination candidates quite clearly and sufficiently mark Caesarius as a disciplinarian of a most rigid and remarkable type, and show to what length his practical ideas of the religious life would legitimately lead him.

A consideration of the council's deliberations on the temporalities of the Church shows us that the possessions of the Church arising from voluntary gifts were very considerable. The will of Caesarius affords evidence that he had almost doubled the wealth of the Church at Arles. The powers of the bishops in dealing with property were carefully limited; funds designed for the good of the whole Church must not be lavished only upon those who serve her in the highest offices. There was a possibility that the bishops might take advantage of the powers and authority vested in them; they were accordingly reminded that they were not the owners but only the stewards of ecclesiastical possessions. It was possible either to forbid altogether the alienation of the Church's goods, or to render it difficult by means of reservations. A check was put upon the possibility of extravagance by requiring the consent of neighbouring bishops before property could be alienated, except in special cases, duly stated, where it was a question of lands of small value, and difficult to make remunerative. Caesarius himself claims this exceptional right on occasion, for we read in his will that he had alienated some Church lands for the good of his monastery, because they were not of great extent, and were too distant. In a similar way, the parochial clergy might not alienate parochial property without episcopal sanction. The State's approval was of course necessary where property and temporalities were concerned. Alaric published an edict sanctioning the canons of the council.

Council of Arles.

The Council of Arles assembled in A.D. 527, on the occasion of the dedication of the Church of the Holy Virgin, in the second year of the pontificate of John I. As at Agde so here, those present were occupied with measures of discipline, but with special reference to the country clergy. We have already noticed how fond Caesarius was of traversing the diocese, knowing and being known by the people of even the remote country parishes. This may partly explain "the rustic tone" observable in most of his sermons. This experience made him anxious to assist the work in secluded and sparsely populated districts. Owing to the scarcity of properly equipped clergy to fulfil the duties in these, there had been, on the part of the bishops, a deplorable lowering of the standard of requirements. There was also a danger in another direction, in the eagerness of lay patrons to accept almost anyone for preferment. Caesarius determined to set his brother bishops free from lay importunity and episcopal weakness alike, and therefore reasserted the age limit for the priesthood and diaconate, and exacted other reasonable conditions.

The Council of Carpentras.

The Council of Carpentras was held on November 6th A.D. 527 (the second year of Athalaric, king of Italy), when fifteen bishops were present. It is curious to note that all but two signed as *peccator* (sinner), not as *episcopus* (bishop). In their deliberations we see in Caesarius that rare combination of the practical man of the world and the saint. As a saint he was most particular that his clergy should be good men; as a business man he would see that they had the wherewithal to live. The Council of Carpentras admitted that, while each parish had the right to keep its revenues for its own use, a bishop who was poor might receive help from rich parishes; where he had sufficient for his reasonable expenses he was forbidden to take anything from any parish, rich or poor. Only one canon was passed, which was to this effect: "If the cathedral church has enough property for its expenses, the parochial revenues shall be employed for the clergy who serve them, or for church expenses and repairs; if the bishop's expenses exceed the income of the revenues of his church, he shall be able to draw what he needs from the richest parishes, leaving them what will suffice for their requirements."

As an illustration of synodical action at this early date it may be mentioned that Agroecius, bishop of Antipolis, was suspended at this council for conferring Holy Orders contrary to the canons. He was doubly to blame in that he had himself subscribed his name to this very canon, and when summoned to state his defence refused to attend. This was, of course, too much for a disciplinarian like Caesarius, who soon brought his delinquent brother bishop to his senses by forbidding him to say mass for a year. This intimation was sent by Caesarius in the following letter: "Caesarius Bishop, and the other Bishops assembled at the Council of Carpentras, to our Venerable Brother, Bishop Agroecius,...Although you might have been present in person, or by deputy, at the council, to give an account of the ordination which you are said to have conferred; and although priests may not ignore the canons, yet the error was almost lighter if, through ignorance, you had done wrong, than if you were a transgressor of the canons to which your hand or that of your deputy had subscribed. But now you are bound fast in a twofold impeachment; since you are acknowledged to have erred heedlessly not only against the decrees of the Venerable Fathers, but also against your own. Wherefore, we have sanctioned this by a mutual deliberation in Christ, that since the statutes, inserted in the canons through you, bind our son Protadius, and bind you by a like vote, you may not presume to perform mass until after the expiry of a year. For it is right that what is established among overseers, God being the Mediator, should be kept undefiledly. For what reverence

10—2

of observance will be manifested by those who come after, if the
law is broken in the first place by those through whom it was
established ? "

Council of Vaison.

Twelve bishops were present at the Second Council of
Vaison. We can again trace the desire of Caesarius to impress
upon the minds of the young the necessity and value of acquiring
knowledge and instruction. Young men must read and give
themselves to systematic study. His personality and his master-
mind left their mark upon the deliberations at Vaison, as seen
in the determination that a parish priest must have young men
at his house for the purpose of imparting religious instruction to
them in preparation for the work of the ministry ; and that, with
a special view to providing for the spiritual needs of country
parishes, the right of preaching, hitherto confined to bishops,
was now given to priests. Where the priests, for some reasonable cause, might be hindered, the deacon could read a homily
culled from one of the Fathers. In an admonition addressed by
Caesarius to his brethren, we have a curious sidelight upon the
incapacity and indolence of some bishops of the period. In
some of the towns in which they lived there was a lack of
religious instruction. The disciplinarian took them severely to
task for their slackness. He expresses his views with the
emphasis of conviction, and with modesty and tact justifies his
action : " If I were to consider my own faults I should perhaps
scarcely presume to offer advice to workers in the country, on
account of what is written, ' Cast out first the beam out of thine
own eye,' and ' He that teacheth another, doth he not teach
himself ? ' But if such considerations might deter me, a greater
thing is said, ' Oh thou wicked servant, wherefore gavest not
thou my money into the bank, that at my coming I might have
required mine own with usury.' On this account I, unprofitable
trader, presume to offer you, with all humility and respect, those
pearls of the Lord, in order that you may be wise and successful
traders. The sluggard and the ignorant, the reluctant or dilatory
can gain no advantage to himself from these ; I offer them to
you so that by the gift of God a crown that doth not fade may

be given to you, and that I may receive the pardon of my sins through your intercession."

If, he proceeds to say, we consider with an honest and anxious heart our grave responsibilities and the enormous weight that rests upon the shoulders of all priests, it is not a light thing that the Lord through the prophet thunders forth to priests : " Cry aloud, spare not, lift up thy voice like a trumpet " ; and that the apostle says : " Remember, that by the space of three years I ceased not to warn every one night and day with tears." If he never ceased night and day, do we neglect to minister the salt of doctrine to the Lord's sheep ? And so, fearing this, the apostle says in the same place, " I am pure from the blood of all men." From what blood did the apostle say he was pure ? From none other than that concerning which the prophet bears witness, " If thou hast not given a wicked man warning of his iniquity, I will require his blood at thy hand "— the blood of souls, not of bodies. Solemnly S. Paul writes to his disciple, " I charge thee before God and the Lord Jesus Christ, who shall judge the quick and the dead at His appearing and His Kingdom " ; and if you ask of what thing it was that he made so terrible a requirement, the apostle adds, " Preach the word, be instant in season, out of season." What is " in season," what is " out of season," if not that " in season " applies to those willing, to whom a warning must be given ; and " out of season " refers to the unwilling, for on the unwilling it must be forced. Thus, then, I suggest that we ought to fear lest any of our sons witnessing against us in the Day of Judgment say that we did not forbid them unlawful things, nor did we urge them to those that were needful. The apostle says also elsewhere, " Give attendance to reading, to exhortation, to doctrine [1]" ; " do the work of an evangelist [2]." Many names are suitably applied to priests ; we are called pastors, and we are named rulers or bishops. If we are in truth pastors, we ought to provide spiritual pastures for the Lord's flock ; if we are rulers, we ought bravely and strongly so to direct the ship of the Church by the help of God, amid the waters of this world, that we may be able without going astray to enter the harbour of paradise with a direct course. For a

---

[1] I Tim. iv, 12. [2] 2 Tim. iv, 5.

bishop is interpreted to be an overseer, and so, since we have
been placed in a higher position, let us by God's help fulfil, with
great diligence, our office, and always be solicitous for the
Lord's flock, fearing what the Lord says concerning priests and
abbots : " I will require my sheep at the hand of the shepherds."
Since we have been appointed by the Lord to rule the ship of
the Church, so with the helm of the two Testaments, let us
guide her by God's help in such a way that turning neither to
the right hand nor the left, we may be able, in spite of difficulty,
to hold a direct course amid the great dangers of this world.
Just as ships' captains, if they become inactive through much
sleep, or fail to issue right directions to their sailors, quickly
suffer shipwreck ; so also, unless the rulers of the Church,
sometimes by severity, sometimes by gentle exhortation, sometimes even by chastisement, have shown the right course to
eternal life, there will be judgment and not mercy. I ask
therefore, and adjure you through Him whom ye serve, that you
pardon my presumption. For I am quite sure that my somewhat crude suggestions may cause asperity, and generate contempt in scholarly ears. Yet, if any will listen to me gladly and
patiently, and believe in God, He is true and faithful, and will
repay obedience with eternal rewards. By introducing these
matters, I am eager to receive absolution at the hands of God.
I am sure that I shall have no fear concerning these suggestions
before the tribunal of the Eternal Judge, because they have
proceeded from a sincere humility and perfect love.

The inference from this *Admonition to Bishops* is that
they were not above making excuses for the neglect of their
plain duty. Some bishops of that day lived under prosperous
conditions ; they were large landowners, and spent most of their
time " inspecting their property, adjusting rents, exacting taxes."
They gave very specious reasons to justify this way of spending
their time ; it was " in the interests and on behalf of their ruined
churches or hungry poor." Caesarius was not slow to see
through these superficial excuses, and dismissed them with
almost biting scorn : " By all means render an account of your
lands, but this is the work of an hour or two a day ; better lose
some of your revenues than neglect the spiritual interests of

those whose care is yours." As for the poor who are dying of hunger, he somewhat sarcastically suggests the bishops might curtail the expenses of their own table! Some of the bishops, either because they feared these excuses would be insufficient, or because they were too sincere to offer them to Caesarius, said they were "quite incapable of preaching." With regard to this lame and impotent excuse Caesarius tries to show them it is not so difficult if they will be content with simple expositions. If they cannot manage this, they can take patristic homilies as models, and copy them if need be. If this is beyond them, he caustically tells them, they can ask the priests and deacons to do the preaching for them! Five canons were passed, to this effect: (1) All country priests shall receive into their homes young unmarried men to read: and, like good fathers, they must spiritually nourish them, making them familiar with the Psalms, and the Holy Scriptures, and instructing them in the law of the Lord. (2) For the edification of all the churches, and the advantage of the whole people, we give to priests the power to preach not only in the towns, but also in all country parishes. If a priest, prevented by infirmity, is unable to preach, the homilies of the holy Fathers shall be recited by the deacons. If deacons are worthy to read what Christ said in the gospel, why are they judged unworthy publicly to read the expositions of the holy Fathers? (3) Since throughout all the Eastern and Italian provinces, an agreeable and beneficial custom has been introduced of saying the *Kyrie Eleison* more often, it has been resolved by us that in all our churches this holy custom shall be introduced, both at matins, at mass and at vespers. (4) It has seemed to us right that the name of the pope be remembered in our churches. (5) As the words, "as it was in the beginning," are said after the *Gloria*, throughout the East, and in Africa and Italy, on account of the deceit of the heretics who blasphemously say that the Son of God was not always with the Father, but "began to be," for there was a time when "He was not," we also decree the words shall be said in all our churches.

The Synod of Marseilles.

The Synod of Marseilles, A.D. 533, was a gathering of bishops, who were constituted a tribunal for the trial of a bishop on a serious charge, which was proved by both clerical and lay witnesses. He owned to his guilt, expressed his deep regret, and was sent to a monastery. Caesarius the disciplinarian expected it would be perpetual excommunication, but the penitent bishop soon fulfilled his own idea of penance, and before a year was out resumed his episcopal work. But it was the fault of the synod, who seem to have acted very languidly in the matter; and even Caesarius himself was not careful to guard this stringent discipline by specific declaration, and so he was foiled and appealed to Rome. The pope decided to deprive the offending bishop of his episcopal functions. The latter made an unexpected counter-appeal to the new pope, in which he maintained an air of injured innocence, and managed to deceive him to such an extent that the pope wrote to censure Caesarius. Whatever be the merits or demerits of the case in question, it will be conceded that our bishop paid dearly for a mistake of which he was rarely if ever guilty, when he failed to ensure that the "finding of the court" was in due form and order.

Semipelagianism, as we have seen, was the doctrinal question of his age and of his country. Caesarius, though a disciple of Augustine, and largely borrowing from his views and sermons, strongly protested against predestination to evil. He also wrote a work "on grace and free-will," which was sanctioned by pope Felix. In it are reflected his practical zeal and his fervent charity; with much independence of thought, he made use of augustinian doctrine in a way most natural to one who referred everything to God and saw Him in every circumstance of life. It must not be inferred that he was weak and vacillating, for though deservedly lauded as thoroughly representative of broad-minded liberalism, he was a man of most courageous convictions, and never feared to give definite and emphatic witness to them.

The Predestinarian Controversy.

The Second Council of Orange, A.D. 529, is chiefly important from the fact that it is the only one of the councils under the presidency of Caesarius which treats of matters of faith. Fourteen bishops were present. The object of the lay signatories was to show that the canons affected the laity equally with the clergy. Besides the preface and conclusion, there were twenty-five canons on grace and free-will. To these were added three propositions. The preface states the aims and intentions of those who met for deliberation and discussion : " After considering matters of ecclesiastical rule, it was declared that there are some who, through simplicity of heart, are willing to think with too little caution concerning grace and free-will, and not in accord with the rule of the catholic faith. Wherefore, it seems to us just and reasonable that, following the suggestion and authority of the apostolic see, we ought to put forth and sign with our hand a few opinions transmitted to us, which have been gathered by the ancient Fathers from the books of the Holy Scriptures, for the purpose of teaching those who hold opinions other than they ought; after reading which, let him, who has not hitherto believed, as he ought, concerning grace and free-will, delay not to turn his mind to those things which are agreeable to the catholic faith."

The general conclusions stated that, according to the view of the Holy Scriptures, and the definitions of the ancient Fathers, we ought with God's help to preach and believe this, namely, that through the sin of the first man, free-will has been abased and enfeebled to such an extent that no one can now either love God as he ought, or believe in God or do good on His account, unless the grace of divine mercy has prevented him. Therefore we believe that, to Abel the just, and Noah, and Abraham, and Isaac, and Jacob, and the whole multitude of the patriarchs, that illustrious faith of theirs, which the apostle Paul praises, was not given on account of any natural good, but by the grace of God. Which grace also, after the advent of Christ, we know and believe may be possessed by all who desire to be baptised ; not as an act of free-will, but conferred by the grace of Christ, according to what has just been said, and

which the apostle Paul preaches: " To you it is given in the
behalf of Christ, not only to believe on Him, but also to suffer
for His sake," and, " God who hath begun a good work in you
will perform it until the day of our Lord Jesus Christ," and
again, " By grace are ye saved through faith and that not of
yourselves; it is the gift of God."   And the apostle says of
himself, " I obtained mercy that I might be faithful " (he did not
say " because I was," but " that I might be "), and, " What hast
thou that thou didst not receive ? " and again, " Every good gift
and every perfect gift is from above, and cometh down from the
Father of lights," and again, " A man can receive nothing, except
it be given him from heaven."   There are, it was stated,
innumerable testimonies from the Holy Scriptures which can be
produced to prove grace, " but they are omitted for the sake of
brevity, and because to him to whom a few will not suffice, more
will be no profit."

The three propositions were : (1) We believe this also
according to the catholic faith, that all the baptised can and
ought to accomplish by the help and co-operation of God, with
the grace received through baptism, all things that tend to their
soul's salvation, provided they are wishful to work faithfully.

(2)   That some are by the divine power predestinated to
evil, we not only do not believe, but, also, if there are any
who are willing to believe such a wicked thing, we say to them
anathema, with every possible abhorrence.

(3)   This also we profess and believe that, in every good
work, it is not we that begin, and are afterwards aided by the
mercy of God, but that He, without any preceding merit on our
part, inspires us with faith and love, in order that we may
faithfully seek the sacrament of baptism, and after baptism, be
able, with His help, to accomplish those things which are pleasing
to Him.   Wherefore most clearly we must believe that the faith
of that thief whom the Lord summoned to paradise, and of the
centurion Cornelius to whom the angel of the Lord was sent,
and of Zacchaeus who was worthy to receive the Lord Himself,
did not come by nature, but was a gift of divine grace.   And
because it is our wish and desire that the definition of the
ancient Fathers, and our own herein subscribed, may be a remedy

not only for the clergy, but also for the laity, it has been decreed
by us that certain illustrious and eminent men, who have been
present with us at the aforementioned dedication, should sub-
scribe it with their own hand.

Thus did Caesarius stoutly deny predestination to evil.
Moreover, he sent emissaries to submit these decrees to pope
Felix IV, requesting his sanction. It was the latter's successor
—Boniface II—however that received the deputation, and ratified
what was promulgated at this council.

His Style of Preaching.

As a preacher Caesarius was vigorous and practical, knew
his Bible well, was anxious his hearers should understand it, and
was fond of showing the connection between the Old and
New Testaments. If his style was not polished in diction, and
intellectual in matter, it must be remembered that we see him
rather as a country parson speaking to simple rustic folk, than
as a scholar addressing his congregation from a University
pulpit. He was adverse to a too studied style because, he used
to say, there were some preachers whose false delicacy was such
that they were far more afraid to offend against purity of diction,
than to inveigh against purity of morals. There were of course
many in Arles who were educated and refined, but Caesarius is
careful to explain his reason for simplicity. In a sermon on
Rebecca[1] he says, "Let the learned accommodate themselves to the
ignorance of the simple, for if the Holy Scriptures are explained
with that order and eloquence which marks the exposition of
the holy Fathers, then the food of doctrine will only benefit the
few scholarly minds, and the rest of the people will go away
hungry; and so I humbly beg that intellectual ears may be
content to receive with equanimity simple words, so that the
whole of the Lord's flock may receive spiritual sustenance in
plain language. Since the unlearned and simple cannot rise to
the altitude of the scholars, let the learned come down to the
ignorance of the simple, because what will be said to these, the
scholars can understand, but what is preached to the scholars

[1] Migne, Vol. 39, *App. Aug. Sermon* 10.

the simple cannot receive." There is no attempt here to excuse himself, or to hide insufficient talent; he was actuated solely by the desire to be helpful to the greatest number. He even encouraged his congregation to make further enquiry into those points which he did not make quite clear in his sermons. He certainly must have sympathised with the weaknesses of human nature, for he did not unduly try their patience, or render attention difficult or impossible. The bishop was one of those who believe it is better to end a sermon while the people still desire more, than to preach to those who have already had enough. Many discourses of his, which are still extant, would certainly occupy but a few minutes in delivery.

He was ready to make allowances for human infirmities, but would brook no weak excuses. There were no seats in the churches, but he was quite willing, with a most fatherly solicitude, to excuse those who from weakness of body could not stand through a service, but when some gave a too liberal latitude to this privilege, he very quickly and sternly reprimanded them : " Some think they may sit down, though they are quite strong and well." Again if any sought to leave the church before the sermon, they feared to face the severity of his reprimand.

While he impressed upon his clergy the importance of preaching, the younger ones must have felt he was almost one of themselves, and knew their difficulties and struggles in the preparation of sermons. He even went so far as willingly to lend his own sermons, and his brother bishops were not averse to utilising his outlines ! He, in his turn, appears to have borrowed largely from the words and works of others, sometimes to such an extent that with the exception of an introduction and conclusion of his own composition, the complete sermon was borrowed. What a precedent for young preachers who would fain borrow (and then with hesitation) the mere skeleton of an idea, to clothe with the flesh of their own words ! There is just a suspicion of artfulness in the way in which he nicely measured his borrowed discourses to the usual length of his own compositions, and with delightful candour he recommended his episcopal brethren to do the same ! " If the words of the Lord and the prophets and apostles are recited by priests and deacons, why not those of Ambrose, Augustine, or of mine, or of any saint? The servant is not greater than his lord. To them to whom is given authority to read the gospel, I believe it is allowed to recite in church the sermons of God's servants or the expositions of the canonical Scriptures[1]." He was by no means a dishonest plagiarist; he was most careful to preserve to each writer the honour of authorship, either by marginal notes, or by the title of the sermon. When his subject was the charity of which he himself, as we have seen, was so bright an example, he, though generally a preacher of short sermons, scarcely knew when to stop.

In treating of the connection between the Old and New Testaments, he was not anxious to find new and unusual explanations, but to emphasise and enlarge those that were already well known through the work of his predecessors. He was the interpreter of the figurative and mystic, rather than of the literal sense, a follower rather of Origen than of Chrysostom. Choosing as his theme the choice by Abraham of a wife for Isaac, Caesarius thus proceeds : " Here is an actual and literal fact, call it even an historical incident. But what possible interest can so simple a fact have for Christians? To marry and be given in marriage are the common occurrences of everyday life in every rank of society. What then is the mystical and figurative interpretation for us? Abraham is typical of God the Father, Isaac of the prophetic word; he sent his son a long journey to seek a wife, even as the Father sent the prophetic word through the whole earth to seek the catholic Church as a bride for His only begotten Son; Isaac coming into the field typifies Christ coming into the world." But his mystical explanations are never so forced, unnatural or far fetched as some of Origen's; they are brief, exact, clear and sober. He would open with an introduction, the details of which were quite familiar to his hearers; a short explanation would follow, and the conclusion would be a resumé in a practical form, and with a definite purpose. Thus his exegesis is continuous, his exposition plain, and his lesson simple.

He seeks to find Christ in every Old Testament saint; their

---

[1] *Vita*, Bk 1, chap. 5, 41.

very names speak of Him; every incident of deformity, wickedness, ingratitude is a type of those who disown Him; each circumstance of most ordinary occurrence speaks of His ministry. When people come out to mock Elisha, they typify the detraction of Christ. When Laban pursues Jacob, it is the devil persecuting Christ. Jacob's well prefigures the waters of baptism. To enforce his practical lessons, he would see in Abraham a model of hospitality; in Pharaoh's punishment the terrible consequences of delayed repentance. In fact all the sermons of Caesarius are interesting and instructive, picturesque and practical, and provide a most fascinating study. We can only give extracts of one of them by way of illustration. It is a sermon on Jacob[1].

(1) The mysteries of Christ are foreshadowed in Jacob.

(2) Jacob carries a staff, Christ the wood of the cross. Concerning blessed Jacob, we do not read that he went out with horses, or asses, or camels, but we read this only, that he carried a staff in his hand: "With my staff I passed over this Jordan." Jacob therefore had only a staff when he received a wife, and Christ carried the wood of the cross to redeem the Church.

(3) What the ladder seen by Jacob typifies. Jacob slept, and saw the Lord standing at the top of the ladder. "What is it to stand on the ladder, but to hang on the cross?" Consider brethren, Who, hanging on the cross, prayed for the Jews, and do not be ignorant Who it was standing on the ladder that called to Jacob from Heaven. But why was this done on the journey, before Jacob received a wife? Because the true Jacob, our Lord, first of all was on the ladder, i.e. on the cross, and afterwards joined the Church to Himself.

(4) Jehovah standing on the ladder prefigured Christ. What Jacob saw in a figure in sleep, this the Lord predicted of Himself in the gospels: "Ye shall see," He says, "the heavens opened and the angels of God ascending and descending upon the Son of Man." If angels descended on the Son because He was on earth, how did these same angels ascend to the Son of Man, unless because He was in heaven?

[1] Migne, Vol. 39, *Sermon* 11.

And so Jacob slept, and He Himself called to Jacob from heaven.

(5) Preachers are angels ascending and descending. For when God's preachers announce lofty and deep things from the Holy Scriptures, which are not understood except by the perfect, they ascend to the Son of Man; but when they preach those things which belong to the correction of morals, and which all people can understand, they descend to the Son of Man.

In this sermon we see how Caesarius was anxious always to leave an abiding impression upon his hearers and was not afraid to reiterate what he had already said. He concludes then by saying: "In order that what we have suggested above may more tenaciously cling to your minds, let us briefly repeat what has been said; Blessed Isaac, sending his son, is a type of God the Father; Jacob who is sent typified the Lord Christ; the ladder reaching to heaven prefigures the cross; in the Lord standing above the ladder, Christ crucified is shown; by angels ascending and descending on it, the apostles and apostolic men and all teachers of the Church are understood, ascending when they preach perfection to the perfect, descending when they introduce to the poor and unskilled simple things which they can understand.

His Practical Teaching and Church Discipline.

In his *Admonitions*[1] we find mystical exegesis and interpretation, and here he inculcates the duties of a Christian life. In them there is much originality of thought, conception and plan. They reveal his character in no uncertain manner. His exegetical homilies were intended almost exclusively for the city of Arles; these *Admonitions* had a far wider sphere of influence, and possess a more than ephemeral value. They were intended for the common people, crassly ignorant of the most elementary notions of Christian duty; they were, therefore, simple without pretence of learning, and of course eminently practical. Doctrines in

---

[1] Most of these will be found in Migne, *Pat. Lat.* Vol. 39, *App.*

themselves were useless if not made use of; faith is valuable only when it issues in good works. "It is in vain that you swear a thousand times that you have faith, if you have not the will to practise and carry into effect all that you profess with your lips. It is by no means a perfect faith to aspire earnestly after rewards if you live as though punishments did not exist." He calls the baptismal questions "a sacramental dialogue," in order to impress on his hearers the solemn contract made therein with God[1]: "When the bishop asks the candidate, 'Do you renounce the devil and his works?' he offers a contract for signature. When the reply is given, 'I renounce,' you have signed the contract." To emphasise this idea still further, he gives a simple, if startling, illustration from the law courts. "How careful a man is not to violate the terms of a deed which he has signed; he will risk the loss of his goods, and even of his life. Should he not much more fear to violate the terms of his faith before Him who reigns above?"

Those who thought the mere rite of baptism was everything and carried with it no further obligation, were asked, "Who would wish to find himself at death in the same state as when he received baptism?" "Who, if he planted a young vine in his field would wish it to be the same at the end of several years as when he planted it?" "Or, who would wish that his child should be, after five or six years, as weak as at its birth?" Then, with the thought in his mind of what was expected from slaves, he turns upon those who exacted so much from them, and he says, "These slaves belong to us entirely; if they followed us with the most serene protestations of respect and devotion, and yet did nothing we told them, how indignant we should be! Yet we did not create our slaves. But we serve God, Who did create us, in this way."

Ritual.

In the same practical way he treats a piece of ritual. The sign of the cross had degenerated into a superstition, and people degraded its use and made it a mockery. Led away by their lusts and temptations, they would make the holy sign, but

---

[1] Those to be baptised made answer with their own lips.

without the least intention of foregoing their desire. "They shut up the devil within them rather than expel him from them."

Eternal Punishment.

Those who held that sins would be expiated in the next world by temporary punishment, based their belief upon the teaching of S. Paul, " If any man's work shall be burned he shall suffer loss, but he himself shall be saved, yet so as by fire." Caesarius accused them of abusing the text, and of constructing a weak argument thereon ; he also denounced conclusions which resulted from their erroneous view, for since they thought the punishment was temporary, they did not trouble about it. He impressed on them his belief that the fire would be worse to bear than anything one could imagine. He refused to make any assertion as to its duration ; the uncertainty was to him a reason to keep us the more on our guard. He could not have belonged to that school of thought which prides itself upon its absolute assurance of salvation here and now ; but he appeals to the hearts of those who, without being morbid or unreal, only dare to hope and pray that their souls may be saved at the latter day. The Judge and the Judgment Day are ever present to his mind, the sentence is decisive : " It is one of two things, we either mount to heaven, or descend to hell, there is no escape[1]." He would never have dared to say or suppose that a man could not fall after baptism, but he thankfully recognises in penitence the means of repairing the ravages of sin.

Penance.

For glaring sin, such as homicide, adultery, perjury, idolatry, or divination, there must be public penance, of which he gives a most vivid picture. The penitent stood before the faithful for the bishop's reprimand. Clothed in sombre garments, the supplicant is further invested by the bishop with a hair-cloth cloak ; he is then expelled from the church as having no right there until his reconciliation. Made to stand at the entrance of the church, all who enter it can see him. After the duration

---

[1] *Vita C.* Bk II, c. I.

and reality of his penance has been adjudged sufficient he would pass through the ranks of the faithful and prostrate himself full length before the bishop. Prayers and absolution followed. Such was the "ancient discipline" of the Church of which the Commination service of the Church of England speaks.

On the question of the sufficiency of death-bed penitence —a view which was becoming general—and in order to try to set at rest a difficult problem, Caesarius took a middle course between two extremes. On the one hand, Augustine taught that grace acted independently of all human merit, and this teaching conduced to great indulgence and a belief that penitence, at the moment of death, was as completely efficacious as at any time; and on the other, there was the rigorous view that death-bed penitence was valueless. About the date of the *Admonitions* the indulgent theory was popular. Caesarius, with that common-sense which is so prominent a characteristic, seeks for the truth in each view, for surely there is some truth even in errors, and he says[1]: "If any one stricken down by serious illness shows his desire to return to God in tears and sorrow, and offers, though late, a sincere and effective reparation, he will be pardoned; but if any one has lived an evil life, reserving penitence till the end of it, and sins in the hope of getting those sins pardoned as a whole; and if, after having done penance, he does not restore what he has unjustly taken, and pardon his enemies with a good heart; and if he has not the firm resolve, should he live, to do penance with much compunction and humility for the rest of his life; if such an one asked for penance and is of an age when he can and ought to offer it, this can be imposed on him, but I cannot assure him of entire security," and he wisely adds: "God, to whom consciences are known and Who will judge each according to his works, sees in what state of mind he is, and with what contrition he has demanded it;" for my part, I fear this penitent has not perhaps in his conscience what he does not show by his actions. Though Caesarius would therefore admit the death-bed convert to heaven, it would be to a place and honour very different from that reserved for those who have lived throughout their days in the

[1] *Sermon* 256.

practice of Christian duty; in his view these only will possess the kingdom, the others will have only rest; the former a crown of glory, the latter repose; the one will be a king, the other a subject.

The opinion Caesarius held on the general value of penitence is that which is best expressed in the well-known words, "Rend your heart and not your garments." As befitted a practical man, he urged upon penitents that contrition of heart is agreeable to God, and the means suggested to test it were almsgiving, frequent prayer, self-denial, and self-discipline, and he was himself willing to dispense with all that was prescribed in formal public penance.

His Teaching on the Eucharist.

About the end of the 5th century a gross inconsistency was too often apparent between the profession and practice of communicants. The authorities of the Church noted with concern that many who came to the Eucharist were becoming more and more careless of their daily conduct and were guilty of making the Lord's Table a table of devils by their luxury and drunkenness, by frequenting pagan shows, and indulging in auguries and superstitions. S. Hilary of Arles had already lamented that many communicants were eager to leave the church, even before the penitents and catechumens. The Council of Agde, which seems to have feared that the Sacrament would fall into entire neglect, had accordingly enacted that "the faithful" must be in a suitable frame of mind to communicate at the festivals of Christmas, Easter, and Whitsunday, the "three times a year at least," enacted in similar circumstances by the English Church. Caesarius himself was at great pains to instruct the faithful on this serious matter, and in a few very homely illustrations he sets before them the necessity for due preparation[1]. These are well worth reproduction, and are admirably fitted to enforce their lessons on present day communicants.

---

[1] *Sermon* 115.

Church Festivals.

The festival at Christmas suggested to him the brilliant anniversaries in illustrious homes, and all the care and anxiety, thought and preparation which they entailed : "Think, I beg you, my brothers, with what anxiety a great man, wishing to celebrate his own or his son's birthday or coming of age, gives the order several days beforehand that all that is untidy in his house may be made neat, all that is unseemly be got rid of, and all that is necessary arranged. The house, lest it should appear gloomy, receives a coat of fresh paint, the floors are cleansed from their stains, and beautified with flowers. The greatest diligence is employed to insure a joyful heart and bodily pleasure. If then you make so many arrangements for your birthday, what ought you not to prepare for thy Lord's birthday ? " True to his love of reiteration he repeats the same lesson under another form, lest that drawn from the customs of the rich should fail to convey an apt illustration to the poor : " Certainly, if an earthly king, or father of a family, invited you to his birthday celebration, what fine clothes you would be compelled to have, if you accepted his invitation. How many new and clean things you would want, lest the age or other defects of the other ones shocked him who sent you the invitation. See then that your soul, costumed in varied virtues and adorned with pure pearls, presents itself in all good conscience at the festival of the Eternal King, in the nativity of the Saviour Lord."

Thus we find in Caesarius an intense reality. In his idea of worship is no formality or mere compliance with custom, no lip-service or outward observance. Thus he insisted on his idea of public preparation for intending communicants, and a right and proper state of heart and life, and consequently to this end he advocated strict discipline in spiritual exercises.

The Laity and Public Worship.

Neglect of public worship was a subject of complaint in his day, and the excuses seem to have been pretty much the same, in character and futility, as they are at the present time. He says: "I ask you, brothers, if shoemakers and workers in gold, and others are industrious that they may provide necessaries for the body, ought we not to rise before dawn for church, that we may be worthy to receive forgiveness of our sins? If business men are accustomed to be vigilant for money, why are we not vigilant for the love of eternal life?"

Prayer.

He urged his hearers to avoid praying in a loud voice, "for we ought to supplicate God quietly and silently." He warned against wandering thoughts: "Let each one before he bends in prayer put aside, God helping him, all extraneous matters, so that holy meditations can find a place in his heart. He tells them for whom and for what to pray, not only for self but for all, not only for friends but for enemies, that God may deign to grant what He knows to be profitable to the soul; he especially commends the Lord's Prayer, for "without doubt He willingly hears the prayer which He himself set forth."

There was an idea in his time, not unknown in our own, that worship was the exclusive business of the clergy. The laity, with some show of gracious patronage, would keep things going financially. Caesarius teaches them by a clear allegory, in the comparison of the elm with the vine[1]. In this sermon the bishop shows that the elm typifies the rich, and the vine God's poor. The elm is sublime, lovely, yet has no fruit; but the vine, though poor and lowly, is known to be full of fruit. What is the remedy to save the rich from being fruitless and the poor from ruin? The rich must put forth their branches, i.e. their hands, well filled with the fruits of their field, and sustain Christ's poor, in order thereby to escape eternal fire. If they are unwilling to join in the vigils, readings and prayers which are necessary, they are as a barren elm, which bears no fruit to sustain human life.

And in another sermon he says: "Some pay no attention, they are only gazers; when they should incline their head for the blessing, most of them hold themselves as stiff as

[1] *Sermon* 307.

columns. What hinders you from kneeling down? With some it is simply negligence, with others it is pride or an anxiety not to spoil their clothes, or they disdain to bend their head beneath the hand of another man." He contrasts the Pharisee's attitude and Christ's: "He who is mercy incarnate prays prostrate on the ground, and he who is in need of mercy does not even bend." He reminds his hearers—and the lesson is needful to-day—that they should think, not of the unworthiness of him who pronounces the blessing, but of the blessing which God transmits through human lips; they should receive it as heavenly dew and rain. This suggests a simple but excellent illustration: "The rain coming down on a lofty mountain does not delay its descent to the valley, so those who humbly incline to receive the blessing make in some sort valleys, where they receive the rain of divine blessing."

The Observance of Lent.

Caesarius does not strongly insist on the necessity of fasting, but this was partly because the faithful were most particular in its observance. He cannot be accused of objecting to it on selfish grounds, for he was most abstemious in his own life, and most stern in his ascetic self-discipline, but he brought to bear upon the subject that sound common-sense which distinguishes the practical Christian. He allows much latitude and when he says that it is a sin not to fast, it is scarcely more than a very venial one. Here are some of his views: "I say to no one, fast more than you can, I impose upon no one the obligations to abstain from wine or meat if his health does not permit it; true mortification is to abstain from sin and to do God's commandments[1]." To his mind, the best spiritual exercise is that which provokes an effort and denotes progress; he would rather revive in the soul the sense of Christian law than afflict the body with useless prescriptions. He makes his meaning and ideas clear by similes drawn from scenes of everyday life familiar to his hearers. He speaks of Lent as of "a place where the soul's ship, damaged by the world's tempests and sin's tumultuous sea, may be housed for repairs." This would appeal to sailors. "Just

[1] *Sermon* 269, 3.

as at harvest time people gather what will suffice for life's needs, so Lent is a time of spiritual harvest and vintage, when we should put in reserve what will make the soul live eternally." This would be clear to the farmer.

A Distinction between Flesh Meats.

A curious sidelight on the distinction between flesh meats is furnished by the reproof that he administers to hunting men concerning their wrong observance of Lent. Caesarius absolutely forbade the flesh of beasts, but allowed and even advised the flesh of flying things for the sick and infirm. This distinction rested on the view that the flesh of birds is less heavy for the body and therefore less enervating for the soul than that of beasts. Huntsmen, however, thought that the flesh of things hunted was quite lawful, and fell under the ban of the bishop for their opinions, not because they desired to eat forbidden meats, but because a desire for dainty dishes betokened a desire for indulgence. He objected to their hunting all day, only because they deprived themselves and their servants of those spiritual exercises, which were specially incumbent upon them in Lent. "Do you think it fasting," he asks, "when a master makes no attendance at the first day's vigil, pays no visit to sacred shrines; awakened with difficulty, he summons his slaves, who would delight to go to church, prepares his nets, sets off with his dogs, searches the woods, spending the whole day at the chase, alternately shouting or giving mute signals for silence, happy when he finds anything, furious if he lacks what he has never had, so great his ardour that he persuades himself the fast was instituted expressly that he may hunt?"

Here is a piece of counsel, culled from the bishop of Arles, which might, with advantage, be appropriately applied to some in high places, though it would doubtless fall on heedless ears: "Devote to sacred reading the time which the excitement of the game of dice has accustomed you to lose, or which you dissipate on a run with your hounds; discourses on the Holy Scriptures make an intermission to foolish conversation, satirical fooling, and venomous lies."

On Almsgiving.

The duty of almsgiving has priority of place as a Lenten observance; it is good to fast, but it is better to give alms when fasting is impossible; almsgiving will suffice, but the fast will not suffice without almsgiving. There must be no saving money in Lent, to spend on oneself afterwards. To save the expense of the evening fast, in order to use it for the morrow's meal, is to accumulate two repasts. The poor had increased and generosity slackened; it was therefore necessary to emphasise the paramount duty of almsgiving. His practical ability comes to his assistance; there is no indiscriminate charity with him; he considers the whole of this complex problem from different aspects, he examines the foundations of it, he describes the effects, he apportions the amount, and regulates the distribution. Its foundation is the precept of Christ, Who identified Himself with the poor when He said, " I was hungry and ye gave Me meat, I was thirsty and ye gave Me drink, I was sick and ye visited Me." When? " Inasmuch as ye have done it unto one of the least of these My brethren, ye have done it unto Me."

How necessary it is to impress upon people what this bishop said so many years ago, that it is an essential part of the Christian law; everyone that calls himself, and claims to be, a Christian must obey that law, not the rich only, but the poor as well, each according to his means, for the poor will sometimes have an opportunity of giving to a brother still poorer " a glass of water to quench thirst, half of his piece of bread, a shelter in the corner of his hut, or some other act of charity." As for the rich, " What pretext can they give to be freed from a duty which is incumbent even upon the poor ? " Thus, " the hand of the poor is a poor-box which opens in the hand of Christ; nothing of what we put therein is lost, it is a portion of our temporal goods which we send before us to heaven as ransom for our soul."

We are almost surprised to find this last thought in the words of Caesarius. The idea of doing good for a reward, of bargaining temporal loss for eternal gain is so sordid and mean, and indeed provides the scoffer with one of those cheap sneers bestowed on the Christian. Caesarius rises to such a height of idealism in so much of his teaching that we are surprised to find this concession to human weakness. He almost teaches that we may substitute almsgiving for penance. As to proportion, he is, as usual, eminently practical : "When you come to church, bring what you can for the poor; if unable to give money bring wine, or even bread, if only a piece ; let those who can do so, bring new or worn clothing. If unable to do these things let them receive the pilgrim and prepare him a bed." He strongly advocated giving away a tenth, and urged it upon his people with vigorous argument. Aware that it was not binding upon them, he appeals to their sense of justice and reason : "God reserves to Himself a tenth of the goods He has given to you. Is this excessive ? What would you say if God had reserved to Himself nine-tenths ? When he takes from you the greater part of what you possess, it is because you were unwilling to give the tenth, that He has taken away nine-tenths. To those who give the tenth, heaven in return for their generosity, dispenses its dew and its sun in good measure." We should, doubtless, pass criticism, or put a reservation on some of this argument, but the principle is good, and the obligation clear, while the need of proportionate giving is paramount. If each would do his share according to his means, there would be an end to begging calls, advertising appeals, monotonous deficits. Method, thought, discrimination, justice, are the preliminary axioms ; these are the underlying principles of genuine Christian socialism. Individual right is strongly acknowledged and gladly conceded, but individual responsibility is sternly emphasised and justly demanded. To those who pleaded, as an excuse for not helping the poor, that they were engaged in the purchase of land, he vigorously replies, that the very method they employ in doing so is dishonest. How can you buy, he says, unless someone is under the necessity of selling ? The position of things in his day appears to have been curious. There seemed to be something far worse than the excuse to be rid of responsibility for the poor. The desire to purchase land was in itself reasonable and right, but there seems to have been that deplorable selfishness among the rich of that period, to which our own presents only too many parallels.

"Some man covets his neighbour's property, to incorporate it in his own domains ; he manœuvres secretly among those who have power to increase the owner's burdens, involve him in public charges, or embarrass him with debts." The poor man is thus led in his extremity to the very man who is the cause of his trouble, and, ignorant that it is he that has got him into difficulty, says, "Give me, I pray thee, some money ; I am in great need ; a creditor presses me"; but he replies, "I have nothing just now," in order to force a sale. When the man has decided to sell, the hypocrite says, "Although I have no money, I will try to borrow it somewhere or other, to come to your aid as a friend !" It is an odious comedy! Well may Caesarius say, "Woe to him in the Judgment Day; nothing shall save him from the terrible sentence, 'Depart from me ye wicked into eternal fire.' If this is the lot of those who have not given clothing to the naked, what fire, do you think, is reserved for those who have made them naked ?" There are some crimes that, even with Caesarius, cannot be atoned for by almsgiving. Neither the amount of money nor the rank of the giver will have the slightest effect, for God will not allow Himself to be corrupted ; "Almsgiving alone does not suffice to wipe out crimes," and he instances homicide and theft. It is false security to think that when men commit crimes daily they can redeem them with daily almsgiving, imagining that God receives money after the manner of corrupt judges. Caesarius begs his brethren not to misunderstand him, or think, he says, that almsgiving cannot do any good on behalf of sin. That is far from his thoughts. "We not only believe it does good, but we confess it does much good, on this condition, however, that he who gives alms also ceases to commit sins."

Superstitions.

Paganism had left its impression upon the people, especially in the country districts. Such was their superstition that on January 1st, celebrated in a manner that was hateful to the Church, they offered gifts for exchange, to which they attached superstitious ideas of their undoubted virtue as securing good fortune for the whole year. On the eve of this day, they would provide tables, with various dishes, to symbolize the prospect of plenty. To counteract the disorders prevalent at this festival, Caesarius instituted a three days' fast, and at the same time denounced the profanities then in vogue in honour of Janus, who was an idol that was "nothing in the world, yet honoured as a God." Those silly people who to-day believe firmly in certain superstitious customs, may be surprised to know that those who lived in the 6th century held very similar views. They considered some days unlucky for taking a journey. One would think that people who believe in an over-ruling Providence would be ashamed to own to superstitions which belittle it. Because his people acted like "howling dervishes" in order to turn away the evil of the darkened moon[1], Caesarius felt it necessary to explain that the eclipse was a natural phenomenon, capable of a simple explanation. They gave special meanings to a false step, to the flight of a bird, to a chance meeting, or to a sneeze! He sternly denounced recourse to divinations during a time of sickness.

The Lord's Day, and Festivals of Saints.

Concerning the necessity of the due celebration of the Lord's Day, and the festivals of the saints, as days of rest, with freedom from all work, because God said by his prophet, "Be still and know that I am God," Caesarius said: "Those who are taken up with the cares of business set this, God's wish, at defiance. Apostles and holy men decreed the observance of the Lord's Day because our Redeemer rose from the dead on that day; it must, therefore, be honoured and revered on account of the hope of our own resurrection, for it is also considered in the Holy Scriptures to be holy, because it was the first day of the world in which the elements were formed; on it the angels were created, the Holy Spirit descended upon the apostles, and manna was first given in the desert. For these reasons the doctors of the Church have decreed that all the glory of the Jewish Sabbath shall be transferred to it. Let him

[1] *Sermon* 265.

come, who can, to vespers and nocturns, and ask from God the
pardon of his sins.   Let him who cannot come, pray at home,
and not neglect to pay to God his vows."

The foregoing will give some idea of the practical views held
by Caesarius, and of the words used by him to counteract the
evils of his day.   It almost requires an effort to imagine we are
dealing with a 6th century divine ; he seems so very modern.
It is yet another exemplification of the truth that human nature
in A.D. 500 and A.D. 1913 is very much the same.

It was fortunate for Caesarius that in his day the preacher
came in contact with his people, and they never doubted the
authority with which he spoke.   But in any generation, and
under any conditions, it will be conceded that the man who
speaks in language suitable to his hearers, and in a manner that
commands their attention, depicting truths by means of simple
and effective illustrations, and showing their value and efficacy
in the daily life of ordinary men and women, will never have
said of him that the pulpit has had its day and lost its power.
There never was a time when sermons were more needed, and
might be more helpful.   Men are wanted who will fire the
doctrines of faith with the spark of living reality, and who can
make men see, and know, and feel that they appeal to their
reason, and desire to enlighten their conscience, answer their
problems and ennoble their lives, expand their spiritual vision
and silence their doubts.   Caesarius, clear and concise, plain and
practical, has merited the eulogium of his admirers.

The Regula ad Monachos.

The *Regula ad Monachos*[1] consists of twenty-six short and
concise articles based upon the Rule of Lerins.   Its obligations
are emphatic and extensive : " This is the Rule which must be
observed in every monastery, whosoever be the abbot," and
there is no doubt it was promulgated, during the lifetime of
Caesarius, in many monasteries. This and the *Regula ad Virgines*
are regarded by modern critics as too pedantic and minute.
The opening injunction is perseverance, the first condition of

---

[1] Accessible in Migne's *Pat. Lat.* Vol. 57, p. 1097.

monastic life. This was an advance on the discipline even of Lerins, where liberty to withdraw was not absolutely forbidden. There was great difficulty in enforcing a permanent profession, especially upon those of good family, who could not altogether forget their pride of race and would not consent to be treated as slaves. It often happened, to the scandal of the brethren, that these would, therefore, suddenly leave, and stir up a spirit of rebellion. Caesarius accordingly felt that stringent rules were necessary for the maintenance of stability, and although of course no one was compelled to take the vow, yet having taken it, the promise was to be deemed irrevocable. With him there was no excuse for a change of mind; it was a bad sign and showed lack of fervour; absolute poverty is a necessary condition, all private possession was suppressed within the monastery walls. He had already practised what he preached, for he gave up all his own patrimony, he had made a valuation of his goods and divided the proceeds between the monastery and the poor. He exacted the same from others as a guarantee of true renunciation. If they had reached manhood, postulants were only admitted on the production of an act of alienation of their possessions in legal form; if minors, they were compelled, when they reached their majority, to confirm by an act of equal validity the renunciation they had verbally made. He allowed them to choose their own beneficiary, and while he emphasises the claim of their parents and the community they join, he strongly objects to their contributing to the pomp of parents already rich; that was, in his idea, a profanation of the vow of poverty. Again, we shall note the desire on the part of Caesarius to repress individualism, to establish a feeling of fellowship, and foster the spirit of harmony and equality. Thus continuity, poverty, and fellowship are the distinguishing marks of his rules for monks.

The *Regula ad Virgines*[1] has earned special attention as the masterpiece of Caesarius, and is regarded as his greatest work. His best thoughts are incorporated in it; no detail of any importance has been forgotten. It is full of good advice, and is more personal than the *Regula ad Monachos*. It was written specially for the monastery of S. John—one of the first

---

[1] Accessible in Migne's *Pat. Lat.* Vol. 57, p. 1103.

for women, mentioned in the documents of Gaul—and was adopted by other celebrated monasteries. Owing to wars and incursions, women dared not go far from centres of habitation; monastic settlements for them were only possible therefore in or near fortified centres, or in places out of the beaten track of invaders. There was also the ground of expense to be considered as another deterrent. But although, before the monastery of S. John was founded there was no community of women, yet by certain vows made before the bishop they were recognised as holding a position of honour in the Church, and it was their duty to catechise unlearned women, and to take care of the church linen. There were two classes—widows and virgins. The veil was reserved for the latter only. With much pomp Caesarius consecrated the mystical marriage of the virgin with the Church. The first inhabitants of S. John's monastery were spared all anxiety about subsistence by the providence of the founder, but misfortune and disappointment soon came to him. Built at first outside the town, the monastery was completely ruined before it was really finished; but with dogged pluck and perseverance, Caesarius set to work to rebuild it. With his practical wisdom and clever foresight he anticipated the possibility of war in the future; he built in the town a place of refuge for the sisters of the convent.

The monastery being built, Caesarius set himself to draw up a Rule, and it is the first of its kind; others before him had compiled treatises for women, but they were exhortations or sermons rather than rules. It was based upon the general principles of the *Regula ad Monachos*, and was suggested partly at any rate by an epistle of Augustine's[1], though it reflected his own originality and independence of character. There was certainly room for and need of a definite authority and settled restrictions. In spite of the supposed vow of poverty, the women had hitherto enjoyed every possible refinement in tapestry, embroideries, dress and art. Designated "servants of God," they seem to have led the life of the world's pleasure-seekers; discipline was conspicuous by its absence. In the men's monasteries the abbot was a man of high ecclesiastical rank

[1] *Ep.* ccxi, Migne, *Pat. Lat.* Vol. 33.

whose word and command was law, demanding and receiving deference from all; but in the women's convents, the seat of responsible government seems constantly to change according to will of abbot and provost, of priest and bishop in turn. Some bishops when asked to lend their support to a convent about to be erected in their diocese only showed indifference or ill-will. Obliged to seek help elsewhere, the sisters were then the butt of episcopal animosity. At another time the convent would itself forget to approach the bishop to choose a priest, or institute a Rule; this betrayed a great lack of discipline and of desire to obey. Caesarius began as he intended to go on, there were no half measures with him, there was no gradual tightening of the reins of government.

The *Regula* consists of forty-three enactments, more numerous and more detailed than those addressed *ad Monachos*. The first restriction is rigorous in the extreme; not content with demanding perseverance, the sisters must promise never to go outside the monastery; this was the most severe as well as the earliest occasion of such a regulation in the history of monastic institutions. His practical prudence, however, established a series of tests to prove whether the postulants were aware of the vows that must be taken by them. He was not one to believe in and to act upon sudden emotions. Before admission, the mother superior questioned the postulant, made her acquainted with this rule, and invited her seriously to examine her supposed vocation. A time of probation followed, of not less than a year's duration, and, at the discretion of the superiors, might be prolonged. She was confined to the care, during this time, of one of the seniors, to whom she could open her heart and thus be warned against illusions. At the end of this probation, the special habit was adopted, and she was admitted to the school. Thus was spent the transition stage between the world and the cloister.

We are not to understand that all communication with the outer world was absolutely cut off. The visits of the bishop, abbots, or priests of recognised merit were welcomed as joyous events. The sisters were asked to cultivate the friendship of pious ladies, and these on certain days were asked to partake of the hospitality of the community. Caesarius did not forbid the exchange of little tokens and souvenirs of friendship; access to the monastery was not forbidden, and interviews were allowed in the presence of a senior.

The precepts enjoining poverty seem to have been intended to teach discipline and equality rather than privation. What ministered to superfluity and vanity was rigorously forbidden, but not what was useful or indispensable. We have already noted in his sermons for Lent that macerations of the flesh did not enter into his ideas. For the sick there were no restrictions of hours, or of quality and quantity of food. Inequality on the ground of health was alone recognised. There was no lack of work, which chiefly consisted of spinning and weaving. In the matter of dress, everything which seemed inconsistent with sisters of poverty was forbidden, but they might undertake elaborate and costly work for the Church or for individuals; Caesarius in his will makes special mention of a mantle that had been made for him by the abbess Caesaria, and he leaves it to her at his death. He forbade all kinds of paintings in the rooms of the monastery, as inconsistent with his idea of poverty.

The precept that they must know how to read and write is interesting because of its object, which was not only to join in the recitation of the office, but to be able to transcribe manuscripts, and to this work may be traced the preservation of some at least of the documents relating to the ecclesiastical history of Gaul. Work was shared in equal proportion, each in turn would do the cooking, lay the table, and in short do the drudgery which did not require aptitude or special qualifications; none but the abbess and the provost were exempted. This taught fraternity, and was a welcome change in the monotonous routine.

The chief and first necessity in a monastery is authority. Caesarius provided it with much wisdom and considerable tact. Though there was a duly constituted and fully recognised authority at the head, there was a division of subordinate powers; there were chiefs of departments. The supreme head was the abbess, but even her authority was tempered by the opinions of other officials. Her chief officer was the provost, who had delegated powers; there were also the "seniors"—commended to the sisters as "Mothers and representatives of God"—who were responsible for the due obedience to the Rule in their own section. Two sisters with special functions and recognised titles were (1) the *Primiceria*, or "character-former" to whom was entrusted the moulding of the novices to discipline and virtue; (2) a *Registraria* or treasurer, who kept all the household accounts, and the keys. These two acted as inspectors, and had the power to reprimand. There were, in fact, all the officials and servants which the exigencies of a large and well ordered house require—cellarer, laundress, nurse, porter, a surveyor of wool, a librarian. The order and arrangement of the household seem to have been well nigh perfect. The faults that were most severely treated were those that involved a breach of charity or modesty. In the matter of faults of charity, the way was always left open to reconciliation, for if the guilty one asked for pardon this request effaced the offence; if the one offended refused pardon, she became the guilty one. On the question of modesty, the sisters were to constitute themselves mutual guardians. The one who was cognisant of her sister's faults must correct her. But Caesarius was no petty tyrant; only serious faults were to be brought to the notice of the superiors. The confession of the fault, and the voluntary acknowledgment of wrong gave immunity from punishment.

Some corporal punishment, on the authority of Holy Scripture, had already been introduced into monasteries. The rule for women allowed the "forty stripes save one," borrowed from the old penal code, but the pride of those punished was probably more wounded than their shoulders. Caesarius preferred spiritual punishments; the use of the rod, which is specified in his *Regula ad Monachos*, is here replaced by excommunication of different degrees, ranging from exclusion at prayer, or the common table, to complete separation, which is, next to expulsion, the greatest punishment. Caesarius impresses upon Caesaria that she must ease her material and temporal anxieties by frequent reading and meditation. There must be no superiority of mere dignity. She must outstrip those under her authority in virtue also; she must be the first in and the last out from prayer; the first at work and the last at rest; the most ardent at the fast, and yet the most abstemious at the feast, in order that it may not be said of her: "It is all very well for our abbess, with a full stomach, to preach abstinence to us; how can she, from whose lips comes the odour of the good food she has eaten, exhort us to be content with bad?" With another flash of true wisdom, he warned against having favourites, and personal preferences.

With a view to securing continuity of policy and safeguarding autonomy for the monastery, Caesarius enacted that the abbess should be elected by her companions; this was of course to their advantage, and avoided all doubt and difficulty. They were also exempt from all outside interference. In his will, he asks his successor to be good enough to institute as priest him for whom the sisters supplicate. The bishop had a limited jurisdiction; he might bless the selected abbess, celebrate from time to time the functions of his office, and interpose in gross infractions of the canons, but he could not interfere in the nomination of the abbess, or in the discipline within the walls of the monastery. By way of insuring the continuity of it and its privileges, Caesarius applied for a bull of confirmation, and obtained it.

It only remains to say that his Rule gained far more than a local and temporal reputation; it was the groundwork and basis of many others, as well as the inspiration of numberless disciples, who, scattered far and wide, attained, some of them, to posts of importance and dignity, and would thus give to their master's work and influence a wide publicity.

Practical to the last, Caesarius prepares to die, but while strength remains he will see the monastery again and bless its inmates. He speaks words of encouragement to the abbess and her "daughters," words which are received by them with a chorus of sobs. We gather from his will that his first thoughts, as his last, were with the monastery, which is made his legatee. He thinks of and looks forward to its future. There was no idea of nepotism, of family influence, or favouritism with him. Zealously guarding it against the possibility of interference on the part of his relatives, he gave it into the care of the Arlesian clergy in general, and to his successor in particular; he confirms the gifts made by him to it, and he contributes to its up-keep by means of the produce of other lands, the ownership of which is given to the metropolitan church. He died at the age of seventy-three; more than half his life, forty-one years, he had been a bishop. Arles as a city mourned his loss, and he was taken to his burial amid every manifestation of universal respect. His body found a resting place in the church of S. Mary, in the suburbs of Arles, but later was removed to a special oratory set apart for it in the monastery.

In A.D. 873, after his sepulchre had been destroyed by the Saracens, Paulus wrote his epitaph[1], the words of which are given in an old Arlesian MS., and of which we venture to give a translation:

> See here the shrine, restored in marble rare,
> The tomb of father, bishop, saint, Césaire;
> Destroyed by ruthless hordes, a frenzied band,
> Whom waves o'erwhelmed by God's command.
> Rostagnus then, at Arles, was titled lord
> When Paulus' reverent zeal this shrine restored,
> Who now, in choir angelic, with Christ doth stay.
> O Reveréd Father do thou in mercy for us pray,
> That God may wash our every sin away.

A possible Author of the Athanasian Creed.

We have elsewhere[2] ventured to suggest Caesarius may have written the Athanasian creed. The first quotation of it at any

---

[1] Cernitur hic vario renovatum marmore tectum
Patri Caesario, pontificique sacro,
Quod Scelerata cohors rabie destruxit acerba,
Hanc virtute Dei sorbuit unda maris.
Praesule Rostagno hac Arelati sede locato
Cernuus id Paulus strenue composuit opus,
Cui Christus tribuat coelestis praemia vitae,
Coetibus angelicis consociat ovans.
Et nobis, venerande Pater, miserere precando
Diluat ut noster crimina cuncta Deus.

[2] *Caesarius Bishop of Arles, claimed as author of the Athanasian Creed*, Journal Company, Rochester, 1903, and *The School of Lerins*, 1905.

length is made by him[1]. The coincidences of language are a most certain indication that Caesarius was steeped in the phraseology of the creed. There is not a sermon of the many attributed to him, in which is not some phrase reminiscent of it. There is also a remarkable similarity in the statement of doctrine. Taking the words of Caesarius on the Trinity as an illustration, we see more than a mere verbal agreement with the creed[2]. The argument of a common authorship is strengthened by a comparison of the rhythm[3], and no less an authority than Dr Burn acknowledges that the same sort of rhythm is found throughout the writings of Caesarius, and he adds that "the *Quicunque* reproduces in small compass but with sufficient exactness the literary qualities and defects of the Bishop of Arles" (Caesarius)[4].

The Athanasian is the only creed that speaks of "works" as well as "faith." Caesarius frequently lays stress upon the twofold necessity of "a right faith" and of a practical creed which is translated in terms of life. These words may be taken as illustrations: (*a*) "As it (faith) is praised with the tongue, so

[1] *Sermon* 244, *App. Aug. Pat. Lat.* Vol. 39, Rogo et admoneo vos, fratres carissimi ut quicunque vult salvus esse fidem rectam Catholicam discat, firmiter teneat inviolatamque conservet. Ita ergo oportet unicuique observare ut credat Patrem, credat Filium, credat Spiritum Sanctum. Deus Pater, Deus Filius, Deus et Spiritus Sanctus, sed tamen non tres dii sed unus Deus. Qualis Pater talis Filius talis et Spiritus Sanctus. Attamen credat unusquisque fidelis quod Filius aequalis est Patri secundum Divinitatem et minor est Patre secundum humanitatem carnis quam de nostro assumpsit ; Spiritus vero Sanctus ab utroque procedens.

Professor Bergmann maintains this sermon cannot be ascribed to Caesarius. Dr Burn has mentioned that in two MSS. (Cod. lat. 14470, 8th and 9th cent. at Munich, and Cod. A 214, 11th and 12th cent., at Rouen) the first omits the whole ; the second all but the first sentence of this quotation. See *The Guardian*, Nov. 13, 1901.

[2] Cum vero in ipsis scripturis ubi invenis secundum humanitatem minorem esse filium, ibi invenis secundum Divinitatem etiam aequalem quomodo ego tibi adquiesco? At ubicumque minor dicitur filius propter incarnationis mysterium, verum esse profiteor : quare tu mecum non vis credere, ubi filius patri aequalis esse scribitur? Ego enim et ubi minor dicitur credo, et ubi aequalis dicitur credo? Novi enim quid secundum Divinitatem et quid secundum humanitatem fuerit dictum; quia minor non dicitur nisi propter carnis adsumptionem. Tu vero qui in ipso evangelio et minorem et aequalem frequentius legis, quare unum credis, et aliud credere non adquiescis?

[3] Notably *Sermon* 228, *ibid.*

[4] *The Guardian*, Nov. 13, 1901. Dr Burn has also drawn attention to a letter of Caesarius to some monks "on humility," which is couched throughout in similar rhythm.

should it be by the life. Let us see what his duty is who wishes to keep the faith. If he believes faithfully and strives to do good with all his heart, let him rejoice that he holds the right faith[1]." (*b*) "What hope can they who do evil have, when they who do no good shall perish[2]." (*c*) "We can see to what punishment they who do evil will be condemned, when those who do nothing good are sent into fire[3]." Again, in the sermons of Caesarius there is always much recapitulation, as if he desired by a repetition of phrases and ideas, in slightly varied language, to make the mysteries of the faith more intelligible.

For some years Dom Morin pointed to Caesarius as the author[4] but has now "marched over the ruins of his own theory," and suggests that the *Quicunque* emanated from Spain[5]. He is not prepared to say definitely that Martin of Braga is the author, but he hazards the opinion that this creed may be the lost *Regula fidei*[6] of this 6th century archbishop.

Martin, who was born at Pannonia about A.D. 510, had spent some time founding monasteries, and was an intermediary of Christian culture between East and West, and in close touch with Gaul. It is more than possible therefore that he had visited Lerins. Dom Morin notes the remarkable coincidence between the entirely special character of the creed and the terms used by Isidore in his description of Martin's rule[7]. The creeds properly so called begin with personal affirmation of belief

---

[1] *Sermon* 264, *App. Aug.*   [2] *Ibid.* 77.   [3] *Ibid.* 78.

[4] "Le symbole d'Athanase et son premier témoin, S. Césaire d'Arles." *Revue Bénédictine*, Oct. 1901.

[5] Four lectures delivered at Oxford in 1910, and published under the title of "L'Origine du Symbole d'Athanase," *Journal of Theological Studies*, January and April 1911, Clarendon Press.

The claim of yet another possible author has been made by Von Heinrich Brewer in *Das sogennante Athanasiansche Glaubensbekenntnis ein Werk des heiligen Ambrosius*, Paderborn, 1909. Father Brewer fixes the date of the composition of the creed between A.D., 382 and 383 and in his argument he says that belief in the Trinity as a condition of salvation is not found in the works of Ambrose before A.D. 383, but frequently occurs subsequent to A.D. 384.

[6] Isidore (*de Viris illustr.* c. 35) tells us that Martin came from the countries of the East into Galicia (Spain), and on arrival there established a *Rule of Faith*, according to custom, for the Suevi who had been converted from Arianism to the catholic faith.

[7] Regulam fidei et sanctae religionis constituit.

at first in the plural but subsequently in the singular person, but the *Quicunque* confronts us with a *constitutum* or dogmatic ordinance to which "Whosoever will be saved" must submit[1].

Dom Morin has evidently found a fairly long list of comparisons in the *Quicunque* and in other authentic works of Martin, but says "the results appeared so insignificant that I have not thought it to the purpose to reproduce them." With delightful and fascinating candour he proceeds to discount his latest suggestion by adding, "I have discovered some traces, almost imperceptible it is true, that decisively prevent me from recognising in Martin the author of the *Quicunque*"; and again, "I do not hesitate to say that it seems impossible at present to put any name at the head of this famous creed[2]."

Until then more definite conclusions are justified and proved, we venture still to uphold, at least tentatively, the claim of Caesarius to the authorship of the creed, but we do not wish to lay ourselves open to Dom Morin's charge when he says this claim is "suggested, affirmed, and put forth with an assurance that is truly astonishing[3]." It would still seem to be true that the arguments for the authorship of Caesarius are more cogent than for any other author. We cannot but express our satisfaction when, for the honour of Lerins in connection with this creed, we read that Dom Morin, is still able to say that "it will always be true that the author manifestly belongs to the theological circle of Lerins; it is in the bosom of this famous monastery that the future *Quicunque* was chiefly elaborated[4]."

An Estimate of Caesarius.

Modern historians who have studied his character and his doings, like Neander, Malnory, Alliez, all agree in the high estimate they put upon this prince of 6th century bishops.

As a bishop he combined in a remarkable degree, saintliness of character, and administrative ability. Thus in him the practical and spiritual sides of Christianity found an admirable exponent. Among his contemporaries he was, in ecclesiastical

---

[1] See also C. H. Turner's *History and use of the Creeds*, p. 66.
[2] *Loc. cit.* April, p. 358.
[3] *Ibid.* January 1911, Lecture 2, p. 181.   [4] *Ibid.* April, p. 339.

eminence, *facile princeps*, and a biographer says that of all the Gallican bishops he would only yield the palm to Martin of Poitiers, Irenaeus, and Hilary.

There were many points in his character which in all ages have been a source of strength to the clergy, and too often have been lacking. He was a man of considerable tact, able to adapt himself to different circumstances and various surroundings. A 6th century bishop (like his episcopal brother of the 20th) had his troublous times, and there were many watching his actions, eager to report his words, and to enlarge upon the most innocent remark, but he went his way, and spoke, and taught, and worked in accordance with the dictates of his conscience—backed by undoubted learning and sanctified common-sense—in faithful fulfilment of the duties of his exalted office. His energies were by no means confined to the city of his bishopric. When health and circumstances allowed, he traversed his diocese from end to end, and thus saw for himself how his clergy were working. Wherever he went his simple messages to the people always had the same effect; they helped and cheered his hearers and deepened their love and veneration for their " Father-in-God." He on his part rejoiced in thus being able to visit his people : " What father does not frequently desire to see his sons, especially when they are good and faithful ? " was the simple explanation of the ties that bound him to all within his rule and jurisdiction. As an administrator he was essentially in advance of his time in thought, method and ideas. He combined a ready sympathy with an earnest enthusiasm. To his spiritual power was added organising ability ; he welded isolated churches into a Gallican Church. Moreover, he knew and realised a valuable secret for the accomplishment of a great work, that is, he understood that he is the best administrator who can with unerring judgment select his workers, and apportion out to each the details for which the individual is most fitted. To him the three chief duties of the episcopate were teaching, preaching, and reading, and he could only devote himself diligently to these things by handing over to trustworthy subordinates the management of matters of less importance. In short, he had the happy gift of making others work. The foregoing pages have provided many illustrations of his disciplinary zeal and dominating will, more especially in his rules for monks and nuns. "Should the abbot find it necessary to reprimand, none shall dare reply; if he call for the attendance of any, disobedience shall be visited with chastisement," is sufficiently eloquent of his ideas of discipline. It was his master-passion, yet he was loved rather than feared, for in his firm strength of will he did not lose the sense of proportion.

His words come with a living message across the centuries, and they strike home to an English reader with no little force, even though they lack the attractiveness of the living voice. The reason is not far to seek, he was above all things manly. He was well abreast of his time; he understood his brother men; he knew their dangers and difficulties, their trials and temptations, aye, and their subterfuges and excuses. He scorned superstition; he would have no dealings with formalism. He brought everything into the clear light of plain fact. While he was most anxious to persuade and help the laity to join in the offices of the Church, he did not forget to give them an intelligent idea of worship; he was at considerable pains to point out the practical significance of their devotions; it was his invariable custom to inculcate the duties which the acceptance of the Christian faith calls forth.

As then, so now, it is just this that so many need. If in our prayers, our praises, our communion, we could change the lip service into heart devotion, and behind all the formality perceive a grand reality, the world would be better than it is, and our own life nobler. The biographer of Porcarius says, "His happiness would have been greater still if the Lord had revealed to him the services that this son of Lerins, Caesarius his pupil, would render during the forty years of his episcopate." Caesarius, as we have seen, loved Lerins, and the monastery was proud of her distinguished son.

CHAPTER X

A NURSERY OF BISHOPS
HILARY, ARCHBISHOP OF ARLES

We have already said that those gathered round the deathbed of Honoratus desired that he would name his successor in the see whom they might summon to direct the Church and rule the diocese. He pointed, as we have before said, to the prostrate form of Hilary. The two men were bound to each other by the ties of a deep affection dating from the great crisis in the life of Hilary. Born in A.D. 401 of a family accounted among the richest and most distinguished in the province, Hilary received an education befitting his rank, and had time and money to indulge his love for the attractions of a worldly life. It was thus in the midst of worldly attractions that S. Honoratus, his compatriot, wrote letters to him, full of tender compassion and of persuasive exhortation and he left the monastery to return to his old home with the special object of saving his friend. The zeal of the young convert was no whit behind that of his cloistered companions, and at the request of Honoratus he accompanied him to Arles. So great was the impression made by Lerins, so deep the love for its secluded joy, that even his devotion to Honoratus could not keep his thoughts from the island home, and so he returned to it. It was in no spirit of ingratitude that he left his dear friend's side, and S. Eucherius, who addressed to him his *Eulogy of Solitude*, said, "You previously showed a brave soul in giving up your country and your kin to seek the desert's solitude, but you show a braver soul to-day in coming back. Honoratus is not opposed to your return. He loves you much but in his love he only desires your good."

Hilary's next visit to Arles was to await as a last sad duty the "passing" of his benefactor, and to learn that at the early age of 28 he would be called to succeed him as archbishop of Arles. Foreseeing what evidently awaited him, S. Hilary hastened, so soon as the obsequies were completed, to return to Lerins, but the people of Arles pursued him, seized him and took him back to the city. For a long time he hesitated to accept the burden that he knew not how to evade. He asked God to make known to him His will, and soon a white dove, as is related, descended from the clouds and rested on his head. The omen sufficed, and all fear was dissipated by the incident. On the anniversary of his elevation to the see of Arles he pronounced the panegyric[1] on S. Honoratus already alluded to above. From this masterpiece of touching eloquence—greatly admired on account of its graceful style—which no one was more fitted to pronounce than he who had been rescued from the attractions of the world which kept him far from God and against which he felt himself powerless to contend, we give a quotation: "It was for me," says Hilary, "that he returned to his own country, for me that he faced danger and fatigue. He came, nevertheless, and when I, a rebel of God, was the slave of the world, he used every persuasion to lead me back to the love of Jesus Christ. I resisted, but with prophetic spirit he replied, "What you refuse me now, God will grant me." What tears he shed to soften the hardness of my heart! At first I gained a hateful victory, but the hand of God took possession of me. Who can describe the contending wills that disputed for possession? When Honoratus was not there, the Saviour took his part against me, and divine pity aroused by my friend's prayers broke all resistance. Honoratus had conquered. He led me away as a glorious triumph, he hastened to make me taste the sweetness of solitude. He fed me at first with the milk of children, and afterwards with the bread of the strong."

[1] *Vita Sancti Honorati Arelatensis Episcopi*, first published by Genebardus in 1578. Also from MSS. preserved at Lerins by Vincent Barralis in his *Chronologia*, Lugd. 1613. See also *Opera Vincentii Lirinensis et Hilarii*, Salinas, Rome, 1731. It is also given in the Bollandists, Vol. II, fol. xi. The text of the former edition was followed by Surius (16 Jan). See also *Biblioth. Maxima Patrum*, Vol. VIII, p. 1228, Lugd. 1677.

In his new position as bishop, S. Hilary continued to live as a monk, sharing the life of his clergy, and being content, as they were, with a cell. He traversed his diocese always on foot and without shoes even in the snow. He was consumed with love for the poor, and for work.

So different an age as ours may learn something from the attitude of this early monastic school towards preaching, and its value. Gifted with an easy eloquence, endued with extraordinary zeal, and with a great power over a multitude, S. Hilary regarded preaching as one of the most powerful means for the sanctification of the faithful. Like the apostle he sought to be "all things to all men," and so fitted his subject and his style to the understanding of his hearers. He was simple when addressing the unlearned, but as his funeral oration abundantly proves, he could rise to the highest eloquence when speaking to the cultured and learned. Sometimes his sincerity offended the proud, but men who loved the truth applauded him. In the work of a monk-bishop in that hard time, when the battles of the age were being fought out, when Romans and barbarians contended inch by inch for possession of Southern Gaul, he displayed a generous solicitude for the bodily wants of his people. He sold all that he possessed to supply their needs, and gave himself up to manual labour that he might have the wherewithal to succour them. He was an inventor also, for he made with his own hands a machine for manufacturing salt[1].

It would be interesting to examine the views held by S. Hilary on grace and predestination if his certain extant works afforded a sufficiency of needful material. At this time the whole Christian world was, as we have noted, alive with these controversial disputes. These old battle cries are rarely heard to-day, but the history of theological controversy is of great importance for the understanding of any age. From the fact that pope Celestine did not include him among the bishops to whom he addressed his letter on this subject some inference may perhaps be drawn as to the attitude he took in this grave controversy. "We know," says Monsieur l'Abbé Goux, "that

---

[1] Salinas expetens automata propriis manibus et sudore confecerit. *Vita S. Hilarii*, chap. XII.

S. Hilary admiring in all else the teaching of S. Augustine, made some reservations touching the question of grace[1]. This is no doubt a reference to Prosper, but, in this case, the words were, "On the question which was then being discussed, he wished himself to write to S. Augustine," and Prosper adds, "I do not know whether he did this, or with what result[2]." S. Hilary believed in prevenient grace, for on his deathbed he said, "In reliance on the heavenly grace which prevents us we have had to sustain on this earth a struggle which no man desirous of attaining to blessedness can avoid." He believed too in the need of being "daily renewed by the Holy Spirit" for he proceeds: "Our envelope of clay cannot without the grace of God prevail against the power of the devil." He must also have held the view that salvation involved human effort to "work out our own salvation," for he states that "the ambush of the tempter can only be foiled by a fierce combat and an incessant struggle." He does not underestimate the use of means, for "God who sees the poisoned arrows shot by Satan, delivers those who know how to pray and weep[3]." He was clearly then no mere Pelagian, for he recognises that salvation could not be effected without the Divine power and presence. In his sermon over Honoratus, he had said, "Thanks be to Thee, good Jesus, that Thou hast broken my chains, and hast surrounded me with the bands of Thy love." He still maintained that salvation was conditional on human effort. The bands of love will deliver me from the chains of sin, "*if* I preserve them in my heart," that is to say, salvation is not absolutely predestinated.

On two occasions Hilary found himself at variance with the pope. He consecrated a bishop to a see, the holder of which was ill but who recovered his health sometime afterwards. His action is however justified by Quesnel[4] and others. This case is of natural interest to us as it is at any rate the first serious struggle between a Gallic bishop and the pope of Rome. His other dispute with the Roman see was in the matter of Celidonius.

[1] *Lerins au cinquième siècle.*   [2] *Epist. ad Augustinum.*
[3] *Vita S. Hilarii*, chap. xx.
[4] Quesnel, *Opera Leonis*, I, Paris, 1675, where the "Panegyric" is also given.

and it cannot be passed over in silence. Hilary had a general supervision over Gaul, and at a synod, held at Besançon, in A.D. 444 he deposed Celidonius on the grounds that his consecration was invalid. The deposed bishop appealed to Rome. Hilary promptly proceeded there. Leo summoned a synod in A.D. 445 but seems to have been prejudiced against Hilary, for he treated him as though he were the accused and not the accuser, and reinstated Celidonius. Hilary claimed that the decision reached at Besançon must be sent back to Gaul for reconsideration, if it was not endorsed at Rome. His freedom and fearlessness of language were such that, according to his biographer, he used words, " which no layman could utter and no priest hear." Leo appealed to the young emperor Valentinian III, who issued the edict that, " no pretended power should arrogate to itself anything against the primacy of the apostolic see," and he empowered the imperial officers to arrest all those who resisted the authority of the bishop of Rome. Tillemont says of this edict that, " in the eyes of those who love the Church's liberty, and know her discipline, it brought as little honour to him whom it praises, as of injury to him whom it condemns[1]." Hilary was deprived of his metro-politan dignity, Arles was reduced to an ordinary bishopric, and the archbishopric of Vienne was revived. Humiliated and insulted as he had been, Hilary was held in deep respect by the Gallic bishops, and had he lived, it is possible that many of the bishops that favoured Arles might have made it very unpleasant for Leo. Be that as it may, the bishops of the province of Arles consecrated Hilary's successor, and in A.D. 450 Leo re-established the archbishopric there, and deprived Vienne of the honour it had recently received.

Though almost all the works of Hilary are lost, his letter to Eucherius, and his panegyric of Honoratus above mentioned are still extant. A poem *Carmen in Genesim* (written about A.D. 429) in which the creation of the world to the flood is described, is usually printed and reckoned among the works of Hilary of Poitiers, but its style and phraseology suit the time of Hilary of Arles, and by some authorities is declared not to be the work of

---

[1] *Mémoires*, Vol. xv, Art. 20, p. 83.

the former. Another work, *de Providentia*, is a poem also
ascribed to him though customarily printed among the works of
Prosper[1]. It will be remembered that as in the case of Honoratus
already mentioned, his claims to the authorship of the Athanasian
creed are not without support.

Waterland maintains his authorship[2]. His arguments which
have still considerable weight, are so well known that only a
brief recapitulation of them must suffice. " Who more likely to
compose such a creed than Hilary, a celebrated man of that
time, and of chief repute in the Gallican Church ? " is Waterland's
introduction to his claims, and he bases his opinion upon the
words of Livius : " If S. Augustine had come after you, we
should have esteemed him less than you "; words which show that
Hilary was " a man of great parts and capacity, of a neat wit
and elegant style." The opinion of Gennadius is also given[3],
and the statement of Honoratus of Marseilles is specially noted,
that Hilary composed " an admirable exposition of the creed."
The admiration of S. Hilary for S. Augustine, whose writings
he had studied, is also emphasised. His *Life of S. Honoratus*
is described by Waterland as clear and strong in style, and it is
remarked that though he touches but little on the subject of the
Trinity, that little is much like a paragraph of the creed " in turn
and expression." Waterland notes also that S. Hilary spoke of
S. Honoratus as " clear and expressive concerning the Trinity."
On the other hand these arguments are characterised by so
careful a writer as Ommanney[4] as " not convincing," and the
passage quoted " contains too slight a resemblance of expression
with the creed to be made the basis of his argument," and his
only other attempt at proof " completely breaks down on
examination."

Worn out by austerities and work, Hilary at the early age of
forty-eight knew that his end was approaching. Like his master
Honoratus, he desired to say a last word to those who gathered

[1] The " opuscula " assigned to him are given in Salinas (Rome, 1731), see also
Bähr, *Christlich-romische Litteratur*, 1 Abtheilung, p. 32, 2 Abtheilung, p. 338.

[2] *History of the Athanasian Creed.*

[3] Ingenio vero immortali, aliqua et parva edidit, quae eruditae animae et fidelis
linguae indicia sunt. *De Viris illustr.* p. 42.

[4] *Dissertation on the Athanasian Creed*, p. 376.

round his deathbed. "We are nearing the harbour of our rest after having struggled against the princes of this world." With prophetic instinct he foresaw the dangers that would beset the faith, and the evils that his people would suffer at the hands of the Arian Visigoths. "Prepare for adversity," he said, "for, if I am not deceived, a great calamity will befall this city. Preserve inviolate the faith of the Trinity, diligently examine the Holy Scripture, fortify your souls by penitence and work." Shortly afterwards in A.D. 449, he died, venerated and loved by all. The whole city shed tears for this zealous pastor, and the Jews lamented over the loss of the man of God, who, in his charities, thought less of creed than of the degree of misery, and they came to chant a Hebrew dirge at his burial[1], because the Christians were so sorrow-stricken that they could not fulfil this duty, and the pope, through whom the emperor's rescript represented the archbishop as "a rebel against the authority of the holy See and the majesty of the Empire[2]," spoke of him as "Hilary of holy memory." His tomb bore a long inscription, in marble, recalling the glory and the virtues of this son of Lerins, who proved himself well worthy to succeed the founder of the monastery, on which master and disciple alike shed lustre and renown.

[1] *Histoire litt. de la France*, II, p. 265.
[2] *Vita Hilar.* chap. XXII.

CHAPTER XI

A NURSERY OF BISHOPS
THE BISHOP OF THE "VIA MEDIA"

Faustus was among the early disciples who came to find in Honoratus a guide and model in the monastic life. He is sometimes called Faustus the Breton, from his alleged birth in Armorica[1]. If, as almost all writers think, he was born in Britain[2], there is an added connection between Lerins and our own country. He was born sometime between A.D. 405 and 410. He had made a great name for himself by his eloquence at the bar; but readily sacrificing an illustrious future he was content to hide his genius in the obscurity of the cloister. His talents could not be thus hidden, and he quickly became proficient in Scriptural knowledge[3]. When Maximus the abbot was elected to the bishopric of Riez in A.D. 433, his pupil Faustus was chosen to succeed him in the abbacy. Of his 25 years' work in this position we have only scanty details, but we know that he had a dispute with Theodore bishop of Fréjus, in which diocese the monastery was situated, on a matter of jurisdiction. From its foundations there had always been intimate relations between the monastery and the see of Fréjus. Perhaps Theodore

---

[1] Oudin, *De scriptoribus eccles.* Vol. I, p. 1293, says that Faustus came from Armorica, but this name was not narrowed into the equivalent for Brittany till the Middle Ages.

[2] The Benedictines in *L'Histoire littéraire de la France* strongly hold this opinion. It is shared by Tillemont, and by Alliez who speaks of "the celebrated Faustus, originally of Great Britain" (*Histoire du Monastère*, I, p. 66). Avitus in a letter to Gundobad (*Ep.* 4, *Pat. Lat.* Vol. 59, p. 219) refers to him as "British by birth" (ortu Britannicus), and Engelbrecht (*Corpus Scriptorum*, Vol. XXI) considers that Avitus desires by this designation to dissociate Faustus from Gaul.

[3] Mundana abdicat...supernas praedicat disciplinas. S. Sidonius, *Ep.* 9. Vir in divinis scripturis satis intentus. Gennadius.

wished to take away some of the privileges granted to the monastery by Leontius, or the abbot may have sought to extend them. Ravennius, bishop of Arles, desirous of ending the dispute, summoned the Third Council of Arles for the express purpose of deciding it, and invited Rusticus of Narbonne and the bishops of the province to attend. The abbot and monks of Lerins were admitted as interested parties. The council preserved to the bishop all the privileges allowed to chief pastors by the canons, and to the abbot all the rights that were necessary for the government of the monastery[1]. Theodore was asked to forget the past, and to renew his friendship with Faustus, to continue the help hitherto given to the monastery in its needs, and to confirm the rights that Leontius his predecessor had conferred. The right of the bishop to give the holy chrism, and to confirm the neophytes, was acknowledged. No strange clergy were to be received in the monastery without his authority. All the seculars were to be under the administration of the abbot whom they themselves had chosen, and Theodore could claim no right to ordain any of them unless requested by the abbot so to do. Incidentally, we see that the community was, at this time, composed of seculars, who made their own choice of superior, and that the bishop had no part in the election. The happy relationship between the bishop and the monastery was thus re-established.

About A.D. 452, again as successor of Maximus, Faustus was chosen bishop of Riez and showed no sign of a slackened zeal for monasticism. He still visited Lerins ; practised asceticism most rigorously, and was very happy in serving the brethren there[2]. In A.D. 462 Faustus went to Rome to attend a synod, which had been summoned to consider the case of Hermes. It appears that Hermes had been consecrated by Rusticus, bishop of Narbonne, to the bishopric of Béziers but was not accepted there. He, therefore, returned to the diocese of Narbonne and assisted Rusticus in its administration. On the

---

[1] Labbé, *Concil.* VIII, p. 635, ed. 1762.

[2] Sidonius Apollinarius thus describes the severe austerity practised by Faustus at this time: Discipulis servire venis, vixque otia somni, Vix coctos captare cibos, abstemius aevum Ducis et insertis pingis jejunia psalmis. *Carmen Eucharist.* XVI.

death of Rusticus, Hermes was elected his successor, but being still canonically bishop of Béziers Leontius, archbishop of Arles, was asked to give particulars of this intrusion to pope Hilarius. The synod decreed that Hermes should remain bishop of Narbonne but without power to take part in the consecration of bishops[1].

The episcopate of Faustus was a period of revolution in the Empire. Euric wished to conquer Gaul, and in pursuance of this desire first turned his attention in the direction of Arvernia (Auvergne); its people bravely fought to uphold the independence of Gaul. Their bishop, Sidonius of Clermont, fearlessly led processions on the ramparts. The Arianism of Euric excited the horror of the people, and their faith and patriotism displayed itself in remarkable examples of heroism. The Gauls implored the aid of Nepos, emperor of Italy, but his own kingdom had suffered loss in dimensions and in resources, and he was unable to render the required assistance, and sent an ambassador to treat for peace. Faustus took some part in the treaty of peace which was concluded in A.D. 475 between Euric and the emperor, and thus had an opportunity of showing his powers of diplomacy, for with Leontius, bishop of Arles, and another, he was appointed to represent the interests of Gaul. At the first conference, Euric demanded the cession of Arvernia, and Sidonius declared with epigrammatic eloquence, " Our country will be more unfortunate in peace than it has been in war." But courageous protestations were of no avail against overwhelming battalions, and Faustus was compelled to sign the cession.

As so often happens, war brought famine in its train, and the town and district of Riez suffered severely. It was then that Faustus showed such generosity and courage that the misery was considerably lessened by his efforts. In A.D. 481 Euric took possession of what still remained to the Roman Empire in Provence, and Riez also fell into his hands. Faustus was exiled to a distant part of Gaul, probably on account of his writings against Arianism, until the death of the Visigothic king. He resumed his episcopal work in the diocese at the instance of Alaric the new king. In the remaining years of his life, he

---

[1] *Concil.* IV, p. 1041.

frequently visited Lerins. He died some time between A.D. 490 and 493 and his body was buried in the cathedral. In spite of his life of controversy, he was regarded by his people as a saint, and they built a church to his honoured memory. He is venerated as "Blessed Faustus, Abbot of Lerins."

The Controversialist.

The theology of Lerins was a mediating theology and Faustus is a notable example of it. He held the *Via media*, or as he also called it, the *Via regia*, in the great, interminable controversy on predestination. If he calls Pelagius *Pestifer doctor*[1] he stigmatises extreme Augustinianism as "a heathenish fatalism[2]." Indeed he himself says, "It is necessary to keep the middle path[3]." To his mind Augustine and Pelagius were both too exclusive, the one allowed too much to human liberty, and the other too little. Like Vincentius, he makes no personal attack on S. Augustine and speaks of him indirectly, and also, like Vincentius, as *Quidam sanctorum*, and he traces his predestinarian theory to its proper source, S. Augustine's Manicheism.

His Writings.

Now in this controversy the writings of Faustus play no inconsiderable part. They were highly praised by Sidonius Apollinarius who described them as important, in the diversity of the subjects, in the forcefulness of their treatment, and in the order of their arrangement under different titles. They "treat serious matters gravely, and carefully examine those that are obscure and difficult." His discourses are "sometimes gentle, sometimes vigorous, but always elegant and edifying[4]."

---

[1] *De gratia*, Bk I, cap. I.
[2] Hinc fatum cum Gentilibus asserunt, inde liberum arbitrium cum Manicheis negant.
[3] *Ep. ad Lucidum*.
[4] Bk IX, Ep. 9.

The Epistle to Lucidus.

Lucidus had carried this doctrine of predestination to bounds which Augustine himself never reached, inasmuch as his theories involved the complete suppression of the human will. He roundly declared that man is irrevocably predestined from his birth, and he expressed himself, and his doctrines, in extremely harsh and utterly repellent language. Faustus begged him to retract his false views, and for this purpose sent a statement for his signature, containing six propositions which he was asked to condemn and censure. They were to this effect: (1) That man was born without sin, could be saved by his own efforts, and could, without the grace of God, keep from sinful ways. (2) That one who had received the grace of baptism, and then fell away through temptation, perished in the original sin of Adam. (3) That in the foreknowledge of God a man might be predestined to eternal death. (4) That no man who perished had been placed by grace in the way of salvation. (5) That a man made as a vessel unto dishonour can never become a vessel unto honour. (6) That Christ did not die for all, and does not desire that all should be saved. From these uncompromising propositions it is possible for us to see clearly what views Lucidus really held. After some delay and reluctance Lucidus signed the condemnation of them.

Two Books on " Grace and Freewill."

It was then that at the wish of a number of brother prelates, this great thinker of the 5th century, Faustus, undertook his work on *Grace and Freewill*[1] in which he argues like a theologian of a much later period in the history of Christian doctrine. There is no doubt that Faustus believed that human salvation was conditional on the possession of a right will, and on human effort. This is for him *Cooperatio voluntatis humanae*, the " co-operation of the human will," *Labor humanae obedientiae*, the "work of human obedience." Overstatement and exaggeration are avoided. Faustus stands midway between S. Augustine's theory of total depravity and its accompanying total disability,

[1] See *Biblioth. Max.* Vol. VIII, p. 523.

on the one hand, and the maxim of Pelagius, "If I ought,
I can," on the other. He ascribes sovereign grace to God,
and full responsibility to man. He maintains that even
before the fall of man, free-will could not without grace attain
to salvation. He vigorously repudiates the contrary opinion
expressed by Pelagius : "Among other abominable doctrines, he
has endeavoured to assert that man's work can prevail without
grace." Faustus says that his opponent, forgetting the fear of
God, forfeits sanity of judgment when he praises human weakness
too highly, and when he affirms the original and unimpaired
liberty of the will, there are others who assert that the human
will has been altogether destroyed. Midway between these two
conflicting errors, the one that extols grace alone, and the other,
human effort alone, Faustus stands, and he maintains that
although after the fall, the human will lost its original power,
nevertheless it was not entirely destroyed, or completely deprived of grace. There. is an indestructible germ and spark
of good that God implanted within, which, if cherished and
nurtured by man, will co-operate with the will of God with saving
effect[1]. Thus, in his opinion, even the heathen might attain to
the salvation of God.

In the second book[2], the writer says that the four attributes
necessary in the work of the Creator in the creation of man,
are power, goodness, wisdom and justice. Faustus asks his
readers to suppose that each of these in turn addressed the
Creator. *Wisdom* asks : What are we to do? are we to allow
man a free will? We foreknow that he will stray into the
by-paths of sin, and we also foresee that he will convert those
endowments which distinguish him among creatures into instruments of wickedness ; and consequently, if we desire that, in his
case, our work should be permanent we must deprive him of the
power of sinning. But *Justice* answers : Not so! It is not in
accord with our principles that a being, who must be tested by
conflict, should have no opportunity of displaying his strength ;
it is not, I say, in harmony with our principles that he whom we

---

[1] Hic in homine ignis interior a Deo insitus, et ab homine cum Dei gratia nutritus
operatur. Bk I, chapter I.
[2] Chapter x.

desire to glorify, by his voluntary service, should be denied the opportunity and condition on which the glory depends ; that he whom we wish to reward, as a matter of pure grace, should have none of the burden of responsibility for his work laid upon him. Rather (says Justice) let all our associated and allied energies be severally displayed in him, and let us individually put forth our strength in his case.   Let it be the endeavour of *Power* to create an exalted creature fit to dwell among all things visible, and especially in a hostile world.   Let it be the part of *Wisdom* to regulate his life with prudence ; of *Goodness* to aid the contest with evil ; of *Justice* to reward the conqueror.   Let us therefore make man for his good and for our glory ; a creature not under necessity to be good, but one who, while understanding the nature of evil, does what is good in virtue of his own choice. Let us make him a creature to whom goodness is natural and evil unnatural ; who may of his choice be good, but is possessed of the possibility of evil ; who naturally desires the good but may do the evil ; who may voluntarily keep our commandments and need not run into moral danger without his consenting will. Let it suffice that we have already formed creatures devoid of moral responsibility, in the cases of those four-footed creatures and other beasts subject to man, and consequently also incapable of the glory of moral conquest.   Certainly, when we are about to confer upon a creature the dignity of being made in our image, he ought not to be made like the beasts of the field. Let us ask with regard to those creatures that we have made unconscious of sin, devoid of reason, and incapacitated for any of the praise of foresight : " Of what moral advantage is its innocent simplicity to an animal, or its fruitfulness to a tree ? " It is clear that we should not be able to bestow the palm of praise on the man we make if we preserve his nature to him by necessity.   It is therefore proper for us to make him a being subject to conditions, free in his choice, perfect in his reason, under a permissive authority and a declared law, that the keeping of our commands may be the means and occasion of reward, for if he have no scope or permission to do evil, he cannot have the praise of virtue.   If while participant in our kindness he does not also by his own effort and toil hold fast by a praiseworthy integrity, this will not be so much innocence as inertia ; and moreover, reward cannot subsist where there is no precedent merit. He cannot keep his blessings who does not know how to gain them. The gift of grace is treated with contempt where there is no devotion of obedience. Besides, it is a shame when he who bestows reward honours the lazy and rewards the sluggish. Nay rather, let him grow worthy by his own effort with co-operant help, and then with a good conscience he can be happy. For there cannot be complete happiness on the part of the recipient, unless there is personal effort, alongside the generosity of the giver. And besides, unless there is, to begin with, the curiosity of the enquirer into ascertained truths, in what way will the kindness of the bestower bring him delight ?

Thus far *Justice* engages in the conversation and then *Foreknowledge* on her part says : Is it not better not to create the human race at all than so to make him as that it may seem he must inevitably perish ? To this *Goodness* and *Justice* answer : Not so. Are we to be deprived of the piety of Abel by reason of the wickedness of Cain ? Are we to be without justice because there is increasing malice in the world ? Are we to have no Peter because at the same time we have Judas ? " Very well then," says *Goodness* : " Let us make the human race in such manner that it cannot sin." *Justice* to this soon made answer circumspectly : " How can we give to man on earth what we have not given to angels in heaven ? Are we to bestow on human frailty what we have denied to the angels. This is how the case stands. It was the work of *Power* to draw immortal man from nothingness ; of *Wisdom*, to make him partaker of reason ; of *Goodness*, to prepare him for blessedness ; of *Justice*, to render him capable of deliberation before he exercises his will."

" A Profession of Faith."

In a preface or dedication Faustus had addressed his monograph on *Grace and Freewill* to " the most blessed and most Reverend Leontius," then bishop of Arles, at whose request it had been written. The Lyons edition of the *Bibliotheca Patrum* separates the preface from the body of the work under the title of *A Profession of Faith*, but it is only a recapitulation of the contents of the treatise on *Grace and Freewill* and written against those who say it is by the will of God alone that some men are led to life while others are thrust down to hell[1]. It is a stern denunciation of the teaching of Pelagius whom it is necessary to confute, because he unduly exalts the work of man, and maintains the all-sufficiency of man in his weakness without the need of grace. " This he foolishly believed and impiously preached," adds Faustus, who declares that grace must be added to obedience. This *via media* bishop who attacks Pelagius, naturally warns against the opposite extreme of fatalism, which the denial of man's power as a free agent would involve. His work had not the approbation he expected, except from Gennadius who shared the views of Faustus. Pope Hormisdas writing to Possessor excludes Faustus from the number of the Fathers who were to be regarded as judges in the difficulties raised by this doctrine of grace and free-will. " We do not receive him among the number of the Fathers" are his words[2], and he says further, " The writings of a certain bishop of Gaul have not the authority of the works of the Fathers accepted by the Church." The work of Faustus was attacked on every side, notably by Fulgentius, Avitus and Caesarius.

" *On the Holy Spirit.*"

Gennadius tells us that Faustus wrote a book *On the Holy Spirit* in which he shows Him to be consubstantial and co-eternal with the Father and the Son. The same biographer says also that Faustus had written another book against the Arians and Macedonians in which he sets forth the co-essential Trinity, and another against those who say there is something incorporeal in created beings. Gennadius clearly distinguishes these two treatises and mentions that he had read both[3]. The work on the Holy Spirit, which is supposed to be lost, is given under the name of Paschasius, a deacon of the Roman Church[4]. Others

---

[1] *Biblioth. Maxima Patr.* Vol. VIII, pp. 523 seq.   [2] *Ep.* 70, *ad Possessorem.*

[3] Legi ejus et adversus Arianos et Macedonianos parvum libellum in quo essentialem praedicat Trinitatem; et alium adversus eos qui dicunt esse in creaturis aliquid incorporeum. *De viris illustr.* sect. 85.

[4] *Pat. Lat.* Vol. 62.

think it is found in the 23rd homily of those that bear the name of Eusebius of Emesa, or is identical with *A Reply to some objections against the Catholic Faith.*

"*A Reply to Some Objections.*"

The style and reasoning of this treatise are sufficiently similar to confirm this last opinion. The increased spread and power of the Arian heresy was due in large measure to Euric, whose ambition was as great as his hatred of orthodoxy. Faustus had felt it his duty to sign the cession of Arvernia, but he would not sacrifice the souls of the people committed to his care. He raised his voice against Arianism, and it was probably on this account, as we have said, that the Arian king banished him. His battles with west Gothic Arianism won him great respect among his contemporaries.

Faustus had been consulted by a bishop, whose name is not mentioned, on three questions[1], namely, (1) What reply should be made to Arians who said that the Son being born of the Father must necessarily be younger? (2) In what sense was it true that in Jesus Christ the Divine Substance had suffered nothing by grief but only by compassion? and (3) what are corporeal and what are incorporeal creatures? Faustus did not put his name to the reply. Although his treatise was not published, Mamertus refuted it, and confined himself almost entirely to the last of the three subjects. The first portion of this work of Faustus is a defence of orthodoxy against Arianism, and gives an explanation of the difference between the technical theological terms *persona* and *natura* in the incarnation. The obscurity of the terms when rendered from Greek into Latin gave rise to much confusion at times. Faustus maintained that the nature of things and the name of things must be distinguished the one from the other. "When you speak of gold and silver, you do not mean the metal, but the designation of the metal, for gold is one thing in its generic quality, and another in the appellation of the word. So too "begotten" and "unbegotten" are a signification of Deity, and not the Deity itself. The

[1] *Biblioth. Maxima Patr.* Vol. VIII, p. 523.

answer to the second question shows that divinity is subject to
passion, and that it is true, in a sense, to say that anger,
repentance and compassion find a place in God.   He explains
that God's anger is really His justice.   The third subject forms
the second portion of the treatise.   It is metaphysical, and
deals with the nature of the soul.   Now this has been a subject
of discussion by the Church from the first century, the corporeal
hypothesis being the more generally held.   Tertullian, for
instance, declares that "the corporeality of the soul is clearly
manifest to all readers of the gospel[1].

As further examples of this teaching we may instance
Arnobius, the Christian apologist, who in the second book
of his treatise *Against the heathen*, does not think the soul is
of divine origin, and scarcely believes it immortal.   He holds
the curious opinion that a belief in its immortality would tend
to remove moral restraint, and would have a prejudicial effect
on human life, and maintains that what is ethereal cannot feel
pain, and so there could be no punishment by fire.   In the light
of modern controversies it is interesting to note that he seems
to have been an "Annihilationist," for in the same chapter in
which he speaks of Plato's view as "not very far from the truth,"
he adds that souls "are cast into hell, and being annihilated
pass away into everlasting destruction...this is man's real death[2].
In a later chapter Arnobius seems to suggest that those who
uphold the immortality of the soul increase the wickedness
of man, who will not be restrained by fear if he is assured that
his life cannot be cut short by any power: "Refrain from
placing man in the highest rank, since he is of the lowest, for
what man is there who if he hear it taught that the soul is
immortal, will not indulge in all kinds of vicious and unlawful
things[3]."   Also Arnobius the younger, a semipelagian of Gaul,
who wrote an allegorical commentary on the Psalms[4] couples
"infinite" and "incorporeal" as the attributes of God[5] only.

---

[1] *De Anima*, v, 7.

[2] Contrast S. Augustine's "The death which men fear is the separation of the
soul from the body; the true death is the separation of the soul from God.   This men
do not fear." Augustine, *Psalm xlviii.*

[3] XI, 2. 29.   [4] Erasmus attributes this to the apologist, the elder Arnobius.

[5] Solus Deus immensus et incorporeus.

Another example is that of John of Damascus, a great theologian of the early eastern Church, who wrote a treatise on *The Fount of Knowledge*, part of which is an exposition of the orthodox faith as relating to the soul, and contains the system of theology, founded on patristic teaching and councils of the Church, from the 4th to the 7th century[1]. In it he expresses the view that "God is incorporeal by nature, but angels and souls by grace[2]." When he states that angels have an incorporeal nature, he explains it is incorporeal "in comparison with the denseness of matter." He draws an interesting distinction between one material being and another, and says "the human body is composed of the four elements, earth, air, water, and fire, and also of four humours, black bile, phlegm, blood and yellow bile[3]. Man shares in the mental processes of reasoning beings, participates in the life of unreasoning creatures, and has something in common with the inanimate. The bond of unity between man and the inanimate creation is the body composed of the four elements, and in the case of plants, there is the added bond of nourishment, growth, and seed. With the unreasoning animals, there is the community of the appetites of desire and impulse, of anger and the like. Man and intelligent creatures share the reasoning faculty. All this paved the way for arguments in favour of incorporeality, but it was in the interests of a literal interpretation of numerous passages of holy writ that the Fathers contended for the materiality of the soul, emphasising the doctrine of the punishment or reward of the soul.

Faustus declared in favour of this teaching, and the argument of the tractate now under consideration proceeds somewhat like this : Everything created is of the nature of matter, and is

---

[1] There is an English translation of the *De orthod. fide* in the Ante-Nicene Library, Vol. IX.

[2] *De orthod. fide*, Bk III, cap. 12.

[3] In a volume of addresses for a retreat, published by Francis Neumayr in 1755, the author calls attention to the excuses that clergy make for their idleness. "I should like to work but I cannot, for I am indisposed." The phrase *non sum dispositus* is delightfully ambiguous. Neumayr then asks, "Do you mean 'I am not able' or 'I do not like' to work? If you are not able, it means that this inability, which is abnormal, must be due to a change in the solid or in the liquid parts of the body." He specifies the liquid parts as, "Humores, sanguis, phlegma, bilis."

corporeal, but the soul is confined within a body. Following
the examples of Tertullian, Origen and others, he thought the
soul in order to inhabit a body had itself need of a bodily
clothing[1], which, after death, became aerial and igneous, but did
not injure its essentially spiritual nature. The soul is permanent,
leaving the body at death, and re-entering it at the resurrection.
He discusses the eternal punishment of the lower regions, and
developing his argument he asks, "Where can the fire prepared
for the devil and his angels be felt if not in the body?" "Tell me,"
he proceeds, "where matter can attach itself if there be no body,
and if it has brought nothing material with it from the higher
regions. In that case, methinks, you will take some one else's
body into torment[2]!" Faustus maintains that a body is under
certain limitations of space, quantity, and quality, and is subject
to pain. This being the case, how can people say that the soul
is not corporeal, and consider it the exception to the universal
rule of material creation[3]. He who made all things out of
nothing, both fashioned them by His workmanship and endowed
them with material form, and "among these things the soul is
included," is the conclusion of Faustus, who anticipates, as a
possible objection, the argument that an admixture of the human
element renders angels susceptible to pain, and that within this
element the pain is felt, and outside it, loses its force; the
answer is that it is not a matter of locality but of body, which
renders pain possible or impossible[4]. Faustus is quick to see
the conclusion that must be drawn from "this shortsighted and
foolish argument" of his opponent who actually admits step
by step that angels are first incorporeal and then infinite,

[1] Vestimentum corporeum.

[2] Ubi inhaerere concretio, ubi haec ipsa nescio quae colligere se potuit crassitudo,
si secum aliquid corporale de illa coelesti arce non detulit? alienum corpus ad
tormentum portabis.

[3] Quae cum ita habeant, quin corporeum dicunt animum? Ergo anima a materia
universae creaturae excepta esse creditur, quae non est corporea, nec localis est, si loco
non continetur, ergo ubique diffunditur.

[4] This would seem to be the line of his argument. His words are, "Si forte
adferendum aliquis putet quod illa angelicae subtilitas naturae quadam contagione
aeris hujus admixtione collecta, flammis inveniatur obnoxia, ergo in aere solo, prout
ait si aerem est quod ardebit, non in illo, sed extra illum poena desaeviret, sed
absque dubio non aliud est, quam substantia corporis, ubi dominari poterit vis
doloris."

and thus the privileges, attributes and majesty of the Creator are ascribed to created beings[1]. Elsewhere, without making any statement as to their spirituality, Faustus seems to protest against the idea of angels, archangels and human souls being reckoned incorporeal[2].

His views were opposed by Claudius Mamertus[3], who in A.D. 470 wrote a book on the condition or substance of the soul, in refutation of the tractate of Faustus. It is possible and not unlikely that Faustus may only have wished to draw a distinction between the Creator and the creature, for though he had said that angels have a body, he was quite definite that nothing is incorporeal but God[4]. In his opinion, "God alone is incorporeal because incomprehensible and everywhere diffused, for He did not take beginning from any created body of matter[5]."

Letter to Gratus[6].

The fruitfulness of his pen is further indicated by his letter, condemning the teaching of the Nestorians and Monophysites, which he addressed to Gratus, a deacon who did not hold orthodox views on the union of the two natures in the Person of Christ, and was probably a Eutychian. This Gratus had lived the life of a solitary, and had practised such austerity that his mind had become affected, and he imagined that he had revelations[7], and, under this delusion, he composed a tractate in which he maintained that in Jesus Christ, God and Man, there was only one nature. He sent this tractate to Faustus who hesitated to reply to it, because it did not seem to merit any answer. He

[1] Vide quo tendat imprudens loquitur et imperita persuasio, qui incorporeum loquitur et jam incomprehensibilem confitetur.

[2] Licet enim non pronuntiemus nonnullas esse spirituales substantias, ut angeli, archangeli, ipsae quoque animae nostrae, tamen incorporeae nullatenus aestimandi sunt. *Epistle* 3.

[3] Gennadius in *De viris illustr.* sect. 68, calls him "Episcopum Viennensem," and in sect. 84, "Viennensis ecclesiae presbyter."

[4] Nihil ergo Deus incorporeum praeter Deum.

[5] Unus ergo Deus incorporeus, quia et incomprehensibilis, et ubique diffusus; ex nullius enim facturae corpore materiale sumpsit exordium.

[6] *Biblioth. Maxima Patr.* Bk VIII, p. 553.

[7] *Hist. lit. de la France*, Bk II, p. 317.

did send a reply, however, in which he tried to persuade Gratus to relinquish his life of solitude, and to submit himself to some experienced abbot for the better regulation of his life. This letter was couched in language of somewhat severe criticism, but was written in sincere humility and unfeigned charity, and with the frankness of a friend, for he desired to cure Gratus with a bitter remedy rather than lose him by the sweetness of flattery. He did not return the tractate, but advised him to suppress what he had written lest it should fall into the hands of others, who loved his person, and his honour, less than his friend did; and in making it public would only bring discredit upon him through its errors. Faustus shows him that in his unwillingness to say that the Virgin was the " Mother of God," he falls into the error of Nestorius. He reproves him for saying there was only one nature, and tells him that although it is quite true to say that in God there is only one nature in three Persons, yet in Jesus Christ there are two natures in one single Person.

Letter to Felix.

Faustus also wrote a letter to Felix, a patrician and prefect of the Praetorium, who was then under the spiritual guidance of Leontius, bishop of Arles. In it he prescribes three remedies against sin. They are: (1) confession of those that have been committed, (2) fear of the last judgment, and (3) a dread of eternal fire.

An Admonition to Monks.

In this epistle Faustus expresses his strong disapproval of monks who return to the outer world, especially if they retain the monastic garb. He points a moral from the lower creation which sets such a different example: " Birds value their nests, wild beasts love the place where they were brought up." He lays stress also upon the importance of the human will; " Resist the devil by the use of your will, cherish all virtues especially obedience and humility," is his message. In similar words he appeals to the human element in religion. Speaking of ex-communication, he says it must only be used as a last resource.

Faustus also wrote on *Deathbed Repentance, The State of the Soul after Death,* and kindred subjects. Sidonius Apollinarius, his great friend, wrote letters and poems to him, lavishing very flattering eulogies upon his writings.

His Homilies.

Uncurbed passions prevailed amongst men of the world, and society was marked by deplorable faults, while the discipline of the quiet monastic life directed and dominated the minds and hearts of the monks. The homilies of Faustus[1], who possessed great powers as an extemporaneous preacher[2], played no unimportant part in fostering this holy temper. " It is not to repose in false security that you have entered this island," he said, " but that you may make vigorous efforts for self-improvement. Our vigour must show no sign of relaxation, our efforts must be constant, for the warfare is endless, and peace with our enemy is impossible. The foe may be vanquished, but friendship between us can never be established. Our profession compels us to renounce all that this present life offers of consolation and of glory ; the delights of earth are not for us ; our thoughts must be towards the eternal promises[3]." Faustus indicates two great means of securing victory in the struggle ; they are the love of solitude and the spirit of obedience. It is evident that from time to time the attractions of outside work and activities proved a strong temptation to the monks, for Faustus asks : " What more dangerous than to leave the place where the Lord has called you, where he has sheltered you as in a harbour from the tempests of the age[4]? " He warns them of the cruel deception of inconstancy. He reminds them that, even in the shelter of the island home, there is danger that the least negligence and the lightest faults act upon the soul, even as drops of water penetrate the ship through imperceptible fissures. He points out also the force of example in its effect upon others, " How blessed is he whose humility has lowered his brother's pride, whose obedience and fervour rebuke lukewarmness and idleness in others[5]." He lays special emphasis upon the necessity and value of obedience :

---

[1] Twenty-two of his sermons are preserved in *Codex Regularum* and a codex of the 9th and 10th centuries.
[2] Gennadius.   [3] *Sermon* I.   [4] *Sermon* VII.   [5] *Sermon* I.

"God refuses the strength needful for the great work of salvation to those who have not learnt how to obey. The habit of disobedience darkens the understanding and misleads the judgment[1]." He warns them that the soul, which is the slave of its own will and passions, is an exile from God.

He bears touching testimony to the influence still exerted by their pious founder: "Let us remember of what an illustrious father we are the disciples and sons! Let each take what he can of this treasured legacy. One can be heritor of his faith, his sweetness, his simplicity, another of his benevolence and his wisdom. Although this friend of God, so rich in virtue, has taken away with him all his possessions, yet he has left them also to us in their entirety, if we desire them[2]." By such exhortations did Faustus maintain the fervour of the monastery's earliest days.

His sermons on some of the festivals show originality of interpretation, and abound in simple illustrations. Preaching on *The Nativity* he says: "Consider I pray you with what anxiety a great man desiring to celebrate his own, or his son's birthday, gives the order several days beforehand that nothing which is soiled and untidy shall be seen in his house. If therefore we make such preparations for our own birthday, what preparations ought we not to make for the Lord's birthday?"

Caesarius, bishop of Arles, defended honest borrowing of the thoughts of others. He was facile enough even to lend out his own sermons which his brother bishops preached or utilised. He borrowed largely from the works of others. This sermon of Faustus is an instance in point. It is reproduced almost word for word in Caesarius[3].

In a sermon on *The Feast of S. Stephen*, Faustus says: "If any distinction can be made between martyrs, he who is first in time would seem to be chief of all. For whilst S. Stephen was ordained deacon by the apostles, he surpassed them in his blessed and triumphal death, and so he, who was inferior in order, became first in suffering, and he, who was a disciple in rank, was a master in his martyrdom."

There are extant several of his sermons on *The Epiphany*. In one of these, he preached on the marriage in Cana. It is an

---

[1] *Sermon* VII.   [2] *Sermon* I.   [3] *Pat. Lat.* Vol. 39, p. 1973.

example of the Origenist allegorical method. He commences by saying that such as Christ was after His baptism, such was He before it, Lord. He interprets the miracle thus: The marriage signifies our restoration, just as on another occasion the younger son is received with dancing and singing. The six waterpots are the six periods of the world, from Adam to Noah, Noah to Abraham, Abraham to Moses, Moses to David, David to the Captivity, and the Captivity to John the Baptist, during which prophecy concerning Christ never failed. The marriage signifies the joy of human salvation, and it was solemnised on the third day to typify either the Trinity or the resurrection.

The Theological Position of Faustus.

It is not altogether easy to define his theological position with complete exactitude. There is no doubt of his orthodoxy concerning the central truth of the Christian faith[1], but orthodoxy in this case is defined without difficulty. It is summed up in one question, Was Jesus Christ or was He not a creature? The difference between Pelagianism and Semipelagianism is one of degree. It has been quaintly said with some clearness and cleverness that Augustinianism represented man as morally dead, Semipelagianism as morally sick and Pelagianism as morally sound. He was a very definite theologian and a stern and uncompromising adversary of Pelagius. He was equally definite in his views on predestination, which he termed "blasphemous, erroneous, heathen, fatalistic and immoral." He may aptly be described, then, as the *via media* bishop, just such a son of Lerins as we have learnt to look for from the mediating influence of that monastery. These men who were trained in the solitude of Lerins were eminently practical, when they went from its cloisters to face the duties of the outer world; they accomplished with honour the mission entrusted to them. Faustus was no exception. In his own words he did not forget the illustrious founder of whom he was a disciple and a son, and

---

[1] In his *De Spiritu sancto*, I, 2, we find these words: "Credo et in Filium Dei Jesum Christum qui conceptus est de Spiritu sancto natus ex Maria virgine" and "(credo et) in Spiritum sanctum, sanctam ecclesiam, sanctorum communionem, remissionem peccatorum, carnis resurrectionem, vitam aeternam."

he did not fail to manifest some at least of the virtues that he had inherited from the master. He maintained the pristine fervour of the monastery and helped to preserve the savour in those whom God had chosen to be "the salt of the earth."

As has been said of other Lerinensian theologians, there are many phrases in the writings of Faustus that are reminiscent of the Athanasian creed. No one has as yet come forward to champion his authorship. It is interesting to note that in one of his letters[1] Faustus answers a question, raised by Paulinus, as to whether one who held orthodox views would be saved in spite of sins against morality. "In things divine, both believing and pleasing are necessary" is the substance of the reply, and in spirit it is in accord with the teaching of the creed, which inculcates not only a right faith, but a right conduct, for in the words of Emerson "a man's action is the picture-book of his creed."

[1] *Ep.* 5.

CHAPTER XII

A NURSERY OF BISHOPS

LUPUS, THE PRINCE OF PRELATES

Lupus was born at Toul towards the end of the 4th century. He was the son of a wealthy nobleman named Epirocus, but lost his parents in infancy. He was educated by an uncle named Alisticus, and seems to have done full justice to his excellent opportunities. He was closely connected by ties of kinship with great ecclesiastics, for his mother was sister of Germanus, bishop of Auxerre, and he married Pimeniola, the sister of Hilary, archbishop of Arles, from whom he afterwards separated by mutual consent in order to devote himself to the conventual life. He too was a son of Lerins, and another illustration of the wide-spread influence of the monastery. He was only there about a year, but it was long enough for him to gain the esteem of the brethren. Connection with it, even if brief, is regarded as one of the glories of a life-time. Eucherius placed his name by the side of those of Honoratus and Caprasius, and, curiously and quaintly punning on his name, compared him to the wolf of the tribe of Benjamin. The point of comparison is that Lupus the bishop and Lupus the wolf are both alike, vigilant and determined to take possession of their prey[1]. It was not distaste for the religious life that caused him to leave Lerins. It was with a view to a fuller renunciation of the world that he went away for a few days, with the set purpose of selling such goods as he still possessed, that he might distribute the proceeds of the sale among the poor. As he was about to return to the monastery, the people seized him at Macon and acclaimed him bishop of Troyes. Of this method of selecting bishops there are of course very notable examples in Ambrose of Milan, and Cyprian of Carthage. This was in A.D. 427 and he occupied the see for the extraordinarily long period of fifty-two years. Sidonius

---

[1] Reverendi nominis Lupum, qui nobis illum ex tribi Benjamin lupum retulit. *De laude eremi.*

Apollinaris, in a flattering description, calls him "the father of fathers, the bishop of bishops, the prince of the prelates of Gaul, the pillar of virtue, the friend of God[1]." A biographer[2] says of Lupus, "his habits were more austere, his activity less varied, (than Hilary's), he lived a hard life, and the severity of it and the assiduity of his prayers were the ceaseless admiration of his contemporaries. He had moreover a cultivated mind and took an active interest in intellectual development. He was anxious about the schools and educational facilities in his diocese, and gave protection to all who encouraged learning." It has been well said also that his ascendancy struck the imagination of men. The story related by Bede of the visit of this eminent prelate to England sufficiently illustrates the saying that he was one of those singular characters that struck the imagination of their fellows.

The Fathers of Gaul had dealt vigorously with the errors of Pelagianism, and when it spread to Britain, the Christians there made an appeal to the Gallican bishops, who thereupon held a synod, and as a result of this they appointed Lupus and Germanus, bishop of Auxerre, to undertake a mission in defence of orthodoxy. Prosper states that this task was undertaken at the request of pope Celestine. The two delegates, by whomsoever sent, preached and taught, and as a climax met the supporters of Pelagianism at Verulam[3]. The story of this public disputation at S. Alban's is worth noting. The two bishops spoke with such power and eloquence that the advocates of Pelagianism were silenced. The rules of debate seem to have been fairly observed, and the Pelagians given every opportunity of fully stating their case. The tomb of S. Alban was visited by Lupus and Germanus who took away with them some earth still moist with this martyr's blood. The heathens were instructed and prepared for baptism. The help of Germanus and Lupus was then sought in defence of the Christians against Saxons and Picts. The well-known and apocryphal story of the "Alleluia victory" (wherever fought) is attached to the visit and to these

---

[1] *Ep.* VI, 1.   [2] Guizot, *Histoire de la civilisation en France*, Vol. I, p. 93.
[3] Bede gives a very full narrative in *Hist. Eccles.* Vol. I, pp. 17–21, which is based upon Constantius' *Life of Germanus*.

names of Gallic bishops. Bede's summary of their mission is
characterised by sound common sense. The varied miraculous
interferences and interpositions, in the story of the "burning
thatched houses, in one of which Germanus lay helpless with a
broken limb, from which the flames scrupulously held aloof," and
the like do not disturb our judgment when we read what he
says·: "Like the apostles, they had honour and authority through
a good conscience, obedience to their doctrine through their
sound learning, whilst the reward of virtue attended upon their
numerous merits." Whether the *Maes Garmon* is the *Field of
Germanus* in Flintshire, or wherever "Alleluia" may have won
a victory, we can easily believe that the piety and learning of
these Gallic bishops produced a great and permanent impression
in favour of the orthodox catholic faith.

His defiance at the gates of Troyes of the fierce barbarian is
another illustration of the impressiveness of his personality. It
was a dramatic meeting. The all-conquering Hun had marched
through unresisted plunder and rapine on this city. Behind him
were the Roman legions, the Burgundians and the Visigoths.
Behind Lupus was a defenceless city! The man of God
triumphed, and the heathen warrior's arms were powerless
under the spell of this soldier of the cross, unarmed with
carnal weapons. The city was saved, the Hun was impressed.
The latter history of the bishop is not known. He returned to
Troyes after accompanying Attila for a time, but the town had
been deserted, and Lupus retired to the mountains some forty
miles from Troyes, where, his biographer states, he spent two
years, in hope of gathering together the people of the episcopal
city. His efforts were in vain, and he went back again to Macon
where he had been proclaimed bishop.

Two letters of his are extant. There is no record of any
other of his writings. The one was written by Lupus to
Sidonius, who had been a prefect of Rome and became bishop
of Clermont. When Euric aspired to conquer Gaul, Sidonius
had conducted operations on the ramparts against him. It was
at this period of anxiety and unrest that he had written to
Lupus, asking his prayers and council. Lupus wrote in reply :
"Very dear brother, I render thanks to the Lord our God who,

in this weakness and affliction of the Church, His spouse, has called thee to the rank of bishop to sustain and console her. You have gloriously endured earthly wars, and now you can with ardour fulfil the ministrations of heavenly battles. You have honourably filled senatorial rank. Once the master of all you must now be the servant of all. Courage, my old friend and young brother. I do in spirit what I cannot do in body. In Christ's presence I embrace and honour no longer a prefect of the republic but a bishop of the church, who is my son in age, my brother in dignity, my father in merit[1]." This letter made a great impression upon Sidonius, and his reply, written in terms of almost extravagant admiration, is extant: " If criminals may be allowed to do justice to one who is at once the model of morals, the pillar of virtues, how great a debt I owe to you who have been so good as to dress, by means of your exhortations, the wounds of a most contemptible worm ! "

The other letter of Lupus was addressed to Talasius who had been elected bishop of Angers in A.D. 453 and was anxious to obtain some information on liturgical matters and ecclesiastical discipline. With this end in view he had written to Lupus and to Euphronius, bishop of Autun. These specific questions on which he desired advice related to the differences in the observance of the vigils of Christmas, Epiphany, and Easter, and to the marriage of the clergy and other officials of the Church. The reply[2] which is sent in the names of Lupus and Euphronius[3] says, "We have carefully read the *Commonitorium* which was sent to us by the hands of Archontius the sub-deacon, and to which, as you have requested, we are anxious to reply." It gives the method of celebrating the vigils, and points out that lections on the birth of our Lord are to be read on the vigil of Christmas, and lections from various books all of which should contain something prefigurative, or prophetic of the passion, and in addition psalms and lections from the prophets or the New Testament may also be included as a

---

[1] This letter is accessible in the *Spicilegium*, but is declared by Mons. Havet (Article in the *Bibliothèque de l'école des Chartes*, 1885) to be a forgery.

[2] Sirmond, *Concil. Gal.* Vol. I, p. 122, and *Instrumenta (Gallia Christiana)*, Vol. IV, Col. 39.

[3] Beatissimo fratri Talasio Episcopo, Lupus et Euphronius Episcopi pariter positi.

voluntary exercise, on the vigil of Easter, but that the festival of Epiphany has its own particular observance, which however he does not state.

With regard to second marriages, the reply states that the Church allows it for all up to the grade of porter, and that where a priest shall have admitted the rule for his own district, the Church will legally guard it, but that she rigorously excludes exorcists and sub-deacons from second marriages. The reply further states that these particulars have been given in order "to explain the custom of our churches of which there is but one rule, but that for anything which conduces to the honour of God which may be introduced in a district, we will allow it, though we may not imitate it." The writers of the letter say further, "We do not allow those who have given themselves to the ministrations of the Church to contract a second marriage," and it concludes, "if either an exorcist or a sub-deacon, or even a porter comes to such a pitch of folly as to bind himself in a second marriage, he is barred not only from his ministrations, but also from the communion of the faithful."

Lupus is described as the "S. James of his age"; "in no way inferior to Moses"; "a sentinel, from a Jerusalem in no way inferior to the first, watching over the Church of God"; and as "indisputably the first of all the prelates not only of Gaul, but of the world." High opinion of this bishop of Troyes is continually expressed in the epistles of Sidonius. He refers to "the wisdom of Lupus[1]," and in desiring to pay a tribute to Aigan, called him "the equal of Lupus[2]."

To speak of his combination of ascetic contemplation, and practical duty, is but to pay testimony to the common characteristic of the sons of Lerins. His bravery in action, his spirituality in counsel, and the honoured position he held in the opinion of his contemporaries justify his biographer's designating him Lupus "of glorious memory," and cause us to regret that we know so little of the life of this "Moses of a later age," who brought lustre to Lerins.

[1] *Ep.* VII, 13.   [2] *Ep.* VIII, 15.

CHAPTER XIII

A NURSERY OF BISHOPS

EUCHERIUS

The name of this, "the most distinguished occupant of the see of Lyons, Irenaeus alone excepted," is said to be derived from εὐχερής, εὔχειρ, ἀνδρὸς εὐχείρος τέχνη. Eucherius was a Gaul of illustrious birth and rank[1]. He was born towards the end of the 4th century. He held a high position in the civil service of the Empire, and there was every promise of a brilliant and successful career in the world. He is an example of the devout layman retiring from an unsettled world whose turbulence wearied a soul naturally devout. It speaks volumes for the miserable state of the world, when a gentleman of birth and education, nearly connected by birth with one Avitus who, if only for a year, was thought worthy to exchange the position of a private noble in the modern Auvergne for the uncertain and dangerous life of a Roman emperor, and to bear the purple of the West, by thought and study realised the vanity of it and so in the prime of life sought the solitude of Lerins[2]. He had for a long time desired the life of an Egyptian solitary, but affection for his wife Galla rendered this impossible and he remained in Gaul. At Lerins he could find an example of piety, and here too his two sons Salonius and Veranus would under Honoratus and Salvianus have a Christian education, and both in their life-time were made bishops. He and his wife dwelt in a hut, much to the regret of her father, who was

---

[1] Orsus ex senatorio sanguine. Schoenemann, *Biblioth. Patrum Lat.* Vol. II.

[2] Viridis aevi, maturus animi, terrae despuens, coeli appetens. Mamertus, *De statu animae.*

estranged from his son-in-law for some years. On the death of Galla, Eucherius retired to Lerins. The desire for Egypt again possessed him, and he consulted Cassian who sent him by way of reply some of his *Collationes* or reports of his conversations with Egyptian solitaries, and he pays a high tribute to the example of both Honoratus and Eucherius whose sanctity the religious who submit to their direction can with difficulty imitate. He compares them to "two lights that illumine the world by their splendid brilliance[1]." Of Eucherius, the author says, "desiring to be edified by the sight of these noble fathers, he has wished to penetrate Egypt, abandoning a land almost benumbed by the hoar-frosts of Gaul; as a pure turtle-dove he longed to fly to the countries, which the sun of justice illumined, and which brought forth in abundance the matured fruits of virtues[2]." Cassian strove nevertheless to dissuade Eucherius from the dangers of the journey. Shortly after his arrival at Lerins, Eucherius had written to Paulinus of Nola, who replied in most affectionate strain, in which he said, "May the Lord extend to you the blessings reserved for those who fear Him. May you have the possessions of the heavenly Jerusalem, and dwell in the house of the Lord for ever[3]."

His works include *A Eulogy of the Desert, Contempt of the World, Instructions, Principles of Spiritual Knowledge, An Exhortation to Monks, An Admonition to Nuns*, and in the opinion of some *The Acts of the Martyrdom of the Theban Legion.*

To form a fair estimate of Eucherius as a writer, it is necessary to take account of the time and place in which he lived and of the influences at work. The 4th century was for the Church what the times of Pericles and Augustus had been for Athens and Rome, and produced, both in the East and in the West, writers who contributed alike to the defence and to the glory of Christianity. The witness of genius was added to the testimony of martyrdom. The 5th century was different, for although the church still had skilful defenders and lofty intelligences, and could number among her sons many bishops and priests, who without attaining to the oratorical power of

[1] *Collationes*, XI, Preface. [2] *Ibid.*
[3] *Epistle*, Migne, *Pat. Lat.* Vol. 61, p. 417.

Chrysostom, the philosophic depth of Augustine, or the scholarship of Jerome, were not without talent and enthusiasm, but in a literary and philosophic comparison the bishops of the 5th century paled before those of the 4th, and chiefly because the disorders, caused by the barbarian invasions, rendered the chances unfavourable. If it cannot be said that Eucherius lacked opportunities of discipline and learning, yet his advantages were minimised by the decadence of the Latin language and the decay of literary taste.

The *Eulogy* and *Contempt of the World* are first in order and the best known. They affect a subjective character, for they lay bare the history of his own soul, and reveal the deep thoughts and sentiments that inspired him to bid farewell to the world. As he speaks from the fulness of his experience, he teaches us the motives that prompted him to sacrifice the brilliant promise of a worldly career for the sweetness of solitude. He is qualified to give two aspects of experience, for he pictures to Hilary the joys of the desert, and to Valerian the counter attraction that had failed to hold his allegiance. Both writings are circumscribed by their subject, but it is reasonable to infer that he might have risen to great heights, had he been called to treat upon some subject of dogma or history.

On " *Contempt of the World.*"

The treatise on *Contempt of the World and of the philosophy of the age* is asserted with some show of evidence to be the first publication that emanated from Lerins, and is of great interest on that account alone. Its precise date is disputed, but Anthelmi mentions A.D. 430, as there is a passage in it, which alludes to the elevation of Petronius to the bishopric of Bologna, which was in that year, and therefore Eucherius could not have written it earlier than this date. The same passage states that Hilary was still a "religious" when Eucherius wrote to Valerian, and as he was appointed bishop of Arles in A.D. 429 the treatise must therefore be anterior to this year.

Whatever may be the date, its contents are worthy of notice, as they express the despair with which the conditions of the time filled Eucherius. It takes the form of a religious "speech at the bar" and is addressed to Priscus Valerianus, a prefect of Gaul and a relative of the emperor Avitus. Its aim is to break the charm that kept Valerianus from Christianity, and to reveal to him the religious insufficiency of Platonism. It is not known whether the writer's object was achieved. Eucherius pleads before his relative at the tribunal of his conscience. While he tactfully recognises his intellectual culture, he appeals to his religious "sense," and points out the imperfection and deficiency of a morality that is purely human; he reveals to the rich and honoured consul the vanity and nothingness of all the advantages of riches, renown, and material joys that the world gives. They are as nothing in the balances of eternity. Eucherius commences with a touching note of personal affection: "the ties of blood are very strong, when friendship comes to bind them closer." He goes on to say: "My well-beloved Valerian, man's first duty is to know his maker and to consecrate the gift of life to the service of God. We pay much attention to the healing of the body, and the hope of health encourages us in the means which we employ; does not the soul deserve a greater vigilance for the cure of its evils? Salvation, our chief thought, should have all our attention, for it is not only our first interest, but it is our only interest." He writes in the hope of inducing his kinsman to abandon his great wealth, and to follow him into retirement, and with this object, he makes a most tender and passionate appeal: "If a rich and illustrious man desired to adopt you as a son, you would brave great and many obstacles. God, the master of the world and of all things, offers to adopt you. You can, if you desire, receive from Him the sweet name of son. Two things bind man to the things of the earth, the pleasures of fortune and the brilliance of honours. These honours offer only vanity, and there is nothing but misery in this pretence of fortune." He proceeds to give a picture of the instability of worldly greatness: "Kings have lived in greatness and power, they shine beneath the brilliance of gold and of diamonds, their mantles are resplendent in metal that art has woven, their crowns dazzle in the reflection of precious stones, their court is luxurious, their will is the supreme rule of mankind, their simplest words are regarded as laws. Of this pomp nothing remains, these immense riches disappear, and with them their possessors. The remembrance of their famous reign remains but as a fable. What have those who possess empires to carry away with them? Nothing, I believe, nothing beyond the treasures of faith and piety." Eucherius proceeds to remind his friend of Clement of Rome, of Gregory Nazianzen, of Basil, Ambrose, and of others who accepted the yoke of the Lord. Eucherius then proceeds to admonish his friend, " Look around you, raise your eyes to our retreat as to a harbour of security and turn the prow toward our shores. It is the only shelter that is open to us, when we leave the storms of the times, wearied by the tempests by which the world is distracted. It is a refuge for all whose hearts are distressed by the upheavals of the Roman Empire. Here the sailor finds a safe anchorage, a peace that nothing can disturb ; he finds a shelter that the fury of the waves cannot reach." In another eloquent passage, Eucherius exclaims, " Nothing is so magnificent as God. If you are attracted by glory, you will find in Him infinite glory. Have you a taste for beauty, truth, and for what is pure and simple? Nothing is so beautiful, so pure as God. Do you seek abundance? He is rich in everything. Do you love faithful hearts? Who can offer a constancy equal to His? Do you desire to be led by severity or sweetness? Nothing is so terrible as His power, nothing so reassuring as His pity. Do you need consolation in affliction, or a guide in prosperity? From Him alone we receive all joy in good fortune, all alleviation in grief. Reason then demands that you should love Him in Whom the most perfect gifts are found. Riches and all that can charm your heart are not only found in Him, but it is He that is the source of them."

The " Eulogy of the Desert."

This work was in the form of a letter to Hilary who had accompanied Honoratus to Arles, and had returned, with some sadness and misgiving, to the monastery of Lerins.

To the mind of the writer the annals of solitude cover a wide period. They commence with the creation of the first man, and culminate in the life of Jesus Christ Who stands at the head of all the great men of the Bible who had preceded Him. "The desert is the boundless temple of God; it is there that He manifests Himself to His saints. When one man asks of another where divinity dwelleth, the questioner is led into the recesses of a vast desert and then is informed that here is the dwelling place of God." Of the retirement of the Saviour to the desert, Eucherius says, "Was it not in the desert that He fed the hungry multitude, and withdrew to pray, was it not there that He was transfigured, and thence was raised to heaven?"

To Eucherius solitude is a halt in the march towards the true country. In the desert everything is silent, and the soul is drawn heavenwards to God on the wings of silence. It is also "the habitation of faith, the arch of virtue, the tabernacle of charity, the treasury of piety, and the reservoir of justice.' Among the blessings afforded by solitude, Eucherius remarks that Providence shows a wonderful tenderness for the inhabitants of the desert. The children of solitude find their manna, and the Lord dispenses their nourishment in mysterious manner. The desert becomes a home whence nothing recalls the solitary, neither fear, nor desires, nor joy, nor sorrow. The hope of heavenly treasures makes him forgetful of and indifferent to everything that the earth can offer. Eucherius speaks in glowing terms of Lerins, of the holy men he saw there, and of the wonderful virtues of which they were the exponents: "Without doubt I owe great respect to all places of the desert that add lustre to the sojourn of saints, but it is chiefly my dear Lerins that I honour, who in her mother's arms welcomes the sailors who flee from the storms of the world. She is worthy to have found such a father (as Honoratus) who possessed the power of the apostles, and in his face the rays of their glory. What congregations, what families of holy men I have seen there! The sweet perfume of their lives is everywhere exhaled. When we see them in contemplation we may call them a battalion of angels[1]." This book has been highly praised. It has been called "one of the most beautiful works issued from Lerins[2]." Isidore of Seville speaks of its "elegant style and lofty thought[3]."

[1] Chapters XLII and XLIII. [2] *Mons. l'Abbé Alliez*, Vol. I, p. 97.
[3] *De script. eccles.* Chapter XV.

Erasmus places his style "above all the productions of the Holy
Fathers[1]."

" The Instructions."

During his episcopate Eucherius wrote other works. *The
Instructions* is a treatise in two books, written about A.D. 441,
and addressed to his son Salonius. The first book deals with
the difficulties of both Old and New Testament by reason of
obscure texts, and it evidences the author's knowledge of the
Biblical criticism of his time. As an illustration of Biblical
difficulties, he instances the action of the Jews in the crucifixion:
"What crime have the Jews committed, in crucifying the Saviour?
The prophet predicted it, because God foresaw that they would
do it. Let us guard against seeing predestination here, instead
of divine foreknowledge. If anyone is dissatisfied with this
solution of a difficult question, let him tremble with me and say,
'The judgments of the Lord are profound, for these judgments,
always just, are often hidden from us.'" The second book is
only a list of names, the etymology of which the author gives.
The treatise was sent to Hilary for perusal, and he replied, " I
have only been able to read it through once; may the Lord
grant me to study this beautiful work of instruction." Salvian
was able to read it at leisure and he expresses to his friend the
impressions he had formed. He found the volume "small but
full of teaching, and altogether worthy of the author's genius
and piety," and he adds, " I am not surprised that you have
written so beautiful and so useful a work for the instruction of
your fortunate children[2]." Cassiodorus places Eucherius among
the number of those who have laid down rules for the understanding of the sacred Scriptures and whose works he had put
in his own library[3].

" Principles of Spiritual Knowledge."

Eucherius addressed this treatise to Veranus, another son. In
it he desires to simplify the knowledge of the spiritual sense of
Scripture. He points out that the Saviour after having spoken

[1] *Ep. Alardo*, Edit. de S. Eucher., p. 530.
[2] *Ep.* VIII.   [3] Cassiod. *Instit.* Chapter X.

to the people in parable, explains to the disciples the hidden meaning of what He had said. Eucherius follows Origen in drawing a distinction between the literal, moral, and allegorical sense of Scripture[1]. As an example of this distinction, the word heaven indicates to his mind in the literal sense, the firmament; in the moral sense, the heavenly life; in the allegorical sense, baptism. In defence of the lawfulness of spiritual allegory, he mentions the use of such words and phrases as "the eyes of the Lord," and "the hand of God," which cannot be taken literally. This work displays a very extensive acquaintance with the Bible and anticipates many favourite usages of mediaeval mystics and hymn writers.

"*The Acts of the Martyrdom of the Theban Legion.*"

By some critics this work is also ascribed to Eucherius. The manuscript is considered authentic by the authors of the *Literary History of France*, by Tillemont and others. The speech addressed to Maximian by the chiefs of the legion "might appear without disadvantage among those of Thucydides, Livy, Sallust, and Tacitus." This is a high eulogy of the author of the history, whether it be Eucherius or not. Other of his works have been lost, but quotations from them are occasionally to be found.

His Views on Incorporeality.

Faustus taught that angels and souls are corporeal. Eucherius is quoted among the authorities against this teaching when he says : "Some ask how God and man could be united in Christ. They ask the explanation of this mystery which was accomplished once, while they cannot explain what is done every day by the union of soul and body in man. In the same way that a corporeal thing is united to an incorporeal, the body to the soul, to make man, so man is united to God to make Christ. And yet the union of the soul with God, both incorporeal, is easier of conception than the union of the body with the incorporeal soul, which forms the person of man[2]."

---

[1] Corpus scripturae divinae, sicut traditur, littera est; anima in morali sensu, qui tropicus dicitur; spiritus in superiore intellectu, qui anagoge appellatur.

[2] Migne, *Pat. Lat.* Vol. 50, p. 866.

When the people of Lyons needed a bishop, they were not unmindful of the virtues of the sons of Lerins, and they approached Eucherius. He refused their invitation, and assured them that he would not leave his grotto-dwelling. This refusal only redoubled their desire. They took violent possession of him, and as he resisted them, they pinioned him, in order that they might take him to their city. On his arrival there, he was acclaimed bishop, and in his submission, his church believed it saw the great Irenaeus ascend its episcopal throne. At the First Council of Orange held on November 8th, A.D. 441, over which Hilary presided, S. Eucherius as metropolitan of Lyons signed the Acts in the name of all his suffragans[1]. He was described by Mamertus as "by far the greatest of the great bishops of the age," and Bossuet calls him "the great Eucherius[2]." He was bishop of Lyons for twenty years, and died in A.D. 449 or 450.

[1] Ego Eucherius Episcopus subscripsi, sanctorum sacerdotum comprovencialium meorum super his expectaturus assensum. See Sirmond, *Concil.* Vol. 1, p. 605.
[2] Second sermon on *The Conception of the Virgin.*

CHAPTER XIV

A NURSERY OF BISHOPS
SOME MINOR PRELATES

Valerian.

So widespread was the influence of Lerins that, generally speaking, it may be said that the bishops and priests from the cloisters of Lerins and S. Victor formed the educated part of the Gallican clergy and episcopate. " In the fifth century there were," says Fauriel[1], "only two monasteries of renown." Great acts of devotion, and noble characters aroused the admiration of the world. It is practical virtue that regenerates mankind. The monks mixed in society, and inoculated it with thoughts and sentiments needful for its moral renovation. The example of a serious life, which the monks gave to the world, exerted a powerful influence. The people soon learnt where they would find pastors worthy and able to feed and guide them, and so again and again, as we have seen, they came to Lerins. Valerian was a son of this monastery. He had been a solitary, and the monks in a neighbouring place[2] had elected him to be their abbot. Before taking up this position he had written them the *Epistolae ad Monachos* on *The Virtues and Order of Apostolic teaching*, which was based upon the doctrine of S. Paul, and was wise and practical. Later he was chosen bishop of Cemélé, and he took part in matters of interest to the Church at that time. Cemélé was once a large town under the metropolitan jurisdiction of Embrun. At the present time there are only ruins on a mountain near Nice. It had its

---

[1] *Histoire de la Gaule Méridionale*, Vol. I, p. 402.
[2] According to tradition, it was a monastery near Nice.

own bishop up to the time of Leo, towards the end of the 5th century, but was then joined to Nice owing to the proximity of the two places. Valerius was bishop of Cemélé before the union.

In common with other monks of Lerins, he was a Semi-pelagian, although it has been said by those who desire to defend the orthodoxy of Lerins, "There is not a part of the homilies, if we except a passage in the eleventh, that cannot be explained in a Catholic sense[1]." The words to which reference is here made are: "God never abandons the will that is animated by the zeal of religion, and Divine consolations cannot be lacking when the acts of a holy life are found. Progress in the religious life is made by vigilance, but God sustains when there is the spirit of religion. Every effort wavers when the help of God is not implored, for faith is certainly in danger if it is not sustained by Divine assistance. It is ours to will, it is Christ who achieves[2], for as the Apostle says, "For to will is present with me, but how to perform that which is good I find not[3]." "You see then," he proceeds, "that the will to a good action must come from us, but its accomplishment depends on the power of God." This is certainly the Semipelagianism of Cassian and Faustus. There are also other passages that bear a similar interpretation. Allowance is made for the use of the will, when he says, "The Christian religion accepts the assistance of free-will[4]," and again, "All these things operate in us by the power of the Father, Son, and Holy Spirit, which procures perfection for our right efforts[5]."

As a theologian, he follows Faustus and Caesarius in the doctrine of grace, but was not a controversialist. He is best known to-day by his homilies, which apart from their historical value in corroborating Salvian's description of the period, are interesting as illustrating the alliterative and other rhetorical artifices of the Gallican rhetoricians. Until Sirmond in 1612 discovered nineteen of these homilies, the only one known was *De bono disciplina*[6]. In this, the need of obedience in a soul

---

[1] *Histoire Littéraire de la France*, Vol. II, p. 362.
[2] Nostrum est bonum velle, Christi vero perficere.   [3] Rom. vii. 8.
[4] Homily III, liberi arbitrii suscepit officium.   [5] Homily VII.
[6] Sirmond found them in a Corbey MS.

created in the image of God is illustrated by the regulated course of the sun and stars, and of the elements, which all obey His will. In two sermons on *The Narrow Way*, Valerian says that it presents difficulties only to the lukewarm and careless, and he gives the example of two men climbing a mountain, one of them is burdened with a heavy weight, and the other carries nothing but a staff on which to lean. The one weighted with his burden gains the summit with difficulty, but the other arrives there with less effort. Similarly one Christian is overwhelmed by the weight of his sins; another has expiated them by penitential tears.

Preaching on the solemnity of promises made to God, he says it is too often man's habit to make vows when he is in danger, and to neglect them when the peril has been removed. Such conduct is compared to the double-mindedness of Ananias and Sapphira.

In a sermon on *The Insolence of the Tongue*, he points out all the grievous effects produced by a malicious tongue, and the difficulty of healing the wounds that are made by it. He advises silence as the only reply that should be made to injuries thus inflicted, and he says that silence is not less perfect than seasonable speech. Closely connected with this subject is a sermon on *Idle Words*; among which he includes those that are destitute of reason and truth, and which are invented either to provoke laughter, or to proclaim as certainties things that are uncertain. Three of his homilies are on *Pity*. The Saviour, he says, who asks for food and clothing is very near. He is waiting at the door with a multitude of His servants, and there can be no mistake in the choice of one to whom charity may be offered. It will be in vain that we give smallness of ability as an excuse for not showing charity. If it were a question of the purchase of a beautiful house, we should give all necessary encouragement to such a purpose. Nor is there any need for us to enquire whether he who asks an alms is Christian or Jew, heretic or heathen, Roman or barbarian, for how can we know in what part of the world Jesus Christ lives? We must believe He is everywhere. Very practical is his teaching when he remarks that " fine words do not satisfy a hungry man, and advice will

not clothe the naked." He blames the conduct of those who
desire to appear charitable, and put off the poor to the morrow
without the slightest intention of giving anything. " It would
be far better at once to refuse help to the poor man than to
deceive him by the false hope of giving him something another
day." The style of his sermons is clear and simple, without any
play upon words, or forced expressions. It is moreover of
interest to note that Sirmond in his preface to these Homilies
mentions an opinion expressed at the time of their production
in Germany[1], " That their appearance during the struggles against
Protestantism showed the intervention of Providence to confound the heretics."

In the dispute between Faustus, who was then abbot, and
Theodore of Fréjus, concerning the independence of Lerins from
episcopal jurisdiction, Valerian took the part of Lerins, and it is
generally supposed that he was present at the Third Council of
Arles, which amicably settled the dispute. The testimony paid
to Valerian's episcopate is that he strove to fulfil the duties of a
good pastor[2].

Of other names less well known and of less theological
importance we may mention Maximus, bishop of Riez ; James,
bishop of Moustiers ; Salonius, bishop of Vienne or Geneva ;
Veranus, his brother, who was bishop of Vence ; Apollinarius,
bishop of Valence ; and Siffred, bishop of Venasque. The mention
serves to illustrate the practical importance, in the Church life
of the 5th and 6th centuries, of this illustrious monastery. We
do not know how far, if at all, the "output" can be paralleled
by any other.

Maximus.

S. Maximus was among the first who placed themselves
under the direction of Honoratus, the founder of the monastery.
Born about A.D. 388 at Comer, a village of Provence in the
diocese of Riez, which belonged to his family, he earnestly
struggled against his passions by means of prayer and penance,
and by the diligent study of holy books. As a proof of his

[1] Quando in Germaniam allatae sunt.
[2] Arnaldus, *Martyrol. Monast.* July 24.

sincerity and with a desire to show the world that he had renounced it, he made a vow of perpetual celibacy, and devoted himself to the practice and austerity of the coenobitic life. To learn this more fully, he came when twelve years old to Honoratus for his guidance and teaching. Like others he manifested a tender love for his brethren, who, in return, gave him the full measure of their affection. When the founder was called to be archbishop of Arles in A.D. 426, he handed over the command of his monastery to this young "religious," in fullest confidence that it would prosper under his fostering care. As Cortesius says, "he received from the hands of Honoratus the government of the barque of Lerins." The monks found in him all the virtues of his predecessor and, as Faustus testifies, "the spirit of Elijah rested on Elisha[1], and sweetness and humility tempered the firmness of his rule." Dinamius Patricius, the author of his life describes him as "walking all night long through the monastery and its dwellings, seeking the suffering who might need his help, and then he would come to the foot of the altar to invoke God's blessing upon the flock committed to his keeping." On the departure of Leontius, bishop of Fréjus, on a missionary enterprise, the people once again came to Lerins to find a successor to take his office, and they came to the conclusion that he who had been considered worthy to take the place of Honoratus as abbot of his monastery might well be chosen as their bishop. They sought therefore, on arrival in the island, to take him by force, knowing that the prospect of episcopal dignity would fill him with hesitating fear. Learning their intention, the abbot endeavoured to leave the island, but taken unawares he could only seek refuge in a neighbouring forest, where he passed three days and nights. *Nolo episcopari* was in these days evidently much more than a mock phrase. His pursuers sought for him in vain, and returned in disappointment. After the election of Theodore, Maximus returned to his dismayed monks who received him with much joy after a painful suspense in which they despaired almost of his life.

---

[1] *Homil. de S. Maximo,* Quasi Helias ad superna migraturus Heliseo discipulo, sic isti pallium pietatis et gratiae ac praeclara meritorum indumenta tradidit (Honoratus), et in se augenda et in aliis multiplicanda.

Saved from the pressing attentions of the people of Fréjus, he was able to devote himself to monastic life only for a time, for the inhabitants of Riez had lost by death their bishop, and they too went to Lerins to find a successor, and to offer the bishopric to Maximus. Again he sought relief in flight, but this time he bowed to the inevitable. To the sorrow of all the monks he left the island monastery, which he had directed for seven years, in A.D. 433. "Happy," adds Faustus his panegyrist, "is the land that brought him forth, happier still the island that brought him up[1]." He was surnamed "the peacemaker." His stature was great and his appearance majestic. The new bishop was anxious that the monks of Lerins should help to build up his diocese, and with this aim he founded a monastery near Moustiers. A writer[2] tells us that what remains of the city of Moustiers is almost all built upon a hill where are to be seen some curious grottos which would serve as cells or retreats, into which Maximus transferred some monks from Lerins.

When it was revealed to this bishop that the day of his death was approaching, he paid a visit to the home of his childhood, and then prepared to die. The date of his death cannot be accurately determined. He lived to a great age. The inhabitants of his early home hoped to watch over his body, but the people of Riez took possession of his remains. Several churches made him their patron saint. After paying their last tributes, they sought his successor, and their thoughts once again were turned to Lerins, where they found what they desired in Faustus, who had succeeded their dead bishop as abbot of the monastery.

James, Bishop of Moustiers.

When Hilary had been constrained to leave Arles and to return to his much loved Lerins, Honoratus summoned to his side James one of his first disciples, and made him his secretary. But he did not enjoy his services for long. He surrendered him to the desires of a people that longed to receive the message of the gospel. The country was "mountainous and inaccessible

[1] Faustus, *De S. Maximo.*
[2] Jean Solome, *Mémoire historique sur la ville de Moustiers.*

almost always buried beneath the snow." Its inhabitants had not been visited by apostolic men, and they envied their neighbours who had enjoyed the light of faith. They therefore sent a deputation to Arles to beg that Honoratus would send some one to preach to them the gospel. James was promptly sent, and so well did he carry out the mission entrusted to him that in a short time he converted the whole province, and established a bishopric at Moustiers.

Veranus.

Veranus was called to be bishop of Vence. Some say he succeeded Eucherius his father in the bishopric of Lyons, but his name does not appear in the list of bishops of this see, which has come down to us from the middle of the 9th century. The list is preserved at Autun, but formerly belonged to the church of Lyons. There is another under the title of, "The names of the bishops of Lyons from the beginning" by Hagues de Flavigny, taken from the preceding list with some alterations. The third is a modern copy of the 17th century, in the library of Lyons. While these three show a general tendency to similarity they agree absolutely in one particular respect. They all interpolate the names of Salonius and Veranus. The interpolation is of ancient date and Duchesne presumes that some one put these names in the margin opposite the name of Eucherius their father, and they passed from the margin into the text[1]. Veranus wrote to Leo concerning the fresh heresy on the doctrine of Christ's person, started by Eutyches, who held that the divine and human natures of Christ, after their union, became so blended together as to form but one nature. Eutyches had been abbot of a monastery near Constantinople and had been a zealous opponent of Nestorius. He was destined to give his name to a heresy which produced a much longer controversy, and a more disastrous schism. The full history must, of course, be sought in histories of Christian doctrine. Domnus, the bishop of Antioch, complained to Flavian. At a meeting of the local synod at Constantinople, Eusebius of

---

[1] Duchesne, *Fastes Epis.* Vol. II, p. 161.

Dorylaeum denounced Eutyches as a heretic. Flavian did his best to dissuade Eusebius from prosecuting the charge, but being unsuccessful, he allowed investigation to be made. Eutyches was cited to a council, and at first refused to present himself. When he did appear, with attendant monks and soldiers, his answers were not regarded as straightforward or satisfactory, and he was deprived and deposed. His monks would not desert him and were put under an interdict by Flavian. Dioscorus admitted him to communion. Leo, bishop of Rome, wrote to Flavian complaining that he had not been informed, but received a satisfactory explanation of the delay. A council was summoned to meet at Ephesus in A.D. 449, at which 126 bishops were present. Leo himself did not attend, but sent by the hand of three representatives a great dogmatic letter to Flavian, bishop of Constantinople, known as the famous "Tome of Leo[1]," in which he treated with intellectual acuteness this intricate dispute. In this monumental work Leo expounded the doctrine of the two natures with singular clearness and detail. It is well known that the proceedings of the council called the Latrocinium were most violent and disorderly and Dioscorus, who was president, tried to prevent the letter being read and it was, in fact, practically suppressed. He pronounced sentence against Flavian and Eusebius. Leo declared the proceedings invalid. He sent a copy of his letter to Flavian to the bishops of Gaul addressed to Ravennius, archbishop of Arles. They received it with great joy, and in reply acknowledged the providence of God which had permitted the heresy which had been so long nourished in secret, to be brought to light. Veranus in conjunction with his brother Salonius, and another bishop named Ceretius made a copy of this letter to Flavian, and wrote to Leo to thank him for having "enriched them with such treasure," and asking him to correct any mistakes or to make any additions he thought necessary, in order that the bishops and laity throughout Gaul might see it[2].

---

[1] *Select sermons of Leo the Great on the Incarnation, with the twenty-eighth epistle called the "Tome."* Translated with notes by Wm. Bright, D.D., J. Masters & Co., London, 1886.

[2] Migne, *Pat. Lat.* Vol. 54, p. 887.

Veranus was evidently a theologian of some repute. That he was regarded as a man of considerable power and influence may be gathered from the fact that he was deputed to enquire into and to determine several controversies of local importance in the Gallic Church. Pope Hilary wrote to ask Veranus, Leontius and Victurus to make themselves acquainted with the dispute that there was between Ingenuus, bishop of Embrun, and Auxanius, bishop of Aix[1]. Veranus must have had some previous correspondence with him, for he refers to his letter. We have already said that the Churches of Nice and Cemélé had been united into one see. Auxanius had evidently separated them. "Moved by a sense of justice," Hilary expresses unwillingness that the privileges of Churches, always enjoyed, should be disturbed. He concludes: "Let our brother Ingenuus have authority in his own province, let none of the Church's law be damaged." Auxanius had resolved that the province of Embrun should be subject to his episcopal jurisdiction[2]. The two places were again to be united. Hilary also asked Veranus and other bishops to investigate by means of a synod the reasons why Mamertus, bishop of Vienne, had without permission of the Roman see consecrated a bishop of Diez in the province of Arles. Veranus took the lead in this synod. A satisfactory reason was evidently given, for Hilary wrote to Leontius and the bishops, who had assembled at the synod, to say Mamertus would not be punished unless he continued to injure the archbishopric of Arles, in which case he would lose the four dioceses that had been added to Vienne for the purpose of its constitution into an archbishopric. As Dr Holmes so well says, "As we look back on the policy of the bishops of Rome, we cannot but allow the wisdom of much which they insisted on." Only a strong outside power could have created the archbishopric of Arles against the opposition of Narbonne and Vienne. But moral influence alone was not what would satisfy the ancient spirit of Rome. She must have the power to command, and her recourse to the emperors for secular powers deprived her of much of that moral influence which she had formerly exercised. If she did not threaten, yet the bishops of Gaul knew that they dare not

[1] Migne, *Pat. Lat.* Vol. 58, pp. 20, 28.   [2] Per obreptionem impenetraverat.

disobey, and the humiliation of wise and saintly men like Hilary of Arles and Mamertus of Vienne may have satisfied the pride of Rome, but it lost her much of the reverence which formerly had been shown. Gaul gained by the help which Rome afforded, but her devotion towards the successors of S. Peter was no longer the same[1]."

Veranus, who had been consecrated bishop by S. Hilary of Arles in A.D. 442, wisely administered his diocese, manifesting a spirit of piety that had been matured within the sheltered cloisters of Lerins. He died peacefully among his people, and his mortal remains are preserved in his episcopal city. According to a biographer[2], he was buried in a marble sepulchre, which was erected against the wall of his church, and to-day serves as an altar in his chapel. His remains were, after a thousand years, removed from this tomb and placed in a coffin of cypress wood, and his skull was enclosed in a beautiful golden shrine.

Salonius.

Salonius was certainly a bishop but the see he occupied is a matter of dispute. Some writers maintain he was bishop of Vienne, others say he was bishop of Geneva. In the letter to pope Leo already referred to, sent by him and his brother, and another bishop named Ceretius, they write as "Bishops of Gaul[3]." He and his brother Veranus wrote a treatise in the form of a dialogue, on the books of Proverbs and Ecclesiastes. Veranus propounded difficulties in the form of questions, and Salonius explained them by way of answer. The style is simple and concise, and most of the explanations have a moral bearing[4]. An extract will suffice to illustrate the method of the teaching. *Veranus.* What must be understood by the words "Wisdom hath built her a habitation?" *Salonius.* Wisdom, i.e. the Son of God, hath built a habitation, in creating, in the womb of the Virgin, the man taken into the unity of His Person. Again Veranus asks how the words of Solomon, "The earth abideth for

---

[1] Holmes, *The Christian Church in Gaul*, pp. 377, 378.
[2] Barcillon.   [3] Migne, *Pat. Lat.* Vol. 54, p. 887.
[4] *L'Histoire littéraire de la France*, Vol. II, pp. 435, 436.

ever," can be reconciled with the words of Christ, " Heaven and earth shall pass away." Salonius replies that the words of our Lord speak of a change, or transformation, and not of destruction. The work was adopted almost word for word by Honorius of Autun in the 12th century, and was published under his name at Cologne in A.D. 1554[1].

The treatise, addressed by Eucherius to his sons Veranus and Salonius, was probably written with the intention of helping them to fulfil worthily the episcopal duties that had devolved upon them, for both were called to the episcopate. He knew well that if the people were to be nourished with heavenly doctrine, the inspired word of God must be the essential foundation of it. Salonius was a pupil of Salvianus who had dedicated his two tractates *On Avarice* and *On Providence* to him. His master calls him "the object of his affection," and it is a testimony to his merits that Salonius is also referred to by him as "the hope of his age."

Apollinarius.

Maximus, abbot of Lerins, and afterwards bishop of Riez, had gathered round him many disciples, and among those distinguished for sanctity was Apollinarius, who was born at Vienne. After some years passed at Lerins, he returned to his home to sell his property for distribution to the poor. While engaged in this work of charity, he was chosen bishop of Valence, about the year A.D. 480. His oversight of the people was wise and conscientious, but his firmness brought upon him the hatred of those who objected to the rein imposed upon their passions. He was one of the bishops who had considered it their duty to excommunicate a man named Stephen for his marriage contrary to the canons. Sigismund, prince of the Burgundians, was persuaded to exile the bishop of Valence. The illness which overtook the prince shortly after was regarded as the vengeance of heaven upon him. The bishop was recalled. His subsequent death was mourned by his people, and his body which had been buried in a suburb of Valence was in the 11th century transferred to the great church which bears his name.

---

[1] Cornelius à Lapide, *Comment. in Eccles.* p. 6.

Siffred.

During the abbacy of Porcarius A.D. 489 to 507 there came to Lerins an old soldier eager to seek repose after his life's work, and to learn the lessons of piety that were so well taught within the monastery walls. He brought with him Siffred, his young son, to be educated there. The father did not live long. His son determined to consecrate his life to the service of his Lord. So well did he progress in this school of piety that the brethren regarded him as their future abbot. This was not to be. He was chosen by the people and clergy of Venasque as their bishop, and was consecrated by Caesarius. He was accompanied to his new home by a large concourse of people. After fully realising the hopes that had been formed concerning him, and as the day of his death approached, he built himself a cell near the church he had erected in honour of the Virgin. Leaving the administration of his episcopal house to his clergy, he became oblivious to the things of this world, and spent his time in prayer. Knowing his end was imminent he summoned the clergy and people, and announced to them his approaching death. "We are your family, why should you leave us orphans?" they cried, "without you, your flock will be the prey of ravening wolves." "Children," said the bishop, "the Saviour will deliver you from the snares of the enemy; tremble not before his threats; oh! that on the day of judgment I may have you as my children, and present you to the Lord." With these solemn words upon his lips, and with his people in his thoughts, he died.

Virgilius.

The last in date of the Lerinensian monks that we propose to mention is Virgilius, a 6th century bishop, who early in his sojourn at the monastery gave promise of a career of exalted usefulness. Virgilius was considered by his brethren to be one of the glories of their cloister. A native of Aquitaine, of rich and powerful family, he had from his earliest infancy displayed a humble and loving spirit. He took the most strenuous measures to reduce his body to subjection, and his biographer says that if he had no outward persecutions to face, he underwent sufficient voluntary suffering to entitle him to the name of martyr[1]. When the call to solitude seemed to him insistent, he left his family, he abandoned his property, and he consecrated his talents to God. He hoped to find what he longed for in the shelter of Lerins. Here he learnt that in order to be perfect he must be indifferent to all things worldly. In due time Virgilius became abbot of Lerins in succession to Florianus. He felt it his duty to do more than set an example of edification to those over whom he was placed. He determined to restore order and sanctity at a time when there was some relaxation of the fervour of former days. In A.D. 589 the city and diocese of Arles lost its archbishop. A succession of distinguished men had occupied this see, and the people were not unmindful of Honoratus, of Hilary, of Caesarius, nor of the abbey which had trained them to such perfection. Once again therefore the clergy went to Lerins and brought away Virgilius, then seventy years old, and in spite of his age, he was able to rule the diocese for some twenty years with wisdom and energy. This son of Lerins took a leading part in the great event that must ever occupy a prominent place in English history. When Augustine and his missionaries were being sent to England, Gregory wrote letters to the prelates of Gaul, commending them to their "priestly affections." After being kindly received and entertained during the winter of A.D. 596, Augustine and his companions landed on the shores of England in the spring of the following year. The events surrounding this visit are too familiar to need recapitulation. When the time was ripe for the appointment of a bishop, Augustine applied to Gregory for consecration and was told to seek it at the hands of the Gallican bishops. He therefore journeyed to Arles and was consecrated by Virgilius on November 16th, A.D. 597. In the letter written by Gregory to the archbishop of Arles, he said, "Your prayers, your help, and if necessary your consolations are desired. If the apostles whom we send shall succeed in their mission, you will yourself share in their reward." The honour of consecrating Augustine was granted to Virgilius as vicar of the holy see in Gaul, and he had

[1] *Chron. Ler.* I, p. 88.

received the pallium by request of king Childebert. The high esteem in which Virgilius was held at Rome may be inferred from extracts of Gregory's letters: "How good is charity! It puts in order what is confused, and hides all imperfections. I know, my dear brother, that you are filled with this virtue. Those who came from Gaul tell me so. No one is ignorant of the source whence our holy faith is spread throughout Gaul. No bishop shall undertake a long journey without your authority. If discussion should arise regarding the faith, or concerning any difference between bishops that may be difficult to decide, summon twelve of your brethren to examine and decide upon the circumstances." This delicate duty was wisely discharged, and Virgilius gained the confidence and friendship of all his diocesans, by the kindness, wisdom, and equity with which he fulfilled the duties of his high position. His death, in the first years of the 7th century, was mourned by many, who realised all the good work that he had undertaken, and appreciated the powers of mind and heart that he had so well displayed.

These "Apostolic Priests," as Bede calls them, filled the whole island with the fame of their doings, and it is not surprising that people came to summon its sons to the highest positions that the Church could offer. The bare mention of those of whom we have in these chapters given some account, would amply justify the title applied to Lerins—"The Nursery of Bishops."

CHAPTER XV

THE MASTER OF BISHOPS

SALVIANUS

One of the most interesting and powerful writers and preachers among the sons of Lerins was Salvian. He was never raised to the episcopate, but he was called by Gennadius "a priest of Marseilles, well furnished with divine and human learning, and not to speak invidiously, the master of bishops." He was born near the city of Trèves about the end of the 4th century. He married Palladia, a pagan, of Cologne. He was soon able not only to convert her to the Christian faith, but after the birth of a daughter who was named Auspiciola, to persuade her to adopt some monastic observances. He passed the latter part of his life in Gaul and was a presbyter of the church at Marseilles. The date of his death is uncertain. He was evidently held in high reputation for his piety, and is referred to by S. Hilary in his sermon on Honoratus as "the most blessed Salvianus." As a commentary on, and a possible explanation of, the title given to him by Gennadius, his words of rebuke to Eucherius for lack of courtesy[1], are certainly those of a teacher or master. He is equally masterful in his letters to other bishops, Agricius[2] and Salonius[3]. The sojourn of Salvian at Lerins has been doubted by some writers[4]. Mabillon[5] inclines to the view that he lived there as a guest, and not as one of the "religious." The tradition of the monastery[6] certainly favours the view that he was one of the monks. Hilary calls Salvian "one of the

---

[1] *Ep.* II.   [2] *Ibid.* III.   [3] *Ibid.* IX.
[4] Notably Tillemont, *Mémoires*, Vol. XVI, p. 746.
[5] *Annals*, Vol. I, p. 16.   [6] *Chron. Ler.* I, p. 376.

dear friends of Honoratus," and in these words conveys an inference in a similar direction. Montalembert[1] says that Salvian spent five years in the monastery, and calls him "the most eloquent man of his age after Augustine."

We scarcely have need again to remind the reader that the early years of the 5th century were troublous times for the Roman Empire; that armies of the barbarians were overrunning and devastating the fair provinces of Gaul, and that it was a matter of little wonder if the spirit of the people was crushed and overwhelmed by the consequent misgovernment and the prevalent licentiousness. Amid the social corruption of the age Salvian stands forth to give his testimony, and in his book *On the Government of God* points to the root of the mischief and to the one hope of its cure. In this work he describes the devastation wrought by the barbarians[2]. His writings are specially valuable not only because they throw light upon the times in which he lived, but also because they treat of them from both social, political and ecclesiastical points of view.

His works are fit to be classed with the best literary productions of the 5th century. "His style is studied and polished, concise and clear, and the beauties of it are acknowledged by all who have a taste for literature. It would be difficult to find discourse more varied, more delightful[3]." Some of his pages are worthy of the great Augustan age, and he is like Sallust, Tacitus, and the elder Pliny in his beautiful descriptions.

His first work in chronological order is a treatise *Against Avarice*, in four books. Written not later than A.D. 430, it is a somewhat extravagant laudation of thorough-going unworldliness. He seems even to have held the view that a father cannot, without sin, leave even a part of his property to his children. To the objection that a father ought to think of his children's future by providing them with suitable position and patrimony Salvian replied, "The most precious heritage he can hand down to them is faith, the fear of God, modesty and holiness, goods

---

[1] *Monks of the West*, Vol. I, p. 248.

[2] He speaks of them as "Gens ignavissima, de loco ad locum pergens de urbe ad urbem transiens."

[3] *L'Histoire littéraire de la France*, Vol. II, pp. 529, 530.

which cannot perish. The happiness of children cannot consist in riches, palaces and property." In another passage, Salvian asks, "Senseless man, are you then born for earth? You cannot ignore what religion says to you, that heaven is your home, that your body, mortal and earthly, is destined to re-enter the earth, but that your soul, immortal and heavenly, is destined to return to heaven. Yet forsooth, so many houses, gardens, castles, so much apparel for your body! And your soul, what are you doing for it? Where do you find it a habitation? What sojourn are you preparing for it? All these thoughts are obscure and confused in your mind; the soul, heaven, immortality do not touch you. Your mind and heart are filled only with earth, they have assumed the nature and qualities of their treasure[1]." Salvian describes the last moments of a rich worldling who without a thought of making reparation for the faults of his whole life, without trying to subdue his avarice by means of almsgiving, proposes to satisfy the cupidity of distant relatives. "My son, have pity on thy soul," says the Lord, "I was hungry and ye gave Me no meat." Taking these words as a text, Salvian asks, "Where are those who pretend that our Lord Jesus Christ has no need that we should place our goods at His service? Here we have witness that He is hungry, thirsty, cold. Ah, you say, 'He is not in need; who tells us He is thirsty?' I go further, I say not only is Christ in need like others, but in much greater need than others. For if I take a great number of poor, the poverty of each is not the same in all respects. One needs clothes, who does not need food; another has no shelter, but has clothes. Many having no lodging, have yet something to eat. Christ is the only one to Whom everything is absolutely lacking in this world. None of His suffer exile, or endure cold or nakedness, but Christ shivers with him. Alone, He is hungry with the hungry, thirsty with the thirsty, and this is why He is in greater need than others. After that, what have you O man to say, that call yourself a Christian? You see Christ in need and you leave your patrimony to people that lack nothing. Christ is poor, and you, you fatten on the multitude of riches.

[1] Book I, Chapter I.

Christ is hungry and you make ready new delicacies for those that are full. Christ complains that He has not even a glass of water, and you fill with wine the cellar of those already drunken. Christ promises you in exchange for your alms eternal rewards, and you give all your property to people who can give you nothing. And you pretend to have faith in your Master, when His rewards leave you without desire, and His anger without fear!" In words of great severity Salvian asks in another place, "When therefore is the time to weep, if that time has been lost? How make reparation, when the days of reparation are gone? Can a man think of reparation when he is *in extremis*? He will wish perhaps to macerate his flesh by hair-cloth, to cover himself with dust and ashes, in order to atone by present austerities for the luxury of his past pleasures. Alas, how can he employ these means when, on the verge of the grave, he is unable to do the very lightest penance?" Salvian paints avarice in the darkest colours. To him, it cannot lose its hold even in a man's last moments; "Oh most miserable of men, you think then only of enriching your heirs, you are anxious concerning the fortune you will leave. You consider who shall profit most by your heritage. You concern yourself with the good things others shall have after you, and you do not think of the horror of your death. When you leave this life, the tribunal of God awaits you, you will be accompanied by angels, the terrible ministers of eternal punishment, and yet you muse of the pleasures your heirs will soon enjoy, you dwell on the thought of the delicacies with which they will be satiated! Senseless man, what have you to do with these vanities, these foolish deceits?" In the resistance of the soul to wise reflection at such a solemn time, Salvian points to very powerful influences in an opposite direction. Gathered round the deathbed, he sees relatives and friends, wealthy men, men of distinguished rank; "What worldly fruit of eternity, to dispense your goods to these indigents! You have just reason to bring to your mind what you will leave to such beggars! We can understand that you are broken by compassion, that you are vanquished by the love that the sight of grief-stricken relatives inspires. You see wealthy men, richly clothed, weeping over your sufferings with dejected countenance and holiday garments, turning towards you eyes that are fashioned to sadness, and seeking to gain your heritage by hypocritical solicitude. Who could resist such affection, who would not be touched by such gentleness, and how, at such a sight could you think of yourself? you see tears flow at command, you hear sighs that are simulated, you witness a pretence of anxiety which far from desiring your health, awaits the moment of your death." It would be difficult to match the bitter irony of this picture.

The greatest work of Salvian undoubtedly is the treatise *On the Government of God*, one of the most remarkable books of the 5th century. It is important not only because, as we have said, it describes the desperate position of the Roman Empire at the time, but also because it throws an interesting light upon the character of the Goths in the days of their predominance. It is in eight books, the 7th and 8th of which are incomplete. He wrote it, he says, "not to please but to correct his contemporaries." In it he draws repeated comparisons between the vices of the Roman and the virtues of the Goth. We see to what depths the Roman Empire had then fallen, in the following denunciation of the Romans: "Where are our riches and our power? Formerly we were the strongest people, now we are become the feeblest. The whole world used to fear us, now we fear the world. The barbarians were our tributaries, we now pay tribute to the barbarians, and they sell to us the repose we enjoy. Have you seen anything more miserable than we are? Into what an abyss have we fallen! It is not enough that we are unfortunate, we are objects of ridicule. The gold that we see taken from us by force, we pretend is given voluntarily; we say it is a "present" which our liberality makes to the barbarians, when it is the price at which we buy our very existence[1]." In his comparison of Roman and Goth he says, "The barbarians are unjust, so are we; they are avaricious, so are we; they are without faith, so are we; they are greedy, so are we; in a word, if the barbarians are given to all kinds of infamy, so are we. But some one will perhaps

---

[1] Book VI, Chapter XVIII.

answer, 'If we are equal to the barbarians in depravity, why are we not their equals in power?' The weakest are the most culpable. Do you ask a proof? Do you say that the barbarians commit the same crimes and yet they are not as unfortunate as we are? Ah, the difference consists in this, our culpability in sinning is much greater than theirs. All the barbarians are either pagans or heretics. Their conduct is not a contempt of heavenly precepts, for the Lord's precepts are unknown to them, and he does nothing contrary to the law, who does not know the law. What wonder then that the barbarians cheat, seeing they do not know that cheating is a crime? We avail ourselves of our name of Christians, we whose acts and lives are such that our title of Christian people seems to become the opprobrium of Christ! Among the pagans, on the other hand, do we see the like? Can it be said of the Huns, 'See what these people who are called Christians do?' Can it be said of the Saxons and the Franks, 'See what these so-called adorers of Christ do?' Do we see our holy law blamed for the fierce manners of the Maurians? Can it be said of any of these peoples, 'Where is the catholic law which they make a profession of believing?' It is of us only that all this can be said. It is in us that Christ suffers opprobrium." We gather from other words of Salvian that the Romans were in no way humiliated or saddened by the disasters that were overwhelming them. The warnings of the Church fell on heedless ears. The monks were ridiculed and persecuted, despised and hated. The one thought of the Romans was amusement. "Three times the chief city of Gaul has been destroyed, thrice it has been an immense funeral pile, and each time after the ruin, the crimes of the inhabitants have redoubled. I have seen—how have I survived the sight?— I have seen the ground littered with the dead bodies of men and women lying unburied, naked, torn, devoured by dogs and birds of prey. The infectious smell from these bodies wrought death among those who might have survived. What happened after all these disasters? The nobles, who had escaped death, demanded of the emperors as a supreme remedy for the ills of their city, permission to have the circus games! Inhabitants of Trèves! you demand the circus when your fields

are ravaged, your city taken by assault! I judged you worthy
of all pity after the destruction of which you were the victims,
but my pity for you is redoubled, when I see you ask for
spectacular shows. I thought that in your wars you had only
lost your fortune, I did not know you had at the same time lost
your sense and your intelligence. O Trèves! you ask for the
circus. Tell me, where will you hold it? On the burning ruins,
or on the bones of your murdered children? Your walls are
blackened with fire, and you wish to clothe them with an
appearance of festival. You insult Heaven, and your impious
superstitions bring down upon you the anger of God. I am not
surprised at the calamities that have befallen you. If three
destructions have not brought correction, you deserve to perish
a fourth time."

In the fifth book[1] his reference to the serf system, and the
evils of vast estates are of great interest. His description of the
condition of the poor, and the awful struggle among the people
who were without bread is not less eloquent in its powerful
condemnation. He vigorously denounces the exactions that
were levied, and here he contrasts the Goths and Romans:
"Can I describe the whole atrocity, its rarity among the
barbarians? its universality among the Romans? I will speak
of the exactions by which one despoiled another. It was the
people who were despoiled; the public taxes were diverted to
personal uses. Those who were guilty of this were not only
men in high places; judges and their servants were alike
rapacious. Where are there—I will not say—cities but even
municipalities and boroughs which have not as many tyrants as
they have citizens? I should not be surprised if this name
flatters them, conveying an idea of power and greatness, for
there are few brigands that do not regard it as a point of honour
and a joy to be thought more cruel than they really are."

How bad the conditions were can be surmised when a
barbarian invasion was regarded by the people as a blessing.
"The poor are despoiled, widows groan, orphans are trodden
under foot, and it was then that we saw many take refuge with
the enemy, in order that they might not be victims of this public

[1] Chapters IV–IX.

persecution. Tired of submitting to the barbarities of the
Romans they asked humanity from the barbarians. They
preferred to live free under an appearance of slavery, to a life as
slaves under an appearance of liberty. Thus this name of
Roman citizen, held once in such high esteem, bought at so high
a price, is repudiated to-day. Can we desire a better witness of
Roman iniquity than to see so many honourable citizens, for
whom the name of Roman should have been the crown of
honour and glory, compelled by the cruelty of Roman iniquity
to desire not to be so called? If it is on the poor that the
weight of the new taxation fell, it is to them that without doubt
the benefit of new reductions should come. But no! the poor
are the first to be charged, they are the last to be relieved. For
when the Imperial Power determined upon some diminution of
payment from cities that had been overwhelmed, it is the rich
alone that benefit by the reductions. In what country, among
what people will such things be seen if not among the Romans?
Where will such injustice be found if not with us? Such crimes
are unknown to Franks, Huns, Goths. Thus the only prayer all
Romans make is never to be compelled to pass again under
Roman government. What the Roman people unanimously
demand is that they may be allowed to continue to live as they
live now, under the barbarian[1]."

Thus we have from the 5th century another proof that the
problems that perplex men's minds never greatly change their
aspect. The inhabitants of the Roman Empire complained that
Providence would punish them the moment they became
Christians. Salvian desires to show that the chastisement is
deserved; "we suffer what we deserve[2]." If the Romans are
conquered, it is because the barbarians are better than they.
The manners of all Romans, clerical and lay, are corrupted.
He gives a satirical picture of Roman society. Social organisation with its slavery and oppression is worth nothing.

Reminded of the perfidy of the Frank, he mentions the new
form of profanity, the oath *per Christum* by which Christians

[1] Freeman quotes these words of Salvian's on Taxation, and discounts them.
[2] Patimur quod meremur.

would "swear by Christ" to take a man's property away from him. With fine scorn he asks, " Is the immodesty of the Hun, the perfidy of the Frank, the drunkenness of the Alamans, the rapacity of the Alan as blameworthy as similar crimes committed by Christians?"

The Christians of this period murmured in their misfortunes against Providence, and charged Him with their authorship. As answer to these doubts, that sound so modern, Salvian wrote the eight books *On the Government of God.* We have seen that he does not minimise the gravity of the evils. He regards the disasters that had befallen Gaul as God's retribution for the unfaithfulness of the Christians. He laid bare the root of the widespread misery and preached as the one hope, the living God. The keynote of the whole book is the overruling providence of God : "Just as the navigator never looses his hold of the helm, so God never ceases His care for the world." The writer boldly proclaims the cause of the misfortunes that had befallen the people, and he justifies God whom many accused, and vigorously and fearlessly maintains that the evils complained of were the just punishment of the crimes which were being committed in Gaul and elsewhere, and in the Church itself. He quoted Pythagoras, Plato, and the Stoics, all of whom confessed a God whose providence governs the world. He called Scripture to witness that God is everywhere present, that He directs all and judges all. It would be the atheists' strongest argument if God did not punish the people who would even swear by Christ that they would commit crime.

We note that Gennadius says that he had read these two and the following other works of Salvian, *An Exposition of Ecclesiasticus, A Poem on the first Chapter of Genesis* and "numerous homilies," so numerous indeed that he could not count them[1]. Judging by his outspoken utterances as revealed in the extracts that have been given from his writings, we have no difficulty in understanding that Salvian was not afraid to say what he felt to be the truth, however unpalatable it might be. But his friendship, ever ready to render a service, was deep and

[1] *De script. eccles.* Chap. 67.

sincere.   He lived to a great age, far beyond the limits of an ordinary life.

Such were the archbishops, bishops and abbots that the monastery of Lerins gave to the Church.   The words of Porcarius to his religious were well spoken : " Lerins is like a vine whose branches have overspread the world, her temples have been multiplied, and her colonies have been more numerous than those of any other monastery[1]."

[1] *Chron. Ler.* i, p. 221.

CHAPTER XVI

WORLDLY PROSPERITY (THE 8TH TO THE 15TH CENTURIES)

The Saracen Invasion.

In the third decade of the 8th century the Saracens turned their thoughts of pillage in the direction of the rich plains of France. In A.D. 721 their armies invaded Aquitaine, and laid siege to the ancient city of Narbonne. In A.D. 724 the invasion was renewed, and strongly defended cities were captured, or capitulated on terms of relentless ransom. Along the Rhine the barbarians carried slaughter, through the valley of the Rhone they wrought destruction. Vienne, Lyons, Besançon, Macon, Châlons, Dijon, and other places were devastated, and their churches were ruined. Lerins did not escape its trials at this time. When it was invaded, Porcarius the new abbot and 500 monks were massacred. Barralis, Surius, Baronius and the Bollandists agree in placing the death of Porcarius at the time of the stoppage of the great invasion by Charles Martel in A.D. 732. Seven days before the Saracens directed their way to Lerins, an angel—so runs the tradition—announced to Porcarius the terrible blow that was to fall upon him and his fellows. He was in the church of S. Stephen exhorting his brethren to suffer martyrdom rather than deny the Faith. He despatched sixteen children and thirty-six neophytes into Italy, as he feared their courage would fail, and he hoped after the storm had passed they would be able to return and restore the monastery. By his instructions the relics had been hidden in a place of safety. When the Saracens arrived, they tried in vain by promises and threats to gain information of the hiding place. Their attempt being futile, they took revenge by wholesale slaughter. Only four escaped and the churches and the monastery were reduced to cinders. The four survivors took refuge in the woods.

Eleutherus, who was one of the four returned with the neophytes in A.D. 752, and was nominated to the abbacy by the pope. He was unable to restore the monastery during the reign of Charles Martel, for this prince was fully occupied in establishing his authority and in fighting his enemies, and so felt himself obliged to abandon the property of the Church to the rapacity of his followers. But when in A.D. 741 his two sons Pepin and Carloman inherited his power, the Church witnessed a new era of prosperity. Pepin became sole master of the empire in A.D. 752 and redoubled his devotion to religion with a view to attaching the clergy to himself. In A.D. 754 pope Stephen II came to France to crown the new king, and profiting by this circumstance, Eleutherus pleaded before Pepin in the pope's presence for the restoration of the abbey, and recalled the services rendered to the Church of Gaul by a monastery that had produced so many saints, and whence so many eminent prelates had sprung. As a result of this interview, extensive lands were presented by the king to the religious. It was then decided to restore the battlements. There was good promise that monastic observances with examples of austerities would again flourish. After being abandoned for twenty years the monastery regained some of its ancient splendour.

After their crushing defeat at Tours, the Saracens only appeared again as pirates, and as such were the terror of the people for many years. In A.D. 810 they ravaged Nice and attacked Sardinia, but were repulsed. In A.D. 838 they arrived at Marseilles. In A.D. 846 they returned to the neighbourhood of Cannes. Struck with the aspect and strategic position of the front range of the encircling mountains they occupied it, and in an almost inaccessible centre they constructed defensive forts which have preserved to this day in Provence their memory in the Fraxinet[1], in remembrance of the forests which covered these heights. Garde-Fraxinet was their capital, and centre of

---

[1] Fraxinetum. Fraxinus, an ash-tree.

operation, from which they sent assailants to levy ransom upon the towns and monasteries of lower Provence.

In A.D. 972 a crusade was preached against them by Mayeul, abbot of Cluny. William I, count of Provence, gained possession of Garde-Fraxinet. This move was decisive. Deprived of their best support on the coast, they ceded little by little the positions they had conquered. They were pursued without mercy, and their power in Provence was ended in A.D. 975. Henceforward their aggressions were isolated acts of brigandage which were stopped by the maritime police. They left an indelible impress behind them. Their name is written on almost every page of the annals of Provence. Every ruin bears marks of their devastating influence. Forts and towns, churches and convents are eloquent of their pillage. Even a chain of the everlasting hills is called after them, for the range that is nearest to the Mediterranean coast is known as the mountains of the Maures.

The Fateful Year.

As the fateful year 1000 approached, which in common belief was to be the end of the world, people had but one thought, and that was to acquire in advance some claim on the mercy of God. Donations to churches and religious houses were popular, and considered the greatest means thereto. A deep gloom fell upon the Christian world, and all classes alike; the rich and powerful dreaded the hour of judgment; the poor and weak awaited with resignation the end of their miseries. The churches and religious houses were now loaded with gifts, for the possessions of earth now seemed useless and unneeded. But when the fateful year passed and no catastrophe befell the world, men again took heart of hope.

Prosperity.

The Church profited both by the past despair and the present hope. She had received the offerings of a terrified people, she now accepted their gifts of gratitude. The monastery of Lerins was abundantly enriched by this liberality, and her landed possessions, especially during the 11th century grew considerably, and continued to increase with such rapidity that by the end of the 13th century, they extended over the entire Mediterranean coast, and northwards as far as the Loire. The jurisdiction of the abbot was exercised over nearly seventy priories and fiefs, and, in addition to the monastery's territorial possessions, it enjoyed many important fishing and shipwreck rights, as well as the right to coin money, and to take salt from the excise store without paying any tax. These privileges were granted by the counts of Provence. A brief account of these possessions and privileges may not be altogether uninteresting to our readers. We do not propose to give a list of names which might prove monotonous, but those who desire precise knowledge of the sources, with names, may be referred to some of the extant cartularies that are invaluable for such a purpose[1]. We will merely say that most of the possessions were situated in the dioceses of Antibes, Grasse, Fréjus, Nice, Riez, Glandèves and Vintimille, and there were others, though less numerous, in Arles, Avignon, Vence and elsewhere. Donations from Fréjus and Antibes were among the earliest to be made. Towards the end of the 10th century William Gruetta, son of Rodoard, count of Antibes, had ceded his property in Arluc to the monastery of Lerins, and in making this gift he says, "I leave the military career to embrace the monastic order. With our persons, my son Peter and I give to the monastery the fourth part of Arluc, its château, farm, and port, with all that is contiguous thereto." The gift bears the date of A.D. 990.

In A.D. 1038 Aldebert, bishop of Antibes, who had already ceded to Lerins all the altars of his diocese with the exception of those of the parish churches, gave the parish church of Cannes, under the name of Notre Dame de S. Nicolas. He also gave Vallauris, and his property in Arluc. In making these gifts he drew up a document in these words: "According to the practice of law from the beginning, under the governance of God Himself, Master and Judge of all things, and by virtue of the law of the Old and New Testaments and of tradition, it is certain that any person, desirous of making

---

[1] See especially *Le cartulaire de l'Abbaye de Lerins*, by H. Moris, Paris, 1883–1905; and *L'inventaire des Archives des Alp.-Marit.* Nice, 1893, by the same author.

a gift of any of his property, can do so with the authority and custom of the past. For the salvation of my soul, I, Aldebert, give to the abbot and monks of Lerins, present and future, all that I possess or that others hold in my name in the place called Arluc. Should any of my heirs, or other person, dare to contravene this gift, let him be smitten with all the curses of the Old and New Testaments, and let him share in the infernal regions the lot of Dathan, Abiram, and the traitor Judas." This benefactor afterwards became abbot of Lerins as Aldebert I, and governed it from A.D. 1046 to 1066. The possessions of the monastery in Arluc were so great that about the middle of this century, its abbot exercised manorial rights as lord of Arluc, and enjoyed fishing rights in the river Siagne. The city was, according to Barralis, of considerable importance till it was destroyed in the wars of the 14th century, and left no subsequent trace in history.

The monastery had the good fortune to be under the governance of Aldebert II from A.D. 1066 to 1102. He deserves to be numbered among those who have been called "The Great." His own personality seems to have attracted more gifts than ever, and in other directions he deserves to be remembered with praise and gratitude for the services he rendered to Lerins. The historian of the monastery says, "There did not pass, I will not say a year, but a month, a week, or a day without some gift being made to Aldebert." Pontius, abbot of the monastery of S. Veranus, sent for him and submitted his person and monastery by a deed of gift in the following terms: "In the name of our Lord Jesus Christ, I, Pontius, give to God, to the Holy Virgin Mary, to S. Honoratus, to the Abbot Aldebert and to all the religious of Lerins, in consideration of the eminent piety which reigns among them, the monastery of Veranus that they may peaceably and perpetually enjoy it. I make this gift in order that the monastery may not lose the good name it has enjoyed since the days of Charlemagne."

Bertrand, bishop of Fréjus, in giving to Lerins a church with tithes and offerings, said: "When I consider what place should be the object of my special affection, I can find nothing more worthy of it than the monastery of Lerins where such eminent virtues shine, and where the Lord has zealous servants from every nation. As Leontius and Honoratus were united by the strongest bonds of friendship, I do not desire to be separated from those who in this sacred shelter consecrate themselves day and night to the service of God[1]."

A more remarkable gift was that made by Boniface and his wife Stephanie. Long childless, they earnestly desired offspring, and following the example of Elkanah and Hannah, they made a vow to consecrate their God-given child to His service. This vow they fulfilled, and with the son they gave a considerable portion of territory.

The gifts occasionally took the form of an act of restitution, as seen from these words : " I, William of Eyras, recognising that it is by God's just chastisement that my body is weak, hand over to the monks of Lerins, absolutely and without restriction, the fourth part of the Château of Arluc which I have unjustly retained to this day, and I implore the Lord and S. Honoratus to pardon my wrong doing and to accord me the mercy that I so greatly need." Parents used to make a gift of some portion of their property by way of remuneration for a son's education.

The history of the monastery in these respects and in some others serves to illustrate the usual history of monastic establishments. With the increase of wealth came the development of estate ownership with requisite officials. How was the property administered ? We are told[2] that the monks or canons regular held large farms under their own management. In order to get the full value from their lands they sent a certain number of the religious to a farm, who took care of the temporalities, and had divine service " in a private chapel." These farms were called *Obediences,* and the superior was called a *Prior* or *Provost,* and the farm in which he resided was called a *Priory*[3]. The officials were called *Obedientiaries,* and the term did not necessarily exclude the prior who was appointed by the abbot. The title of prior was loosely applied before the 13th century to any monk who by reason of age, experience, or acquirements ranked

---

[1] *Cartulaire,* f. 6, v.   [2] Héricourt, *Lois Ecclesiastiques,* Part II, p. 211.
[3] See also Dr Gregory Smith, *Christian Monasticism,* p. 138.

above his fellows. It was a personal rather than an official position. A conventual prior may therefore be the superior of an offshoot from some larger monastery[1]. Similar testimony is given by Du Cange, who says[2], " The prior who is first after the abbot, is also called *Praepositus*. He is of more honour than the others, and has the chief place in chapter, choir and refectory. The name prior in the sense of *Praepositus* is of later date, and was not in use till the end of the 13th century." Benedict had enjoined on the younger monks the duty of reverence to their priors, but by this term he evidently means elders[3]. At the beginning of the 13th century some abbots allowed certain of their religious to live in an obedience and to administer the property as perpetual farmers. Pope Innocent III regarded this as an abuse that was contrary to the vow of poverty, and he condemned it in a decretal[4]. In spite of this, the abuse increased, and when the priors saw that the abbot and other officers of the monasteries each took a share of the abbey's resources, they took the revenues of which they had previously been only the farmers. The Council of Vienne in A.D. 1312 established definite regulations, and among these it was forbidden to confer a priory, even if it was a conventual, on any clerics others than professed religious at least twenty years of age.

The great glory reflected upon the monastery of Lerins by the saintliness and erudition of the monks, and by the eminent services that were rendered to Christianity, constrained popes and kings to accord to it many important privileges, and those already enjoyed were confirmed[5]. It was defended from enemies within and without, and placed under the protection of the most powerful and influential. It was taken under the direct care of the see of Rome by successive popes. No appeal at the court of Rome to the prejudice or detriment of the monastery was allowed to be made by any beneficed clergyman. It was exempted from the visits of the ordinary, and from the jurisdiction

---

[1] See Cassell's *Encyclop. Dictionary.*
[2] *Glossary Lat.*   [3] *Reg. Bened.* 63.
[4] Nec alicui committatur aliqua obedientia perpetua possidenda tanquam in sua sibi vita locetur, sed cum oportuerit amoveri, sine contradictione qualibet avocetur. *De statu Monachorum et Canonicorum Regularium.*
[5] See *Inventory*, already quoted.

of the bishops of Grasse and of the metropolitan[1]. Again and again those who tried to usurp its goods were plainly warned against any such action, and those who were guilty of it were promptly ordered to make immediate restitution. Arbert, bishop of Avignon, was enjoined by Urban II and Pascal II to allow the monks of Lerins freely to possess the church of Laurade. Calixtus II wrote three letters on their behalf. The abbot had complained of the bishop of Nice, and the pope's letter shows us the quaint form of the complaint: "Our well-beloved son Peter, abbot of Lerins, and his brethren have said much of your brotherliness and how you love, protect, and show favour to their monastery and their persons with quite a fatherly affection, but they complain that some of your clergy have taken possession of a church which is one of the dependencies of their monastery, and has been in their lawful possession for many years. We order you to make immediate restitution[2]." To the bishop of Fréjus he wrote on behalf of the same abbot to this effect: "Chevalier Troandus has pillaged a farm belonging to the monastery, and despoiled the religious as well as the laymen that live in it. It is also complained that Aldebert and his brother Raymond have set fire to it, and caused considerable loss. We order you to compel Troandus to restore this property to the monks and to abstain from further vexation. Against the incendiaries promulgate sentence, unless the abbot and your own discretion desire an indulgence after satisfaction has been made[3]."

In the anxieties of hostile invasions, it might have been thought that fellow Christians would at any rate have been sympathetic. On the contrary, they appear to have pillaged and seized possessions belonging to the monastery. Honorius, bishop of Rome, wrote as follows to the bishops of Riez, Fréjus, Vence, and Antibes: "Our sons, the abbot and monks of Lerins, exposed to the attacks of the Saracens and threatened with pillage, slavery, and death, complain bitterly to us that you seek to take away their churches by violence. When they should

---

[1] For these and other privileges see H. Moris, *L'Abbaye de Lerins: Histoire et Monuments*, pp. 68 seq., Paris, 1909.

[2] *Chron. Ler.* II, p. 158.   [3] *Ibid.*

have found in you defenders, they find themselves the victims of your injustice. We command you to make restoration without delay[1]."

Adrian IV and Clement III placed the monastery under the care of the consuls of Grasse who were requested to lend their assistance "when Saracen pirates or wicked Christians attacked them[2]." Alexander III forbade the bishops of Nice, Fréjus and Antibes to take the tithe belonging to the monastery, and he commissioned the archbishop of Embrun and the bishop of Riez to compel these bishops to respect its rights[3]. Celestine III commanded the bishops of Provence to prevent the faithful from retaining anything that belonged to the monastery[4], and Nicolas V excommunicated Antony Bonnefay, a beneficed clergyman, and other individuals of Grasse, for striking a monk.

From the 12th century the island had been the burying place of many of the faithful who were for the most part benefactors or other privileged persons, but Adrian IV authorised the abbot to receive the bodies of any who had expressed the wish to be buried there[5]. When certain bishops, jealous of their rights, forbade the faithful to select the island as their burial place, Clement III ordered them to respect the injunctions of his predecessor[6]. Indulgences were granted to the faithful who made the pilgrimage of the island, or sojourned three months there, who helped in the building of the tower, or assisted the monks in a crisis.

Kings and princes always manifested their favour towards the monastery by their gifts, by their protection, and by privileges that were most advantageous. As a reward for the château fort built and guarded by the monks, to which we shall refer presently, the counts of Provence gave them the right (no small one at a time when salt was very dear), to deduct twelve bushels of it from every ship that brought it to the storages of Cannes and Grasse. This right was enjoyed until A.D. 1453.

The monastery possessed exclusive fishing rights over a

---

[1] *Cartulaire*, f. 134. [2] *Inventaire Arch. des Alp.-Marit.* II, II.
[3] *Ibid.* II, I, f. 203. [4] *Ibid.* H. II.
[5] Quidem nobiles laici elegerunt sibi locum sepulturae in insulâ et ecclesiâ Lerinensi. *Chron. Ler.* II, p. 168.
[6] *Invent. Arch. des Alp.-Marit.* II, I, f. 210.

C. M.   17

very large stretch of sea[1]; originally given by Alphonsus of Aragon, count of Provence in A.D. 1193; and when the people of Cannes, Grasse, Antibes and other places protested in the 15th century, the privilege was confirmed. The Statutes of Cannes[2] were drawn up about this time by the abbot Andrew de Plaisance, and included the regulation that no stranger may fish where an inhabitant of Cannes is already in possession, under a penalty of £25, to be shared between the abbot and the informer, and these privileges were continued, defined, and protected by authority.

The charter of the gift of the principality of Sabourg and the right to coin money there, are points of some debate. The château and domain of Sabourg, a village of 20 families, are supposed to have been presented to the monastery by Gui, count of Ventimille, towards the end of the 12th century; and at a date that cannot accurately be determined, its abbots claimed the title of "Prince of Sabourg." A lease of the mint was granted in A.D. 1666 to Bernardine Bareste. By its terms he was allowed to manufacture certain kinds of gold, large and small, and also certain silver pieces, and from time to time he was under obligation to submit samples of all to the abbot[3]. The king (Louis XIV) ordered the mint to be closed and the lease to be cancelled. The monks drew up a letter of supplication in which they traced the origin of their rights. "We have always coined money, which however has never been current in France, but only in Italy where the mint is situated, and no prince of Italy has ever complained." The appeal concludes "His majesty surely would not desire to deprive poor monks of this privilege, and of the revenue of seven or eight hundred pounds, which they annually draw, and which forms almost the whole of the income of this principality." In spite of this request the council of state annulled the lease and the privilege. As the principality was of no further use, the monks sold it to the duke of Savoy in A.D. 1697.

The increase of wealth brought a new danger to the monks, for it tempted the cupidity of pirates. In earlier days the

---

[1] *Invent. Arch. des Alp.-Marit.* H. 24.   [2] *Ibid.* H. 473.
[3] *Cartulaire*, II, p. 188.

treasures of the monastery were of a different sort. Intellect and saintliness were not the kind of booty to attract the cupidity of marauders; and to such persons the only possible value of a monk would be his price for ransom. In the abbacy of Aldebert I, Saracens had appeared at Lerins, and the invaders, having pillaged the sacred objects, carried away some of the younger monks to Spain to sell them as slaves. The elder monks went to Marseilles to implore the help of the old abbot of the monastery of S. Victor, and through his kind offices the captives were redeemed.

It was necessary that the monks should have some protection for their property and their persons. Defensive works were urgent, and it was determined that one fortress should be erected on the island, and another on the mainland. It was Aldebert II who conceived the idea of these fortresses, and in A.D. 1073 he laid the foundations of both. It was during his abbacy that the chapel of the Holy Cross, the church of "Our Lady of Pity" and the great church of S. Honorat were consecrated. The fortress (of which we give a picture[1]) was intended not only to protect the island, but also to communicate information to the whole sea board for the purpose of defence. As soon as suspicious sails appeared on the horizon, the watchman of Lerins raised the signal which was repeated from other towers. Aldebert, who died at the age of seventy-two, devoted himself for thirty-six years to the realisation of his project with wonderful ardour and perseverance. Yet he never forgot that it was not enough to build walls for the protection of the bodies of the monks, and realised that the monastery had been entrusted to his care for the salvation of souls. His vigilance was everywhere manifest, and in his administration the fervour of Lerins was reminiscent of its best days; it continued to attract men from all ranks of life, and from all parts of the Christian world. He did not live to see the completion of the building, which indeed was not finished until more than a hundred years later. It was not sufficiently advanced to provide safety for the monks during piratical incursions in A.D. 1107, when many were victims of fire and sword. It was then that Pope Calixtus II wrote a letter in

[1] Frontispiece.

support of the appeal that was being made by Aldebert's successor, Peter I, and reminded the people both far and near of "all that the monks have so long suffered from the attacks of the Saracens."

It was in A.D. 1133 that Raymond-Berenger visited the island, and in proof of his love for it addressed to the monks in chapter assembled, these words: "I give and confirm to you the château formerly called Marsellinum, exempt and free from all charges and taxes. By reason of this freedom I wish the château to bear the name of Francum[1]. I take under my protection the monastery, and all you possess in Provence within the boundaries of my jurisdiction. If any one takes anything away from you by violence, or contrary to justice, I will be your defender." It will be remembered that this Castrum Marsellinum was an earlier name for Cannes.

The Saracen pirates continued to make frequent incursions against the island, and the erection of the fortress was from time to time impeded, but Augier, who was elected abbot in A.D. 1172, took up the work of completion with great activity, and, with the assistance of many influential people, he achieved his object. It was recognised by Pope Innocent II that the position of the island made it an easy prey to barbarians, and he therefore accorded in A.D. 1139 the same indulgences, that his predecessor had given to the Crusaders, to those who would go and inhabit it for three months in order to defend it in case of attack. He also recommended the nobles of Grasse and others to help the monks with all their power, and if need be with their arms. These powerful families placed their treasures and arms at the service of the community. In subsequent raids upon the monastery, the monks recalled the promise of the nobility of Grasse, and begged their assistance, which was immediately forthcoming. Antony of Villeneuve, Luke de Grimaldi, and Bertrand of Grasse, Lord of Cagnes, were among those who led the people of Grasse, Cannes and the neighbourhood against the pirates and forced them to retreat.

In the year A.D. 1400 Genoese marauders made a night attack upon the monastery under the leadership of a redoubtable

[1] "Franc" is the French for "exempt."

chief named Salageri. He carried out his plans so silently that ladders were already placed against the walls before the monks were aroused. The strength of numbers prevailed, though the defenders made a brave, if ineffectual attempt, to ward off the assailants, and soon the Genoese were masters of the position, and of the place. The defenceless monks gathered in the chapel of the Holy Cross and there awaited the invaders. These were, for the moment, impressed by the majesty of the surroundings, but soon their habitual contempt even for the most holy things restored their audacity. They took possession of the relics and other sacred objects. One seized the bust of S. Honoratus and broke off its head; another took the pastoral staff and made mimicry of a bishop's ceremonial acts. Then they imprisoned the monks and installed themselves in the fortress, where they remained for sixteen days. It was their design to use their latest possession as the centre of their operations in Provence. Fortunately the news of the invasion spread, and George de Marles, Seneschal of Provence, levied an army in which both the nobility and the people were willingly enrolled. It was soon seen that the fortress would not be recaptured without great loss of life, and a capitulation was therefore arranged, by the terms of which the pirates were to take away a sum of money and some valuable vases as compensation for their withdrawal. The monks were greatly cheered and encouraged by the munificence of Louis II, king of Provence, who in his will dated April 27th, 1417, left a legacy of £600 for the purchase of church ornaments to replace those of which they had been so ruthlessly despoiled. These perpetual raids upon the island were not the only troubles that befell the monastery. Others, greater and deeper, were threatening.

The Sojourn of Popes at Avignon[1].

During the period of the papal schism when the Church was embarrassed by two rival popes, the one resident at Rome, and the other in France, Lerins gave unfaltering allegiance to the

---

[1] A most interesting and illuminative study of the Avignon Papacy has been made by Mons. G. Mollat, who has just published *Les Papes d'Avignon*, Librairie Lecoffre, Paris, 1912.

one at Rome; but the proximity of the monastery to Avignon obviously meant new difficulties. Rostan had been directly nominated to the abbacy by Boniface IX in A.D. 1399, and put in possession by a cardinal-legate sent expressly from Rome for the purpose. The pope at Avignon (Clement VII) endeavoured to nominate Nicolas, who would have endeavoured to persuade the monks to oppose the Roman pontiff. Clement next sent a cardinal of Spain to depose Rostan, and to despoil him of his position; and this deposition was maintained by Benedict XIII who actually held his court at Lerins, whilst, by calculated tardiness, he tried to avoid meeting his competitor Gregory XII[1]. Happily the schism was terminated in A.D. 1417 when the Council of Constance pronounced the fall of Benedict, "the most obstinate and redoubtable supporter of the schism," and elected Otto Colonna, who took the title of Martin V. He soon gave his attention to the monastery of Lerins, and laid upon himself the charge of finding it an abbot. His choice fell upon Geoffrey de Mont-Choisi, a monk of S. Martin of Tours. The monks were surprised to find themselves deprived of their right of election, and loudly protested that they would resist any attempt on the part of the new abbot to take possession. This is the first sign of the cloud that presaged the gathering storm. The monks were as good as their word, and the rejected abbot was only able to make his entrance under the escort of some soldiers of the king. He managed to ingratiate himself later by tactful means. He obtained from the pope several favours for the monastery, specially the annulment of some contracts by which property had been sold under injurious conditions. Under him studies once again flourished. He himself had some literary ability, for he wrote on *The Perfection of Monks*. He also put in order the library which was renowned as the finest in Europe, and had been enriched by the counts of Provence, the kings of Naples and others with most rare books in every language. This was not all, for he carried out the repair of the tower. In the end the appointment proved to be excellent in every way. Discipline was completely restored. He gained the gratitude of his monks by abridging *The Book of*

[1] Salembier, *Le grand schisme d'Occident*, p. 233.

the Professions, which was too long and wearisome[1]. He also enriched by a gift of stalls the choir of the chapel of the Holy Cross at his own expense.

In A.D. 1436 he was nominated to the abbacy of S. Germain, near Paris, after he had been present at the Council of Basle as ambassador of Louis III, king of Naples. The monks of this monastery had elected a man of their own choice to the abbacy, but Geoffrey's death, poisoned (so it was said), at the instigation of his rival, put an end to the difficulty. There is evidence that the discipline and piety introduced by Geoffrey were not maintained by his immediate successors. The first of these was Louis du Pont, who was not in favour with the king because he was a Nicois, and he was forbidden to enter the monastery. He attempted, however, to govern it in absence, and nominated John de Bolliers and John Maynier to administer in his name. The monks were left in want of the barest necessaries, and made a complaint. Meantime the abbot was admitted again to the king's favour, and effected an exchange with Antony Rostan, abbot of Thoronet. The new abbot held a general chapter, the statutes of which have been preserved, and they show how urgent was the need of reform. Among the enactments, every monk was ordered to communicate on solemn festivals, under pain of spending a whole day on bread and water. A fine was levied for continued absence from the monastery. No monk was permitted to leave the island without the abbot's permission, under pain of excommunication. Statutes were also promulgated which specified the rights and duties of the various officers of the monastery. The obligations of the abbot in his relations with his community were also enumerated. Among them, he must supply the monastery with bread, wine, wood and salt ; "the wine shall be pure and good." He must also provide "splendid repasts" on the first Sunday in Advent, at Christmas, and other customary festivals. He must pay and keep for the service of the monastery, a cook, barber, night watchman, and gardener, maintained one year by the abbot, and the year following by the monastery. He must also

---

[1] *Inventaire de Mme la Ctesse de Saint-Seine*, f. 13, quoted by H. Moris, *L'Abbaye de Lérins*, p. 204.

furnish arms and ammunition for the protection of the fortress ;
a fisherman, a boat and three oarsmen ; linen for the table,
kitchen, refectory, and pantry; plates and dishes, and kitchen
utensils, storeroom accessories ; linen for the monastery, and all
ropes for the wells.

At the death of Rostan, William Vaycière obtained possession
of the monastery, and gives the first indication of what was
to follow.   He replied to the protestations of the monks by
excommunicating them ; but they were absolved by the pope,
and Vaycière was deprived.   His successor, Andrew de Plaisance,
was regularly elected by the chapter.   This did not end the
disputes, for Vaycière was again put in possession, meanwhile
Andrew de Plaisance laid his case before the court at Rome.
The latter seems really to have had the direction of the monastery
until he was appointed in A.D. 1464 to the bishopric of Sisteron.

We see indications of the growth of abuses.   Property and
ecclesiastical rights gradually became transmissible by heritage
and gift.   Prelatures were regarded as fiefs, and manorial lords
received the fruits of religious properties.   We even see women
put in possession of monasteries, and seculars, appointed abbots
by the sword, going to live with their families in offices the
first rule of which should have been the removal of all that can
recall the agitation and vanity of the world.   Thus was the way
prepared for the introduction of a system of abbots-commendatory which struck the last blow at the moral grandeur of
the monastery.

CHAPTER XVII

THE DAY OF DECAY

The Day of Decay is from the period of the *Commendam*[1] to the time of secularisation in the 18th century. In this period there is much of parallelism with the history of the decay of monasticism in England, but the parallel is far from close. From the 6th century onwards the rights and uses of monasteries began to be abused. Vacant abbacies were given to bishops expelled from their sees by barbarian invaders. From the time of the conquest of the Gauls, the Franks had not differentiated between the rights of ecclesiastical and any other property; to them neither was sacred. In the 8th century bishoprics were regarded as fiefs, and were given as a reward for military services, and in this way the king's henchmen were permitted to draw the revenues of the office.

In the 9th and 10th centuries, Franks and Burgundians became titular abbots of various monasteries, and appropriated the revenues to their own use. Sometimes the canonical possessors were left to fulfil, under certain restrictions, the functions of the sacred ministry. At other times mere seculars were appointed by the power of the sword; and in the words of Bede, "they received the tonsure to possess abbeys." The Church naturally protested against this usurpation of her rights; popes and emperors realised the injustice, but were powerless to alter it. In this way the old relations between the abbot and

---

[1] The gradual growth of the claim, made by despotic rulers, to bestow the revenues of a monastery, and the title and position of abbot upon any ecclesiastic, or even a layman, without the necessity of his residence there, or of conformity to its rules, attained its utmost limits in the Church of France. The procedure is technically known as the "Commendam." A monastery is held "in Commendam" as a *provisional* trust, in contradistinction to a permanent appointment which is held "in Titulum."

the brethren grew estranged. Many attempts were vainly made
to regulate the appointments. The right to nominate laymen
was ecclesiastically abolished in A.D. 1122, and the Council of
Trent[1] decided that vacant monasteries should only be bestowed
on pious regulars, and that the principal house of an order and
its daughter priories should no longer be placed *in Commendam.*

Hitherto Lerins had been more fortunate than most of the
monasteries; and with one or two very temporary exceptions,
due to internal troubles, had been ruled for a thousand
years by abbots who were elected with all regularity by the
"religious" themselves, and resided on the island. The relationship between abbot and monks had been hitherto that of
an united brotherhood. But in A.D. 1464 Lerins was put *in
Commendam* and remained so for more than three hundred
years. This year, therefore, marked an eventful change in the
history of the monastery, which now entered not only upon the
period of its greatest trials and difficulties, both from within and
from without, but upon the commencement of a decadence from
which it did not recover, and as a result of which it was ultimately
secularised.

In future, the successors of the poor and humble solitaries,
who had ruled the brotherhood of Lerins, were great lords of
high rank, bishops and cardinals, and even princes of the blood,
who possessed numerous fiefs, priories in various dioceses, and
great revenues of money and goods, and its claustral abbot
ended by assuming the title of " Prince of Sabourg,"—a town of
one hundred inhabitants. Thus the abbey of Lerins lost its
former simple grandeur, and its unique reputation. It indeed
gained a new fame, but the men who earned it were no longer
the scholarly and saintly ascetics that brought honour and
renown to the island of Honoratus in its golden age. Its fame
was of a different and less praiseworthy sort.

The first of the abbots-commendatory was Isnard, bishop of
Grasse, who held the position for twenty-five years. He was a
poor man, and part of the revenues of his bishopric belonged to
Lerins. It was in fact on this account that he received the
appointment. He was solemnly received at the monastery and

---

[1] Session 25, Chap. XXI, *De regularibus.*

appears to have respected its rights. He was succeeded in A.D. 1489 by John Andrew de Grimaldi, who had commenced his ecclesiastical career at the court of Rome. He combined the offices of referendary to the pope, provost of Grasse, abbot-commendatory of Lerins, and then bishop of Grasse; whilst his nephew Augustine de Grimaldi acted as his coadjutor in the see. John Andrew's name is preserved in the annals of the monastery in part by his gift in A.D. 1499 of the chest which is now in the cathedral of Grasse, and of which a description will be found in the Appendix. He made an effort to carry out reforms in the monastery, but was frustrated by the opposition of William Saletta, the claustral prior. In A.D. 1500, being now of advanced age, John Andrew resigned his abbacy in favour of Augustine. The first official act of the new abbot was the dismissal of the prior, and the firm administration of his government rendered the period memorable in other directions. Like his uncle before him, he held more than one office, and was lord of Monaco as well as abbot of Lerins and bishop of Grasse. But this great position did not preclude him from a laudable desire to see restored to the isle of the saints the pristine fervour of former days; and with this intention he asked the king (Francis I) to send him the grand prior of Cluny to reform the monastery. In order to carry out the reform, the abbot-commendatory conceived the idea of uniting Lerins to the congregation of S. Justina of Padua (Monte-Cassino), which for two hundred years had rendered signal service to Christianity. The pope pronounced the union in a Bull of January 29th, A.D. 1515, and it was confirmed by the king. In order to make the union doubly sure, Augustine resigned his position as commendatory, but took care to reserve to himself for life the revenues of the abbatial[1] income, and the customary honours, privileges and powers, as well as temporal jurisdiction in Cannes, Arluc and other places.

In A.D. 1516 he caused Jerome de Montferrat, the prior elected by the chapter of Monte-Cassino, to be put in possession of the monastery. This prior brought with him ten monks to

---

[1] The revenues appropriated to the maintenance of the monks were called "conventual income."

carry out the reform and among them were Gregory Cortesius and Denis Faucher of whom we shall give some account later.

In A.D. 1522 the newly elected pope (Adrian VI) came to Lerins, on his way to Rome, and Augustine Grimaldi went there to pay his respects to him. Much touched by the hospitality extended to him on the occasion, the pope granted a plenary and perpetual indulgence for the festival of the five hundred martyrs of Porcarius, to all the monks present and future[1].

The Emperor Maximilian died in A.D. 1519, and Francis I aspired to the imperial power, but the electors preferred Charles V, and war between the two rivals ensued. The constable of Bourbon, who was now an enemy of France, put himself at the head of Charles' troops and arrived in A.D. 1524 on the banks of the Var with 25,000 infantry and 2000 cavalry, supported by a fleet of thirty vessels of the Spanish fleet that had been sent by Charles to revictual the constable's army. A French naval force, under the command of Admiral Fayette, with Andrew Doria then in the service of France, met the hostile fleet. In spite of its victory, the French fleet, powerless against a huge army on land, was compelled to retire to Marseilles. The enemy had no difficulty, therefore, in taking possession of S. Laurent, Villeneuve, Antibes, Cannes, Grasse and the islands of Lerins. Charles entered Provence with an army of 48,000 Germans, Spaniards and Italians. It was at this time that the town of Cannes suffered so severely. He was crowned king of Arles and Provence. His soldiers, the prey to hunger, lost 20,000 of their number on the passes of the Esterel, where fifty brave Provençals "with no defence but their courage and the difficulty of the passage," barred their way. In A.D. 1525 a Spanish ship with Francis I on board as a prisoner of war, touched at the island, and the king stayed a night at the monastery. In remembrance of his visit he made a present to the monastery of a silver chest bedecked with vermilion. The truce of Nice between Charles and Francis was not of long duration, and the struggle recommenced in A.D. 1536, when a Spanish squadron again sacked the island under the leadership of Andrew Doria, one of the most celebrated sailors of his century, who after bravely serving

[1] *Chron. Ler.* II, p. 183.

France, lent his aid to Charles. In the absence of details we are left to the supposition that the prince failed in his enterprise and was forced to retire. A treaty was signed in A.D. 1538 and hostilities ceased. Before making its descent upon Lerins, the fleet had stayed for a time in the port of Monaco, and was welcomed by Augustine de Grimaldi, whose presence there was due to the assassination of his brother Lucian, and it fell to his lot to take in hand the affairs of the principality as lord of Monaco. As he had taken the part of Charles V, it was only natural that Francis I should notice such disloyalty, and seek some means of retaliation. This he did by confiscating all the revenues and benefices Augustine held in France. Seeing that the king had declared him a rebel, and guilty of high treason, the monks of Lerins hoped to get possession of the properties he had reserved for his enjoyment for life, but an order of the court ordered them to be paid into the treasury, and they were afterwards ceded to Cardinal de Bourbon. Augustine was on the point of recovering them, but died suddenly. There was some suspicion of poisoning. Some of the monks who had disagreed with his policy of reform proceeded to elect Monsignor de Jarente, bishop of Vence, as his successor, but the king nominated John de Bellay, bishop of Bayonne. In the absence of the abbot-regular, the monks protested against the king's nominee, and the monastery gates were closed against the representatives of the new commendatory. The king was much annoyed, and sent a company of soldiers to force an entrance. The letters-patent approving the union with Monte-Cassino were withdrawn in A.D. 1542 ; all strangers were forbidden admittance to the island, and all Italians were ordered to leave it. In A.D. 1548 John de Bellay, now bishop of Paris, and cardinal, and later archbishop of Bordeaux, made an arrangement with William Pelicier, bishop of Montpelier, by which he exchanged the abbacy of Lerins for that of Échailly. The Italians were recalled in A.D. 1558.

The history of this period thus presents us with a picture of a continual struggle of the monks against their commendatory-abbots, many of whom were, however, really remarkable men. When in A.D. 1568 the monks protested against the appointment of Cardinal de Bourbon, who was archbishop of Rouen, and a noble and powerful person, parliament retorted by seizing all the revenues of the monastery. In the hope of suppressing the *Commendam*, the Cassinists made an offer to the cardinal that they would at their own expense erect a tower on the island of Sainte Marguerite to accommodate fifty monks, and promised to guard the port. When this proposition had been refused, the island was ceded to the people of Cannes for a payment of 200 crowns a year and other dues.

When Henry IV in A.D. 1591 nominated John Baptist Romans d'Agoult as commendatory-abbot, the Roman curia refused to sanction an election that had been made by a protestant prince ; but in spite of this, Henry insisted on his nomination and ordered his nominee " to take real and actual possession of the abbey." As a result of negotiations with Rome, this prince confirmed the union with Monte-Cassino, but made it a condition that the monastery should be under the governance in things both temporal and spiritual of a religious who was "a good Frenchman." This proved a happy solution ; and the community once more enjoyed its rights, under abbots regularly elected, during the next twenty years. The *Commendam* was in danger of being re-introduced in A.D. 1611, when the prince of Joinville demanded the abbacy, but to avoid the re-establishment of this fatal system, the monks, with the pope's authority, offered him the island of Sainte Marguerite, and obtained in return an ordinance to the effect that " the king in council has revoked and declared null and void the gift to the prince of Joinville of the abbey of S. Honoratus"; the prince renounced the position of abbot, and the chapter were thus able to proceed to the election of a successor. The monks gave as one of their reasons for the cession, that they desired to place the island of Sainte Marguerite in the hands of some powerful lord, who would construct a fortress there and purge their shores of the pirates who frequented them.

In A.D. 1635 the Spanish fleet again appeared on the coasts of Provence. The islands of the Lerins offered little resistance and soon capitulated. They proved an important strategic position to the Spaniards, who during the ensuing two years added to the fortifications on the island of Sainte Marguerite, and, having sent away the monks from the island of Saint Honorat, they fortified this also; using the chapels for defensive purposes, until Marshal de Vitry assembled the nobility of Provence to raise an army against the enemy. The states assembled at Fréjus and granted a subsidy of 12,000 francs. The French naval force was placed under the command of Count Harcourt and the archbishop of Bordeaux, and took up a position under the forts of Sainte Marguerite and Saint Honorat. It was unfortunate that these two commanders quarrelled about the supreme command and blows were exchanged. This provoked the Provençals and they remained in a state of inactivity. The king wrote as follows to the archbishop: "I cannot tell you the displeasure with which I see my armies and these preparations ineffectual, and am aware that all the world knows that those to whom I confide such important designs have spent their time in quarrelling." Richelieu could scarcely restrain his anger and wrote to de Vitry: "It is so little creditable to a man of your profession and quality to be willing to offend a person of such a position as the archbishop (which they say you have done), that unless I had seen this error committed, I could not persuade myself that it had been done." The king wrote to the archbishop urging that he and the count should act on so important an occasion "for the welfare of my affairs, and for the reputation of my arms." Still there was delay. Richelieu wrote again: "I am extremely astonished at the delay. You know as well as any one how important it is to recapture these islands. You will oblige as much by making this matter successful as if you gave your life. I conjure you to believe this." M. de Noyers also wrote to this effect: "The long delayed attack exhausts our patience, and obliges his majesty to say that if, eight days after receipt of this letter, you see no opportunity, it shall be postponed to a more convenient time, when minds are more prompt and more disposed to recover this portion of France." In his letter to the archbishop, Richelieu said, "If you can attack the islands, you will do the most glorious action in the world, and will render his majesty so signal a service that he will be ready to forget the past." The archbishop, thus spurred on, redoubled his zeal. An attack was made. The stone entrenchments of the Spaniards were broken down and part of the fort was destroyed, but a sudden tempest delayed operations. When it had passed, a second attack was made and the French landed and seized the entrenchments. The king then wrote to congratulate the archbishop on his success. This was all the reward he obtained. He had shown the greatest courage, but his enemies accused him of dereliction of duty, and he fell into disgrace. The Marquis Duquesne, a distinguished French naval officer, who began his career in the merchant service, obtained his first distinction in naval warfare by the capture of the islands from the Spaniards on this occasion. The fort on Sainte Marguerite was repaired according to the plans of Vauban, and the monks, who had taken refuge at Villauris, were recalled to the monastery. It was about this time that Monsignor de Sourdis, archbishop of Bordeaux, addressed a memorandum to the court on the importance of the coast, and of the shelter afforded by the islands of the Lerins. He drew attention to its "most beautiful situation." Among the advantages of its position on the Mediterranean he mentions that "no navigation can be unseen. If for instance we desire to make war with the Turks, they cannot sail the sea and escape discovery. If there is war with Spain, Genoa or Savoy, the enemy would not be able to leave their ports without the fear of being seen. If there is universal peace, it is the most splendid repository for merchandise; no better ever existed."

The court was advised that in the best interests of France it would be wise to get rid of Italian monks and other strangers, lest they should betray the island into the hands of an enemy. The fear may have been, and probably was, entirely groundless, but the suspicions aroused at the time, by this mixture of nationalities, were a cause of continual disorder, especially among those monks who were by birth half Italian and half French.

After the expulsion of the Spaniards, Cardinal Richelieu, at whose instigation the assault had been made, was anxious to reward Cardinal de la Valette, derisively called Valet, by making him abbot-commendatory. Louis XIII therefore by an edict disunited Lerins from Monte-Cassino and annexed it to S. Maur. It was Monsignor Godeau, bishop of Grasse, who had advised the king to take this course. His motive was not unimpeachable. He had a spite against the monks of Lerins because they had refused to sell him the church and house which they owned at Grasse, and he was jealous of the jurisdiction their abbot exercised in his diocese. Through his efforts, the Cassinists were sacrificed in spite of the fidelity that they had always shown towards France, and they were dispossessed of the monastery which they had occupied from A.D. 1512 to A.D. 1638, and the monks of S. Maur were brought in. After Richelieu and Louis XIII were both dead, the power of Godeau weakened, but he wrote a letter to the count of Brienna in which he said: "I have been told that what the late king, of glorious memory, has done is on the point of being changed, and that the Benedictines of S. Maur whom I introduced, are to be withdrawn. None can tell you, better than I, what is the truth concerning the state of this house before the entry of these fathers; and the consequences of the change. It is not only the evil life of the monks that has brought down God's anger upon the island of Saint Honorat so long inviolable. There has been no regular practice of charity, or virtue. The superior officers have thought only of filling their own purses, and bad management is clearly proved by the debts that have been contracted. Dom Maynier cannot say, 'Silver and gold have I none.' I fear to see the return to the monastery of people who have been the cause of so many scandals. My diocese is much edified by those who are now there in possession." This letter had not the desired effect. The Cassinists prevailed; the union was signed in A.D. 1645; and the monks of S. Maur were sent away.

By the help of the archbishop of Aix, Louis Maynier, abbot-regular of Monte-Cassino, endeavoured to supplant Godeau in the bishopric of Grasse. In a letter to the king asking that Antibes might be united to the abbey of Lerins, and suggesting that as the Lerinensians possessed a large priory there, it would be better that their residence should be in that place, Maynier makes a curious statement. Sufficient monks will be left at Lerins to conduct the services, but the installation of the

majority at Antibes "will much more conduce to the glory
of God and the edification of the people than in a desert island
where, for habitation, there is only a tower occupied in great
part by soldiery whom the king is compelled to maintain there
for the preservation of the place, but who impede the monks
in their religious fervour, when they should be free from all
noise and tumult." This petition was unavailing.

For the next hundred years, during which the abbots-
commendatory, who governed Lerins after Cardinal de la Valette,
succeeded one another almost without interruption, the monastery
was directed by abbots-regular, chosen by the general chapters
of the different congregations to which Lerins was joined from
the 16th to the 18th centuries. One of the first duties of these
regulars was to defend themselves against the great lords who
were chiefly concerned to secure for themselves the revenues
furnished by the monastery, and who for the most part never
visited it. At de la Valette's death, Armand de Bourbon, prince
of Conti, became abbot-commendatory in A.D. 1642, but owing to
differences between the court of France and the pope, the bulls
were not granted till A.D. 1645. The king forbade this prince to
cede his *Commendam*, and his majesty was not allowed to
nominate a successor in case of death. But in spite of the
clauses contained in the patents of nomination, the prince of
Conti abandoned his *Commendam* to Cardinal Mazarin in A.D. 1654,
to whom the monks were to pay a life pension, in order to obtain
union with Monte-Cassino. In exchange for the annuity, the
monks asked for other privileges besides the confirmation of the
union; they desired the ratification of their right to take salt
free from excise duty, which had been accorded by the counts
of Provence and was no longer recognised; they also requested that they should no longer have soldiers quartered on
them whose habits and inclinations were not helpful to monastic
ideals. They insisted upon this point because they were incom-
moded not only personally, but in the service of God, for as they
said in their letter to the cardinal, "The monks cannot give
attention to study or to spiritual exercises amid continued dis-
turbance, and moreover from the contrariety of the two professions association is incompatible." The monks also addressed a

petition to the king that they might enter into possession of the
properties of the abbatial income, the revenue of which the cardinal
continued to take. His death in A.D. 1661 did not materially
alter the position—for Louis XIV gave the monastery to Cardinal
Louis de Vendôme—except that the new abbot entered into an
agreement[1] with the monks, to whom he conceded, together with
the confirmation of the union, such privileges and advantages as
the right to institute and to deprive claustral officers, fishing and
shipwreck rights, and the revenues of certain priories. They were
also freed from any liability to maintain the pensioners sent by
the king, as lay monks, to Lerins as to other monasteries of
France[2].

Louis de Vendôme was succeeded in the abbacy in A.D. 1670
by his brother Philip who took possession by nomination of the
king solely, as the papal bulls were refused. It was during his
abbacy that the "religious" made a complaint to the king in
A.D. 1692 to the effect that the abbots of Monte-Cassino sent all
their most scandalous monks to Lerins, who were received there
without any difficulty. Complaint was also made that they
could not educate the youths, as there was no one who could
teach. The number of abbots in the monastery is so large, it
was said, that the rents and revenues were squandered. In
expressing a desire that their monastery might be freed from
union with Monte-Cassino they said, " It is a matter of nothing
less than the preservation of one of the illustrious monasteries of
your kingdom." Their wishes were endorsed by the archbishop
of Aix. Thus were attempts being continually made to dis-
possess the Cassinists. The pretext was always the same, it was
a question of nationality. It was argued that the subordination
of French monks to Italian superiors aroused antipathy and

---

[1] *Inventaire de Mme la Ctesse de Saint-Seine*, f. 51, quoted by H. Moris, *Histoire
et Monuments*, p. 52.

[2] A decree in Council of A.D. 1611 drew up regulations for the maintenance of
" poor gentlemen, disabled captains and soldiers," who were to receive assistance
from the religious houses of the kingdom of France. In A.D. 1624 Louis XIII laid all
monasteries under an obligation to pay an annual sum of one hundred pounds for the
maintenance of disabled soldiers, and an edict of A.D. 1629 directed that poor
captains and disabled soldiers should be distributed for maintenance among the
abbeys and priories of the kingdom.

defiance. The real causes of any disaffection were probably jealousy and ambition. It was a pity that questions of nationality, and feelings of jealousy should have divided the monks at such a time, and diverted them from what might have been the common interest of striving for the suppression of the *Commendam.* On the death of Philip de Vendôme in A.D. 1727 they did resolve to make a supreme effort to secure its extinction, and with this object they approached Monsignor d'Anthelmy, bishop of Grasse, who was quite ready to make himself the mouthpiece of all those who alleged grievances, whether rightly or wrongly, against the union. In seeking to receive the full enjoyment of the abbatial revenues, they promised that if he should succeed on their behalf, they would give him an annual pension of £4000, and make this sum a perpetual donation to the bishopric of Grasse.

The monks little knew that their negotiations would give birth to strife that would last for twenty years ; nor did they imagine that the bishop of Grasse would use this opportunity to further his own designs, and they could not have suspected that those designs were in the direction of the secularisation of their monastery. With this object in view, he did not scruple to aggravate the situation. He denounced the disorders, and painted a very dark picture of the position. His first step was to delay the nomination of an abbot-commendatory, and two years passed without any action being taken in the matter, and as the author of *The Island and Abbey of Lerins* quaintly puts it, " The bishop had in this interval of his indecision a means of consolation, an abbey with a rental of seven thousand pounds to which he was nominated[1]." He was popular at Court and successful in all he undertook, and the monks awaited the happy termination of their affairs, the more so because the bishop's letters were full of bright hope. To their amazement he then wrote to say that the king desired to make a nomination to their monastery in the person of himself, and that their union with Monte-Cassino was improper. His acceptance of the abbacy made the monks think that, in spite of the declarations of Cardinal de Fleury to the contrary, their proxy had not performed his mission with

[1] *L'île et l'abbaye,* p. 214.

all the zeal that was desirable. The abbot-regular, Dom Jordany, wished to go to Paris in order to uphold the interests of the community, but was dissuaded from doing so by the bishop who said there was no need to take the journey as he would find everything completed. To the grief and consternation of the monks, they learned that the king had joined their monastery to the bishopric of Grasse under a warrant dated January 14th, A.D. 1732, and in a second one on the 26th of the same month, it was stated that his majesty had ordered that the vacancy in the abbacy should cease from that date, and the bishop of Grasse would on that day enter into possession of its revenues, and would make all speed to obtain the necessary bulls at the court of Rome ; but later the need of this formality was withdrawn and d'Anthelmy received an ordinary warrant dated January 26th, A.D. 1732 ; and instead of the pension that was offered to him in the event of his success, he obtained, in his defeat, the full and entire possession of all the revenues. Cardinal de Fleury wrote to the abbot-regular to assure him that the bishop had not abused his confidence, or suppressed any of the reasons by which the claims made by the monks were supported, but that the king had had them examined and they were found defective, and that His Majesty had the right of nomination. The monks again made their protest, and gained their cause, but the bishop, as a rejoinder, obtained a decree of the council of state that ordered the monks, " To give an account of the bulls, letters patent and other titles of virtue, by which they pretend that the monastery has been united to the congregation of Monte-Cassino, and ought to be exempted from the royal nomination." As this did not seem sufficient, he demanded that his opponents should recall their opposition at the court of Rome. This request was renewed in A.D. 1738 and A.D. 1739.

Another warrant issued in this latter year annulled the bull of Leo (which united the monastery to Monte-Cassino), and enjoined the monks to conform to the laws of the kingdom and to unite with a French congregation of the order of S. Benedict, without any particular one being specified to them, and in default of so doing they would be submitted to the jurisdiction of the

ordinary.   Conformably to this warrant they besought union
with Cluny from Cardinal d'Auvergne, the abbot-general of
this order, and he issued a decree accordingly.   Now it is the
turn of the bishop of Grasse to protest, and he demanded
definite submission.   Two warrants of A.D. 1741 and 1742 cancel
the decree because it was issued without royal authority.   And
now at last in A.D. 1743 the bishop thought it time to pay a
visit to Lerins in his capacity as abbot, to which he had been
nominated eleven years previously.

The record of his reception is pathetic.   Dom Benedict, who
had succeeded Dom Jordany as abbot-regular, two monks and
the cellarer were present to receive their visitor.   Three other
monks were prisoners in their cells and guarded by soldiers,
guilty it seems of quarrelling and fighting, of disobedience, and
of subverting discipline.   The old prior, quite unable to restore
or to maintain discipline, had found it necessary to appeal for
help to Captain Audry, commandant of the fort at Sainte
Marguerite.   Two letters from this officer are extant[1].

Writing to the bishop of Grasse, he says : "I must not leave
you in ignorance that Dom Benedict wrote the day before
yesterday to ask me to send him an officer to guard three
monks who have grossly insulted him.   I have placed six men
and a sergeant there to prevent greater violences.   As I have
no right to punish these monks, I do not know whether to
withdraw this guard or to renew it.   I will act according to the
advice you are pleased to give me."   He duly received a reply,
and in thanking the bishop for it, he writes again, "I have
delayed until to-day informing the court of this incident, and
I now send you a minute of the report I have drawn up and
which these two officers have signed, in order that you may
kindly tell me if it is necessary to add or withdraw anything."
The prior informed the bishop that these three mutineers "no
longer appear at the refectory, or attend the conventual
services ; they are unwilling to celebrate mass in their turn,
they no longer observe the fasts, and they make fun of my
orders and call me 'the old man.'"   The prior also wrote to the
father of Dom Caesar Alziary, one of the recalcitrants, "Help

[1] *Les Archives des Alpes.-Marit.* G. 169.

me to inspire him with better feelings, and if he will return from the evil of his ways, I will forget all the past[1]." The recalcitrant monks also wrote to the bishop, and to their parents, retorting with charges against the prior and justifying themselves. D'Anthelmy proceeded to hear and determine these counter-charges. The monks complained that, when they asked to be present at the divine office, the prior replied, "Give them something to eat and drink, that is all they want.' They also complained that they were refused a light in the evening and were not allowed to write to their parents. Alziary said he had had the fever but only saw the doctor once. "It ill becomes the old man to accuse us of living as we like, when he gives himself all he wants, and keeps his Lent with woodcock. Let him ask the soldiers their opinion of us." When he recommended them to thrash us well, they said, "They are angels." Asked why they had dealings with the boatmen, one of the rebel monks said, " He had to send some things to his mother." They were by the king's orders, relegated, as a punishment, to different monasteries of Cluny.

Another matter in dispute with d'Anthelmy concerned the depredations committed in the island and monastery at the time of the war in A.D. 1746. The united forces of France and Spain on the one side, and of the Austrians and Piedmontese assisted by the English navy, on the other, carried their struggle for supremacy into Italy, not far from the frontiers of Provence. The Austrian army under the command of General Brown crossed the Var, and he established himself at Vence. From here he issued a manifesto in somewhat grandiloquent terms as follows: "We Maximilian Ulysses Brown, Count of the Holy Roman Empire, Councillor of State and War for her Imperial Majesty Queen of Hungary and Bohemia, Commandant General in Provence of the Imperial Army and of that of His Majesty King of Sardinia. We make known to all the inhabitants of Provence and other provinces of her very Christian Majesty that so long as they do not bear arms against the royal allied troops, and are not guilty of violence and opposition, and remain quietly in their homes and possessions, they shall enjoy our protection, but if they make armed resistance, or use any violence, we

[1] Quoted by L'Abbé Tisserand, Vol. v, pp. 40, 41.

reserve the rights of war, and of fire and blood without distinction of grade or condition." On arrival at Cannes he found it practically deserted, as most of the inhabitants had taken refuge in the islands of Lerins, whither they had taken their children and their treasures. As these islands offered useful facilities, he resolved to capture them. They were garrisoned only by a company of cadets who guarded prisoners of state, and by three companies of invalided troops. They were summoned to surrender, and General Brown took peaceful possession, and stayed there some months, protected by the English fleet under Admiral Byng. During their sojourn in Provence the troops committed terrible ravages everywhere. The island was re-taken by Chevalier de Belle-Isle, and fifty Austrians, who formed the garrison, were made prisoners of war. The thickness and solidity of the walls of the tower were proof against the bullets of the French artillery, but they entered through the windows and made great havoc of the marbles, floors, and partitions. These were repaired later by Dom Maximus the prior. This is the last episode in the military history of the Lerins that merits any record.

This occupation by strangers was a ruinous time for the monastery, as the Austrians levied a heavy contribution on it. Apart from this the damage done was estimated at a very large sum of money. The monks accused the bishop of Grasse of wishing to take possession of the right of indemnity, and of an intention to leave the interior of the monastery unrepaired and uninhabitable. The bishop then drew up a memorandum demanding the secularisation of the monastery. It was not the wish of the monks who inhabited it, and they replied in a letter, which did not arrive in time to be read by him, as in the meantime he died. It was received by Louis Sextus de Jarente, bishop of Digne, who succeeded him in the *Commendam* in A.D. 1752 and was the last to hold the office at Lerins. The new abbot was most favourably inclined towards the monastery, and the monks added prayers " for the preservation of his days." Maximus Rainbert, the prior, in a letter of congratulation said : " We are twenty persons in all, including monks and domestics. We have demanded, and still demand our union with the order of Cluny, and we have no wish to be secularised." A council of state confirmed in A.D. 1756 the decree of union that had been issued by Cardinal Auvergne. But the catastrophe came nearer. Such an old institution declines almost insensibly; "the salt had lost its savour," and Lerins was to bear the consequence. During the next thirty years, the history of the monastery can be written in the one word, decadence. It will be seen from the preceding account that it was due in great measure to the abbots-commendatory who were selfishly bent on drawing the revenues for their own use, and prevented the monks from being governed by their natural superiors, and rendered all reform difficult, if not impossible. They made the cloister-life languish, and led the monks into distaste for their holy vocation. The abuses of the *Commendam* had no small share in the preparation of the way that culminated in the secularisation of the monastery. The decadence continued year after year until in A.D. 1768 King Louis XV asked Monsignor Prunières, bishop of Grasse, for information concerning the various orders of his diocese, and the picture presented by this prelate was lamentably sad. Lerins could only muster seven monks and these were not resident the whole of the year. As Monsieur l'Abbé Tisserand has well said[1]: "Far be it from us to belittle the praises which have been showered upon the monks of Lerins, but we have the documents in our hands from which to publish the truth." The celebrated abbey was closed because all reforms were judged to be impossible, and, in point of fact, it shared in the general deterioration of all the monasteries in the 18th century.

These pious establishments have their human side, and their divine side, and if the institution gravitates towards the worldly and the secular, and loses its savour of spirituality, becoming materialistic in its aims, God forsakes it and ruin falls on it. Monks can only carry out their vocation by the constant exercise of chastity, poverty, humility and obedience. Prayer and mortification are essential. For their ideals more than the common virtues are necessary. The monastery of Lerins had not been without warnings. Godeau's motives may not have been unselfish, but he spoke the truth when he declared that

[1] *Chronologie des Abbés*, Vol. v.

there was no regularity. The monks too had heard many fervent sermons which were calls to penitence. The memory of their predecessors had been recalled. They had been reminded that the island had been a citadel of which rules and vows were its walls of defence, and piety its arms; while now it is come to be regarded as a hateful prison from which men long to escape.

The bishop of Grasse was compelled to declare that reform was now impossible. The final blow was not long delayed. It fell in A.D. 1788 and when the commissioners arrived on the island, they found but four monks. So ingloriously was closed the monastery that had lasted for nearly fourteen centuries. It may be generally true that Englishmen remember monasteries only in their decay, but this can never be said of Lerins. The decadence of its latter years is forgotten in the remembrance of the splendour of the work it did in the golden age, and of the names of its sons, who were more than worthy to be added to the roll of fame, and achieved an honour that will remain as long as the world shall last.

CHAPTER XVIII

SOME LATER WRITERS OF LERINS

In the golden age, as we have seen, there were men taking refuge in the island of Saint Honorat from the disorders and misfortunes of the Roman empire who added to the monastery's renown in many ways, and not least by their contributions to literature that have had a permanent value. The *Commonitorium* of Vincent is immortal, and has been praised by the learned in every century. We have dealt too with the writings of Salvian, Hilary, Eucherius, Faustus and of other scholars who added lustre to the records of Lerins. In the Middle Ages study continued, but did not flourish in as great a degree as formerly, and the monastery produced no serious and important publication during this period. We search in vain for names that will bear comparison with the pioneers of Lerinensian literature. A few writers made a brave, and not altogether unsuccessful, attempt to connect the present with the past, and in this connection reference must be made to four ; they are the troubadour Raymond Feraud, of the 13th century, and the theologians Denis Faucher of the 15th century, Gregory Cortesius of the 16th century and Vincent Barralis, the historian of the monastery, of the 16th century.

Raymond Feraud, the Troubadour.

Provençal literature is confined within limits both of time and space. It took its rise in the 9th century and disappeared in the 14th. Its geographical area does not far exceed the linguistic limits of Provence. It embraced Gascony and Catalonia, and was for a short period cultivated in Upper Italy. It was never popular with the people, for it was intensely artificial, and made its appeal to the aristocracy. It imposed itself upon the whole of feudal Europe with the imperiousness of a fashion, and gave a lead to the lyrics of most of the modern nations, notably of northern France, Germany and Italy. Of its literature there are three kinds, lyric poetry, both religious and secular, epic poetry, legendary and narrative, and didactic literature, which was a development of the 13th century, and was both dogmatic and narrative. To this category belongs *The Life of S. Honoratus*, interesting by reason of the frequent allusions to epic legends. Lyric poetry is the most characteristic of Provençal literature; the impress of its originality made it successful. Love is almost the only theme, but it is a love that is quite peculiar, in which the head has a larger share than the heart.

Catalonia, which had maintained relationship with Provence, shared its most brilliant tastes, and even surpassed them. Barcelona the last centre of the empire of the Visigoths lost none of its splendour, and when Raymond Berenger married the daughter and heiress of Count Gilbert, and joined his estates to those of Provence, his court was the brilliant home of the life of culture and elegance. The cult of poetry became the favourite occupation of the higher classes, and association with this movement came to be regarded as the inseparable mark of aristocratic breeding. The poetry of the troubadours was universally disseminated, and all who made any pretensions to rank desired to speak, and affected a love of, the Provençal language. Raymond Berenger left a daughter to inherit his estates in Provence, and Blanche de Castille, mother of Louis IX, intrigued to secure her as the wife of her other son, Charles d'Anjou. This prince added to his warlike pursuits a taste for pomp and show. Like his predecessors, he favoured literature as an amusement, and drew to his court the most successful exponents of it; and in all this was cordially supported by his wife. Days of misfortune were to follow, and Charles, at his death, left to his eldest son an involved estate, a host of enemies, and a reduced Provençal nobility; but the new ruler bravely undertook the difficult task thus set him. By avoiding war and complications he paid his father's debts, re-established the finances of his kingdom, and died just as his efforts seemed crowned with success and happiness. These two reigns were the most glorious times of the troubadours, and were also the beginning of their decadence. Provence, threatened by the desertion of the most illustrious families, was, after all, only an annexe of the kingdom of Naples. It is during the period just reviewed that Raymond Feraud, the author of *The Life of S. Honoratus*, lived and wrote. He was born in A.D. 1245, and died about A.D. 1325. Like most of the troubadours he is only known through one or two brief notices[1].

John Nostradamus[2] assures us that he had seen and read two large volumes, illuminated in gold and blue, in which the lives of the Provençal poets were written in red, and the poetry (eighty pieces) in black letters. He also states that Raymond Feraud, "translated several books into Provençal poetry, which brought him great favour from Robert, king of Naples."

John Nostradamus also tells us, on the information supplied by Hugues de S. Césari, that when Raymond Feraud assumed the monastic habit, he took the name of Porcarius as a title of honour, but that the monk of Montmajour[3] in ridicule played on the name, and implied that it meant he was a swineherd, and that, after he had served for a long time in this capacity, he was

[1] John Nostradamus, *Les vies des plus célèbres et anciens pöetes Provençaux.* Caesar Nostradamus, *L'Histoire de Provence.* Gioffredo, *Storia delle Alpi Marittime.* Papon makes no reference whatever to Feraud in his *General History of Provence.*

[2] The title-page of this book reads: "A collection of the works of several authors, named in the following pages, who compiled and wrote them in the Provençal tongue, and they have since been translated into the French language by John Nostradamus." A list of these authors is given, and among them are : "A Religious of the monastery of S. Honoratus in the isle of Lerins, surnamed Le Monge des îles d'or." "Another Religious of the same monastery, his companion, whose name we do not know." Another Religious of the same monastery named Hermentarius." "A Religious of the monastery of S. Peter of Montmajour, surnamed 'the Scourge of the Provençal Poets.'" "Another Religious of the same monastery named Césari." In his preface the author says, "The lives of our Provençal Poets have been collected from several authors, and from the 'Monge des îles d'or,' and Hugues de S. Césari, who have also assisted me in my collection of the works of the 'Monge de Montmajour,' surnamed 'the Scourge,' because he has written against the Provençal poets."

[3] M. Diez (*Leben und Werke der Troubadours*, p. 607) says this person should be identified with the monk of Montaudon near Auvergne, and that Nostradamus has assigned him to Montmajour near Arles. M. Meyer says "the fraud is palpable" and that this "monk of Montmajour" is "only the creation of his own mind." *Derniers Troubadours de la Provence*, p. 134.

allowed by the monks to live at ease with plenty to eat. We need not lay much stress upon the words of a monk who "entered the monastery of Montmajour against the wishes of his parents[1]." The value of any information, supplied by John Nostradamus, is very negligible if the following criticism is just: "He only furnishes the names of the most celebrated poets of Provence; the accounts he gives of them are so manifestly fictitious that the critic can only reject them absolutely. We can either regard him as the inventor of the facts he mentions, or admit the reality of 'the monk of the Golden Isles' and of Hugues de S. Césari, those pretended biographers in whose authority he takes refuge[2]." There is a MS. in the library of Carpentras containing a collection of notes on various subjects of history and archaeology, among which are some fifty leaves relating to the history of Provence; and in the opinion of the librarian, "these fragments appear to be by the hand of John Nostradamus, and form part of the documents which his nephew Caesar Nostradamus used in the composition of his history of Provence[3]."

Caesar Nostradamus tells us that Feraud was graciously welcomed by all in the monastery, and soon became so proficient in poetry, rhetoric, and theology, that none of his contemporaries equalled him. On this account he was asked by the monks to take charge of the monastery library. He did his work so well that in a short time he put the library in order, and arranged the books according to their subjects.

This biographer also gives some details of the life of Feraud, who, in the spring and autumn, retired for some days with a friend into his little grotto on the islands of the Steccades, or Hyères, where there had been from the earliest days a little church, a dependency of the monastery, which gave to him his title of "the Monk of the Golden Isles[4]." Here he listened to the sweet murmurs of fountains, and to the songs of birds, the beautiful variety of whose plumage he studied. Among his

---

[1] John Nostradamus, p. 216.

[2] Paul Meyer, *Bibliotheca de l'école des Chartes*, 6th series, Vol. V, p. 253.

[3] M. Lambert, *Catal. des MSS. de Carpentras*, III, 152.

[4] Le Monge des îles d'or. "Monge" is an archaic word still in use in some parts of France, and signifies a monk.

books, found after his death, was a collection of drawings and paintings showing the situation of neighbouring villages, all kinds of herbs, plants and trees, the perspective of the mountains and other information of the natural beauties of the district. He died at Lerins surrounded by his brethren.

Caesar Nostradamus also reproduces from his uncle's account some details of the life of Feraud who "had been all his life very amorous, a true courtier, and withal a good Provençal poet"; and that Mary, queen and wife of Charles II of Anjou, retained him in her service because he wrote well and cleverly in all sorts of rhymes as may be seen in the *Life of Andronicus, Son of the King of Hungary, surnamed S. Honoré of Lerins.* This was translated by him into Provencal rhyme from the Latin, at the request of Mary[1] to whom he dedicated his work in A.D. 1300, and as a reward for which she gave him a priory, which was one of the dependencies of the monastery of S. Honoré of Lerins in Provence.

We learn from the same authority that there is nothing of the merely amatory in Feraud's writings, for he feared to exercise an evil influence upon youth, and therefore consecrated all he had done to Vulcan rather than Venus. Gioffredo adds the information that he had seen and read Feraud's works in the library of Lerins, and that he was the author of another poem besides the one which had gained him renown[2].

John Nostradamus asserts that Feraud was of insignificant birth, and rose by merit alone to the highest circles, till he gained the favour of his sovereign. But Gioffredo adds another piece of valuable information when he describes Feraud as "one of the Lords of Ilonse[3]." This has enabled Carlone to trace the branches of certain families in the Maritime Alps, and to show that the fief of Ilonse passed at the end of the 12th century to

[1] This is not in accord with Feraud's own statement that he had undertaken to translate the Latin life into Provençal at the instigation of Gaucelin, abbot of Lerins from 1295 to 1309 ("Monseu Guancelm l'abat agut en ay mandat").

[2] Feraud himself tells us that he had translated *The life of S. Alban*, put into verse a *Treatise on Computation*, and composed a lament *On the death of Charles of Anjou.*

[3] Ilonse (formerly Ylonse) is a village in the Department of the Maritime Alps, in the district of Puget-Theniers.

the house of Thoramus, which family was ultimately merged with that of Glendevey[1]. It would thus appear that Feraud really belonged to one of the feudal families of the old countship of Nice[2]. He was the grandson of William Feraud who withdrew to the monastery of S. Victor, and whose second son married a daughter of the house of Agoult who became the mother of our troubadour. It was the custom of the time for children of illustrious families to leave the paternal roof, and enter the service of the prince, or of one of the nobility, not as an act of servility, but to gain experience of life and the world. In this way, Raymond Feraud was sent to the court of Charles I, where his natural ability was helped by court influence. It is possible that he followed Charles in his expedition to conquer the kingdom of Naples, and as we have already said, he was attached to the court of Mary, the wife of Charles II. He obtained the priory of Roquesteron before he had put his hand to the last page of his poem, for in the concluding words of the appendix he says, " In the year of the Lord one thousand three hundred, the prior finished his romance to the honour of God and of His Saints." In La Roche was his dwelling place, a priory in the valley of Estaran[3].

His " Life of S. Honoratus."

It is the only one of his writings now extant. Though it is only a legend in verse, in which there is little or no true history, and the marvellous oversteps the limits both of taste and reason, it is yet characteristic of epic poems in certain respects. Its aim is to exalt the virtues of Honoratus, and to identify him with the house of Hungary. Feraud takes full advantage of " poetic licence " in the matter of time, and so sweeps away any

---

[1] The genealogy is traced in the *Annales de la Société des Lettres, Sciences et Arts aes Alpes Maritimes*, Vol. II, p. 31. (Nice.)

[2] Up to 1860 the city of Nice was the capital of the countship of Nice.

[3]   Que l'an de Dieu mil e tres cent,
          Compli le *priols* son romans,
          A l'onor de Dieu et del santz.
          En la Roqua tenc sa mayson,
          Priols en la val d'Estaran.

difficulty of date[1]. The poem relates how Andronicus, son of the emperor Constantine VI, married Hellenborex. The sons of this union, the eldest of whom bore his father's name, were sent to the palace of Constantine, near Nicomedia. Thither Caprasius was sent by God in order to bring them into a place of instruction. Caprasius baptized Andronicus under the name of Honoratus, and Germanus, his brother, under that of Venantius. Then follows the description of a series of adventures. Honoratus was sent to Spain to deliver Charlemagne[2] who was in captivity, and after a successful mission returned to France and founded the monastery. The period that embraces these and other incidents of his life covers five hundred years! Surely nothing can better prove the popularity of the memory of Honoratus among southern races than this poem of Raymond Feraud, in which the biography of the founder of Lerins is strangely confused with the fanciful traditions of Charlemagne's time.

Lerins is clearly the place of its composition, for Feraud says at the commencement of his prologue that *The Life of S. Honoratus* had been found at Rome and brought to Lerins by a monk of the abbey[3]. For a long time scholars have been perplexed by the results of the comparison between the Provençal translation, and the *Life* found in the Latin MS. published at Venice in A.D. 1501, and re-edited in A.D. 1511, as the Provençal translation contains so many details and quotations not found in this Latin MS. But doubts have been almost set at rest by the discovery that the text of A.D. 1501 is only an extract of a much larger work. A MS. in the library of Trinity College, Dublin, and another in the Bodleian Library at Oxford, would appear to show the original source of Feraud's information.

It may be asked why he should have based his poem upon legend that has but a slight connection with history, when the panegyric of Hilary was at his disposal for inspiration. It must not be forgotten that Hilary's masterpiece was addressed to

---

[1] Did not Virgil make Dido contemporary with the siege of Troy?

[2] The deeds of this powerful emperor second the efforts of the hermit and *vice versâ*, although Honoratus came into the world 400 years before the son of Pepin.

[3] De Roma l'aportet uns monges de Leris.

C. M.

men of letters, whereas the legend would appeal to a multitude of pious pilgrims, whose imagination it was necessary to strike. Then too it would be easier and more attractive to translate into a poetic form.   Feraud says, " If any one finds fault with my language and my words of romance, let him excuse me since my tongue is the true Provençal[1]." This poem is therefore valuable as a specimen of dialect, and as one of the last monuments of old Provençal literature.

Denis Faucher.

In the 16th century we see a decided commencement of that process of change from the feudal world which has been going on ever since.   There are now new forces, religious and secular, that are at work like ferment.   New horizons are appearing in view.   The new learning and religious changes are transforming Europe.   In the words of Guizot, it was " the time of great men and of great things, when the activity of the human mind was manifested in every department, and not least in the relations of man with his fellowmen, and his relationship to material and intellectual forces."   At his birth, Faucher stands on the threshold of this momentous and stirring period. He was born at Arles in A.D. 1487, and his parents were of distinguished rank.   The family was possessed of culture, and manifested literary aptitude.   Denis was a theologian of repute, his brother was a lawyer, his nephew a physician.   Denis spent the time of his novitiate in the convent of Padolirona, and assumed the monastic habit in A.D. 1508.

At this time there were grave disorders at Lerins.   These were in part caused, as we have seen, by the abuses of the *Commendam.*   In an attempt to remove disorders and abuses, the monks of Cluny had been summoned to the island ; then, hope was fixed upon annexation to the monastery of Monte-Cassino which was under the Rule and discipline of Benedict. Among those sent to regenerate the monastery were Denis Faucher, and Gregory Cortesius.   It was a dreary picture that

---

[1] From the period of the extinction of Latin in Italy, the common Provençal had been the dialect of the countship of Nice.   Feraud thus distinguishes between the literary Provençal of the troubadours and the dialect of the common people.

was presented to them, but they received a hospitable and generous welcome which heartened them in their difficult task[1]. To the debates and disputes that centred round the abbots-commendatory, the placid mind of Faucher gave no heed. Nourished on the love of literature, educated in a respect for the monastic Rule, penetrated with the excellence of learning, his endeavours ever kept a well-defined aim in view, and that was to combat heresy, to restore discipline, and to spread the desire for knowledge. What concern had he with the revenues of rich prebends, which were disputed with such animosity? He applied to himself his own definition of the ideal monk[2].

He had no long space of time afforded to him to carry out his ideals, for he was summoned to direct the monastery of Tarascon, the discipline of which had also been greatly relaxed. This convent took its beginning from Lerins, and had been placed under the government of an abbess who was assisted by some monks. The delicate mission was entrusted to Faucher in A.D. 1530. He was promptly successful in his efforts, but the nuns were equally prompt to grow weary of the strict *régime*, and sought, first by flattery and then by reviling him, to obtain some relaxation of his stringency. He was obdurate, and indeed redoubled his firmness. He described the position to cardinal de Bellay, and in stating the difficulties he had to endure, he recalls "their silly words, and their loquacity," though he is not unmindful of the virtue and piety manifested by some of them. For a long time the reformer faced calumny and imputation, and resistance to his discipline was not confined to the inside of the convent walls. He had found it necessary to expel some unworthy monks, and these carried the grievances of the nuns to the papal legate at Avignon, and did their best to poison the mind of de Bellay, the abbot-commendatory, against him. Several times he was summoned to make his defence, and did so with the consciousness that his honour had been outraged, and with an energy that would make no

---

[1] Tam variis sudoribus, omnem non movit lapidem. *Chron. Ler.*

[2] Monachus est castificatum corpus, expiatum os, et animus divino semper lumine irradiatus.

compromise with duty. Full success at last crowned his earnest efforts, and he went back to Lerins.

It may be noted that he evidently held strong views as to the necessity of the higher education of women, for in an account of the work done at the convent he says : " We explain the letters of Cyprian, Ambrose and Jerome ; we comment together on the *Offices* of Cicero, and on his letters, and I explain to them the *Proverbs of Solomon.*" He says further that the nuns " unreservedly give themselves up to the study of polite literature, and apply themselves to turn the pages of their books with the same zeal that they devote to turning the spindle of their distaff [1]."   In writing to a friend on another occasion, he says : " I cannot be enough astonished that people find it so difficult to admit that a young girl can succeed in learning Latin, as if nature had imparted to women less intelligence than to men, as if the diction and style of our sister were not sufficiently elegant, and furnished with enough serious and varied thoughts to prove that a young girl, who will devote herself with zeal to the study of polite literature, will enjoy and possess it with fruition. Note also how frequently men are inept, and approach us with the cry that it should suffice that nuns should learn to say, like so many magpies in a cage, psalms that they do not understand ; that it is far better that they should be taught to turn their spindle-wheels, and not the leaves of a book, and that it is as strange to make them study polite literature as to make an ass drink wine [2]."   In support of his opinion, Faucher quotes Ambrose and Jerome who wrote, " that young women consecrated to the religious life should be clever, and give themselves to the study of Greek and Latin."

In A.D. 1548 Faucher was elected prior of Lerins by the community. His affection for the monastery is manifested in his words, " Let him who desires to escape the tempests of a senseless world and to shelter himself from the snares of Satan ; let him who wishes to live deaf to the voluptuous appeals of a too passionate temperament, and to remain chaste in advancing years, come to Lerins and its shelters of solitude. There is not a safer retreat in all the world." He does not seem

---

[1] *Chron. Ler.*   [2] Barralis, *Opera Faucheri.*

to have sought his new office, for he remarks : " I should feel happy if I did not hear myself called by this name prior ; which I bear without deserving it. I only hope that at the approaching assembly of the Fathers, they will free me from this burden, the weight of which is far beyond my powers." This election was nevertheless confirmed, and it was a wise decision at a critical time. De Bellay resigned the abbacy to William Pelicier, bishop of Montpelier, and received in exchange another abbey, and in confiding to Faucher the care of defending the interest of Lerins at this moment, the community counted upon the disinterestedness of his motives. All this time Tarascon was much in his thoughts, and for the benefit of the nuns he wrote a treatise[1], in which he expounded the advantages of grace, charity, obedience and poverty.

Literature and painting were among his accomplishments, and both these talents are combined in *A Book of the Hours*, which is in his own hand, and is ornamented with initials and figures of exquisite workmanship[2]. This he sent to his brother John with a charge that it should be preserved as a family heirloom in perpetual remembrance of the author's affection for him and his people, and as a remembrance of him before God. Barralis mentions that in his day it was still in the hands of a member of the family, Francis Faucher, an advocate of Arles[3].

Entrusted with the task of teaching literature to novices he found he must, in this way, take up much time that he desired to consecrate to study. Writing to Gregory Cortesius, his old teacher, he epigrammatically says : " I hoped to have gained the crown, but it is necessary that I should take the grindstone...happily love that endures everything turns the grindstone with me and shares a good part of the work[4]."

---

[1] *De reformatione mentis.*

[2] Horariae preces manu propria ipsius Dionysii scriptae et miris figuris penicillo subtiliter adornatae. *Chron. Ler.* ii, p. 223.

[3] According to Tournaire (p. 95), it remained in the family of Faucher till it passed in A.D. 1731 to the house of de Vigueiro by the marriage of Marie de Faucher to James de Vigueiro; at the commencement of the 19th century Madame de Latour, heiress of Marie de Vigueiro, gave it to M. l'Abbé Mercier, of Marseilles.

[4] *Chron. Ler.* ii, p. 276.

He wrote several books, among which *The Annals of Provence*, in five books, is included by some, but its authenticity is questioned by others; Barralis does not speak of it, but Mouan[1] says, " Faucher wrote with exactness in his *Annals* what related to the administration of the country, its wars and principal events." Barralis attributes to his pen *An Explanation of S. Paul's Epistles*; and the Latin translation of three Italian works, *The Mirror of the Inner Man, Discretion*, and *Mental Prayer*. A dialogue on *The Natural Causes of Occult Things* is also ascribed to him. He addressed some 150 letters to persons of piety, erudition or rank, which dealt with the customs and institutions of his time.

He was a poet of no mean order, and possessed great facility in Latin verse of every form and metre. He employed this gift to the glory of God, and to sing the happiness of rural life. He addressed himself to notable persons of his age, to kings and princes, and cardinals, to pupils and to friends. He was very modest about his work, for when sending some of his poetry to a friend, he said : " I wish to send you these verses which I composed some years ago when in Italy, and which I have just discovered among my papers. I hesitate to send them, because I do not judge them worthy of being submitted to the appreciation of so learned a person. Now I address them to you that you may have a little diversion in reading my poetic reveries for what they are worth." Addressing Marguerite of Navarre, he puns upon her name[2]. On another occasion he was asked to write an epitaph on Antony Vitalis, and could not resist the temptation to play upon the words, even though it was unworthy of the solemnity of the tomb[3].

As prior he had to defend the monks and the revenues of the monastery against the cupidity of the agents of the abbot-commendatory. In A.D. 1557 he appealed to the bishop of

---

[1] *Études sur Denis Faucher.*

[2] Sic tua si fueris virtute, et moribus almis splendida,
Margarito est mens pretiosa magis.

[3] Antonii Vitalis in hoc sunt ossa sepulchro
Condita, mens coelum, carne soluta, petiit.
Nam licet ipsa maris, potuere obnoxia morti,
Corpora, vitalis mens perire nequit.

Montpelier for justice, and complained that too favourable attention was paid to the enemies of Lerins; who seem "born to torment good people who long for Divine justice." A reiteration of his complaint against calumny led to his withdrawal from his monastery, and it was during his exile that he composed an epilogue or poem of a hundred verses, in the form of a dialogue between two monks, which dealt with the desolation of the monastery[1]. Though the officers were changed and the monks were replaced by those of Cluny, the Cassinists soon returned, and Faucher with them. "The latinity of Faucher," says a writer[2], "is not sufficiently elegant, and his verse is often harsh and cramped. But whether in prose or verse there is fire in his works, and we feel he is a man of genius and of taste for literature, and in especial possesses zeal and piety."

He lived to have the somewhat unusual experience of reading his own obituary notice! The rumour of his death spread among his friends and relations, and he reassured them with the quaint remark that he had "derived great benefit from the rumour that had been falsely circulated. All my friends have prayed to God for me. Continue your prayers in this sense, for at my age, death cannot long delay its coming." According to Barralis he died in A.D. 1562 at the age of seventy-five. He was one of the last representatives of the studious men sheltered in the cloister-cells during the middle ages. The persistent struggles between monks and abbots-commendatory distracted the minds of men, who would otherwise possibly have pursued learning and added to the reputation of this *Alma Mater*. It was this constant predominance of material interests that led to the decadence of the monastic foundation on the island of S. Honoratus. On this sufficient has already been said.

Gregory Cortesius (16th Century).

It will be remembered that when the monastery of Lerins was reformed in A.D. 1516, Jerome de Montferrat was nominated by the monks of Monte-Cassino to go there as abbot to undertake the task of reformation. Gregory was one of the ten brethren

[1] *De desolatione monasterii Lerinensis et de extrusione monachorum.* Barralis.
[2] Moreri.

that accompanied him on this occasion, and succeeded him as abbot-regular in A.D. 1524, having previously occupied for some time the position of prior.

Born in A.D. 1483 he came of an old family of Modena, and was a skilled theologian, and one of the most distinguished humanists, with a profound knowledge of the Latin, Greek, and Etruscan languages. He wrote in Latin, both prose and verse. His skill in these classic languages was noted by cardinal Medici, afterwards pope Leo X, who was anxious to have him near him and appointed him legal auditor in the Curia. He had studied jurisprudence for five years at Bologna and Padua, but such an office was utterly foreign to a nature aspiring after peace and the austerities of the cloister. Accordingly, he bade farewell to this worldly calling and embraced the monastic life of the monastery of Padolirona near Mantua, and was soon chosen to take direction of that of S. Peter at Perusia. He returned to Padolirona to become abbot, and it was from there that he departed for France in the company of Montferrat. He spent twelve years at Lerins, nine as prior, and three as abbot. Much against his own wishes and preference, he left Lerins to undertake the direction of the monastery of S. George-the-Greater at Venice. It was here that he came in contact with cardinal Caraffa, afterwards pope Paul IV, who made known his merits at the court of Rome, for Cortesius was considered one of the most learned men in Italy, and corresponded with the greatest scholars in Europe. Through this influence, Gregory Cortesius was nominated visitor-apostolic for the whole of Italy, and then, as a distinguished theologian, he was one of the colleagues of cardinal Campeggio attending the council at Worms in A.D. 1540. Here he rendered valuable services and proved himself "the most capable of the four theologians that had been sent with the cardinal"; and there is no doubt that it was in recognition of his merits on this occasion that he received a cardinal's hat. In A.D. 1542 the pope selected him as one of the members of the committee of cardinals appointed to make preparations for the Council of Trent. He only lived six years to hold his honour, for he died at Rome in A.D. 1548. His only regret was that he could not draw his last breath in the cloister among his brethren. As the moment of his death drew near he said to those who were gathered round his bed : " For some years I have been a cardinal; what will remain to me of this honour now? It would have been sweeter to die in the cloister, where the dangers that menace salvation are much less." He was buried in the Basilica of the Twelve Apostles, before the altar of S. Eugenia.

He is mentioned by an Italian writer as being among the cardinals who presented a treatise to pope Paul IV in favour of the reform of the Church[1]. His numerous works have been much praised by ecclesiastical writers, but are little known[2]. They include *A Tract against anyone who denies that the Blessed Apostle Peter was at Rome*; and some letters to his friends and family, written in Latin. These two works were published by his niece, Hersilia Cortesius, who dedicated them to pope Gregory XIII. Among other writings may be mentioned a Latin translation of the New Testament from Greek texts; a book on the Disruption of Genoa; some theological and philosophical treatises; extant fragments of Hilary and Eucherius, as well as hymns, poetry in praise of S. Peter, and verses in honour of the holy Virgin, of S. Honoratus, and of Lerins. He was passionately fond of the island, as his poem clearly indicates. In reproducing it, of course, something of the unique beauty of the original, and the delightful rhythm of its stanzas is necessarily lost:

> Though small in size, 'tis great in fame,
> In Lerins isle men praised the Triune name.
> From whence five hundred saints have passed to glory
> Whose crimson blood has stained that island's story.
>
> As stars that shine in clearest night
> So many are its saints, whose lives were bright.
> In piety their holy lives they spent
> In quiet solitude, on holy duties bent!
>
> O island home! the land of peace!
> Where troubled souls found sweet release!
> The worldling shunned that sacred shore
> Where peaceful monks found joy for evermore.

---

[1] Furono dunque congregati in Roma sceltissimi Prelati, cioe il Contareno,...il Cortese; quali, dall' anno 1546 fino all' anno 1538, faticarono in lavorare una scrittura che poi la presentarono al Papa et la chiamarono Consilium de emendanda Ecclesia. Carragioli, *Vita di Paulo*, Vol. IV, p. 93.

[2] They were published in two volumes by Gradenigo at Padua in 1774.

The north wind's blast the sea-girt isle defies,
Shut in by sheltering rocks the island lies,
Nor Nereus with his weeds, nor Neptune's blast
Could shake that island home, in ocean fast.

A lofty castle stands upon its rocks
Hurling defiance at the ocean's shocks,
Like eagle swooping through the sky
Scaring the timid doves with piercing eye.

Winter is soft as elsewhere balmy spring,
Here autumn tints the golden apples bring,
The laurel and the myrtle as on Paphos' isle !
And, all around you perfumed flowers smile.

The waves are limpid on the sparkling sea,
Where Proteus' offspring sport as cattle on the lea,
Here lissom dolphins play and roll at large,
Tumbling in joyous glee on Lerins' marge.

Here summer's heat is tempered by the breeze,
And soft winds blow from tossing seas,
In sheltering woods cool spots are found
And haunts of peace and love abound.

Here when men see how all is wrought
They say farewell to envious thought.
All wrath those smiling landscapes banish
And in their sight all trials vanish.

The trials which men's spirits lashed
When ambitions were by disappointment dashed !
Not in Lerins' island were such worldlings found
But far from hence, and in the world around[1] !

Vincent Barralis.

An account of the history of the Lerins would not be complete without the mention of the author of *The Chronology of the Saints and other illustrious men, and of Abbots of the holy Island of Lerins*[2].

Vincent Barralis, the historian of the monastery, was born, it is generally agreed, at Nice. He entered the congregation of Monte-Cassino in A.D. 1577, and from there was sent to the convent of Monte-Real in Sicily, where he classified the archives

---

[1] I am indebted to Rev. J. S. Hill, B.D., for this rendering.
[2] This work was abridged by Dom Delisle, a monk of Lerins, in the 18th century, and the MS. is in the Municipal Library at Grasse.

and the library. He was at Lerins in A.D. 1595, charged by the chapter of the monastery to negotiate the giving up by the prior of Roquesteron of the capitular revenues[1].

It was about this time that he began the collection of historical materials for the book on which he spent some years. It was published at Lyons in A.D. 1613 and consists of 856 pages. It was adorned with a view of the island of S. Honoratus, as it appeared in his day, and was inscribed "This is a faithful picture of the holy island of Lerins." As a frontispiece, S. Honoratus is depicted vested in his episcopal insignia, and seated on a throne in the centre of the island, trampling under his feet the serpents that infested it. On either side of him are the two most celebrated martyrs of the monastery, Aygulphus and Porcarius, clothed in the monastic habit, each holding a palm in the right hand, and in the left the abbatial cross. The first of the two volumes of his book commences with a detailed description of the island, and with Isidore of Cremona's eulogy in Latin verse. It also contains the *Life* of the founder by Hilary, that of S. Odilo abbot of Cluny and of Lerins by Father Damian, and the *Lives* of Faustus, Virgilius, Attalus and many other monks of the monastery. The second volume deals with *The Life of Columba, the Apostle of Ireland*, that of Maximus, bishop of Riez and formerly abbot, and others, and gives besides a list of all the abbots, the history of the foundation of the château fort, and the works of Denis Faucher and Eucherius.

The task of collecting information from this valuable work of Barralis is rendered extremely difficult, because it has the great and unpardonable defect of having no index, and the arrangement of the subjects is quite unmethodical, and may almost be said to be haphazard. Here is an opportunity for some lover of Lerins, and student of its history, to elucidate this mine of information, some of which is not to be found, so far as we know, anywhere else. A methodical redaction of this work in chronological order, with an index of the subjects therein contained, offers a useful field for patient exploration. No

---

[1] A.D. 1595 le 24 Avril, D. Vincent de Luceran feust depute par le Chapitre de Lerin, pour traicter avec maistre Honoré Boqui, prieure, pour la remission du dict prieure a la mense capitulaire. *Inventaire de Mme la Ctesse de Saint-Seine*, f. 105[1].

English writer has given us a history of the wonderful monastery, and our own effort has in consequence been rendered the more difficult. We should welcome any attempt to throw light upon a remarkably interesting subject, and no better means can be suggested than by bringing this annalistic masterpiece of the 17th century within reach of those who have neither the aptitude or ability, nor the inclination and opportunity to read the original.

CHAPTER XIX

FROM SECULARISATION TO THE PRESENT DAY

The story of the last days of the monastery, before its secularisation in A.D. 1788, makes very sad reading. Only a few monks wandered through its corridors, and its vaulted roof no longer echoed with sounds of many footsteps or resounded with psalms of praise. "Divine service could not be decently celebrated, ornaments that seemed indispensable were missing, and others were in a neglected state." Even the half-dozen monks that were left were only resident there for a part of the year. The number was at last reduced to four, and these received a lump sum of £1500 to console them for the great ruin that was consummated before their eyes. The monastery was to suffer much humiliation for the ensuing seventy years. First, it was put up for auction at Grasse in A.D. 1791, where it was bought by M. Alziary de Roquefort for £37,000. He outbid an Irishman, named Welsh who, descended from one of the families devoted to the Stuarts, was driven to take refuge in France, and desired to dwell in the place that once had sheltered Patrick, the patron saint of his country. The monastery that had played such a glorious part in the religious history of France must lose even its name, for the name of the island, Saint Honorat, was changed to the island of Pelletier, whilst its sister island, Sainte Marguerite, was called by the name of Marat[1]. By a strange caprice of fortune, it next became, for some years, the home of a queen of comedy, for it passed into the hands of Marie Blanche Alziary de Roquefort, a daughter of the new proprietor, and a follower of Voltaire. She was born at S. Paul du Var near Nice in A.D. 1752, and under

[1] Pinatel, *Quatre siècles de l'Histoire de Cannes*, p. 149.

the name of Mademoiselle Sainval gained fame and reputation at Paris, after making her *début* at the Comédie Française in A.D. 1772 ; she retired in A.D. 1792. Round her talent surged jealousies and calumnies, and after many struggles with contemporary mediocrities she retired from the world, and, like a queen dethroned, departed to hide her disappointments and regrets in the château fort, the eastern part of which she restored for occupation. She left the island in A.D. 1813 at the instance of her family, and went to live in retirement at Dragugan where she died at the age of eighty-four in A.D. 1836[1]. Once again it changed hands, and by another caprice of fortune became the property of the vicar of a parish in Ireland, named Sims, who "although a Protestant, respected the objects that had been consecrated to Catholic worship[2]." He conceived the idea of a restoration, and had actually commenced the work when his death in A.D. 1857 put an end to his project.

During this time astonishment had been frequently expressed that no bishop of Fréjus had purchased a place so rich in memories, and one of the glories of that diocese. It is only fair to say that more than one tried to do so. Monsignor Jordany, who had made more than one effort in this direction, succeeded in buying it in A.D. 1859, to be used once more for religious purposes. It was in the fitness of things that he should buy it, whose ancestor had once been abbot of Lerins. It was fitting also that he should invite the archbishop of Aix, Arles, and Embrun to accompany him when a solemn possession of the island was taken. Nothing more appropriate can be imagined than that a successor of Honoratus in the ancient see of Arles, and a successor of Leontius in the bishopric of Fréjus should together visit the ruins of the monastery which had been founded by their predecessors fourteen centuries before, and "renew the chain of her glorious traditions." The arrival of Monsignor Jordany and the archbishop was acclaimed with exultant joy, with the roar of guns, the fanfare of trumpets, and the shouts of the people. Some English were among those present, led there perhaps by curiosity. Seeing them, Monsignor Jordany reminded them that a bishop from

---

[1] *Gazette du midi*, December 25, 1873. J. B. Sardou.
[2] Alliez, *Les îles de Lerins*.

Lerins had consecrated the illustrious Augustine, and assuming they were Protestants and therefore, from his point of view, "heretics," he endeavoured to show them from S. Vincent the refutation of their fundamental errors, and the easiest and surest means to discover the truth[1].

The robed procession of priests, canons and vicars-general, led by the cross, marched towards the church. They were prepared for what they would see. Like Eleutherus after the massacre of Porcarius, they saw desolation everywhere. The marble altar had formed a balcony for the actress who had lately lived on the island. The celebration of Mass amid the desolate ruin was, to those who participated, the emblem of hope. Thoughts of sadness were submerged in the joy which anticipated the restoration of the ancient walls presently to resound with the music of festal song. The bishop so interpreted this occasion. His words really touch the heights of eloquence : "When we go back in thought to the primitive days of this monastery, and recall the memory of the illustrious saints who came here to seek a shelter, and peacefully to cultivate knowledge and literature at the time that Europe was desolated by barbarians, it is impossible not to have a feeling of sadness at the sight of these ruins. The works of man die with him, but the works of God have a principle of life which renders them imperishable. A great writer has said, and history confirms his words : 'God only effaces to write a fresh inscription.' If the sight of these ruins has in it something heartbreaking, then lest hope may fail, there is also that which says 'These ruins shall be restored.' More than once since the days of Honoratus and Leontius, storms have beaten against these walls, even as the waves surrounding us have rolled in fury to hurl themselves upon this coast and to whiten it with their foam. The earth we tread has been stained with the blood of five hundred martyrs. God has taken account of the fervour of her first sons. From heaven, all the saints she has produced have kept watch over her. It is their prayers that have led to the present hope of speedy restoration."

---

[1] Alliez, *Les îles de Lerins.*

The archbishop made reply in the following eloquent words : "The seventy years captivity are ended. Let us rejoice. From the foot of this altar, so recently profaned, I embrace at once the past, the present and the future. The past, these ruins; the present, yourselves; the future, God."

In May of the same year three brothers of the Order of S. Francis of Assisi were installed, but did not remain there long. They were replaced in A.D. 1861 by the monks of S. Peter-in-Chains, a congregation founded at Marseilles. For the ensuing eight years they occupied themselves in developing the land, and in directing an orphanage which the bishop of Fréjus had founded. This paved the way for a return to the monastic uses of former days. The death of abbot Fissiaux, the founder of the order then in possession of the island, offered the desired opportunity. The monks were discharged, and the bishop then invited the monks of Citeaux to rebuild the ruined abbey and to people its cloisters. Thus after seven hundred years was fulfilled a wish that Cistercians might bring restoration, which had been expressed by pope Celestine III, in the days of the monastery's decline in the 12th century : "Restore the order and peace of the religious life in the abbey of Lerins, and to this end establish there some monks of Citeaux." In these words he had written to the archbishop of Arles, and not till A.D. 1870 was his wish fulfilled. It was then that pope Pius IX writing to Marie Bernard, abbot, vicar-general of the congregation of Senanqua, said : "It is our desire that a monastery so illustrious should be restored, and it is with supreme joy that we learn that this revival is about to be accomplished, thanks to the zeal and efforts of the excellent bishop of Fréjus, and we note with equal pleasure that the difficult task of consummating such an end has been confided to you. We fervently exhort you to allow yourself to be conquered by no obstacle, but to persevere with your intentions, trusting in the Lord. We implore on your behalf His abundant help, and we accord to you and to all your congregation our apostolic blessing."

This congregation had a monastery in the diocese of Avignon, built in the 12th century, devastated at the time of the revolution. Father Marie Bernard had undertaken to restore it to religious uses, and from the time of his arrival there, this abbey of Senanqua had adopted the rule of Citeaux.

Dom Marie Bernard made no delay in carrying out his instructions. The abbey of Lerins was restored in A.D. 1871, and he transferred his permanent residence to the island the following year. Here he spent sixteen years of strenuous work at restoration. Full of faith and zeal he attracted to the place a large number of monks; cells were built round the ancient sites "like a frame round venerable and precious relics," and the present church was built on the foundations of the old church of S. Honoratus. This venerable abbot died in A.D. 1888, leaving to his successor a task more laborious still, the consolidation and completion of what had been so happily begun. Dom Marie-Colomban, who had been for fifteen years the right hand of the late abbot, was elected by the community to succeed him in the abbacy. He developed the plans of his predecessor. The workshops have been enlarged; the printing and carpentry machines, and the pumping of the well of S. Honoratus, are now worked by steam, and a dynamo supplies the monastery with electric light. The church has been embellished; and Dom Marie-Colomban was also able to acquire the island in full right. Hitherto, during all the years it was in the occupation of the monks of Senanqua it had been the property of the episcopal revenue[1] of Fréjus. Under the auspices of the bishop, the abbot undertook to obtain the authority of the government for its purchase; he went to Paris for the purpose, and the object of his journey was promptly and satisfactorily attained. The decree was signed by President Carnot. One important consequence of the acquisition was the right to apply the title of abbey once again to Lerins. Such was the esteem in which he was held by his community that he was elected abbot in A.D. 1893 for the second time, and a petition was sent to the pope asking for a modification of that article of the constitution of the congregation of Senanqua according to which the abbot is only elected for six years. An exception, quite personal, was made in his favour, and Dom Marie-Colomban was declared abbot for life.

[1] Mense episcopale.

At his death, the present abbot, Dom Patrice, was elected to succeed him. In mentioning this fact we take the opportunity of thanking him for his great courtesy and ready kindness and favour extended to us on several occasions. It is by his permission that many of the illustrations appear in this book, for they are reproductions of photographs that are the exclusive property of the monastery. He accorded us a gracious reception when we subsequently visited the island, and allowed us to take photographs of buildings which the monastery had not photographed, with authority to reproduce them.

We had long anticipated with pleasure a visit to the island of Saint Honorat, and on one occasion when in the vicinity we put many questions to the people of Cannes and the surrounding neighbourhood concerning it. For many, the island had no interest; few knew it, fewer still were acquainted with its history and its reputation. The little steamer that plies twice a day between the mainland and the islands of the Lerins always carried a full complement of passengers, but most of them regarded the excursion as one of the recognised picnics undertaken by all visitors, and the island of Sainte Marguerite, with its cypress-avenue and the prison house of the Man with the Iron Mask, was the resort favoured by most of these excursionists.

Many thoughts crowd in upon those who approach the island of Saint Honorat as visitors to an honoured shrine, and much sadness and disappointment await them there. In us, the words of Charles Lentheric found a sympathetic echo, when he says, " The traveller who to-day sets foot on this island-rock, so full of memories, is struck at once with the number and mass of ruins that he sees around him. In some places, débris of defaced materials, bits of Roman tiles, fragments of arches and colums, and marble strew the ground[1]."

On the island there seems little respect for antiquity, and the aggressiveness of the new makes little appeal to the pilgrim. It is true that the ancient cloister remains in part, and that sundry stones and inscriptions are preserved in the lapidary museum, but if they are of any value at all, they should not be exposed to " the open windows of heaven." We are informed

[1] *La Provence Maritime, Ancienne et Moderne*, p. 427.

by those who have some claim to speak authoritatively that "the seven chapels occupy an important place in the religious history of Lerins," but they are left to crumble into decay. In a description concerning some at least of these buildings, we read they "offer nothing very remarkable." We turn with interest to the chapel of the Holy Trinity, "the most curious of them all." It is slowly perishing of neglect. When we cross the island and visit the chapel of S. Saviour "which merits the attention of travellers," we find it whitewashed, and when we peer through the window we note with a sigh of regret that it is used—apparently by the proprietor of the inn—for the storage of his bottles, while the chapel of S. Cyprian and S. Justina described as "not much altered," has been turned into a poultry-shed[1].

There is unconscious irony in the words of a local historian, "Seven chapels built at different points, the remains of which are still to be seen *more or less preserved*, used to serve as places of prayer for each group of cells situated in their neighbourhood." Sic gloria transit mundi!

We do not presume to comment in any detail upon the modern buildings, for we readily acknowledge that the old must often be supplanted by the new, even if, to all lovers of the past, the aggressiveness of the present brings little pleasure, but one critic expresses the opinion that "all these modern restorations aroused the just criticism of the friends of art and archaeology. The new church does not harmonise with the great ruins that surround it. We may replace ruins, but we cannot remake the past; and the past of the Isle of Saints was sufficiently glorious to be preserved in its entirety as a precious relic. For the man of taste, knowledge and faith, the island of Honoratus should remain a grand ruin, the monastery a great memory[2]."

It is scarcely likely that the island will ever again occupy the position of former days, but as we recall its past, we cannot be unmindful of the gratitude that we owe to the distinguished men who found their aptitude for work and prayer in the

---

[1] H. Moris, *L'Abbaye*, p. 385.

[2] Lentheric, *loc. cit.* p. 430; see also Leon Palustre, *Destruction de l'abbaye de Saint Honorat par les religieux Bernardins*, 1876.

discipline of the famous monastery, and rejoice that in an age of failing culture and crude theology, the lamp of intellect and industry, of faith and love, of prayer and saintliness, was kept brightly burning in the brotherhood of Lerins.

Whatever be in store for the island in the days that are yet to come, the past can never be forgotten. The memory of her gifted sons can never die. The names of her philosophers, theologians, and moralists are known far and wide; their writings are quoted in many books and in various languages. These men and their works can never perish, and so the chief monuments of her past are preserved intact to demand and deserve the gratitude of succeeding centuries to the end of time.

The Lapidary Museum.

Reproduced by kind permission of the Most Reverend Father Abbot Dom Patrice.

The Chapel of S. Honoratus.

Reproduced by kind permission of the Most Reverend Father Abbot Dom Patrice.

The Chapel of S. Saviour (west view).

From a photograph specially taken by kind permission of the Most Reverend Father Abbot Dom Patrice.

The Chapel of S. Saviour (east view).

From a photograph specially taken by kind permission of the Most Reverend Father Abbot Dom Patrice.

The Chapel of the Holy Trinity.

Reproduced by kind permission of the Most Reverend Father Abbot Dom Patrice.

The Chapel of S. Cyprian and S. Justina.

Specially photographed by kind permission of the Most Reverend Father Abbot Dom Patrice.

The Cloister.

Reproduced by kind permission of the Most Reverend Father Abbot Dom Patrice.

The Château Fort.

Specially photographed by kind permission of the Most Reverend Father Abbot Dom Patrice.

The interior of the Château Fort (ground floor).

Specially photographed by kind permission of the Most Reverend Father Abbot Dom Patrice.

The interior of the Château Fort.

Specially photographed by kind permission of the Most Reverend Father Abbot Dom Patrce.

The Chest, now in Grasse Cathedral.

The Chest, now in Grasse Cathedral.

APPENDIX

ANCIENT MONUMENTS, BUILDINGS AND TREASURES

Only one inscription has been discovered on the island of Sainte Marguerite. It is bilingual (Greek and Latin) and was unearthed in 1818, near the fort. It has been lost again and only an imperfect account of it has been preserved. It was dedicated to the god Pan. If it does not prove that there was originally a temple on the island in his honour, it shows at any rate that Greek navigators frequented it, and that a Greek population existed side by side with the Roman.

The island of Saint Honorat, on the contrary, is rich in inscriptions and monumental ruins, which attest that it was very early occupied, and was of considerable importance long before the Christian era. Most of these are now preserved in the lapidary museum of which we give an illustration.

In the court of the château fort is a votive stone, with an inscription as below[1]. It would seem to be a column erected "To the emperor

[1] IMP . . . .
　　　FL . . . . VAL . . . .
　　　　　　. . . . . . .
　　　TINO P . . F . . . . .
　　　　AVG . . . .
　　　　. . . . . . .
　　. . . . .
　　　　NEPOTI
　　　　. . . . . . .
　　. . . . .
　　　　. . . . . . .

The full inscription may be conjecturally restored as follows:

IMPERATORI CAESARI
FLAVIO VALERIO
CONSTAN
TINO PIO FELICI
AVGVSTO
DIVI MAXI
MIANI AVGVSTI
NEPOTI
DIVI CON
STANTI AVGVSTI
PII FILIO.

Caesar Flavius Valerius Constantine, pious, blessed, Augustus, grandson of the divine Maximinius Augustus, son of the divine pious Constantius Augustus[1]."

There is an interesting inscription which recalls a college or association of boatmen who plied between Cannes and the island[2]. It may perhaps be thus read: "Gaius Julius Catullinus raised this monument to the honour of the college of the Utriculars[3]." These Utriculars used inflated leather bottles, covered with planks, to transport travellers and merchandise across the river, or an arm of the sea. As these rafts were very light, and only drew a little water they could, even if heavily loaded, navigate shallow water more easily than any boat. This inscription was originally in the chapel of S. Stephen.

On a block of limestone, forming a lintel or head-piece of a door, some letters are very clearly cut[4]. It is probably part of a tomb prepared for himself and his family by one who had had his name engraved thereon, "Desiderius Ferox during his lifetime made this tomb for himself and his family." The position of this mutilated stone, in the very shadow of the present church, has moved a writer to see a vivid contrast between one who was self-named the ferocious, whose pagan relic now lies almost on the ground, and the magnificent basilica of the humble S. Honoratus whose memory will be immortal. This writer also makes an interesting alternative suggestion that the first word of this inscription should read "Lerius." As the first letter has disappeared, the supposition finds some support. It may then be

---

[1] M. Edmond Blanc, *Épigraphie du Département des Alpes-Maritimes*, Partie I, No. 2125.

[2] COLLEGIO
VTRICLAR
GIVLIVS
CATVILLINVS
DON POS

It should probably be amplified to read thus:
COLLEGIO
VTRICVLARIORVM
GAIVS IVLIVS
CATVLLINVS
DONO POSVIT

[3] We are again indebted to M. Edmond Blanc for an interpretation.

[4] ERIVS FEROX SIBI ET
SVIS V F

The full inscription may be restored thus: "Desiderius Ferox sibi et suis vivus fecit."

conjectured that the monument is part of a dedication to Lerius or
Lero whose altars Honoratus destroyed[1].

Another limestone column is in honour of Neptune[2]. It consists
only of three proper names, and may be understood without difficulty :
"Veratia Montana raised this monument to Neptune." This was
formerly in the chapel of Caprasius.

In the old cloister there is a stone which serves as the capital
of one of the columns. It is upside down. The two first words of
the short inscription are quite clear, the last is indistinct[3]. It is reasonable to assume that it is the offering of some freedman to his master.

The Chapel of S. Honoratus.

The original building, partly in ruins, was still standing so late as
A.D. 1876. A learned and well informed archaeologist[4] gives a very full
and interesting account of the church as it was in A.D. 1835. The walls,
he says, have a Roman appearance, but the layers, which are quite
parallel, are of unequal thickness, and the stones, although cut square,
are not joined with that perfection which was characteristic of early
times to the end of the 4th century. He tells us that the interior
of the chapel was divided into three naves by two rows of six pillars,
each of which sustains a Gothic vault. He presumes that the chapel
took the form of a Latin cross. In no part was any sign of painting
to be seen "except mean whitewash which is to be found everywhere."

An architect to the French government has published a monograph on
the ancient chapel as he saw it in A.D. 1869[5]. He expresses the opinion
that "this sanctuary goes back to the highest antiquity, according to
tradition, and was founded in the 7th century, although the general form
of this early date has entirely disappeared." Both these writers are agreed
that the chapel was of great antiquity although not contemporaneous
with the founder of the abbey. The use of very ancient materials and
especially of tumular stones indicate a barbaric age. According to

[1] *Monographie de l'île Saint Honorat de Lerins*, 1880, p. 237

[2] NEPTVNO
VERATIA
MONTANA

[3] NVS   LIBERTO
INCOMPARABILI

[4] Prosper Mérimée, *Voyage dans le midi de la France.*

[5] Rohault de Fleury, *Une visite à l'île de Saint Honorat, Mémoires de la
Société des Sciences*, Cannes, 1869. This book is now out of print, but we were
able to see it in the municipal library at Nice.

tradition[1], the chapel was rebuilt and consecrated in A.D. 1088 by abbot Aldebert II, who had originated the fortress tower. Alterations and additions were made until completion in the second half of the 12th century, and in this form the building remained until the 17th, when considerable ruin necessitated important reconstruction.

The Cistercians, who were put in possession of the monastery after the secularisation, were unable to adapt the old chapel to their new needs. They therefore pulled it down and built a new one in its place. According to a modern writer[2], the new building reproduces the ancient gable of the old chapel; "in a word the whole architecture concurs in perfect reproduction, but in better harmony with the ancient building."

The Seven Chapels of S. Honoratus.

Barralis, the historian of the abbey, tells us that round the island of Saint Honorat were seven chapels, all of them on the sea-shore, and most of them terraced with two cannon, and that in the period of indulgences, pilgrims visited them before preparation for Holy Communion[3]. He gives the names as follows: The Holy Trinity, SS. Cyprian and Justina, S. Michael, The Transfiguration of our Saviour, S. Caprasius, S. Peter, and S. Porcarius. They served as places of prayer for groups of cells.

The Chapel of the Transfiguration of our Saviour.

By far the most interesting is the chapel of the Transfiguration, known as S. Saviour. It is situated on the north-east of the island, not far from the present landing stage. Its architectural beauty is seriously disfigured by being almost entirely covered with a thick coating of whitewash. It is octagonal in form, with a very low semicircular apse. The roof is shaped like a slightly raised dome. The arched door in the front is low. The absence of all characteristic ornament renders the date of construction very problematic. But its simplicity, and the relationship it bears to the buildings of the old monastery, suggest it was erected about the same time, if not earlier. It was probably the first chapel to be built on the island. Its size too would suggest that it was anterior to the large

[1] Barralis, *Chron. Ler.* I, p. 376.
[2] *Monographie de l'île Saint Honorat de Lerins*, 1880.
[3] Circa gyrum insulae, Viae stratae ad peregrinorum solamen visitantium.... *Chron. Ler.* Descriptio situs.

addition of monks in the later years of the history of the monastery. Prosper Mérimée[1] makes the interesting, and by no means unlikely, suggestion that this chapel was really a baptistery. There is something to be said both for and against this theory. On the one hand, there was a custom in the first centuries for the new converts to pass some time in the monasteries in preparation for baptism, or for instruction. The Council of Arles, regulating the rights of the bishop of Fréjus and the immunities of the monastery, enacted that the bishop alone should give the chrism, that is confirm the neophytes, but that the abbot possessed the right to give holy baptism. In the primitive churches the baptistery was generally in a separate building. On the other hand, this chapel is a long way from the monastery. No baptismal font or laver has been discovered, and no conduit for the water. Barralis says nothing about it, and local tradition is equally silent.

The Abbot's Grotto.

Not far from this chapel is the "Abbot's Grotto." It is entered from the sea through an opening between two rocks. The historian of the abbey tells us that Columbanus and Eleutherius probably hid here[2] at the time of the massacre of Porcarius and the five hundred monks. It received its name from the fact that Eleutherus subsequently became abbot of the monastery.

The Chapel of the Holy Trinity.

Situated at the opposite end of the island, and facing the islet of S. Ferreol, is the chapel of the Holy Trinity. No whitewash or plaster has defaced this construction which has impressed all archaeologists who have visited and examined it. "At first sight," says Revoil[3] "this singular edifice leaves us in very great uncertainty as to the period of its erection, but after a more close survey, it is recognised to be much anterior to the 11th century." Mérimée places it in the 7th or 8th century, and remarks that "it is difficult to imagine a more barbaric structure[4]," and he adds his opinion that "we do not believe there

[1] *Voyage dans le midi de la France.*
[2] Columbanus et Eleutherius discedentes a ceteris in quodam antro prope littus insulae. *Chron. Ler.* I, p. 222.
[3] *Architecture romane du midi de la France; Édifices religieux, Chapelles et Oratoires,* pp. 4-8.
[4] *Voyage dans le midi de la France.*

exists in the west a more ancient dome than that of the chapel of the Holy Trinity." Composed of regular layers carelessly placed, devoid of architectural proportion, and without the least decoration, this chapel can be cited as one of the first built in Christian Gaul. There is a nave, with semi-circular vault, divided into two parts by a groin. A narrow arcade separates the nave from the three apses which terminate it. A small dome with circular base, and conical in shape, surmounts the space between these apses. This remarkable construction may not belong either to the Christian era or to the Roman period. Its enormous stones, and its lack of ornamentation are not inconsistent with the period of the Greeks or Phoenicians.

The Chapel of S. Peter.

The site of this chapel is indicated by a mass of ruins near the position of the old monastery. It was dedicated to S. Peter, the first patron of the island of Saint Honorat. Its foundations were buried under thick bushes, and only saw the light of day in recent years. The chapel had fallen into ruins towards the end of the 15th century, and was rebuilt by Antony Saramand, prior of Vergons, with the concurrence of Andrew Grimaldi who was abbot-commendatory at that time[1]. It was destroyed by the Spaniards in A.D. 1636, in order to make a bastion of the materials.

The Chapel of S. Caprasius.

This chapel, which Fournier calls S. Caprasius, and places opposite the fort of Aragon, was in the western part of the island, but has now entirely disappeared. Its stones were used for the construction of a battery. It was built in honour of Caprasius, the guide and companion of Honoratus and Venantius, near the place in which he had lived a hermit's life. From motives of humility he never received Holy Orders, but, in spite of this, he was always regarded as the patriarch of the monks. He survived Honoratus and died a centenarian in A.D. 434. The cell of brushwood, occupied by this old hermit for 55 years, became a holy meeting place, and it is not surprising that a chapel should have been erected in commemoration of him. Only a few unimposing ruins remain.

---

[1] *Inventaire de Mme la Ctesse de Sainte-Seine.*

The Chapel of S. Cyprian and S. Justina.

This chapel is now in the precincts of the orphanage ; and still preserves its architectural features, and is in a good state of preservation. It is a simple structure with arched vault, and is lighted by two lancet windows. It is jointly dedicated to S. Cyprian the Magician, and S. Justina, two illustrious martyrs who suffered death the same day at Nicomedia under Diocletian. The relics of Justina were venerated in the church of the Benedictines at Padua ; and when the Bénédictines came to assist in the reformation of the monastery of Lerins, they established there the memory and veneration of their saint, and consecrated this small chapel to her. The building thus serves to commemorate the transitory union of the monks of Saint Honorat with those of the congregation of S. Justina, or Monte-Cassino.

The Chapel of S. Michael.

This chapel was situated on the northern extremity of the island, opposite Sainte Marguerite. Very little of the building remains except the base of the front wall, for the materials were used for the construction of a little rotunda for the storage of the rigging of a ship. It was built in honour of Caprasius at the place where S. Michael was said to have appeared when he announced the approaching death of this aged monk, and, judging by the foundations, it was of somewhat small dimensions. The dedication is not altogether special, for in the middle ages there was an almost universal devotion paid to the Archangel. There was, however, an added reason for this dedication at Lerins, for according to the legend, the prince of the angels appeared not only to Caprasius but also to Aygulphus and others.

The Chapel of S. Porcarius.

Porcarius and his martyred monks were supposed to have been buried by Eleutherus and his three surviving companions in a long grave hollowed out between the chapel of Porcarius and the new monastery. This chapel is within the abbey walls, and is the only one of the seven where mass is now celebrated. This is done once a year on the festival of the Martyr-Saint. This appears to be the only one of the seven chapels which the Spaniards spared. Of all the others we read that they were terraced with cannon, and used for some military or other temporary purpose. It offers nothing of interest from the point of view of archaeology, but historically it ranks among the oldest buildings on the island.

Indulgences for Pilgrims.

Reference has already been made to the grant of indulgences, by various popes, to those who visited the island during the period from the Ascension to Whitsuntide. The chapels were then the objects of special worship on the part of the faithful who went in procession, chanting canticles, the whole length of a path traced round the island. They came from all parts, both far and near, and jealousy on the matter of precedence was not unknown. The two villages of Rians and Pertuis, situated at some distance from Cannes, seem to have been as jealous as they were fervent, and in order to avoid any dispute in the future, the abbot found it necessary in A.D. 1633 to make an ordinance determining the order and rank that each one should hold. It is entitled "An ordinance of the Abbot of Lerins, relative to the order of precedence in processions, between the inhabitants of Cannes, Pertuis and Rians[1]." It is to this effect: "In order to avoid in the future every kind of dispute and contention about rank, order, and right of place in the procession which is annually made at the feast of the Ascension, in the island of S. Honoratus of Lerins, between Cannes, Pertuis and Rians, and in order that union, peace and concord may be continued among them and all present, and that devotion may in no way be disturbed, We, Dom Honorius Dubrais, Abbot of the Monastery, on the advice of the Reverend Father Benoist of Aix, Prior, and of the Reverend Father Louis, of the said Aix, Cellarer and Procurator-General of the said monastery, have determined the rank, order, and place in the procession as follows: First of all shall march the chief and captain of the company of Cannes with his armed men disposed and ranked as customary. After them shall follow the great cross of our Monastery with the candles. Then shall follow the cross and banner of the confraternity of Rians, the priest-prior and other colleagues two and two. Afterwards shall march the cross and banner, priests, priors and other colleagues of Pertuis, two and two. Immediately afterwards shall march four ranks of musketeers of the Cannes company. Then shall march our chapter in order, and after them those who carry the relics of S. Honoratus and S. Aygulphus, one priest of Pertuis and one of Rians. Pertuis shall go first and return last." The processions were

---

[1] There is a similar Norwich order of precedence extant.

forbidden by the archbishop of Aix in A.D. 1743 within a radius of more than a quarter of a league round the parishes. The community of Rians which did not wish to renounce so ancient a devotion on any account, decided that a delegate should go in its name every year to carry the offerings reserved for the saint, as long as the prelate should maintain his prohibition. At Pertuis, the devotion to Honoratus was not less than at Rians. According to local tradition he was born near this place, and about A.D. 1397 a chaplaincy in the parish church was established in his honour. In A.D. 1655, the consuls of Pertuis themselves went to Lerins. These processions ceased altogether in the middle of the 18th century.

The Cloister.

Not less interesting is the old cloister, the darkened galleries of which still survive. The Cistercians rebuilt the new church round it. According to tradition it was here that Porcarius and his companions were murdered. The cloister communicated with the ancient church through the right transept, and this position has been maintained in the new church. The cloister is very low built, and very dark. Mérimée[1] says of it: "Nothing is ruder than the construction of the cloister; the capitals of the columns are never the same height; the breadth of the windows varies continually; in short, as an indication of barbarism, the capital of one column is formed by a stone with an inscription upside down[2]."

Rohault de Fleury is not more complimentary, except that he says the cloister is "one of the oldest examples of monastic architecture in the west." In the almost entire absence of features which give the ordinary indication of the date of a building, he will not precisely specify its date. We find, he says, "in front of thick-set arcades, coarse mouldings without any special characteristics." He sees in the construction some indication of date, for he notes that it is partly Roman, and may be ascribed to the 7th or 8th century. The introduction of the rule of Benedict at Lerins in A.D. 661 would be a sufficient motive for the erection of the cloister. The new horizon which Christianity opened out to modern art had not yet appeared, and builders had, as models, only ancient monuments, and as materials, only their ruins. Those they used in their work, without showing any power or originality in reconstruction. This writer realises with a shock that "these heavy

[1] In his work already quoted.
[2] The *Incomparabili*, already referred to, p. 311, note.

and dark galleries replaced the entrancing cloisters of the Middle Ages, those marvels of architectural elegance such as we admire at Rome, Pisa, and Arles. Here we see no ornament, no symmetry, nothing picturesque."

The Château Fort.

The most modern and the largest monument is the château fort, constructed for the defence of the island against the Saracens. It is built with beautifully cut stones of a yellow tint, on the edge of the sea which it proudly commands. Its high walls and crenelated parapets are mirrored in the dark blue of the Mediterranean, and still seem to protect the ruined church which was once the sanctuary of the first monks. It is a characteristic type of the forts, both military and religious, erected on the shores of Provence from the 10th to the 14th centuries. These forts serve to remind us of the disorder and violence characteristic of the Middle Ages. Beneath the ground floor is a large dungeon. The ground floor itself contains a small, square court open to the sky. It is supported by six columns, one of which is red marble, three are granite, and two are common stone. On one of them are the remains of the inscription to Constantine already noted. In the middle of this court there is a 15th century cistern with a large water capacity, which was built at the expense of Gastolius de Grasse, who also paid for a chapel in the western part of this floor. It has since been destroyed. It was in this chapel that the abbots came to take official possession of the abbey. The eastern wing was added at a later date, and consisted of a large kitchen and offices, and a dining hall, and on a slightly lower level the bakehouse.

The first floor is also of Gothic form and corresponds with the lower. The columns here are not so high, and their diameter is less. The chapel of the Holy Cross was in the western portion, and the body of Honoratus was placed here, but was transferred with other relics to various parishes in the neighbourhood of Grasse at the time of the secularisation of the monastery. The choir was built by abbot Geoffrey in A.D. 1432.

The second floor shows the remains of several rooms, some of which were in the occupation of the monks at the time of the secularisation. To the west was the library. The most remarkable work it contained was a Bible in two volumes with two columns, on vellum. The commissioners, appointed to make an inventory at the time of the secularisation in A.D. 1788, noted that it had suffered considerable damage. The prior and other "religious" observed that the books were very old, and they had heard say the tradition was that, to prevent them being taken away, they had been buried, but they did not know who had cut, torn, or taken away the leaves that were missing.

The tower is surmounted by a terrace floored with stout bricks, with an open parapet, which is still well preserved. This is recognised as part of the Spanish construction. In the whole building there were nearly ninety apartments altogether, among which were thirty-six cells for monks, five for strangers, and others for servants. There were four chapels, two cisterns, two staircases, four kitchens, and "in a word all that was necessary for a well-ordered monastery[1]."

This splendid building was commenced in A.D. 1073 by Aldebert. It stands partly upon old Roman foundations and partly on the natural rock. The second floor was covered in about fifteen years afterwards, and this haste shows the dangers that the "religious" ran. In A.D. 1190 the tower was completed. In A.D. 1295 much of the interior work was undertaken by abbot de Mayreris[2].

In A.D. 1400 the cloisters and winding staircase were commenced[3]. It was in this year that Genoese corsairs attacked the monastery, and approached the tower which was courageously defended by the monks, till an entrance was forced. The chapel was also invaded and nothing was respected.

Twenty years later, further building was undertaken by Gastolius. In A.D. 1524 the Spanish fleet, tempted by cupidity, took possession of the monastery, and in A.D. 1536 it was taken, for Charles V, by Andrew Doria. In A.D. 1746 the Germans captured it, but it was retaken by Chevalier Belle-Isle the following year.

The Chest.

This curious relic is now at Grasse, stowed away in a recess of the cathedral, and its existence is apparently unknown to the inhabitants generally. It is a small, arched, wooden box two or three feet in length, and a foot and a half in height, with curious archaic figures in bas-relief, and is supposed to have contained the bones of the founder of the monastery.

The painted figures are still in a remarkably good state of preservation. One of the sides with the top corresponding to it only shows rude decoration. The front is in three panels of unequal size, separated

---

[1] In summâ, omnia quae ad bene ordinatum monasterium requisita. *Chron. Ler.* II, p. 214.   [2] *Ib.* p. 170.   [3] *Ib.* p. 214.

by figures of trees carved in the woodwork.   On the left panel is depicted the arrival of Honoratus at Lerins.   Three people are rowing towards the island.   In the centre panel, much smaller than the other two, Honoratus, three-quarter length, is pointing with his finger to one of the trees.   The sculptor either meant this to refer to the traditional palm tree, in which case Honoratus should have been depicted as mounted on it; or more probably he wishes to indicate in this way the fertility of the island.   To the right, Honoratus is shown chasing away the monsters that swarmed there at the time of his arrival.   With hands joined he awaits the "Host" which an angel is bearing to him from heaven, while two serpents and a stag flee from him, and two women of repulsive ugliness, doubtless figuring the evil genii of the place, are seen above.   Beneath are two shields, with a golden band across them. Three scenes are also depicted on the top of the chest : the arrival of a pope at Lerins, his reception by the abbot, and his departure.   This cannot be Adrian VI, who visited Lerins in A.D. 1522, for this relic, presented as previously stated by John Andrew Grimaldi in A.D. 1482, was in existence forty years before his pontificate.   The scene may merely commemorate a legendary visit.

Both ends of the chest have carved work.   The lower portion of the one shows Honoratus giving the Holy Communion to three monks ; and the upper panel depicts Christ leaving the tomb.   The other end in the lower panel shows Honoratus celebrating Mass, and in the upper there is a representation of the resurrection in which Christ appears to be carried, or escorted, by two angels to heaven.   The subject is probably another version of that shown on the other end, the ideas in both being practically identical, and perhaps represents a vision seen over the altar by Honoratus as in the "Mass of S. Gregory," or a similar legend[1].   The artistic value of this chest is not great, but still it merits

---

[1] I am indebted to Dr James, the Provost of King's College, Cambridge, for this suggestion, which he very kindly allows me to reproduce.

The legend of the Mass of S. Gregory is a late one, and artistic representations of it are very common from the beginning of the 15th century.   There are several variations of it.   Mrs Jameson in *Sacred and Legendary Art*, Vol. II, p. 316, gives this description of it : "On a certain occasion when S. Gregory was officiating at Mass, one who was near him doubted the Real Presence ; thereupon at the prayer of the saint a vision is suddenly revealed of the crucified Saviour Himself Who descends upon the altar surrounded by the instruments of His passion." This writer says she has "met with it in every variety of treatment and grouping ; sometimes several saints are introduced in a poetical manner as witnesses of the miracle, and the crucified Saviour descends from the cross and stands on the altar, or is up-borne in the air by angels."

attention, and is valuable inasmuch as reliquaries of the Middle Ages in sculptured wood are comparatively rare[1].

The Library.

Caesar Nostradamus tells us[2] that the monastery library was in the 14th century "renowned as the most beautiful in Europe," and that a "Monge des îles d'or" made a catalogue of the books. This, if it ever existed, has been entirely lost, as well as one said to have been compiled by Hermentarius; but four others are still preserved which date from the 17th and 18th centuries. Two of these[3] form part of an inventory of the property of the monastery at the time of its cession to a French congregation in A.D. 1742, and at the secularisation in A.D. 1788. The greater part of the manuscripts named were not then found at Lerins, and Monsieur Moris says that "search for most of them has been so far in vain[4]." Only "the Bible of S. Honoratus" appears in the official entry, and this book has in its turn now disappeared. The inventory of A.D. 1742 speaks of "a small missal in vellum with capital letters, and illuminated pictures." It is a lectionary of the 13th century, and is to-day in the departmental Archives of the Maritime Alps[5]. It contains a homily of Gregory the Great, a sermon of Fulgentius, a prayer of Gregory, two homilies of S. Augustine, and an *Order of the Divine Office of the Monastery of Lerins*[6]. There are no traces of the writings of the great men of the golden age.

The Monastery Treasures.

The oldest inventory of these dates from A.D. 1638, others were made in A.D. 1685, 1742 (as part of the one to which reference has just been made), 1757, and 1788. There are also occasional notes by Barralis in his *Chronology*. At the time of the secularisation most of these treasures were distributed by Monsignor Prunières, bishop of Grasse, to the churches in the neighbourhood, and some were sold.

[1] We confess to a feeling of disappointment and regret that on our visit to the cathedral at Grasse in search of this remarkable chest, the caretaker was not apparently instructed to regard it as of value or interest, for he did not show it until much pressed as to its whereabouts, and when produced, part of the roof or lid was broken in, and gave the impression of an old box that was not wanted. We have seen many relics treasured on the continent which seem to receive undue notice and veneration. In this case, the chest might with advantage be placed in a position more in keeping with its archaeological and historic interest.

[2] *Histoire de Provence*, pp. 443–5.   [3] *Archives des Alpes-Maritimes*, II, 126, 127.
[4] *L'Abbaye*, p. 409.   [5] II, 138.   [6] See H. Moris, *L'Abbaye*, p. 411.

C. M.   21

BIBLIOGRAPHY

INTRODUCTORY

GIBBON. Decline and Fall of the Roman Empire.
E. A. FREEMAN. Western Europe in the 5th Century. Macmillan. 1904.
A. W. HUTTON. The Church and the Barbarians. Rivingtons. 1906.
GUIZOT. Histoire de la civilisation. 3 vols. (Bohn's Standard Library.)
FLEURY. Histoire Ecclésiastique.
DÖLLINGER. History of the Church.
G. W. KITCHIN. History of France. 3 vols. Clarendon Press. 1896–1903.
T. HODGKIN. Italy and her Invaders. 8 vols. Clarendon Press. 1892.
T. HODGKIN. The Dynasty of Theodosius. Clarendon Press. 1899.
BEDE. Ecclesiastical History.
F. J. FOAKES-JACKSON. The Christian Church. Cambridge. 1909.
S. DILL. Roman Society in the last Century of the Western Empire. Macmillan. 1899.
S. CHEETHAM. A History of the Christian Church during the first six Centuries. Macmillan. 1894.
S. CHEETHAM. A Sketch of Mediaeval Church History. S.P.C.K. 1899.
I. GREGORY SMITH. Christian Monasticism. Innes, London. 1892.
E. C. BUTLER. Monasticism : in The Cambridge Mediaeval History, 1912. Vol. I. pp. 521–542. And BIBLIOGRAPHY, pp. 683–687.
O. ZÖCKLER. Askese und Mönchtum. Frankfurt. 1897.
J. O. HANNAY. The Spirit and Origin of Christian Monasticism. London. 1903.
URSMER BERLIÈRE. L'Ordre Monastique des origines au XIIᵉ siècle. Maredsous. 1912.
AUGUSTE MOLINIER. Les sources de l'histoire de France. Paris. 1901–1906.

GENERAL

VINCENT BARRALIS. Chronologia sanctorum...ac abbatum sacrae insulae Lirinensis. Lyons. 1613.
P. GOUX. Lérins au cinquième siècle. Paris. 1854.
MONTALEMBERT. Les Moines d'Occident. Paris. 1860.
TILLEMONT. Mémoires pour servir à l'histoire ecclésiastique des six premiers siècles. Paris. 1693–1712.
ALLIEZ. Histoire du monastère de Lérins. 2 vols. Paris. 1862.
ALLIEZ. Les îles de Lérins, Cannes et les rivages environnants. Paris. 1860.
TISSERAND. Chronologie des Abbés de Lérins. (Mémoires de la Société des Sciences, &c.) Cannes. 1873-4-5.
TISSERAND. Chronique de Provence. Histoire civile et religieuse. Nice. 1862.
REDAN. Dom Marie-Bernard. Lerins. 1907.

GUIGOU. Histoire de Cannes. (La Société des Sciences, &c.) Vol. VI. Cannes. 1876.

PROSPER MÉRIMÉE. Un voyage dans le midi de la France. Paris. 1835.

C. LENTHERIC. La Provence Maritime, Ancienne et Moderne. Paris. 1897.

The Author of "Vera." The Maritime Alps and their seaboard. 2 vols. Tauchnitz. 1898.

GASPARD D'ANGERY. Le trésor de Lérins. 1644.

LHUILLIER. Mémoires sur les îles Lérins. 1824.

AZAIS. Les îles Lérins. Nimes. 1862.

ALZOG. Handbuch der Patrologie. 1876.

J. PUVEREL. Les îles Lérins et le monastère Saint-Honorat. Antibes. 1869.

PAPON. Histoire Générale de Provence. Paris. 1777–86.

P. LAHARGON. De schola Lerinensa. Paris. 1890.

GASQUET. English Monastic Life. (The Antiquary's Books.) Methuen. 1904.

A Monk of Lerins. L'île et l'abbaye de Lérins. Lérins. 1909.

Anon. Monographie de l'île Saint de Honorat. Lérins. 1880.

ROHAULT DE FLEURY. Une visite à l'île de Saint-Honorat. (La Société des Sciences, &c.) Vol. I. Cannes. 1869.

A. L. SARDOU. L'histoire de Cannes, des îles de Lérins. Cannes. 1894

PHILIPPE PINATEL. Quatre siècles de l'histoire de Cannes. Cannes.

H. MORIS. L'Abbaye de Lérins. Histoire et Monuments. Paris. 1909.

H. MORIS. L'inventaire des Archives des Alpes-Maritimes. Nice. 1893.

H. MORIS. Cartulaire de Lérins. Nice. 1883.

BERNARD. La primatie de l'église d'Arles. Avignon. 1886.

SILFVERBERG. Historia Monasterii Lerinensis usque ad annum 731. Copenhagen. 1834.

HELYOT. Histoire des Ordres Religieux et Militaires. Paris. 1792. Vol. V. pp. 116–125.

J. M. BESSE. Les Moines de l'ancienne France (période gallo-romaine et mérovingienne). Paris. 1906.

M. HEIMBUCHER. Die Orden und Kongregationen der Katholischen Kirche. Band I. Paderborn. 1907.

JEAN MABILLON. Annales Ordinis Sancti Benedicti. Tom. I. Lucca. 1739.

LUCIEN DAVID. Les grandes abbayes d'Occident. Bruxelles. 1907.

ULYSSE CHEVALIER. Répertoire des sources historiques du Moyen Age. Topo-Bibliographie. Montbéliard. 1894–1902.

BIOGRAPHICAL

ACHARD. Hommes illustres de Provence. 1787.

BARDENHEWER. Les Pères de l'Église, leur vie et leurs oeuvres. (Translated from German by P. Godet.) 1899.

BARONIUS. Annales ecclesiastici. 1588–1607.

SIRMOND. Concilia Galliae. 1629.

BOUCHE. Essai sur l'histoire de Provence. Marseilles. 1785.

C. NOSTRADAMUS. L'histoire et chronique de Provence. Lyons. 1614.

BELLARMIN-LABBE. De scriptoribus ecclesiasticis. 1587.
CEILLIER. Histoire des auteurs sacrés. Paris. 1747.
LE COINTE. Annales ecclesiastici Francorum. 1665.
GENNADIUS. De viris illustribus.
MIGNE. Patrologia Latina.
MABILLON. Acta sanctorum ordinis sancti Benedicti.
LA BIGNE. Magna Bibliotheca. Lyons. 1618.
LA BIGNE. Maxima Bibliotheca. Lyons. 1677.
OUDIN. De scriptoribus Ecclesiae antiquis. Frankfort. 1722.
ADAM CLARKE. Succession of Sacred Literature. London. 1830.
SURIUS. Vitae sanctorum. 1618.
SMITH AND WACE. Dictionary of Christian Biography.
Catholic Encyclopaedia. Robert Appleton and Co., New York. 1907–12.
Benedictines of S. Maur. Histoire litteraire de la France. Paris. 1735.
SPENCE-JONES. The Golden Age of the Church. S.P.C.K. 1906.
McCLINTOCK AND STRONG. Cyclopedia of Biblical and Ecclesiastical
    Literature. New York. 1867–87.
SCHAFF-HERZOG. Encyclopedia of Religious Knowledge. Funk and
    Wagnall. 1910.
E. CAPELLE. Un Moine : le père Jean, Abbé de Fontfroide. Paris. 1903.
AUGUST POTTHAST. Wegweiser durch die Geschichtswerke des Euro-
    päischen Mittelalters bis 1500. 2 vols. Berlin. 1896.
ULYSSE CHEVALIER. Répertoire des sources historiques du Moyen Age.
    Bio-Bibliographie. Paris. 1905–1907.

CAESARIUS

ARNOLD. Caesarius von Arelate. Leipsic. 1894.
PAUL LEJAY. Saint Césaire, évêque d'Arles. (Revue du Clergé Français,
    Nos. 97, 487.) Paris. 1895.
PAUL LEJAY. Les sermons de Césaire d'Arles. (Revue Biblique, IV. p. 593.)
    Paris. 1895.
PAUL LEJAY. Le rôle théologique de Césaire d'Arles.
A. MALNORY. Saint Césaire, évêque d'Arles. Paris. 1894.
BRUNO GELLERT. Caesarius von Arelata. Leipsic. 1892.
A. C. COOPER-MARSDIN. Caesarius, Bishop of Arles. Rochester. 1903.
URBAIN VILLEVIEILLE. Histoire de saint Césaire d'Arles. Aix. 1884.
J. M. TRICHAUD. Histoire de S. Césaire d'Arles. Arles. 1858.

SALONIUS

COLLOMBET. Saints du diocèse de Lyon. Lyons. 1835.
J. J. GRYNNAEUS. Monumenta S. Patrum Orthodoxographa. 1569.

HONORATUS

TILLEMONT. Mémoires. Vol. XII.
A. E. BURN. An Introduction to the Creeds. Methuen. 1899.
L. PIERRUGUES. Vie de S. Honorat. Paris.
GALBERT. Saint Honorat et son Monastère. (Bulletin de l'Acad. delphin. X.)
    Grenoble. 1896–7.

EUCHERIUS

P. ALLARD. La Persécution de Dioclétien et le triomphe de l'église. Paris. 1890.

A. GUILLOUD. Saint Eucher et l'église de Lyon au cinquième siècle. Lyons. 1881.

F. DUMAS. S. Eucher, évêque de Lyon. (Revue du Lyonnais.) Lyons. 1886.

P. ALLEGRE. An article in " Revue de Marseille." Vol. VIII. Marseilles. 1862.

COLLOMBET. Saints du diocèse de Lyon. Lyons. 1835.

TILLEMONT. Mémoires. Vol. XV.

Revue du Lyonnais, CVI. pp. 422–446. Lyons. 1868.

Corpus Script. eccl. Latinorum. Eucherius Lugd. Ed. C. Wotke. 1866–1895.

FAUSTUS

ENGELBRECHT. Studien über die Schriften des Bischofes von Riez, Faustus. Vienna. 1889.

ENGELBRECHT. (Text.) Corpus Scriptorum ecclesiasticorum. Vol. XXI. Vienna. 1889.

A. KOCH. Faustus, Bischof von Riez. Stuttgart. 1895.

DOM MORIN. Article in " La Revue Bénédictine." 1892.

EDM. SIMON. Étude sur Fauste de Riez. Riez. 1879.

G. F. WIGGERS. Versuch einer pragmatischen Darstellung des Augustinismus und Pelagianismus. Hamburg. 1833.

G. F. WIGGERS. An historical presentation of Augustinianism and Pelagianism. Translated from the German by R. Emerson. Gould, Newman, Andover (Mass.). 1840.

DORNER. Augustinus, sein theologisches System. Berlin. 1873.

HELLER. Fausti...fides in exponenda gratia Christi. 1854.

The sermons of Faustus are published by Fathers Durand and Martenne. Paris. 1733. (Vol. IX.)

His works on dogma and discipline are accessible in " Bibliotheca Magna." Vol. III. p. 50.

GENNADIUS. De viris illustribus. 85.

TILLEMONT. Mémoires. Vol. XVI.

HILARY, BISHOP OF ARLES

D. CEILLIER. Histoire des auteurs ecclésiastiques. Vol. XIII. pp. 523 seq

TILLEMONT. Mémoires. Vol. XV.

WATERLAND. History of the Athanasian Creed. Parker, Oxford. 1870.

SALINAS. Edn. of Remains. Rome. 1732.

LEVESTRE. Dict. Patr. II. pp. 192–201. Paris. 1854.

MIGNE. Patrologia Latina, I. pp. 1213–1292.

Bibliotheca Maxima Patrologia. Vol. VII. Vita et Ep. ad Eucherium.

SMITH AND WACE. Dict. Christ. Biog. III. pp. 67 seq.

CAVE. Hist. Lit.

HOOK. Eccles. Biog. Vol. VI.
MOSHEIM. Ch. Hist. I. 340.
A. EBERT. Litteratur des Mittelalters, I. 499 seq.
CLARKE. Succession of Sacred Lit. II. p. 191.
MILNER. Hist. Ch. Christ. II. 317.
RIDDLE. Christian Antiquities.
MILMAN. Latin Christianity, I. 272.
FESSLER-JUNGMANN. Institutiones patrologiae, II. 2, p. 336 fol. Innsbruck. 1896.

LUPUS

J. HAVET. An article in the "Bibliothèque de l'école des Chartes." 1885.
HOEFER. General Biography, XXXII. 16.
HERZOG. Realencyklopädie, VIII. 564. Leipsic. 1900.
MIGNE. Two letters. Vol. LVIII.
GALLANDIUS. Bibliotheca Veterum Patrum. Vol. IX.

VERANUS

E. BLANC. An article in the "Bulletin Monumental." 1878.

VALERIANUS

L. DUCHESNE. Fastes épiscopaux de l'ancienne Gaule. I.
N. SHACK. De Valeriano seculi quinti homiliae Christianae. Copenhagen. 1814.

VINCENT OF LERINS

LEON BRETENIER. Essai sur Saint Vincent. 1854
J. MARTIN. Vincent de Lérins. 1859.
TILLEMONT. Mémoires. Vol. XV.
C. A. HEURTLEY. Vincent of Lerins. Nicene and Post-Nicene Fathers. Vol. XI. Oxford. 1894.
OMMANNEY. Dissertation on the Athanasian Creed. Oxford. 1897.
BRUNÉTIÈRE AND LABRIOLLE. Vincent of Lerins. Paris. 1906.
POITEL. De utroque Commonitorio Lerinensi. Nancy. 1895.

THE COMMONITORIUM

Vincenti Lerinensis Commonitoria, in Florilegium patristicum. Ed. G. Rauschen. Bonn. 1906.
Commonitorium. Editio princeps by Jo. Sichardus. Basel. 1528.
Commonitorium. Antidotum contra diversas omnium fere seculorum haereses. Edition by Pithoeus. Paris. 1586.
Veterum aliquot Galliae theologorum scripta. Edition by Bartholomew Petrus Duaci. 1611. With notes and dissertation.
    Edition by Baluzius. Salviani et Vincentii Lir. opera. Paris. 1663, 1669, 1684.
KLÜPFEL. Common. S. Vincentii Ler. Vienna. 1809. (With excellent Commentary, and references to the Latin Fathers.)
D. A. JÜLICHER. Vincenz von Lerinum. Mohr, Freiburg and Leipzig. 1895.

HURTER. Opuscula selecta. Vol. IX.

ELPELT. German translation and notes. Breslau. 1840.

HEFELE. Beiträge zur Kirchengeschichte. (In Tübingen Quartalschrift.) 1864.

Anon. Vincentius of Lerins against Heresy. The translation is a revision of one published in A.D. 1651 in the Bodleian, with an extract from Bishop Beveridge. Appendix of extracts from Jewel, Hammond, Usher, Ridley. John Henry Parker, Oxford. 1841.

S. PATRICK

J. B. BURY. The life of S. Patrick. Macmillan. 1905.

J. HEALY. Life of S. Patrick. Dublin. 1905.

N. J. D. WHITE. Paris MS. of S. Patrick's Latin writings. Hodges, Figgis and Co., Dublin. 1905.

W. B. MORRIS. Life of S. Patrick. Burns and Oates. 1908.

W. B. MORRIS. Ireland and S. Patrick. Burns and Oates. London. 1907.

W. B. MORRIS. The Apostle of Ireland and his modern critics. Reprint from the Dublin Review. Burns and Oates. 1881.

J. H. TODD. S. Patrick. 1864.

E. J. NEWELL. S. Patrick. The Fathers for English Readers. 1907.

WHITLEY. The Tripartite Life of S. Patrick. London. 1887.

STOKES. Ireland and the Celtic Church. Hodder and Stoughton. 1892.

F. E. WARREN. Lesser Western Rites. Irish Rite. Bradshaw Publications. Vol. IV. 1893.

F. E. WARREN. Liturgy and Ritual of Celtic Church. Oxford. 1881.

H. BRADSHAW. Collections of Canons (Hibernensis). Macmillan. 1885.

A. RYAN. S. Patrick, Apostle of Ireland. Gill and Son, Dublin. 1890.

J. S. SMITHSON. S. Patrick, the Missionary of Ireland. Dublin. 1867.

C. WORDSWORTH (Bishop of Lincoln). S. Patrick, the Apostle of Ireland. London. 1853.

L. A. H. T. POOLER. S. Patrick in County Down. C. K. Assoc. Dublin. 1904.

T. J. SHAHAN. S. Patrick in History. Longmans, New York. 1904.

CASSIAN

E. C. S. GIBSON. John Cassian. Nicene and Post-Nicene Fathers. Vol. XI. Parker, Oxford.

MEYER. J. Cassian, sa vie et ses écrits. Strasburg. 1840.

WIGGERS. De Johann. Cassianus.

F. PAGET. The Sorrow of the World, with preface on "Accidie." London. 1912.

J. S. HILL. Haering's "Ethics of Christian Life."

GODET. Dict. de Théol. Cath. Paris. 1906.

A. HARNACK. Dogmengeschichte. Tübingen. 1897. (English translation. Boston. 1899.)

SALVIAN

BOISSIER. La fin du paganisme. Vol. II. pp. 410–422.

J. BONNET. De Salviani libro ad gubernationem Dei. 1851.

LOUIS MERY. Salvien, prêtre de Marseille et son époque. 1849.

ROUX. De Rutilii itinerariis et Salviani opera. 1811.
BÄHR. Geschichte der Röm. Literatur. Scriptorum eccl. Lat. 1866–1895.

THE SARACENS

CARLONE. La domination Sarrasine dans la Narbonnaise. Nice. 1865.
E. A. FREEMAN. History and conquest of the Saracens. Oxford. 1856.
S. OCKLEY. History of the Saracens. Bohn's Library.
A. GILMAN. Magna Charta Stories. 1882.
A. GILMAN. The Saracens. Story of the Nations Series.
SIR E. S. CREASY. The Fifteen Decisive Battles of the world. 1852.

RAYMOND FERAUD

CARLONE. Études historiques sur l'ancien Comté de Nice. Ann. de la
    Société des Lettres, des Alpes Marit. Vol. II. Nice. 1873.
C. FAURIEL. Histoire de la Poésie Provençale. Paris. 1847.
DIEZ. Die Poésie der Troubadours. Zwickau. 1827. New edition by
    Bartsch. 1883.
DIEZ. Leben und Werke der Troubadours. Heidelberg. 1882. New
    edition by Bartsch. 1882.
RAYNOUARD. Choix de poésies originales des Troubadours. Vol. II. Paris.
    1817.
PAUL MEYER. Les derniers troubadours de la Provence. Revue des
    Sociétés savantes. Paris. 1871.
GASTON PARIS. Histoire poétique de Charlemagne. 1865.
A. L. SARDOU. La vida de Sant Honorat. Nice. 1875.
JOHN NOSTRADAMUS. Les vies des plus célèbres et anciens poëtes
    Provençaux. Lyons. 1575.
GIOFFREDO. Storia delle Alpi Marittime, Monumenta historiae patriae.
    Turin. 1839.
LA CURNE DE SAINTE-PALAYE. Histoire littéraire des Troubadours.
    Paris. 1774. English edition. London. 1807.

DENIS FAUCHER

MOUAN. Étude sur Denis Faucher. Bulletin des travaux de l'Académie
    d'Aix. Aix. 1847.
ROBERT DE BRIANÇON. Études sur Denis Faucher.
H. TOURNAIRE. Faucher, Prieur du Monastère de Lérins. Mémoires de
    la Société des Sciences, &c. Vol. III. Cannes. 1873.

GREGORY CORTESIUS

HERSILIA CORTESIA DE MONTE. Vita Gregorii Cortesii.
    The works of Cortesius were published by J. A. Gradenigo, at
    Padua, 1774, in 2 vols.
ANSAR. Vie de Grégoire Cortés. Paris. 1786.

INDEX

212; at the siege of Troyes, 213; extant letters, 213; on Church lessons, 214; on second marriages, 214, 215, character of, 215

Mabillon (quoted), 239
Malnory on Caesarius, 182
Mamertus on Lerins, 133, 205 (note), 233
Man with the iron mask, 35 ff; theories of, 37
Manhood of Christ, Cassian on, 122
Manicheans, 69
Marcellinum, old name of Cannes, 23, 25, 260
Marcion, 122
Marguerite, Island of Sainte, 30, 33, 35, 39, 129, 270, 271; fort on, repaired, 272; history of, 35 ff.
Marius Mercator, 52
Marles, George de, 261
Marriages, second, Lupus on, 215
Mars, M. de Saint, 35, 37, 39
Martell, Charles, 249, 250
Martin of Braga and *Quicunque*, 181
Martin of Poitiers, 183
Martin of Tours, 16, 17, 44, 95
Martin, S., of Gallinaria, 17
Martin V, 262
Massilians, 73
Massorah and Kabbalah, 57
Matthioli, 37, 38
Maur, S., monks of, 273
Maximian, speech of, 223
Maximilian, emperor, 268
Maximus, abbot and bishop, 46, 131, 192, 193, 228; made bishop of Riez, 230
Mayeul, abbot of Cluny, preaches crusade against Saracens, 251
Mérimée, 313 (note)
μεσημβρινοῦ, Vulgate of psalm 91, 108 (note)
Milman (quoted), 7
Mishnah, 57 (note)
Mollat, Mons. G., *Les Papes d'Avignon*, 261 (note)
Monachorum Chori, 16
Monachorum, Historia, 13
Monachos, Regula ad (Caesarius), 172, 173, 174, 175
Monastery, coat-of-arms of Lerins, 41; prosperity of, 251; possessions of, 252-3; treasures of, 321
Monasticism, rise of, 1, 11 ff.; origin of, 14 ff.; coenobitic, 15; anchoretic, 16
Monophysites, 205,
Monte-Cassino, monastery, 274 ff.
Montmajour monastery, 285, 286

Morin, Dom (quoted), 82, 181
Moris, M. (quoted), 321 (note)
Mother of God (see *Theotokos*), 120
Mulling, bishop of Ferns, 98

Napoleon at Cannes, 31
Narbonne, 249
Narrow way, (sermon, Valerian's), 227
Nazarus, abbot, 47
Neander, 97
Nemthur, birth-place of S. Patrick, 85
Neoplatonism, 14
Nestorian controversy, 81
Nestorius, 55, 67, 68 (note), 76, 119, 126, 127, 182, 205, 231
Neumeyer, address at retreat, 203
Nice, 19
Nicholas V, 257
Noris, cardinal (quoted), 73
Nostradamus, John (on Feraud), 285 (note), 286-8

Obedience and obedientiaries, 154
Ommaney, on the *Quicunque*, 81, 190 (note)
Orange, Council of (see Councils)
Ordinands, age of, 145
Origen, 54, 55, 78, 204
Origenistic controversy, 101 (note)
Orosius of Tarragona, Histories (quoted), 3, 17
Ottley, *Doctrine of Incarnation* (quoted), 67 (note)
Otto Colonna (Martin V), 262
Oubliettes or secret dungeon, 39
Oudin, 192 (note)
Oxybians, 19, 20, 21, 46; Roman conquest of, 22, 23

Pachomius, 15
Palladius, Lausiac History of, 13, 15, 17
Palladius and Ireland, 84
Pantaenus, 58 (note)
Papal power, 7
Paphnutius, abbot, 112, 125
Papon (quoted), 22
Paschasius, on Holy Spirit, 200
Patrice, Dom, present abbot of Lerins, 307
Patrick, S., 45, 83; origin of name, 84, 86; birth-place, 84, 85; sources of information, 86; *Confession* of, 85, 86 ff.; in Gaul, 88; at Lerins, 88; at Marmoutier, 88; at Sabhall Padhrig, 89; in Connaught, 90; biographies of, 90; teaching of, 91; legends of, 88-90; monastery of Armagh, 92; his writings, 93; place-names from Patrick, 91, 92; monastic organisation, 95; *Ecclesiastical*

For EU product safety concerns, contact us at Calle de José Abascal, 56–1°, 28003 Madrid, Spain or eugpsr@cambridge.org.

 www.ingramcontent.com/pod-product-compliance
Ingram Content Group UK Ltd.
Pitfield, Milton Keynes, MK11 3LW, UK
UKHW010351140625
459647UK00010B/997